Intimate Relationships

Intimate Relationships

Issues, Theories, and Research

Ralph Erber

DePaul University

Maureen Wang Erber

Northeastern Illinois University

Allyn and Bacon

Boston • London • Toronto • Sydney • Tokyo • Singapore

Executive Editor: *Carolyn O. Merrill*
Editorial Assistant: *Lara M. Zeises*
Senior Marketing Manager: *Caroline Croley*
Editorial-Production Administrator: *Annette Joseph*
Editorial-Production Coordinator: *Holly Crawford*
Editorial-Production Service: *Lynda Griffiths, TKM Productions*
Composition Buyer: *Linda Cox*
Electronic Composition: *Peggy Cabot, Cabot Computer Services*
Manufacturing Buyer: *Megan Cochran*
Cover Administrator: *Jenny Hart*
Cover Designer: *Suzanne Harbison*

Between the time Website information is gathered and then published, it is not unusual
for some sites to have closed. Also, the transcription of URLs can result in unintended
typographical errors. The publisher would appreciate notification where these occur so
that they may be corrected in subsequent editions. Thank you.

Library of Congress Cataloging-in-Publication Data

Erber, Ralph.
    Intimate relationships : issues, theories, and research / Ralph Erber,
Maureen Wang Erber.
        p. cm.
    Includes bibliographical references and indexes.
    ISBN 0-205-18706-4
        1. Intimacy (Psychology).   2. Man-woman relationships.
    3. Interpersonal relations.   I. Erber, Maureen Wang.   II. Title.

    BF575.I5 E73 2000
    306.7—dc21   00-025104

Printed in the United States of America

10   9   8   7   6   5   4   3   2   1   05   04   03   02   01   00

To our boys:
Brian, Kekoa, and Kai

Contents

10 *Communication and Relationship Management*   **161**

11 *Fidelity and Jealousy*   **180**

12 *Relationship Violence and Abuse   207*

Preface

This book has been a long time in the making. Although the actual writing was completed during the last couple of years, its origin dates back to the time when, during the course of a job interview, I (Ralph Erber) was asked if I felt comfortable at the prospect of teaching a course on close relationships. Given the circumstances under which the question was asked, my answer was, of course, an enthusiastic "yes." However, on the long plane ride home, as I reflected further, I realized that teaching such a course could be an instructor's dream, especially if it could be on intimate relationships and include issues of attraction, courtship, and marriage. After all, such relationships frequently take center stage in people's lives and how these work often affects individuals profoundly. Thus, it seemed as though this could be the one course that would not require special tricks to generate and maintain interest among students.

At the same time, the prospect of teaching a course on intimate relationships was also quite frightening. One worst-case scenario held that students might fall into two diametrically opposite groups. On the one side there could be those who, through personal experience or previous exposure to pseudo-scientific treatises about differences in the makeup of men and women, felt that they already knew a lot about intimate relationships. How could I help them separate fact from fiction? On the other side might be those who were so troubled by aspects of their relationships that they might desperately look to me for solutions. How could I help them deal with their very real problems? A final challenge was provided by questions about the suitability of my own background as an experimental social psychologist to teach a field to which many social sciences have contributed significantly.

The solution to these challenges was to design a course that looks at relationship issues in terms of raising the following questions: What are the issues in important relationship processes such as attraction, communication, conflict, and the like? What theories, if any, have been proposed to explain these and other relationship phenomena? What does the relevant research have to say about the veracity of these theories? What are the implications of theory and research on relationships and people's lives? Because we found this general approach to be a useful one, we incorporated it into how we presented the relationship issues in this book. In doing so, we were especially selective in choosing the work we included and emphasized. Research that tests theories and their implications receives somewhat more attention than research that is simply interesting but not well grounded in theory. As a result, we are not biased against research based on its age. According to many, the study of close relationships as a field in its own right is a relatively recent occurrence, and consequently much of our understanding of close relationships comes from research published during the past few years. However, social scientists, and social psychologists in particular, have speculated about many important issues for a long time. And unlike some fields, where everything published three or more years ago is considered hopelessly outdated, much of the early work on relationships is still relevant today. In some cases, it has established enduring truths or important controversies and therefore provides an important context in which to evaluate current concerns in the literature. Because we want to tell the story of intimate relationship *research*, we found ourselves faced with a task similar to the one incumbent on a writer of novels. For the actions of the protagonists to make sense, their characters must be well developed. Thus, on occasion, we ask our readers to join us on little trips down psychology's memory lane. These reflections will be particularly important for those readers with little or no background in psychology; however, even seasoned veterans of psychology will likely find them enjoyable.

Finally, the field of intimate relationships is truly interdisciplinary, with many important studies coming from a variety of social sciences. Although we agree wholeheartedly with most contributions, we also realize that at least occasionally we are biased toward our own backgrounds as social psychologists. Thus, we are most comfortable telling the story of intimate relationships primarily from this viewpoint. We hope you will enjoy reading it as much as we did writing it.

Like most textbooks, *Intimate Relationships* follows the introduction with some customary yet important considerations of research methods. There are good reasons for proceeding in this way. First, as we know firsthand, when it comes to understanding and doing research, redundancy is the mother of expertise. Second, the study of close relationships poses a number of unique challenges for research methods that were initially developed to study the behavior of, for example, a single rat running through a maze in search of food. Chapter 2 talks about some of the advantages and limitations of traditional social science methods in the context of studying intimate relationships. More recent approaches that were specifically developed to meet the unique challenges of the subject matter are also discussed.

The next chapters are devoted to issues, theories, and research pertaining to attraction. Chapter 3 describes the topic of physical attraction. Much of the relevant research on this subject was conducted 25 to 30 years ago; however, the recent emergence of evolutionary approaches to understanding human behavior has put a new spin on physical attraction issues that we found worthy of some exploration. Chapter 4 looks at the psychological bases of attraction. It covers everything from the implications of general psychological theories to such phenomena as secret relationships and fatal attractions.

Chapters 5 and 6 examine the processes that unfold after initial attraction has taken place. Chapter 5 focuses on how flirtation, self-presentation, and self-disclosure help transform the attraction between two people into romantic relationships. Chapter 6 discusses the interactions that follow in terms of whether they should be considered as an exchange of resources, as is the case between strangers or casual acquaintances. The chapter also highlights a view advocating that interactions in close relationships may operate on communal rather than exchange principles.

Chapters 7 and 8 are broadly concerned with something germane to intimate relationships: love. Chapter 7 is particularly concerned with the processes that initiate love between two people and the many different types of love that exist. Chapter 8 looks at the emotional bonds between two people in terms of attachment. It specifically examines the relationship between attachment to caregivers in infancy and attachment to one's romantic partner in adulthood. There are two reasons for discussing this in a separate chapter. First, research on adult attachment flourished in the 1990s and forced us to rethink how people conceptualize love. Second, it allows us to present a number of nonobvious predictions regarding partner choice, relationship satisfaction, and relationship stability.

Sexuality is the focus of Chapter 9. Some classic research on sexual attitudes and sexual interactions are reviewed, followed by several issues that are particularly relevant today. Specifically, we look at theories and research pertaining to sexual orientation and homophobia.

Chapter 10 deals with issues related to communication and relationship management and critically examines theories and popular notions about sex differences in communication. It debunks many current myths found in best-selling advice books and replaces such prescriptions for improving relationships with suggestions derived from current research.

Chapters 11 through 14 examine the darker side of close relationships. Chapter 11 discusses why people become jealous, how jealousy is different from envy, how it differs between men and women, and how individuals can cope with it. Chapter 12 looks at the causes and consequences of relationship violence, including sexual violence, and discusses what can be done about it. Chapter 13 is concerned with conflict in relationships. Rather than looking at conflict exclusively as something detrimental to an intimate relationship, the chapter considers the possible benefits of conflict as well. Finally, Chapter 14 acknowledges the sad fact that all intimate relationships will eventually end. The chapter focuses on variables that help predict whether a distressed relationship will continue or be terminated. The ramifications of losing a partner to death concludes the chapter and the book.

Acknowledgments

Even though we'd like to make everyone believe that we sweated for every word of every sentence in this book all by ourselves, we fully realize that we couldn't possibly get away with it. We owe a debt of gratitude to the many people who have helped us in many ways. Sean Wakely was our editor in the early stages and, through his insightful criticism, influenced the direction we took. Carolyn Merrill then provided just the right amount of encouragement and persistence to get us to the completion of the book. Our colleagues Chris Agnew, Bella DePaulo, Susan Fiske, Theresa Luhrs, John Pryor, Glenn Reeder, and Neal Roese provided us with valuable feedback along the way. We also thank the following reviewers for their helpful comments: Christopher R. Agnew, Purdue University; Ellen Berscheid, University of Minnesota; Steve Duck, University of Iowa; Paul Mongeau, Miami University; Elizabeth L. Paul, College of New Jersey; Constance Pilkington, College of William and Mary; Ann L. Weber, University of North Carolina at Asheville; and Robert L. Weiss, University of Oregon. The students in our relationships courses kept us informed about what should be covered in a book like this and how it should be presented. Randy Andrews and Jennifer Poe came through for us by putting together the references. The people in the office of DePaul University's Psychology Department—Tuesday Anderson, Michele Kmetz, and Lucinda Rapp—could be relied on in times of crises. Andrea Iorio and the members of the Wang family proved to be capable cheerleaders: Asking us at every turn how the book was coming had its desired motivational consequences. Our children showed an incredible amount of patience and understanding when they kept seeing us sitting in front of a computer for days on end without playing even a game or two. The fine products of Carlton & United Breweries in Melbourne, Australia, and Bayview Farm in Honaunau, Hawaii, helped to provide the appropriate states of consciousness. A special thanks to Iwa for so diligently keeping us supplied with Kona coffee. Finally, we thank Michael Jordan. His retirement from professional basketball in December 1998 eliminated all reason to watch the Chicago Bulls, thus providing us with ample time for the "final push."

Intimate Relationships

1

Strangers, Friends, and Lovers

Why Is Life So Complicated?

*Man is by nature a social animal; an individual who is unsocial naturally
and not accidentally is either beneath our notice or more than human. . . .
Anyone who either cannot lead the common life or is so self-sufficient as not
to need to, and therefore does not partake of society, is either a beast or a god.*

—Aristotle

Aristotle wrote these words a long time ago. Chances are he intended his insights
to apply to men and women alike. In any event, the idea that humans, by nature,
are social creatures is as old as or older than civilization itself, and it permeates
the social sciences to this very day (e.g., Aronson, 1992). If nothing else, it seems
that many of our daily activities require the presence of others to make them
enjoyable or even possible. Dancing, playing ball, or going on a date are practically impossible to do if not for the presence of at least one other person. Other
things, like going out to dinner or taking a vacation, can be awkward if done in
solitude.

More importantly, there is reason to believe that most humans will not do
well when they are deprived of contact with others. In the pilot episode of Rod
Serling's popular 1960s TV show, *The Twilight Zone*, fittingly entitled "Where Is
Everybody?" the protagonist found himself alone in a small town somewhere in
America. Everywhere he went, he found tangible signs that other people had been
there—a lighted cigarette in an ashtray, a steaming cup of coffee on a kitchen
table, the receiver of a phone off the hook, and a partially eaten breakfast on the
counter of a diner. Faced with all these traces of human existence, he developed
the singular preoccupation of trying to find somebody, anybody for that matter,
to the point where he appeared to be losing his mind. Fortunately for the protagonist, the situation in which he found himself was an experiment conducted by the
space program designed to test how prospective space travelers would fare in social isolation. In light of their observations, the researchers decided to terminate
the experiment and concluded that prolonged social isolation was simply too
much for any human to bear.

Interestingly, the idea of being completely isolated was intriguing and outrageous enough to resurface as the theme in at least one other episode of *The Twilight Zone*. In that particular episode, Archibald Beachcroft, a misanthropic office
worker, was given the power to make anything happen by merely wishing for it.
Granted such powers, his first wish (after making his landlady disappear) was for
everyone to go away. And while the resulting situation was not one that was
thrust upon him as part of a cruel experiment, he quickly came to realize the difficulties of living a life of complete solitude. He was soon faced with the utter
pointlessness of such seemingly trivial activities like shaving and going to work.
Moreover, the elimination of the nuisance previously created by the presence of
others came at the price of complete boredom. To alleviate it, he wished for diver-

sions, such as an earthquake, which he found too exciting, and an electrical storm, which he found too dull. Another wish for everybody to come back and be just like him created a situation he quickly found intolerable, and thus, with his final wish he asked for everything to be the way it used to be.

It appears that Rod Serling's fantastic explorations into the effects of physical isolation were not very far off, as there is at least anecdotal evidence for the detrimental effects of social isolation throughout the recent history of human existence. For example, early settlers of the Midwest, after having received huge parcels of land, proceeded to build their homesteads somewhere near the center of their property, equidistant from its borders. Unfortunately, this put them at a maximum distance from everyone else who used the same strategy. Frequently, torrential rains and harsh winters kept people confined to their property for long periods of time, and, as a result, they often spent months deprived of human contact. Rod Serling would probably not have been surprised to learn that occasional visitors described these settlers as appearing wild and having a crazed look in their eyes. The twentieth century brought with it reports of brainwashing among prisoners of war, particularly during the wars in Korea and Vietnam. And although the phenomenon of brainwashing has thus far eluded serious scientific investigation, perhaps in part because of the ethical issues involved, it appears that most people who were thought to have been brainwashed had spent a great deal of time in social isolation.

Of course, to attribute the detrimental effects of social isolation to the notion that humans are social animals does not provide much of an explanation in and of itself. Instead, we need to identify the particular aspects of human nature that appear to make being by ourselves so intolerable.

The Need for Affiliation

One of the reasons why life in complete solitude is likely to leave us with that wild-eyed demeanor has to do with the importance that others play in defining ourselves. Some (e.g., Murray, 1938; McClelland, 1985) have argued that humans are hardwired to seek out others to varying degrees, and have attributed this tendency to a need for affiliation. Without comparing ourselves to others, it is difficult to ascertain whether we are good or bad at something, whether our personal habits are appropriate, or whether our taste in music is cutting edge, to name only a few examples. Additionally, much of what happens in the world around us carries a certain amount of ambiguity or uncertainty that we often cannot resolve by ourselves: Is my boss being nice or is he sexually harassing me? Is it good or bad to have a Republican president? Is Chicago a good place to live? Frequently, we find the answers to such questions by consulting others to see what they think. Of course, if this is true, then people should be most likely to affiliate with others in situations that carry a high degree of uncertainty. Some time ago, Stanley Schachter (1959) found an ingenious way to test this idea in the psychological laboratory. He recruited undergraduates to be research participants for a seemingly routine psychology experiment. However, once they arrived at the lab, they were greeted by a serious-looking experimenter who claimed to be from the university's medical school. He explained that the purpose of the study was to examine the physiological effects of electric shocks. Half the research participants were told that the shocks they were about to receive would be harmless and wouldn't cause as much as a tickle. The other half were told that the shocks would be intense and quite painful. It is this latter group that is of particular interest here.

Faced with the description of the experimental purpose, the students were likely to ponder any number of questions: Just how painful are these shocks going to be? Will my health be in jeopardy? Is there any way I can get out of this ludicrous experiment? Should I call security on this guy? As it turns out, the experimenter asked research participants to wait for a few minutes, ostensibly to get his equipment ready. At this point, they were given a choice of either waiting by themselves or waiting with another person. Not surprisingly, nearly two-thirds of the research participants expecting to receive the painful shocks opted to wait with others rather than by themselves. Of those expecting to receive the painless shocks, only one-third chose to spend the waiting period with someone else. In a second experiment, Schachter varied the nature of his study by telling research participants that the other person was or was not participating in the experiment. Under these conditions, 60 percent of the research participants expecting to receive the painful shocks opted to wait with the person who shared their fate.

Schachter (1959) concluded several things from these observations. First, it appears that misery doesn't love just any sort of company; instead, misery seems to love miserable company in particular. Second, and more importantly, he inferred that his research participants probably preferred to wait with someone who shared their fate because this enabled them to reduce the uncertainty involved in expecting the painful shocks. Even if research participants never spoke a single word to each other, they could look for signs that would inform them whether the other person was anxious or relaxed, eagerly anticipating the beginning of the experiment or dreading it. In essence, then, we affiliate with others because they help us reduce uncertainty.

Of course, it is safe to assume that Schachter's research participants were probably frightened as well as feeling uncertain at the prospect of receiving painful electric shocks. As it turns out, fear comprises another set of circumstances under which people are likely to seek the company of specific others. For example, coronary bypass patients who had a choice of sharing their hospital room prior to surgery with someone who either was about to have the same surgery or someone who was recovering from it, preferred the latter by a margin of almost four to one (Kulik & Mahler, 1989). Presumably, being with someone who survived the somewhat frightening operation aided in reducing the fear of anticipating it. Similarly, and perhaps less dramatically, we seek the company of like-minded others when we expect to be in a situation in which we have to defend our beliefs (Kruglanski & Mayseless, 1990). When our self-esteem is threatened, we tend to seek out others who are doing less well than we are in order to come out ahead in the case of failure (Wills, 1991; Wood & Taylor, 1991).

Fear and uncertainty are dramatic conditions that motivate people to seek the company of others. However, many of our everyday activities involving the company of others have little to do with such conditions. After all, we don't go to parties to reduce fear and uncertainty but to have a good time. On other occasions, we may prefer solitude over company. Regardless of the specific reasons for such shifts in preference, it appears that affiliation motivation is geared toward achieving an optimal balance between social contact and solitude. From this perspective, affiliation motivation can be understood as a homeostatic process. Prolonged social contact will lead people to seek a period of solitude, whereas prolonged solitude will lead people to seek out social contact (O'Connor & Rosenblood, 1996).

The Need for Intimacy

The need for affiliation predicts why people generally try to establish and maintain interpersonal relationships that are at least somewhat rewarding, such as friendships. After all, having friends around can be comforting because it saves us from turning to complete strangers when we are uncertain or frightened. However, by itself, it does not explain why we may feel compelled to look for that special someone with whom to share our thoughts, our feelings, and perhaps our lives. Some (McAdams, 1982) have argued that such tendencies are motivated by a need for intimacy. Unlike the need for affiliation, which produces a desire to establish and maintain many rewarding interpersonal relationships such as friendships, the need for intimacy triggers a desire for a warm, close, and communicative relationship with one person in particular. Additionally, people with a high need for affiliation tend to engage in active, controlling social behavior with an emphasis on the quantity of social relationships. They tend to communicate more with others and generally find the company of others as well as social activities more enjoyable than people whose need for affiliation is low (McClelland, 1985). On the other hand, a high need for intimacy results in more passive and less controlling social behavior with an emphasis on the depth and quality of social relationships (McAdams, 1988). Generally, people high in need for intimacy tend to be more trusting and confiding in their relationships, and they report a greater sense of well-being than people whose need for intimacy is low (McAdams & Bryant, 1987).

It is important to note that although need for affiliation and need for intimacy are not mutually exclusive, they preclude each other to some extent. Someone whose need for affiliation leads him or her to be a social butterfly will likely experience some difficulty initiating and maintaining a single, close relationship. By the same token, someone who is high in need for intimacy may be unsatisfied with a social life that primarily revolves around friends and acquaintances. But who is better off in the long run? It appears that need for intimacy is a better predictor of a person's overall psychosocial adjustment. A study that measured need for affiliation and need for intimacy among a group of men at age 30 and again 17 years later found that those who scored high in need for intimacy at age

30 were happier with their jobs and more satisfied with their marriages than those whose need for intimacy had been low. Need for affiliation, on the other hand, did not predict differences on these kinds of indicators of middle-age adjustment (McAdams & Vaillant, 1982).

The Need to Belong

A recent proposal (Baumeister & Leary, 1995) does away with the idea that humans have separate needs for affiliation and intimacy. Instead, it suggests that our tendency to seek and maintain relationships of breadth as well as depth are caused by an underlying need to belong. According to this hypothesis, humans "have a pervasive drive to form and maintain at least a minimum quantity of lasting, positive, and impactful relationships" (Baumeister & Leary, 1995, p. 497). Although this need to belong is to some extent innate, our evolutionary history may have done its part to make it a dominant form of human motivation. Forming social bonds may have important survival and reproductive benefits. Banding together in groups helps to supply mates and enables the sharing of food as well as the care of offspring. Moreover, groups have a competitive advantage over the single individual when it comes to acquiring scarce resources and defending against predatory enemies. From this perspective, evolution has provided humans with a set of internal mechanisms that predispose them toward seeking relationships with others.

There is ample evidence supporting the belongingness hypothesis. First of all, it appears that social bonds among humans form quite easily, even in the absence of specific circumstances that might make these bonds particularly advantageous. For example, when people are assigned to be members of a group by some arbitrary criterion, they quickly develop strong feelings of loyalty and allegiance to the point where they discriminate against nonmembers in a variety of ways (e.g., Brewer, 1979; Sherif et al., 1961; Tajfel, 1970). Similarly, infants develop attachments to their caregivers long before they are able to figure out the benefits (Bowlby, 1969).

At the same time that humans form social bonds easily, they react to the loss of such bonds with a measure of distress. People often have a hard time leaving family, neighbors, and friends behind in order to go to college or move to a new city. Interestingly, they experience distress even when the separation has no practical or instrumental ramifications (e.g. the loss of neighbors). In addition, people are often reluctant to dissolve relationships that are abusive (Strube, 1988). Even if people dissolve a bad relationship through divorce, they often maintain a sense of ambivalent attachment to former spouses, suggesting that the relationship changed rather than ended altogether (Vaughan, 1986; Weiss, 1979).

Support for the belongingness hypothesis can also be obtained when one realizes the importance of social relationships for individuals' cognitions, emotions, and health. For example, we think about others more when we expect to have a relationship with them (Berscheid et al., 1976; Erber & Fiske, 1984). Many of our strongest emotions are related to belongingness. The initiation of a relationship is generally accompanied by positive emotions associated with a sense of acceptance, such as happiness, elation, love, and joy. The end of a relationship is generally associated with emotions associated with rejection and loss, such as anxiety, grief, jealousy, and loneliness. It appears that even those who initiate the breakup of a romantic relationship are no exception, as any initial feelings of relief are soon replaced by feelings of guilt (Baumeister, Stilwell, & Heatherton, 1994). Finally, there is evidence that marital relationships serve as important buffers against stress (DeLongis, Folkman, & Lazarus, 1988) as well as physical and mental health problems. Compared to people who are single or divorced, married people have a lower incidence of heart attacks (Lynch, 1977), fewer problems with immunocompetence (Kiecolt-Glaser et al., 1984), and a higher chance of survival from cancer (Goodwin et al., 1987).

The belongingness hypothesis is appealing for a couple of reasons. For one thing, the need to belong can explain a variety of important psychological phenomena. For another, the need to belong explains our tendency both to seek and maintain relationships of breadth as well as depth. It is thus more parsimonious than any explanation that attributes these same tendencies to more than one motive (e.g., need for affiliation for one and need for intimacy for another). On the other hand, people may be attracted to relationships because they meet multiple psychological needs. Weiss (1969) suggested that people have five important needs that can be met only through close relationships with others:

1. The need for *intimacy* compels us to share our feelings with another.
2. The need for *social integration* requires someone with whom to share our concerns and worries.
3. The need for being *nurturant* is best met by being with another whom we can take care of.
4. The need for *assistance* involves another who will help us in times of need.
5. The need for *reassurance* of our own worth requires that we are with someone who will tell us that we are important.

Within this framework, the success of a relationship is defined by the extent to which two people meet each other's needs.

The Inevitability of Social Relationships

The need for affiliation, the need for intimacy, and the need to belong explain why most people would like to have friends, have a romantic partner, and be part of a group. At the same time, explanations of this kind are also somewhat problematic. To some extent, need-based theories often observe a behavior, such as people's tendency to seek out others. They *explain* it as being caused by an underlying need, such as a need for affiliation, and then go on to *predict* the behavior based on the corresponding need. In other words, the argument takes on a somewhat circular nature, which detracts from its explanatory power. Of course, if we conveyed such reservations to someone who subscribes to theories that explain human behavior as being caused by needs, we would probably be asked what the alternatives are. This is not an easy task. However, one possibility would be to point out that interactions with others, and perhaps relationships as well, are an almost inevitable outcome not so much of human nature but human existence. Planet Earth is, after all, a heavily populated place, which makes a life of complete solitude almost impossible. Even if we built ourselves a log cabin in the most remote wilderness, it would be impossible to escape interacting with others entirely, if for no other reason than to buy food, clothing, and supplies.

In reality, most people spend their lives in a heavily populated social context. We are raised by one or more parents in a home that is part of a neighborhood and a larger community. We may have siblings and an extended family that descends upon us on holidays. And even before our proud parents bring us home from the hospital, we have been checked, assessed, measured, and poked by pediatricians and nurses. In due time, we go to school with other children and eventually are employed in a setting that usually features superiors, underlings, and coworkers. The point is that, whether we want it or not, relationships with others cannot easily be avoided, and it may be that this inevitability holds an important piece in the puzzle of explaining why and how people initiate and maintain social relationships.

Some time ago, sociologist George Caspar Homans (1961) proposed a number of fairly straightforward principles with regard to the relationship between social interaction and relationships. The first principle states that people with equal status are more likely to interact. Students, for example, are more likely to interact with other students than with their professors. Clerks are more likely to interact with other clerks than with their managers. Of course, if equal status were the only basis for interacting with others, there would be a copious amount of possibilities. However, over time, we end up interacting with others who are similar to us, like students who have the same major or share a similar taste in music. This is the second principle. The third principle states that the more frequently we interact with others, the more we will like them. And finally, the fourth principle stipulates that frequent interaction and increased liking will result in increased sentiments of friendship.

Homans' (1961) four principles do a decent job of explaining why people interact more, and perhaps form relationships more with some but not others. They also explain a variety of phenomena without adding the flavor of a circular argument. However, by focusing almost exclusively on the situational context of social interactions and relationships, the principles fail to take into account individual differences in the level with which people desire to initiate and maintain close relationships. As is often the case, the truth may lie somewhere in the middle. Needs for affiliation, intimacy, and belonging may predispose people to desire relationships with others to varying degrees. The rewardingness of interactions with others because of equality of status or similarity may help determine with whom we form relationships marked by sentiments of friendship or love.

Intimate Relationships Yesterday and Today

The Way We Were

Intimate relationships can take on many different forms, but most Americans who are asked to describe the prototypical intimate relationship will probably respond by naming the heterosexual, married couple. This may sound biased or even discriminatory to those considering alternative forms of intimate relationships, but it is not entirely surprising. In fact, current estimates hold that roughly 90 percent of all young adults between the ages of 18 to 24 believe that they will eventually get married (Norton, 1987). This certainty with which we believe that we will someday get married may be traced back to a couple of factors that shape us in important ways. First of all, many people spend most if not all of their childhood exposed to Mom and Dad as the predominant model of adult intimate relationships. Even children who grow up in something other than the nuclear family often desire to have a more traditional relationship as adults. Moreover, there is a widespread belief that the family is an important aspect of the fabric from which our social culture is woven. During the 1980s and 1990s, politicians of all colors and backgrounds wore on their sleeves a concern with "family values." This concern was underscored in 1996 when President Clinton signed a bill that made marriage the exclusive prerogative of a man and a woman.

Although it is not clear what a return to family values implies, it conjures up the image of the traditional family as portrayed in such 1960s TV shows as *Leave It to Beaver*. For the benefit of those readers who are either too young to have watched the show when it originally aired or do not have cable where it can occasionally be seen in reruns, it (as well as others of the same era) depicted the family in a rather unique way. There was Ward Cleaver, the husband and father who sprinted off to work early each morning. Then there was June Cleaver, the wife, homemaker, and mother who took pride in what she did. Both believed that their relationship would last forever, and together they worked hard to create a happy homelife for themselves and their two children who were basically good kids who loved, honored, and obeyed their parents as they struggled to grow up. The children, Wally and "The Beaver," were expected to work toward starting their own families, of course modeling them after their own.

Historically, the so-called traditional American family is an institution that was relatively short-lived. Its beginnings can be traced back to the industrial revolution of the nineteenth century. Prior to that, the home was the site of production, and every member of the family unit contributed productive labor toward tending the farm, raising cattle, or manufacturing goods. Compared to today, affection was less likely to be a basis for marriage, and relationships among family members were more formal, less companionate, and less child centered. The industrial revolution shifted the site of production to a physically separate workplace and brought about an increased specialization of husband and wife. In part because the woman has a biological advantage when it comes to rearing very young children, the husband became the provider and by necessity took on a reduced role in the family life. At the same time, the wife's economic role decreased as increased emphasis was placed on her skills as a homemaker and mother. Finally, the return of huge numbers of soldiers from World War II triggered a housing boom, which created the suburbs (in which June and Ward Cleaver raised their children).

The Way We Are Now

In addition to being short-lived, the image of the traditional family has also been culturally bound, as it is mostly descriptive of the white middle class. But even within this confine, since the 1970s, a number of important changes have taken place that had a profound impact on the traditional American family. Perhaps most dramatically, the Cleavers are now older when they get married, as many Americans put off marriage longer than their counterparts of the 1940s and 1950s. According to the U.S. Census Bureau, the median age of a first marriage is currently 26 for men and 24 for women, compared to 22.4 and 20 in the late 1950s.

Today, June Cleaver is also more likely to have a job, partly because the economic realities of the 1980s and 1990s led many women to seek employment. Whereas in 1940, only 27.4 percent of women worked outside the home, in 1987, a full 56 percent of all women were part of the workforce, and 54.7 percent of them were married (Footlick, 1990). It is not clear whether this is a blessing or a curse. Although part of this increase may be due to a growing tendency on the part of women to pursue careers, in many instances their employment comes out of necessity, and frequently employment is a chore that is added to the already existing responsibilities within the home.

Finally, the nuclear family has been modified in yet another way. The rising divorce rates of the 1970s and 1980s resulted in a proliferation of stepfamilies (a fact that popular culture tacitly acknowledged via the 1970s TV series, *The Brady Bunch*). By the mid-1980s, a full 46 percent of all marriages were marriages in which at least one partner had been married before, and roughly 16 percent of married couples included spouses with at least one child from a former marriage (Norton, 1987).

Changes in the age of first marriage, women's employment outside the home, and the existence of stepfamilies could be taken as indicators that the traditional family is still basically intact, having merely adapted to external pressures in relatively minor ways. However, other changes have led to alternative forms of relationships that for many have taken the place of traditional marriage and family. If one assumes that media portrayals of relationships reflect what goes on in real life, albeit somewhat exaggerated, a week's worth of TV watching in the late 1990s revealed the diversity of relationship arrangements of the present day. Yes, there were still shows about couples and families (*Mad about You*), but some of the most popular shows depicted dysfunctional ones (*Cybill, Married with Children, The Simpsons*). Other shows included depictions of singlehood (*Seinfeld*), cohabitation (*Friends*), and relationships with others of the same sex (*Ellen*), to name only a few.

But, as is often the case, people's real-life experiences often outstrip those concocted by writers who create them for the purpose of entertaining an audience. Consider, for example, the case of one of the authors' students. Aixa took the authors' course during her sophomore year in college in large part for very personal reasons. At the time, she was living with her African American mother and her Latino father, who, after twenty-some years of marriage, were contemplating a divorce. Matters were complicated by her mother's chronic illness that triggered frequent and often dramatic medical emergencies. After a great deal of contemplation, Aixa decided to escape the strained life at home by moving in with Ramon, her fiancé of six months. At first, life with Ramon was blissful. But less than a year after they moved in together, he lost his job and, in Aixa's words, simply came apart. Unable to find another job he liked, Ramon became verbally and physically abusive to the point that Aixa decided to terminate the relationship. She subsequently moved back in with her parents, who by then had gotten divorced but nonetheless kept living together. Aixa is now dating again, although for the time being she is not looking for a serious relationship, which could get in the way of her aspirations to pursue a medical degree.

If nothing else, Aixa's example is maximally removed from the *Leave It to Beaver* model of dating, marriage, and family. Life at home is not necessarily a safe haven from which to explore the world, and it often provides models of relationships that are more frightening than soothing. As for dating, the rules of the game have changed to include arrangements that were unheard of 30 years ago. At the same time, the stakes are higher and, as a result, the consequences of false starts can be profound.

Of course, it is one thing to lament that "things are different now." Anyone with minimal observational skills can probably cite numerous examples of relationships that have strayed from the traditional trajectory. To make sense of it in a theoretical manner is an altogether different story, however, and it is not certain that anyone has a clear-cut answer. Instead, the state of affairs resembles a just-opened puzzle. We don't quite know how the pieces fit together, and we are not even sure if the manufacturer included them all. In this particular case, the solution to solving the puzzle may begin with the recognition that relationships do not exist in a vacuum. Instead, how we think and feel about them along with our conduct is to some extent influenced by the larger physical and sociocultural context (Werner et al., 1992).

Levinger (1994) identified three sets of interlinked social forces that have contributed to the changing landscape of close relationships:

1. First, historians and economists alike have long pointed out that Western societies have become increasingly concerned with issues of autonomy and personal control. Some (e.g., Dizard & Gadlin, 1990) have attributed this to the spread of commerce and industry, which operates by stimulation of consumer need. Commerce flourishes more easily when people have a sense of independence along with the ability to make choices in the marketplace. At the same time, this individualistic orientation toward independence and freedom of choice helps erode people's dependence. As a result, elders try not to burden their adult children, parents put a greater emphasis on work and leisure often at the expense of not attending to their children's support needs, and spouses develop careers independently from one another. It is possible to respond to these changes in vastly different ways. Some may be compelled to re-create rigid traditional forms of relationships (e.g., return to family values), whereas others may try to avoid any sort of permanent commitment (e.g., remain single, cohabitate). But regardless of which solution is adopted, everyone has become more preoccupied with the conduct of their relationships.

2. To some extent, the economic changes just described have empowered women to the point that their relationships with men are less and less defined in terms of "owner-property" relationships (Scanzoni, 1979). Instead, male-female relationships have come to be more and more defined in terms of intimacy. Intimacy, by definition, implies equality, and this has put pressure on women to be more assertive and independent and pressure on men to be more sensitive and caring. Of course, at this point we are still short of having achieved complete gender equality. However, the notion that equality may be within reach may lead many to monitor their relationship more carefully. Such monitoring may paradoxically magnify even small inequalities and consequently lead to increased levels of dissatisfaction (Levinger, 1994). Interestingly, a process of this nature may help explain why wives in traditional marriages are often more satisfied with their relationship than wives with stronger expectations about equality (Hackel & Ruble, 1992; Peplau & Hill, 1990).

3. Finally, the increase in autonomy and independence and the push for equality have been accompanied by a reduction in the legal, economic, religious, and social barriers against the ending of marriages. In some ways, the idea that marriages do not have to last "until death do us part" can lead to the perception of perpetual choice, and thus it promotes the possibility of exiting a relationship when careful monitoring suggests that its outcomes fall below one's expectations. Of course, to see others get divorced further highlights exiting a relationship as a viable solution to marital dissatisfaction, which, among other things, shows that the microcontext of a close relationship (i.e., how individuals conduct themselves in it) can become part of a larger social force. The reduction in barriers against exiting a relationship and a corresponding reduction in barriers against entrance have triggered many to seek alternatives to marriage, including staying single and cohabitation. Just as importantly, they have provided a context that enabled people to have interracial and same-sex relationships.

These changes in relationships brought on by the changes in the macrocontext in which they take place are dramatic indeed, primarily in terms of the speed with which they happened. As late as 1967, a Columbia College male and a Barnard College female were denied graduation upon disclosing their unmarried cohabitation (Levinger, 1994). Miscegenation laws prohibiting marriage between people of different racial backgrounds were not finally abolished until that same year. And it was not until 1974 that psychologists dropped homosexuality from their compendium of psychological disorders.

At the threshold to a new millennium, we find a great deal of diversity in terms of how we live. According to data from the U.S. Census Bureau, in 1970, nearly three-quarters of the 63 million U.S. households were married couples. By 1998, the percentage dropped to 53 percent and included those who were divorced and remarried. At the same time, more than 9 million households are headed by single parents—a 200 percent increase over 1970. At present, they account for 27 percent of all households. Also on the rise are the number of adult children living with their parents. Current estimates put the number at 18 million—a 43 percent increase over 1970. Finally, about 5 percent of all households consist of two or more unrelated people, including roommates, unmarried heterosexual couples, and about 1.8 million gay and lesbian couples. Despite all these changes in the social landscape, many of our nation's laws, policies, and procedures still seem to have the traditional family in mind. An adult son cannot include his mother on the medical insurance provided by his employer. Even though they share a home, there is no provision to add anyone other than a spouse or a child. The same logic has similarly deprived gay and lesbian partners of sharing work-related benefits, but change in legislation is beginning to occur in this area. Legislators have similarly ignored the plight of many single mothers in dire need of adequate child care to work one or more low-paying jobs.

Yes, a lot has changed over the past 30 years, but a lot has also remained the same. Just as they have done in the past, people will always fall in (and out of) love, except that they now have many more choices in terms of partners and the types of relationships they form. And although this can make things very complicated, the life of virtually any intimate relationship can be conceived of as unfolding in a predictable number of stages. In the *sampling* stage, people look at and compare characteristics of others to determine their suitability for an intimate relationship. In the *bargaining* stage, they exchange information about each other to determine whether they will be able to maintain a long-term, exclusive relationship. The *commitment* stage is marked by such behaviors as getting married, buying a house, and having children, with each behavior reducing the likelihood for alternative relationships. Finally, just as all close relationships have a beginning, they will eventually end as well, either through a breakup, divorce, or death. This is the *dissolution* stage, which has unique ramifications for all involved. This book is written as a journey that will take the reader through all these stages. After a brief sojourn into the methods social scientists use to study relationships, the journey will begin in earnest by looking at the kinds of things that attract us to others in the first place.

Summary

Issues. Humans do not do well in solitude. Instead, they seek out relationships with others, marked by both breadth and depth. Intimate relationships have changed in significant ways when compared to the prototype of the married couple at the core of the nuclear family. Among these are an increase in the age at which people get married, rising numbers of women pursuing careers, and an increase in the number of stepfamilies as a result of second marriages. Consequently, intimate relationships today manifest themselves in a myriad of ways that are markedly different from the ones common a few decades ago. At the same time, much has also remained the same. People will likely continue to fall in love and establish relationships with one another according to a relatively predictable pattern of sampling, bargaining, and commitment.

Theories.   Some researchers have identified a set of psychogenic needs that explain the distinctly social nature of humans. The need for affiliation compels us to form relationships of breadth for support and uncertainty reduction. The need for intimacy compels us to look for a one-on-one relationship of depth with another. The need to belong perhaps helps explain both tendencies. Others have traced the origin of our social nature to the human condition. Explanations for the changing nature of intimate relationships center on changes in the macrocontext in which they occur.

Research.   Much research conducted during the past 30 years supports many hypotheses suggested by need-based accounts of intimate relationships, both directly and indirectly. Research on the changing nature of relationships is necessarily descriptive, and thus many explanations derived from it are at least somewhat speculative yet nonetheless intriguing.

2

Methods to Study Relationships

SEATTLE—Most couples bent on beating the divorce odds have never heard of John Gottman. His nine-page list of accomplishments, tracking his weighty impact on the growing marriage education field, tells some of the story. So does an article in Psychology Today, *which stacked Gottman's academic credentials up against those of John Gray, the oft-quoted author of* Men are from Mars, Women are from Venus. *Gottman has formally studied 760 couples, some for as long as 20 years, Gray none. Gottman has written 109 articles in marriage and family journals, Gray none.*

—Shirley Barnes, *Chicago Tribune,* August 2, 1998

Despite the marked difference in their scholarly accomplishments, it appears as though many of us are more likely and willing to take the advice of the unproven John Gray rather than the established John Gottman. Not surprisingly, Gray's ideas and lingo (starting from his catchy book title) have infiltrated popular culture, whereas Gottman's name and research are largely unknown to the general public. Perhaps part of this oversight is due to our misgivings about and unfamiliarity with science and the scientific method. Further, as interested observers of human behavior and especially of romantic human behavior, many of us might be dubious about the use of the scientific method to understand it. In fact, one might wonder exactly how such methods could be applied to a topic so personal and intimate.

The Science of Intimate Relationships: Controversies and Issues

The *science* of intimate relationships? Former U.S. Senator William Proxmire voiced just such a sentiment when in the 1970s he denounced the National Science Foundation for funding the scientific study of romantic attraction. Proxmire bestowed the Golden Fleece award to social psychologists Ellen Berscheid and Elaine Walster because he doubted that they could uncover the secrets of love. Furthermore, he expressed skepticism that anyone other than the researchers themselves would want to know about the results of such experimentation!

Despite such opposition, the scientific investigation of close relationships has thrived and grown. Indeed, we have come a long way from the days when a university professor could be fired for studying the seductive effects of whispering into someone's ear. Furthermore, we have developed and refined several different methods for studying close relationships. However, before discussing these research methods, it might be worth noting that there are several assumptions (e.g., empiricism, determinism, testability, and parsimony) and goals underlying the conduct of scientific research. Although a complete discussion of these assumptions goes beyond the scope of this chapter, it is important to address here one of the goals implicit in all methods of scientific research: objectivity. No matter the method—quantitative or qualitative, field or laboratory—researchers strive to collect objective, unbiased data. The goal of objectivity is what sets the scientific pursuit of knowledge apart from the layperson's astute observations and interpretation of behavior. Data that are collected through objective methods result in a truer picture of the phenomena of interest. Objectivity helps to ensure that a researcher's beliefs, prejudices, or biases will not color either the collection or interpretation of the data. Thus, psychologists are careful to use objectivity and objective methods to gather evidence to support their claims.

Ironically, objectivity may be the most difficult goal to maintain when attempting to study highly personal topics such as love, partner selection, abusive relationships, and divorce, to name a few areas covered in this text. However, perhaps even more of an issue is the question of how best to study relationships. How does one go about studying something intangible, something that can't be seen? For while it is easy to operationally define *couple,* so much of what truly defines and shapes relationships lies in the interactions that occur between people. This is more difficult to quantify and analyze. Of course this problem is not unique to the examination of intimate relationships; however, it is probably especially acute in this arena. For example, observing couples may seem like a sensible solution to this problem, but exactly how does one go about observing a couple engaged in courtship or lovemaking or conflict? Ah, the researcher must be creative, indeed! This book will cover a range of methodologies that relationship researchers use in their quest for the truth; however, the masterful researcher will recognize both the strengths and weaknesses inherent in each methodology. In other words, there is no single perfect way to study relationships. Instead, the canny investigator is careful to match the question to the method, the theoretical assumptions underlying the method to the relationship issue being studied (Duck & Montgomery, 1991).

Before plunging into a discourse on methodology, let's back up a few steps and start at the very beginning. Basically, when psychologists are conducting a research study, they are testing a hypothesis, or the relationship between two or more variables. For example, we might want to test the following hypotheses: Blonds have more fun (or more formally, attractive individuals get more dates); insecurity leads to jealousy in romantic relationships; and people who are in love spend more time gazing into each other's eyes.

However, before we hurry out the door to collect our data, we must first operationally define our concepts. That is, we must specify, in concrete, measurable terms, what we mean by "attractive," "jealousy," and "love." We could operationalize "love" as a person's score on a questionnaire, or a person's heart rate or pupillary dilation when gazing at or thinking about the target of his or her affection. Thus, operational definitions specify exactly how our concept should be measured and the process through which we will measure it. Further, it allows others to understand and replicate our efforts. Finally, these functions ensure objectivity in the measurement and investigation of our variables.

It is important to add, however, that although operationalizing our concept lends objectivity, clarity, precision, and the possibility of replication to our experiment, it also detracts from the depth and breadth of the concept being operationalized For example, if we were to rely solely on a single operationalization of "love" (e.g., pupillary dilation), many would agree with the late Senator Proxmire's criticisms regarding the sterility and futility of conducting a science of relationships. It's clear that this definition alone doesn't fully capture what most of us would call love. Thus, a single operational definition taps into a limited set of the relevant features of the concept and clearly doesn't capture the entirety of the concept. It is for this reason that some researchers (e.g., Judd, Smith, & Kidder, 1991) suggest using multiple operational definitions to define complex concepts such as "love." This caveat is probably even more important to topics of study in close relationships, in which many of the constructs are complex, broad, and therefore more difficult to operationalize. The practice of carefully defining and constructing our variables, formally identifying and measuring them, is indeed a first step.

Methodology: Data Collection

Archival Research

Once we have arrived at a suitable operationalization of our variables, we can proceed to the data collection stage of our study. However, at this stage, we have at our disposal many options on how to proceed. One method of investigation is archival research. This methodology uses already existing data that have been collected for purposes other than those of the archival researcher, who then reanalyzes them to address a whole new set of questions. There are many sources for archival data. One source, *statistical records,* includes information such as census data, school and hospital records, sports statistics, and business records. *Survey archives,* on the other hand, are archives such as those maintained by the National Opinion Research Center (NORC) and the University of Michigan, which compile the results of a variety of surveys and opinion polls. *Written records* or "personal accounts" such as diaries, journals, and letters are another source of archival data. Finally, *mass communications,* including newspapers and journals, radio and television broadcasts, and film, represent the last and richest category of archival data.

In order to examine our particular research question through this methodology, we could review TV footage of talk-show interviews involving couples. After gathering a sufficient number of these interviews, we would then submit them to a content analysis. A *content analysis* is a way of coding archival data into measurable units of analysis. Categories are developed by the researchers or coders, and the data are then analyzed to establish the frequency of occurrence of data within those categories. Thus, in conducting archival research, investigators must (1) decide on a sampling strategy and the medium from which the data will be drawn,

(2) determine what type of coding categories will be used, (3) establish inter-rater reliability measures for interpreting the data, and (4) analyze the coded data.

Some of the advantages of this approach are that it enables researchers to study phenomena that take place over long periods of time. For example, we could conduct an archival study on the nature of love by analyzing and comparing love letters written early in the century to more current romantic epistles.

The archival method also enables us to collect, economically, data that span broad geographical areas. We could tap into census data to get an idea of the changing composition of the American family, or we might analyze marriage announcements in newspapers from different cities across the country to get an idea of what might bring couples together. A final advantage of the archival method is that it allows us to examine the effects of nonmanipulable phenomena such as suicides, spousal abuse, natural disasters, accidents, and so on.

One of the major disadvantages of this method is that the researcher does not have control over the objectivity and accuracy of the data collection. Records may be incomplete, carelessly maintained, or biased. Codes for interpreting data may be lost, confusing, or incomplete. Further, inaccuracies in the interpretation of records may result from the passage of time. Finally, it is difficult to determine causality with this method.

Systematic Observation

Another method of data collection is through observation. There are many different ways in which we can observe human behavior and interaction: from naturalistic observations to laboratory observations, from unstructured observations to systematic and structured observations.

Indeed, in defining the different types of observation, we see how complex and varied observations can be. For example, although we generally tend to equate field or naturalisitic observations as unstructured, we can impose structured observations in the field (e.g., observing personal space violations in a public restroom; Middlemist, Knowles, & Mather, 1977). Likewise, we can conduct fairly unstructured observations in the laboratory (e.g., observing children interacting in a free-play situation) (Sillars, 1991).

Let's examine this methodology via our question of whether we are attracted to others who are similar to ourselves. We might decide to answer this question by observing couples in transit. We would position our researchers at stoplights and have them record the physical similarity and positiveness of the exchange between our targeted passengers (i.e., men and women). Clearly, one of the advantages of this research method is that we have a high degree of certainty that the behaviors we observe are unaffected in any way by our presence. Our research participants, unaware of our presence or intent, behave in a natural way, in a natural setting. Further, since no manipulations are used to induce conversation in our couples, the treatment is also a natural one. The advantage of this naturalness, however, is offset by the utter lack of control we are able to exercise over this situation.

This lack of control reduces confidence in our results. For example, we have very little certainty, in this study, that the passengers we've observed are indeed couples. That is, although we observed men and women in the act of commuting, we have no control over or knowledge of their actual relationship. We may be observing coworkers, neighbors, siblings, or carpoolers. Thus, we clearly have poor control over the countless variables that may be influencing the situation or behavior. This is an important issue and one that we will return to later in this chapter.

Observations are usually conducted in a more controlled, structured manner than this example suggests. In fact, some observation methods are quite complex—a far cry from our fictitious traffic study. For example, researchers in marital relationships (e.g., Bradbury & Fincham, 1989) use an observational technique in which couples are seated at opposite ends of a table and are observed while they interact. While trained observers rate the couples on several behavioral dimensions, couples also record their own perceptions of the behaviors as well as their feelings about their interaction. Information is gathered on several levels, not only through observation, but also through self-reports and behavioral ratings. Further, the interactions and data collection procedures are more structured and controlled.

William Ickes and his colleagues developed an ingenious method of making observations in the lab: the dyadic interaction paradigm (Ickes, 1982; 1983; Ickes et al., 1990). This method enables researchers to collect and analyze data on both overt behaviors as well as on thoughts, feelings, attitudes, and perceptions. In the dyadic interaction paradigm, participants' interactions are videotaped surreptitiously while they are awaiting the arrival of the research assistant. The study, in other words, begins *outside* the lab proper, and the waiting room becomes the natural setting for the observation. This, however, is only the first component of the dyadic interaction paradigm. After the interactions between participants (e.g., strangers, lovers, friends, etc.) are videotaped, the interpretation phase begins. Participants are seated in separate cubicles where they report their thoughts and feelings while viewing the videotaped interactions. Thus, this paradigm yields a wealth of data on both the behavioral and cognitive components of social interactions that occur *naturally*.

Thus, in systematic observation, procedures for sampling and observing behaviors are developed to conduct an objective measure of behaviors and other observable phenomena. The advantages of systematic observation are its naturalness: naturalness in setting if conducted in the field, naturalness in behaviors that are observed, and naturalness in treatments. Some research questions can be addressed only through this method. Many treatments are either impossible or unethical to manipulate. We cannot, for example, manipulate things such as droughts, hurricanes, and earthquakes (i.e., forces of nature); crime, unemployment, and social economic status (i.e., social forces); or introversion/extraversion, sociability, and sense of humor (i.e., person variables). Other events—for instance, relationship dissolution, high-risk sexual behavior, and conflict—would simply be unethical to manipulate. Research questions dealing with topics such as these would be served well by either naturalistic observation or field experimentation. However, as mentioned earlier, the weakness of this methodology resides in the absence of control that we have over other extraneous variables. This lack of control leads to problems in interpretation, and, most importantly, to an inability to perform causal analyses.

Interviews and Surveys

By now, many readers might be thinking, "If you want to find out how similarity affects attraction, just ask!" Thus, we might conduct either an interview or create a survey to answer our question. Interviews can take place in face-to-face sessions or via the telephone, and their format can be either structured or open ended. Although one of the most costly and time-consuming forms of collecting data, the main advantage of the interview is that it yields the highest quality data of any research methodology (Judd, Smith, & Kidder, 1991). Additionally, interviews usually have the highest response rate, and able interviewers who establish a good rapport with their respondents are able to elicit highly accurate answers from them. Further, during an interview, the interviewer can detect any confusion on the part of the participants and clarify questions they may have. The disadvantages of the interview stem directly from its advantages. First, as already mentioned, interviews are costly. Second, the rapport established by the interviewer can lead to bias and experimenter demand. Respondents may frame their responses in ways that they believe will please the interviewer. Finally, with regard to sensitive topics, the face-to-face interview might be less conducive to frankness and openness than other more anonymous and private data collection procedures.

In the survey method, questionnaires are distributed to large numbers of people who respond to questions in either structured or open-ended formats. Surveys address a wide variety of topics, ranging from self-reports of respondents' behaviors, feelings, beliefs, attitudes, and recollections of their past, to topics dealing with respondents' assessments of issues, events, institutions, political candidates, and so on. For example, if we decide to use survey research to investigate the relationship between similarity and attraction, we might have our respondents evaluate their previous relationships and rate the degree of correspondence they feel existed with regard to their attitudes, beliefs, values, interests, and activities.

Survey research is an attractive alternative to the interview because of the low cost entailed in producing and reproducing the survey itself. Further, the ease of distributing and responding to surveys and therefore of collecting data from a large number of respondents makes surveys both time and cost effective. Another advantage is that survey respondents are anonymous and therefore more likely to reply honestly. A disadvantage of both the interview and the survey methods is their reliance on respondents' self-reports, which can be unreliable. In their efforts to recall past events, respondents may reconstruct their memories in the process. Further, as psychologists (Nisbett & Wilson, 1977) have found, people really don't have an especially good understanding of their own behavior. Although we think that we have privileged insights into the whys behind what we do, we often make erroneous attributions and self-reports. Berger (1980) and Duck and Sants (1983) have made similar observations in studies involving interpersonal relationships and interactions. Indeed, they find that not only do participants overinterpret their self-insight, but that researchers are also overly confident in people's abilities to have self-knowledge.

Other considerations to take into account when using surveys are decisions of how to construct the survey and who will receive it. In survey construction, researchers must exercise care in determining how to word survey items as well as how to arrange the items or questions. Not surprisingly, the manner in which questions are phrased makes a difference in how they're answered. For example, we might ask the same question in two ways: "Do you approve of interracial relationships?" or "Do you disapprove of interracial relationships?" We may think that we're asking the same basic question (simply worded differently), but the differences inherent in these two sentences can make a world of difference when collecting survey data. Positively worded statements generally tend to prime approval-related thoughts; that is, they bring to mind thoughts that reflect the respondents' positive feelings and beliefs about the topic. Negatively worded statements, on the other hand, will tend to prime negative thoughts and lead to retrieval of negative information related to the question being asked.

Thus, one of the challenges for survey researchers is to ask (often sensitive) questions in as unbiased a manner as possible. Another challenge in the construction of surveys has to do with the sequencing of survey questions. Researchers (e.g., Schuman & Presser, 1981; Schwartz & Clore, 1983; Tourangeau & Rasinski, 1988) have found that different sequences of questions can have different effects on survey questions. For example, Schwartz and Clore (1983) telephoned research participants and asked a series of questions in different orders. Participants phoned on fair, sunny days usually responded to the question "How satisfied are you with your life?" with a positive statement. Participants who were asked the same question on an overcast, dreary day responded more negatively. However, if participants—on either a sunny or cloudy day—were first asked about the weather ("How's the weather down there today?") and then asked about their life satisfaction, the so-called weather effect was gone. Indeed, Schuman and Presser (1981) found that order effects can be as large as 15 percentage points!

In general, context effects are more likely to be found when asking general questions ("Do you think it should be possible for individuals to be involved in romantic relationships with those of different racial and ethnic backgrounds?") than when asking specific questions ("Do you think it should be possible for an Hispanic to be involved in a romantic relationship with an African American?") (Tourangeau & Rasinski, 1988). Thus, when constructing a survey, we might want to start with general questions first and "funnel" down to the specific (Judd, Smith, & Kidder, 1991).

Imagine you were asked to answer several questions about someone, say an actor such as Mel Gibson or Alicia Silverstone. The first item on the survey requests that you rate the sex appeal of the actor. The ensuing items ask that you give your opinion of a particular movie in which the actor starred (e.g., *Braveheart* or *Clueless*), your evaluation of the person's acting skills, his or her humanitarianism, his or her talent as a painter, and so on. According to research, another context-based bias called the *halo effect* might influence your answers to these questions. In this case, your response to the first question (i.e., the sex appeal of the actor) might color or influence your responses to subsequent questions—whether or not these questions have anything to do with the initial question. That is, an actor's sex appeal, although good for box office drawing power, may not necessarily have anything to do with the quality of a particular movie, the actor's actual acting skill, or whether he or she cares about Greenpeace, Amnesty International, or freeing Willy. Nonetheless, if we are smitten by Mel Gibson or Alicia Silverstone, we might find ourselves giving rave reviews to their movies and lauding their art work.

Thus, if in our attempt to discover the relationship between similarity and attraction, we were to ask first about the nature of the relationship or the respondent's feelings toward his or her partner, we might find a bias in our respondent's response to our target question. Thus, survey construction and, more specifically, item ordering are important considerations when using survey methodology.

Still other drawbacks of survey methodology include its high boredom potential. That is, it can be fairly easy for respondents to become bored with and detached from the survey process. When this happens, respondents become disengaged and answer items in a careless or haphazard fashion, thereby threatening the internal validity of the survey. This drawback is not specific to survey research alone; however, the survey format makes this methodology more susceptible to this hazard. Finally, surveys do not give us information on the causal relationship between variables. That is, we cannot ascertain whether one variable was actually instrumental in causing the occurrence or nonoccurrence of another.

In sum, a major weakness of surveys, like observation, archival research, and interviews, is their inability to yield information on causation. Rather, these methodologies tell us about the relationship that exists among two or more variables. This type of relationship is commonly referred to as a *correlation*. We will return to a discussion of correlations later in this chapter.

Experimentation

For many of us, the mere mention of laboratory experimentation probably conjures up images of the bespectacled scientist in his or her white lab coat, supervising mazes full of hapless rats or equally hapless college freshmen hooked up to electric shock delivering devices. The gap between this image and our very personal, emotion-laden beliefs concerning our most intimate relationships is likely responsible for the cynicism that Senator Proxmire expressed for the possibility of a scientific study of relationships.

Exactly how can the scientific approach deal effectively with issues of love, romance, divorce, jealousy, and marriage? Suppose that in our ongoing quest to determine the relationship between similarity and attraction, we decided to conduct an experimental examination of the topic. How might we accomplish this?

Three key elements of a successful experiment are control, random assignment, and comparison. Essentially, researchers attempt to hold all variables constant while allowing only the variable of interest (i.e., the independent variable) to fluctuate. Any changes observed in the behavior of interest (i.e., the dependent variable) can then be attributed to changes in the independent variable. Or, the independent variable is largely responsible for changes in the dependent variable: a causal relationship.

Control is an essential feature of the experiment, and this is one of the main reasons that many experiments are actually conducted in laboratories. The sterile surroundings of the typical lab setting facilitates the type of control that increases our confidence in our findings. Once outside the laboratory, a myriad of factors—factors beyond the researcher's control—affect or have the potential to influence the behavior of interest. Although it is not impossible to conduct experiments outside the lab, greater care needs to be taken to protect the internal validity of the study.

Upon hearing the results of experimental research—such as viewing pornography leads to dissatisfaction with one's partner (Zillmann & Bryant, 1988)—many students often challenge the results with personal anecdotes illustrating how their friends are exceptions to the finding. Another kind of reaction falls under the rubric of "Who were the research participants?" Were there any Asians in the study? Were gays included in the sample? Were any depressed or introverted individuals in the experiment? What the student of experimental research should understand is that results represent a group outcome, an average score that comes to represent a range of scores. In response to the "Who were the research participants?" questions, random assignment to condition should ensure that individual differences are distributed evenly across conditions.

Through *random assignment* (e.g., flipping a coin, drawing random numbers), everyone who participates in an experiment has an equal chance to be assigned to any of its conditions. Another way of explaining the function of random assignment is to imagine what would happen without it. Suppose, for example, that research participants in the pornography experiment were allowed to choose the condition in which they would participate (i.e., subject self-selection). Suppose, further, that devout, religious men chose to view the *National Geographic* videos, whereas the "party animals" and playboys selected the pornographic video condition. In this case, we have two variables covarying in a systematic fashion: type of video (pornography, nature) and research participant variables. It is impossible to decide what caused differences in relationship satisfaction (dependent variable). With random assignment, however, our devout research participants and our party animals would be evenly distributed across all conditions. Changes in the outcome can then be attributed to the independent variable or variables.

Finally, the idea of *comparison* is implicit in the two points already addressed. In the interest of making it explicit, experimental designs usually include two or more conditions. In the simplest two-group design, the outcome of one group (a control group or pretest) is compared to that of the treatment group (or a posttest). Other types of between-group comparisons include varying the level of the treatment (e.g., no pornography, three hours of pornography, six hours of pornography, etc.).

Now that we have all the elements of experimentation in place, let's apply them to our question regarding similarity and attraction. How can we study this issue in the lab? Suppose we were interested primarily in attitude similarity with an eye toward eliminating physical appearance from our equation. One possibility for testing our hypothesis might include the following. First, we might have our participants complete some type of attitude measurement instrument. Then, if we had the ability, technology, and skill, we could randomly assign participants to computer chatrooms that are occupied by a supposed cyberperson of the opposite sex who is attitudinally either similar or dissimilar to the participant. At the end of their dialogue session, we could measure several things: attraction, liking, intimacy of conversation, number of topics discussed, interest in actually meeting their cyberdate, and so on.

Thus, true experiments are attractive because they give researchers greater control over the variables of interest as well as control over unwanted variables. Further, as a result of this control, researchers are able to test the nature of causal relationships that may exist among variables. Not surprisingly, the drawbacks of the experimental method are the antithesis of those of the nonexperimental methods—that is, what experiments gain in control, they lose in real-world realism.

Experimental and Mundane Realism.   As already mentioned in passing, the laboratory setting is usually sparse and sterile. Studies that attempt to investigate topics as hot and sexy as obsessions with secret lovers (Lane & Wegner, 1994; Wegner, Lane, & Dimitri, 1994) might include having participants play a game of Battleship while they use their feet to tap out coded communications with their partners—a far cry from clandestine meetings in smoke-filled bars and humid backseats. Yet, is this degree of realism truly essential to the successful experiment? Well, it depends.

The answer to this question hinges on the type of research one is conducting: theoretical or applied. And, more precisely, it depends on the type of generalizability the researcher is seeking (Mook, 1980). For example, in basic, theoretical research, researchers are interested in generalizing or inferring a general set of principles—their *findings* or a set of theoretically based predictions—to all others. Applied researchers, on the other hand, are interested in generalizing results of the study to a specific setting or to a specific population of people (e.g., assembly-line workers in love, people who cruise leather bars, sex habits of the HIV positive, etc.). The aims of these two types of research differ along with the importance of realism.

In the first case, that of theoretical research, because the goal is to generalize a set of principles, an exact duplication of the real world is less important than is *experimental realism*. This type of realism requires that experimental participants be fully involved and absorbed by the experiment and interpret the manipulations in just the ways that the researcher had envisioned. In other words, the impact and experience of the experiment must be real and meaningful to the participant. This ensures that the variables of interest are interpreted correctly and that results therefore speak to the desired theoretical issues.

Whereas experimental realism is fundamental to theoretical research, *mundane realism* is key to applied research. Mundane realism refers to a resemblance to the real world. Because an applied researcher's interest lies in generalizing results to specific settings or populations, obtaining as close a resemblance as possible to those settings or populations strengthens the generalizations that can be made.

In sum, the experimental method provides researchers with a powerful tool to test different predictions. Yet, despite its advantages, it too is not without its weaknesses. Thus, a more accurate view would be that all methods of data collection have both their advantages and disadvantages. And, returning to issues raised earlier in this chapter, perhaps the most important determinant of which methodology to use is the topic being addressed. With this in mind, the researcher as well as the consumer can weigh the pros and cons of the method against the question it is addressing.

New Directions in Data Collection

Upon close inspection, most of the methods discussed thus far deal largely with two categories of social interactions, or domains of experience (Reis, 1994): the domain of *reconstructed experience* and the domain of *exemplary experience*. The third type of experience, that of *ongoing* social interactions and experiences is, according to Harry Reis (1994; Wheeler & Reis, 1991), woefully underrepresented in current approaches to the study of relationships.

Let's take a closer look. First, the domains of reconstructed and exemplary experiences have been used extensively to study relationships. Any type of self-report measure that asks participants to recall particular events, thoughts, feelings, or relationships is asking for a reconstruction of the issue under scrutiny. And although this method might yield a lot of interesting information, there are some drawbacks to its usage. Cognitive and social psychologists have established that many factors affect recall: the way the question is asked, the context in which it is presented, the mood of the respondent when asked (e.g., Erber, 1991), and so on. Indeed, reconstruction of past events can be viewed as taking place within a frame of facts; however, like the artist who interprets reality, the details that are used to fill the frame may be generated not from actual events but from a variety of other influences. Thus, caution should be used when interpreting data gathered through the domain of reconstructed experience, and this should by no means represent the sole method for studying relationships.

If the domain of reconstructed experience is like a movie flashback in which respondents attempt to dredge up and analyze past experiences, the domain of exemplary experience is like a studio portrait of the participants. Just as we put on our best faces for that portrait, so too do participants in laboratory studies. Knowing that our behaviors are being studied and analyzed may increase self-presentation concerns: We might become extremely concerned about being perceived in the "right" way. In addition to capturing the best portrait, research in this domain also attempts to discover what is "typical." Like the Norman Rockwell portraits of America and Americans in the 1950s, what is typical may apply to many but certainly not to all. This approach fails to capture the details and minutiae of everyday experiences. Although problematic, this criticism is by no means an indictment against laboratory research, but merely a caution that this too should not be the only way to investigate ongoing close relationships.

Reis (1994) suggested that in the third domain, that of ongoing relationships, the humdrum everyday ebbs and flows of life are the stuff that define and influence interpersonal relationships. Unlike a flashback or a portrait, this domain is like a video camera running silently from the corner of the room. Participants forget its presence as it records the mundane, spontaneous aspects of their daily lives—not only the cataclysmic, distinctive, joyful, or otherwise significant life-changing events but also the "smaller" moments that fill in the gaps. Since relationships are defined by the social interactions that comprise them, then perhaps studying the continuous flow of interactions is what will ultimately reveal them to us.

Methods for studying this domain can be categorized into three types: interval, signal, and event recordings (Reis, 1994). In *interval-contingent recordings*, participants record their experiences at predetermined and (usually) regular intervals: every morning, every evening, after every meal, and so forth. Participants giving *signal-contingent recordings* report on their experiences whenever they are signaled by the researcher. Signals may include beepers, pagers, or telephone calls, with participants being signaled an average of 7 to 10 times daily. Thus, unlike the interval-recording method, reports collected via the signal-contingent method can be more numerous and their occurrence more random. Finally, the *event-contingent recording* methodology elicits participant reports after well-defined and predetermined events have taken place. Once the event has occurred, participants make the appropriate recordings and perhaps complete short questionnaires about the event.

The three domains of inquiry, although very different from one another, are not mutually exclusive. Indeed, data gathered across all three domains, together, should give us the clearest picture of the phenomenon under investigation. For example, data gathered via the domain of reconstructed experience tell us about how people understand and *interpret* their lives, whereas data gathered through experimentation (exemplary experience) tell us how people react in particular, specific situations. Finally, research conducted on ongoing experiences provides us with immediate and continuing data on people's thoughts, feelings, and behaviors. Like converging operations, information assembled across the three domains should give us the most comprehensive and inclusive understanding of behavior (Reis, 1994).

Diaries and logs enable us to tap into the domain of ongoing experience. Unlike the diary of archival research discussed earlier in this chapter, these types of recordings are structured, standardized, and goal directed (Duck, 1991). Wheeler and Nezlak (1977) developed the Rochester Interaction Record (RIR) as a structured means of capturing unfolding interactions and daily events. Not only does the RIR provide a means of collecting factual information (e.g., date, time, place of interaction, number of partners, length of interaction) but it also allows researchers to gather information about participants' own insights and judgments regarding their interactions (see Figure 2.1).

The potential for this methodology is exciting. Logs can be modified to fit a wide variety of research questions. Duck's (1991) Iowa Communication Record (ICR) is another type of diary log. It is similar to the RIR in many respects; however, it focuses more closely on the communication process itself. Participants using the ICR will answer questions regarding the topic of their conversation, the quality of the conversation, its impact, as well as what they were doing before and after the exchange. Thus, the ICR allows access to everyday talk—the conversations that really define our interactions and relationships.

Let's now return to our investigation of similarity and attraction. If we were to apply this approach to our question, we would include our previously discussed survey study, along with our electronic laboratory investigation. However, to round out our investigation, we would now launch an investigation in the domain of ongoing experience. Perhaps an event-contingent recording would be best suited for our question; that is, participants would keep a log after each social

FIGURE 2.1 *Adaptation of the Rochester Interaction Record (RIR)*

Date: _____	*Time:* _____	*Length of Conversation:* _____
Initials:		
Sex _____	*No. of males:* _____	*No. of females:* _____
Nature: Work ____	Task ____ Pastime ____	Conversation ____ Date ____

Intimacy:	superficial	1 2 3 4 5 6 7	meaningful
I disclosed:	very little	1 2 3 4 5 6 7	a great deal
Other disclosed:	very little	1 2 3 4 5 6 7	a great deal
Quality:	unpleasant	1 2 3 4 5 6 7	pleasant
Satisfaction:	less than expected	1 2 3 4 5 6 7	more than expected
Initiation:	I initiated	1 2 3 4 5 6 7	other initiated
Influence:	I influenced more	1 2 3 4 5 6 7	other influenced more

Source: Wheeler, Reis, and Nezlek, 1983. Reprinted by permission.

interaction. In addition to gathering information about interpersonal similarity, we might ask our participants to evaluate the tenor of and satisfaction with each social interaction. Together, data accumulated from these three domains give us the most complete picture of our question.

Analysis: Before and After Data Collection

Now that we have collected our data, we need to analyze them and interpret our results. Although an in-depth discussion of specific statistical techniques is beyond the scope of this text, it is important to emphasize the importance of the relationship between the data collection method used (design) and the type of analysis to be used. That is, data analysis should really begin with the design of the study. Design drives analysis.

One topic that will be addressed is the difference between correlations and true experiments. Finally, the section will conclude with a discussion of some innovations in data analysis techniques.

Correlations

A *correlation* describes the relationship among variables. For example, returning to our ongoing research into the relationship between similarity and attraction, we might ask couples to answer two different self-report questionnaires: one that gathers information about their individual attitudes, beliefs, hobbies, goals, and economic and educational backgrounds, and another that asks them to rate their partner on several dimensions of attractiveness. Upon submitting this information to a correlational analysis, we would be able to get a picture of the relationship of these variables to one another. What is meant by "relationship between variables"?

Several different outcomes are possible with correlational analysis. First, such an analysis can reveal that there is *no relationship* among the variables of interest; that is, changes in one variable are totally unrelated to changes (nonchanges) in other variables. A second outcome is called a *positive correlation*. This is the case when increases in one variable are related to increases in the other. Thus, if we found a positive correlation between similarity and attraction, we would conclude that the greater the similarity between partners, the greater the attraction, or as similarity increases, so too does attraction. A third type of correlation is a *negative correlation*. In this type of relationship, one variable increases in value or intensity while the other decreases. A negative correlation, in our example, would translate into the following: As similarity between partners increases, attraction decreases.

Correlational analyses are especially useful for investigating variables that cannot be manipulated: natural disasters, political events, personal attributes, births, deaths, suicides, disease, and the like. That is, variables that cannot be manipulated due to either physical impossibility or ethical reasons can be studied with the correlational method. Rather than physically manipulating the variables of interest, researchers simply measure them and then determine what type of relationship exists between them.

One of the main disadvantages of the correlational method is that it does not speak to the issue of the causal relationship among variables. Thus, while we can learn about the nature of the relationship among variables (positive, negative, none), we cannot know with any certainty that changes in one variable actually *caused* changes or variations in the other. For example, the following provides a vivid illustration of the care that must be taken in interpreting correlational analyses.

Research conducted in third-world countries reveals a positive correlation between intelligence and height. In other words, the taller a person, the smarter. Aside from the fact that this finding would make the National Basketball Association an intellectual powerhouse rivaling the best universities, there are other major points to be taken from this example. First and foremost is the fact that correlations *do not* imply causation. Therefore, although we are now aware of the relationship between height and intelligence in Haiti, we are unable to make causal statements about this relationship, or to suggest that one causes the other (height causes one to be smarter? or higher intelligence causes one to be taller?).

Indeed, as is frequently the case, a third variable may in fact be responsible for changes in both observed variables (i.e., height and intelligence). In our example, note that this finding is confined to third-world countries. Perhaps a mediating variable, the causal component, is socioeconomic status. Children growing up in wealthy homes not only eat their Wheaties every morning, but they actually attend school—good schools—and stay awake to learn. Wealth provides them with both nutrition and educational opportunities. On the other hand, children born to poverty not only miss meals but they are probably also unable to get much of an education (or to benefit from one): Poverty leads to poor nutrition and health as well as poorer educational opportunities.

Most of the previously discussed data collection methods have various advantages, usually revolving around naturalness and feasibility. Additionally, they all share a common disadvantage: the inability to determine causation. The only method that yields information on causality is the experimental method.

New Directions in Data Analysis: The Social Relations Model

Kenny's (1988; 1994; Kenny & Kashy, 1991) Social Relations Model provides an example of a creative methodology that pursues and highlights the complexities of interpersonal relationships. The model is notable for many reasons, two of which are its innovation in design and analysis. The Social Relations Model uses two specific research paradigms to collect data: a round robin and a block design. In both designs, groups of participants interact in various combinations such that each person is observed with multiple partners. Thus, several measures are drawn from each participant, and these multiple measures reveal the degree to which effects are due to the individual actor, his or her response to others, or his or her response to a specific relationship. Although this data collection paradigm is exciting and innovative, this text will focus on the Social Relation Model's contribution to data analysis. In this regard, a major innovation of the model has to do with its treatment of variance.

Let us back up a few steps and start at the conceptual beginning. One of the main goals of the Social Relations Model is to measure and analyze the degree of interdependence (or agreement or similarity) that exists between actors in a dyad. Social scientists have long attempted to define and measure the intangible element of social interactions that transcends the participants themselves: the "something more" that results when we interact with one another. Wegner, Erber, and Raymond (1991) suggested that transactive memory between couples is a type of transcendence wherein the members of the couple demonstrate interdependence of knowledge and, together, demonstrate memory abilities that exceed the sum of the individual units. In a similar vein, Kenny proposed that what transcends the individuals in a relationship is their interdependence. Thus, the partitioning and analysis of interdependence is an integral part of the Social Relations Model.

Kenny and Kashy (1991) have suggested that there are two types of interdependence: within dyad and between dyad. *Within-dyad interdependence* refers to what is shared or exchanged within the couple. It is a longitudinal measure of a single couple's (dyad's) interactions. For example, if Monique responds to Harry's queries with impatience and aggravation, Harry might react with anger and defensiveness. Monique may in turn be hurt by Harry's response and become withdrawn and hostile. This give-and-take demonstrates how one partner's reactions are dependent on his or her partner's preceding actions.

Between-dyad interdependence, on the other hand, is completely different from within-dyad interdependence (Kenny & Kashy, 1991). It represents the degree of similarity or agreement at a single point in time when measured across several dyads or couples. This type of interdependence is of particular significance to social scientists and to the discussion here because it impacts directly our statistical analysis of relational data.

In the Social Relations Model, interdependence is comprised of three parts: individual, dyadic, and occasion specific. The model allows researchers to partition variance and ascertain the degree to which variables are caused by effects occurring at the level of the actor, the dyad, or the specific occasion. For example, self-disclosure can be viewed from the individual level (Harry discloses to everyone), the dyadic level (Harry discloses to one person in particular), and the occasion-specific level (Harry, along with everyone else, demonstrates a high degree of self-disclosure while flying on airplanes). Thus, whereas traditional researchers often treat interdependence as a statistical nuisance, Kenny's model focuses on it and examines interdependence in order to get a clearer picture of the origin of different relationship effects and, ultimately, of the "stuff" that transcends our individual selves. In other words, one person's trash is another's treasure!

Summary

Even the most casual of readers will notice that each research type has its unique set of strengths and weaknesses. More precisely, each method has weaknesses. Thus, instead of being left with the easy task of simply choosing the "best" method, we are forced to weigh the pros and cons of each and to find the balance between them (e.g., how much control versus how much naturalness?).

Yet another consideration when choosing from among the many different research methods has to do with the hypothesis. Methods should be chosen to match the question being asked. That is, instead of shopping for a method based on personal preference or convenience ("I'll use this because I think it has the most strengths and fewest weaknesses"), we should be careful to base our choice of methodology in the specific research question we are asking. In other words, the methodology should be the slave to the question.

One paradoxical principle of data analysis is that it starts before the data collection even begins. That is, design and data analysis are intertwined; thus, data analysis considerations should be at the fore when designing a study.

Studying relationships and interactions present special problems for the social scientist. In this regard, innovative methods have been developed both to collect and to analyze data. These methods attempt to measure the intangible and preserve the true essence of relationships while enabling objective analyses. Approaches such as the framework suggested by Reis and creative methodologies such as the Social Relations Model provide increasingly sensitive methods for measuring a difficult area of study. Thus, as discussed throughout this chapter, careful study can effectively illuminate our understanding of close relationships. Current approaches along with good, old-fashioned creativity are likely to push relationships research into new frontiers.

3

Physical Attraction

A thing of beauty is a joy forever.

—John Keats, "Endymion"

*In recent weeks . . . suspicion—that beauty blights our better judgment—
has again crept into the public conversation. In critiques of the passionate
response to John F. Kennedy Jr.'s death, and in reports about the upcoming
auction of Marilyn Monroe's clothes, shoes, jewelry and other personal
effects, is a persistent mutter that Kennedy and Monroe are undeserving of
such attention. . . . If they're beautiful, the thinking goes, they can't be deep.
There can't be more than what meets the eye.*

—Julia Keller, *Chicago Tribune*, August 15, 1999

The two opposing views depicted above illustrate both our absorption with
beauty and our simultaneous misgivings with this predilection. Is it any surprise,
then, that much of the early literature on intimate relationships was devoted to
exploring the physical basis of attraction? That such issues can be investigated
with relative ease did not hurt either. They are highly conducive to being studied
in the context of tightly controlled laboratory experiments in which the physical
attractiveness of another can be varied while everything else can be held constant.
Any differences that are obtained on a dependent measure can therefore be attributed to the variations in attractiveness employed in the experiment. And even
though there were reports as far back as the early 1970s indicating that understanding (initial) attraction between two people may tell us little about what happens in their (ongoing) relationships (Levinger, Senn, & Jorgensen, 1970; Levinger
& Snoek, 1972), the field was relatively slow to shift its attention to issues going
beyond attraction. Furthermore, despite the fact that many of the towering figures
in research on physical attraction were women (Karen Dion, Ellen Berscheid,
Elaine Hatfield), much of the early attraction research focused amost exclusively
on heterosexual men's perceptions of women's attractiveness. And although more
recent research has freed itself from its early androcentric bias, most of the more
current work is limited to cross-gender perceptions of attractiveness by heterosexual men and women.

These shortcomings aside, there is a second, and perhaps more compelling,
reason for starting this book by discussing physical attraction, and it has to do
with its importance for the initiation of close relationships. Simply put, we are
more likely to initiate relationships with people who have physically attractive
characteristics. This could be due to a number of reasons. It could be that physically attractive individuals are simply more noticeable. In the course of any given
day, we tend to encounter a large number of people—on the train, in school or at
work, at the grocery store, and at our favorite watering hole. The vast majority of
the people we encounter in these ways are quickly forgotten. It may be that attrac-

tive people catch our attention more than others—we look at them longer, think about them more—and therefore they have an edge over others when we feel inclined to form a relationship of any kind. Of course, there is a problem with this kind of reasoning. If relationship initiation were solely dependent on the salience of another, unattractive people should have a similar edge, because standing out in context often requires little more than that a person is different from the rest (e.g., Taylor et al., 1977).

Moreover, our predilection to seek relationships with attractive others is still present when their noticeability or salience is held constant, especially in dating relationships. In other words, given a choice among several possible dates, we tend to prefer those whom we perceive to be most attractive. This chapter addresses the importance of physical attractiveness in dating and beyond, and discusses some of the explanations social scientists have advanced to account for it.

Physical Attractiveness and Dating Choices

One of the first studies to look explicitly at the relationship between physical attractiveness and the initiation of close relationships dates back to 1966. For some, 1966 is a distant memory; for most, it is a part of history. Here is a recapitulation of some of the events of that year: President Lyndon Baynes Johnson was still convinced that the war in Vietnam could be won by sending increased numbers of young men to fight in its jungles and rice fields. Closer to home, the Green Bay Packers had just won the first Superbowl ever played. On the pop music circuit, a young and somewhat obscure guitar player from Seattle by the name of Jimi Hendrix went on tour as the opening act for a group called The Monkees, whose lead singer, teenage heartthrob Davy Jones, sang about the importance of good looks by proclaiming to have become a believer at the sight of a pretty woman's face ("I'm a Believer"). Critics and just about anyone with a taste in music were quick to point out that the Monkees' phenomenal success that year was less due to the quality of their music than the physical appeal of its lead singer. Needless to say, they were neither the first nor the last to base their success on something other than the quality of their "product." However, the relative obscurity The Monkees have attained by now allows us to ask a larger question without offending the musical tastes of the readers of this book. That is, to what extent are our thoughts, feelings, and behavior toward others influenced by such peripheral aspects as their good looks?

A provocative answer to this question was provided that same year (1966) in the form of a field experiment conducted at the University of Minnesota (Walster et al., 1966) that looked at the role of physical attractiveness in the context of dating choices. In this study, more than 700 freshmen participated in a "Computer Dance" held the week before classes started. Research participants were told that if they chose to participate, they would be assigned a date by a computer. Tickets could be obtained only by appearing in person at the Student Union. When students came to pick up their tickets, they were asked to show their photo ID to one person, sign for their tickets with a second person, and pick up the tickets from yet a third person. As it turns out, the people handling the ticket distribution were employed by the experimenters to rate independently the physical attractiveness of research participants who were about to participate in the Computer Dance. Participants were then randomly assigned a date of the opposite sex with whom they spent the evening at the computer dance a few days later. During intermissions, all research participants were asked to rate their dates on a number of dimensions, including how attractive they thought their dates were, how comfortable they were with their dates during the dance, and whether they would like to date their partners again.

As it turns out, the only predictor for research participants' answers to these questions was the attractiveness of their dates. How much the students liked their dates, how comfortable they felt during the date, and how much they wanted to date the person in the future was solely determined by their dates' physical attractiveness. This finding was somewhat surprising, especially in light of the observation that research participants' responses were not at all influenced by such variables as their own level of attractiveness, self-esteem, and general level of aspiration.

The idea that we base our dating choices solely on our dates' physical attractiveness is somewhat disheartening. After all, it seems to fly in the face of such admonitions as not to judge a book by its cover and that beauty is only skin deep. However, the phenomenon has shown to be fairly robust (e.g., Sprecher, 1989a) and universal (Hatfield & Sprecher, 1986), even extending to homosexual couples (Sergios & Cody, 1986). At the same time, this phenomenon is not without its limitations. For example, men tend to place a higher premium on physical attractiveness than women do (Feingold, 1990, 1991), although it appears that this is mostly the case when we look at what men and women *say* about how important attractiveness is to them. When we look at what men and women *do*, the difference is somewhat weaker, albeit still in existence (Sprecher, 1986). Consistent with this sex difference, among married couples the physical attractiveness of the wife is the main determinant for some aspects of dyadic adjustment. Specifically, husbands reported lower sexual satisfaction as the physical attractiveness of their wives declined as a function of age, although the same was not true for wives (Margolin & White, 1987).

One frequently heard argument against the seeming importance of physical attractiveness for dating is that its role changes as people get older and as couples continue dating. Under such circumstances, people may become more realistic in their choices. Instead of reaching for the fairest of them all, they may look for others who match their own level of attractiveness. This idea that romantic couples in ongoing relationships are matched in their level of attractiveness has received some empirical support (Murstein, 1972; Price & Vandenberg, 1979). And while some studies indicate that matching levels of attractiveness are primarily found among long-term, committed couples (Murstein & Christy, 1976; White, 1980), other studies suggest that matching may be especially important during the early stages of relationships (Feingold, 1988). There is even evidence that matching is important for same-sex friendships (Cash & Derlega, 1978), although once again men are more likely to base same-sex friendship choices on attractiveness than women (Feingold, 1988).

One of the earliest and most dramatic demonstrations for the veracity of the matching hypothesis in the initiation of romantic relationships comes from a study (Berscheid et al., 1971) that used the same "Computer Dance" techniques previously employed by Walster and colleagues (1966) with one major difference. Rather than being assigned a date, research participants could choose from several possible dates who varied in their level of attractiveness. As it turns out, research participants chose dates that matched their own self-reported level of attractiveness. This occurred regardless of whether research participants thought that their potential date might accept or reject them.

At first glance, the findings of this second "Computer Dance" study seem to be at odds with Walster and colleagues' observation that the date's level of physical attractiveness was the only thing that mattered. After all, people can't very well seek the most attractive dates and at the same time those who match their level of attractiveness. However, a closer inspection of the results shows that the findings may be complementary rather than contradictory. Matching may most readily be observed in an initial dating choice when there is a range of potential dating partners, as was the case in the Berscheid and colleagues' study. On the other hand, when fate or a computer arranges a date with a highly attractive person, as was the case in the Walster and colleagues' study, people tend to attempt to maintain that contact, especially after they already had some interactions with the date. In other words, matching may be a motive in achieving a date, whereas attractiveness may be a motive in holding on to that date.

Even with issues of timing aside, there appear to be few people who think of themselves as unattractive. In a survey of 2,000 men and women, Hatfield and Sprecher (1986) found that most *adults* are quite happy with the way they looked. Only 4 percent of the men and 7 percent of the women they surveyed indicated that they were dissatisfied with their appearance. From this perspective, the results of the two "Computer Dance" studies are quite compatible: People look for dating partners that match their own level of attractiveness, but since they think of themselves as pretty attractive, they tend to look for others who are also high in attractiveness. Either way one looks at this matter, the physical attractiveness of another is of paramount importance for the initiation and maintenance of romantic relationships.

Standards of Attractiveness

It has been said that beauty is in the eye of the beholder, and in some ways nothing could be more true. Standards of beauty vary from one culture to another in terms of what parts of the body are important and what characteristics these parts should take on. For example, Ford and Beach (1951) looked at the value that 100 "primitive" cultures placed on body build for female beauty, and found that a slim body build was considered to be beautiful in 5 cultures, a medium body build was considered beautiful in another 5, and a plump body build was considered beautiful in 18 cultures. What is interesting about this discovery is not only the variations in importance placed on different body builds but also the fact that body build was not considered important by the vast majority of cultures. On the other hand, there is also evidence suggesting that cross-cultural variations in standards of attractiveness may have been at least somewhat overstated. Specifically, one study that looked at judgments of women's facial attractiveness across three cultures (Cunningham et al., 1995) found that Asians, Latinos, and Whites favored faces with many similar features, including large eyes, small nose, and small chin, regardless of whether the face in question was that of an Asian, Latino, or White woman. The only exception was that the attractiveness ratings made by Asian research participants were less influenced by features indicative of sexual maturity and expressiveness than those made by Latino and White research participants. It is important to note that the extent to which participants had previous exposure to Western media (portraying Western ideals of beauty) did not influence attractiveness ratings.

Perhaps there is more variation in what is considered to be attractive in the context of one culture over time. The beauty ideals exemplified by the voluptuous women portrayed in Baroque paintings have little in common with the busty yet slim-waisted ideals exemplified by Marilyn Monroe and Jane Russell in the 1950s, the sensuousness of Racquel Welch and Sophia Loren in the 1960s, and the athleticism of Cindy Crawford and Elle MacPherson of the 1980s and 1990s.

On the other hand, when one takes a snapshot of the standards of attractiveness of Western culture at the beginning of the twenty-first century, it appears that beauty is, if not in the eye of the individual beholder, in the eye of the collective beholder. For both sexes, bodily aspects, facial features, as well as facial expressions appear to be important in determining another's attractiveness. Men tend to value a waist-to-hip ratio of 0.7 (Singh, 1993), low weight (Franzoi & Herzog, 1987), and physiques with less curvature (Horvath, 1981). In terms of facial features, men prefer women with large eyes, small nose, small chin, narrow cheeks, and high eyebrows (Cunningham, 1986). Further, men like smiles (Cunningham, 1986), along with facial expressions generally indicative of happiness (Mueser et al., 1984; Raines, Hechtman, & Rosenthal, 1990). Interestingly, both facial cues and bodily cues seem to be of equal importance in determining a woman's physical attractiveness, although the presence of an unattractive body can decrease overall ratings of attractiveness even in the presence of an attractive face (Alicke, Smith, & Klotz, 1986).

By and large, women like men with a muscular upper body (Franzoi & Herzog, 1987), although they tend to favor moderately broad shoulders over more exaggerated features (Lavrakas, 1975). Large eyes, prominent cheekbones and chin, along with high-status clothing and indications of good grooming habits are other characteristics that determine men's physical attractiveness in the eyes of women (Cunningham, Barbee, & Pike, 1990). Interestingly, women's judgments of a man's attractiveness are also influenced by his waist-to-hip ratio. However, although women like men with a 0.9 ratio of waist to hip, their perceptions of attractiveness are equally influenced by cues suggesting a high financial income (Singh, 1995).

But what about those who are attracted to members of their own sex? Intuition would seem to suggest that they should be attracted to sex-typical features. Specifically, gay men should be attracted to men with masculine characteristics, and lesbian women should be attracted to women with feminine characteristics. One study that examined gay and lesbian preferences as expressed in personal ads as well as by direct responses from a Chicago sample finds this to be the case, with some qualifications (Bailey et al., 1997). Gay men consistently search for men who look and act masculine. In fact, masculine looking and straight acting were among the most common descriptors in the personals of gay men. Lesbian women consistently searched for partners they believed were female looking; that is, they rejected potential partners with masculine characteristics, such as short hair, muscular build, and high waist-to-hip ratio. However, they did not look for sex-typical behavior to the same extent that gay men did.

While our perceptions of others' attractiveness are to a large extent determined by the nature and configuration of facial and bodily features, this is not the whole story. Perceiving others does not take place in a psychological vacuum. Instead, our judgments of others' physical attractiveness are often profoundly shaped by the context in which our perceptions take place as well as our dispositions, such as our moods and whether we are currently in a romantic relationship.

Context Influences

How attractive we perceive another to be depends in part on the attractiveness of other people to whom we are exposed. Simply put, our perceptions of an average-looking person can be adversely affected if we had prior exposure to an extremely attractive person. Perceptual contrast effects of this nature are most pronounced when we are conscious of the prior stimulus (Martin, 1986) and when there is a large discrepancy between the prior stimulus and the one to be judged (Herr, Sherman, & Fazio, 1983). In the domain of attractiveness judgments, this effect has been demonstrated in a number of experiments. In one study (Kenrick & Gutierres, 1980), male dormitory residents were asked to rate a photograph of an average-looking female. Half the research participants made their ratings after watching an episode of *Charlie's Angels,* a TV show featuring three strikingly attractive women, while the other half made their ratings after watching other TV programs. As it turns out, men who had watched *Charlie's Angels* rated the photograph as less attractive than men who had watched programs not featuring attractive women. This contrast was subsequently replicated in more controlled laboratory settings as well (Kenrick & Gutierres, 1980, studies 2 and 3).

Prior exposure to relatively unattractive others sends this contrast effect in the opposite direction: Research participants rate the photograph of an average-looking female as more attractive when it is presented *after* a series of photographs depicting faces low in attractiveness. Note that timing seems to be essential for this contrast effect to occur. It is primarily obtained when attractive or unattractive stimuli *precede* the one to be judged. When the same moderately attractive picture is *embedded* in a series of pictures either low or high in attractiveness, exactly the opposite effect is observed. Under these circumstances, the perceived attractiveness of the average-looking person is assimilated to the context. It is perceived as less attractive when it is embedded in a series of pictures depicting people low in attractiveness, and it is perceived as more attractive when it is embedded in a series of photographs depicting others high in attractiveness (Geiselman, Haight, & Kimata, 1984; Wedell, Parducci, & Geiselman, 1987).

The lessons from the work on perceptual contrast and assimilation are straightforward: Attractive people are tough acts to follow. Massive attractiveness not only affects how attractive others perceive us but also decreases perceptions of one's own desirability as a mate (Gutierres, Kenrick, & Partch, 1999). Consequently, if we are concerned with being perceived as attractive by others as well as ourselves, we are better off being surrounded by attractive others.

Dispositional Influences

Our perceptions and evaluations of other people are to some extent influenced by our transient moods. Generally speaking, we tend to look at others more favorably when we are in a good mood and less favorably when we are in a bad mood (Erber, 1991; Forgas & Bower, 1987). This seems to include our perceptions of others' physical attractiveness. In one study (May & Hamilton, 1980), female research participants rated photographs of men who had been previously judged to be physically attractive or unattractive. They rated the photos while listening to either positive mood-evoking rock music or negative mood-evoking avant-garde music, or no music at all. As one might expect, all photographs were rated as more attractive by research participants in whom a positive mood had been induced and less attractive by research participants in whom a negative mood had been induced, regardless of how attractive the men in the photographs actually were.

Our perceptions of others' physical attractiveness are also shaped by whether people are presently involved in romantic relationships. Relative to people not involved in ongoing dating relationships, people who are dating someone tend to perceive opposite-sex persons as less attractive than people who are not in a dating relationship (Simpson, Gangestead, & Lerma, 1990). This perceptual shift does not appear to be influenced by such extraneous factors as self-esteem. Instead, it may be a powerful mechanism for the maintenance of relationships because it reduces our susceptibility to temptation. This effect can sometimes go in the opposite direction, however. Consistent with the findings on perceptual contrast, one study (Kenrick et al., 1994) reports that male research participants who had been exposed to photographs of *extremely attractive* females evaluated their current relationship less favorably than research participants who had been exposed to females who were of average attractiveness.

On the other hand, unattached people who desire a dating relationship seem to become less discriminating as they become progressively more desperate. A study (Pennebaker et al., 1979) was conducted to provide an answer to country and western singer Mickey Gilley's 1975 question (and song title): "Don't All the Girls Get Prettier at Closing Time, Don't They All Start to Look Like Movie Stars?" Male patrons of bars in Charlottesville, Virginia, were approached by an experimenter at 9:00 P.M., 10:30 P.M., and 12:00 P.M. and asked to rate the collective attractiveness of the female patrons. The results provided an affirmative answer to Gilley's question: Men rated the female patrons as more attractive when their number of possible choices decreased as closing time (12:30 A.M.) approached. Interestingly, this change in perceptions of attractiveness does not appear to be caused by increases in alcohol consumption. Furthermore, women's perceptions of men's attractiveness show a change similar to that in men's perceptions of women, suggesting that the boys, too, get prettier at closing time. Finally, as one might expect, these effects are not limited to the particular geographic location in which the study was originally conducted (Gladue & Delaney, 1990).

Although contextual and dispositional variables can often alter our perceptions of others' physical attractiveness, the fact remains that it is of paramount importance for the initiation, progress, and maintenance of romantic relationships. But just why is physical attractiveness so important? At this point, we have no definite, clear-cut answers. However, there are a number of theoretical perspectives that shed some light on this question.

Evolutionary Perspectives

Evolutionary perspectives on human behavior look at psychological processes in terms of their adaptive value. Evolution has a way of selecting against maladaptive processes, selecting instead for processes that aid in the survival of the species (Darwin, 1871). As it turns out, humans are not so much concerned with collective survival as they are with the survival of their own genes (Wilson, 1975). From an evolutionary perspective, dating is considered to be a precursor to mating. In other words, dating is a process of sexual selection with the ultimate goal of reproduction. In nonmammalian species, there is often a wide discrepancy in the parental investment males and females have in their offspring (Trivers, 1972). Generally, males become relatively expendable once fertilization has occurred, leaving the female in charge of gestation and raising of the offspring. In most mammalian species, where both fertilization and gestation take place inside the female, males and females have more even levels of parental investment (Trivers, 1972). Nonetheless, the nature of men's and women's parental investment is such that they play the dating game according to different rules. For reproduction to occur, males need to find females who are likely to produce viable offspring. Thus, men tend to look for cues indicative of women's fertility (how likely she is to produce offspring) and reproductive value (how long she will be able to produce offspring). These cues can be found in a woman's physical appearance. Given that women's reproductive capacity is relatively short, men should be attracted to females who have physical features associated with youth, such as smooth skin, good muscle tone, lustrous hair, and full lips (Symons, 1979).

Among other things, this perspective helps explain why men generally place a higher premium on physical attractiveness in their mate than women do. Because men can produce offspring until they reach a fairly old age (in 1997, actor Tony Randall fathered a child at the age of 77), physical indicators of youth are of diminished importance. What is important instead is men's ability to provide resources related to parental investment, such as food, shelter, territory, and protection. Among modern-day humans, resources typically translate into earning potential. As a result, women should be attracted to men who are ambitious, industrious, and otherwise convey possession or acquisition of resources. Interestingly, recent advances in reproductive technology that enable postmenopausal women to bear offspring have the potential to level the playing field. However, at present, the promise of this technology seems to be offset by a double standard that considers having a child late in life as a sign of virility on the part of the father and as a sign of irresponsibility on the part of the mother.

Speculations about the differential importance of youth and good looks versus ambition/industriousness were confirmed in a study that assessed the importance of these characteristics for men and women in 37 cultures from Belgium to Zambia (Buss, 1989). Males in all cultures preferred spouses that were younger than they, at an average of 2.66 years. The preferred discrepancy was as low as 0.38 year in the Netherlands and as high as 7.38 years in Zambia. Women, on the other hand, preferred men who were, on average, 3.42 years older than they. In all but three cultures (India, Poland, and Sweden), men more so than women rated good looks as important. In all cultures, with the exception of Spain, women rated earning potential as significantly more important than men. The highest ratings were obtained in Indonesia, Nigeria, and Zambia, and the lowest ratings were obtained in the Netherlands, Great Britain, and among South African Zulus. Analogous results were found for the evaluation of ambition and industriousness. On this variable, sex differences were obtained for 29 of the 37 cultures (in case the reader is wondering about the "deviant" cultures, they are Iran, Finland, The Netherlands, Norway, Spain, Sweden, and Colombia).

Considering the diversity of Buss's (1989) sample and the consistency with which the predicted differences were obtained, his findings seem to provide overwhelming evidence for the veracity of the evolutionary perspective on physical attractiveness, including its differential importance for males and females. At the same time, aggregate data like the ones presented by Buss often obscure some important nuances in the perception of physical attractiveness. For example, Buss's respondents were merely asked to indicate the importance of good looks without specifying what they thought constituted attractiveness. Youth is just as correlated with the facial features of small eyes and a large nose as it is with large eyes and a small nose. But while the combination of small eyes and large nose is generally considered unattractive in women by Western cultures (Cunningham, 1986), there may be cultures that consider it attractive.

Moreover, men's preference for attractive, and relatively younger women and women's preference for older men with economic resources may have little or nothing to do with adaptation to evolutionary pressures. Instead, this general tendency may reflect societal arrangements characterized by a division of labor rendering men as breadwinners and women as domestic workers. Compared to older women, *young women* often lack independent resources, making it more likely that they find the domestic worker role acceptable. Compared to younger men, *older men* are more likely to have acquired the economic resources to be optimal providers (Eagly & Wood, 1999). Support for this alternative explanation for the importance of female youth and attractiveness comes from reanalysis of the Buss (1989) data. Across cultures, the value men place on physical attractiveness is equaled by the value they place on a woman's ability to be a good cook and housekeeper (Eagly & Wood, 1999)! Thus, it appears that gender-based division of labor may provide a better, and certainly more palatable, explanation for the sex differences in mate preferences than an account based on adaptation to evolutionary pressures.

There is a different problem with the evolutionary approach's overemphasis on reproductive issues. It has been argued that men's and women's dating choices are not exclusively based on factors related to reproduction, but instead are influenced by multiple motives (Cunningham, Barbee, & Pike, 1990). From this perspective, reproductive interests constitute but one of many motives entering into our dating choices. Women may in fact be attracted to men who, through their physical features, convey that they might successfully compete against other men and provide the resources necessary to ensure the survival of her offspring, as the evolutionary perspective would suggest. At the same time, however, they may also wish to cooperate with their mates, and perhaps even nurture and protect them. Men may similarly look for attributes in women that convey things other than fitness and youth, such as sexual maturity, approachability, and kindness. There is evidence for the presence of such multiple motives in research that had research participants judge the attractiveness of facial photographs that differed in terms of their neonate and mature features (Cunningham, Barbee, & Pike, 1990). Women preferred men with an optimal combination of these features, such as large eyes and small nose (neonate features eliciting nurturance) combined with prominent cheekbones and large chin (mature features indicating dominance). Similar findings were obtained when men judged photographs of women who varied in terms of their neonate and mature features.

These findings as well as others (e.g., Berry & McArthur, 1985), suggest that evolutionary theories may explain some aspects of the importance of physical attractiveness in dating choices. On the other hand, because of their exclusive focus on reproductive issues, they do a less than optimal job explaining variations in terms of the physical features that people find attractive. To suggest that our perceptions of physical attractiveness as well as our dating choices are due to the operation of multiple motives is certainly an important modification, which helps account for deviations from the evolutionary norm. At the same time, even the multiple motive hypothesis assumes that dating and mating are inextricably linked. One could even argue that such features as approachability and kindness are at least indirectly related to mating. After all, it may be difficult to produce offspring with a woman who is not approachable, and a perceived lack of kindness on the part of a woman may be taken as an indication that she may be less than willing to nurture the offspring. However, this line of reasoning could easily be carried to the point where every physical or psychological feature could somehow be related to the production of offspring. As a result, the utility of the theory in explaining the importance of physical attractiveness would be greatly undermined.

These issues aside, the evolutionary account rubs many people the wrong way because it deemphasizes the possibility that humans may date for reasons other than selecting a mate for reproduction. Clearly, most of us have dated without a reproductive motive. If this were not the case, the world would have busted at its seams a long time ago. In many cases, our desire to date may be motivated by a need for affiliation (Schachter, 1959) or a need for belonging (Baumeister & Leary, 1995) rather than a desire to reproduce, even though in some cases the two may go hand in hand. This point of view suggests that we may need to look elsewhere for additional explanations of why physical attractiveness is so important in dating.

Social Psychological Perspectives

One of the reasons we seem so drawn toward people high in attractiveness may be related to our propensity to make inferences about what physically attractive and unattractive people might be like. It appears that our perceptions of physically attractive others are to some extent shaped by a stereotype suggesting that attractive people are better people in terms of their personality. It is through this process that we judge a book by its cover: If it looks good on the outside, it must be good on the inside as well.

The "What Is Beautiful Is Good" Stereotype

The nature of people's stereotype about beauty was discovered in a classic study in which male and female research participants looked at photographs of men and women of varying levels of attractiveness (Dion, Berscheid, & Walster, 1972). Research participants were asked to evaluate the men and women depicted in the photographs in terms of their personalities and to rate the quality of their lives. As one might expect, attractive people were perceived to be warmer and more sensitive, kind, interesting, strong, poised, modest, sociable, and outgoing than people who were merely average or low in physical attractiveness. Attractive people were also perceived to have happier marriages, better jobs, and more fulfilling lives. The only dimension in which attractive people did not come out ahead was on research participants' judgments of their parenting skills. Perhaps they thought attractive people have such busy social lives that they could not imagine them engaging in such unpleasant activities as changing diapers or driving the kids to baseball practice.

Given the positive characteristics with which we imbue physically attractive people, it is not surprising that they receive preferential treatment when it comes to dating. Additionally, simply being associated with a physically attractive person appears to turn us into better people in the eyes of others, although this is primarily true for men with attractive partners (Sigall & Landy, 1973). But discrimination on the basis of physical attractiveness is not limited to dating situations. Rather, good-looking people enjoy a number of other advantages in terms of how we perceive them. For example, we tend to think of attractive people as higher in status, especially those aspects that are inherited (Kalick, 1988). We tend also to evaluate the work of attractive people better than that of less attractive people, especially when that work is objectively poor (Landy & Sigall, 1974). Perhaps this is one of the reasons why attractive people often have an edge in promotion decisions (Morrow et al., 1990).

To some extent, the advantages attractive people enjoy are not so much an outcome of a stereotype for beauty but may stem from a complementary stereotype for low attractiveness. In other words, what is beautiful is good and what is ugly is bad. A number of research findings support the existence of a stereotype about ugliness. In one study (O'Grady, 1982), research participants were asked to indicate the extent to which people of varying levels of attractiveness might be at risk for a number of mental illnesses. Not surprisingly, research participants' risk assessment was strongly influenced by the attractiveness of the person they rated, with the likelihood of risk increasing as attractiveness decreased. But the story does not end there, as this bias extended beyond categories of mental illness that are often accompanied by a neglect in personal hygiene, such as disorganized schizophrenia, which could alter a person's appearance so as to appear unattractive. Moreover, this bias occurred regardless of whether research participants were told that the targets had been diagnosed by a psychiatrist as having or not having the illness. And finally, even when research participants were explicitly instructed that attractiveness was irrelevant to their "diagnosis," they still continued to attribute psychological disturbances differentially to unattractive targets (Jones, Hanson, & Phillips, 1978). This latter finding is of special importance, as it suggests that the attractiveness stereotype is so ingrained that even conscious attempts to control it may fail to eradicate its application.

The results of the studies on the relationship between attractiveness and perceived risk for mental illness are mirrored by analogous findings in the legal domain. In general, research participants who were instructed to act as though they were jurors in a legal case tended to be more lenient in terms of the perceived guilt and the recommended sentence when the offender was high in attractiveness (Efran, 1974). In some cases, the locus of this effect can be traced specifically to the stereotype about attractive people. In one study (Solomon & Schopler, 1978), male research participants were asked to judge a case of a young woman accused of embezzling $10,000. The woman was either highly attractive, of average attractiveness, or unattractive. Not surprisingly, the attractive woman received the most lenient sentence (12 months in prison), whereas the average-looking woman received a sentence of 19.5 months. Interestingly, the unattractive woman was not penalized because of her looks. The sentence for her was even somewhat shorter (18.5 months) than the sentence for the average-looking woman.

In other cases, differences in punitiveness can be traced to our stereotype about *unattractive* people. In one study (Esses & Webster, 1988), research participants were given hypothetical information about an attractive, average-looking, or unattractive sex offender and asked to decide whether he met the criteria of a dangerous offender (which would mandate stiffer penalties). As it turns out, research participants perceived the unattractive offender as significantly more likely to meet those criteria than the average-looking or unattractive offender.

Why this leniency for attractive people and this harshness for unattractive people? One possible answer may be that our attributions of responsibility are influenced by the attractiveness of the person under consideration. Simply put, we may hold attractive people less responsible for situations that have negative outcomes. Perhaps we are more apt to take mitigating situational information into account ("She needed the money to care for her dying father") when the offender is attractive. After all, our stereotype holds that attractive people are "better" people and thus we may try to attribute responsibility to causes that are external to them. By the same token, people lower in attractiveness are far from having superior personalities and thus we are more likely to think that the causes for their transgressions might be related to their dispositions.

Having said this, it is important to note that the attractiveness-leniency effect appears to have some clear boundaries. The attractiveness of a defendant seems to matter little when his or her transgressions are particularly heinous. For example, the law was equally harsh to mass murderers Ted Bundy and John Wayne Gacy despite their obvious differences in physical attractiveness. At the same time, unattractive defendants can level the playing field somewhat by smiling. People who smile are perceived as more attractive, sincere, sociable, and competent (Reis et al., 1990), and their transgressions are consequently judged more leniently (LaFrance & Hecht, 1995).

These issues aside, attributional processes may be important when we try to render judgments about the perceived responsibility of *victims* of a crime. To blame victims for what happened to them is an all too common reaction to hearing about their misfortune (Lerner, 1970). However, we frequently assign more blame to unattractive than to attractive victims. This is especially true in rape cases. Although attractive women are more likely perceived as victims of rape, unattractive victims are often believed either to have provoked the attack (Seligman, Brickman, & Koulack, 1977) or not to have resisted enough (Burt, 1980). Interestingly, this proclivity to differentially blame unattractive rape victims for the attack is just as strong when the rape is committed by an unattractive offender, although such rapists are perceived to be more likely to commit rape as well as other crimes and antisocial acts in the future (Gerdes, Dammann, & Heilig, 1988).

Of course, one could question the extent to which the findings on attractiveness-based discrimination would apply to real-life mental health or legal settings, especially since they were obtained with undergraduates participating in experiments. In real life, diagnoses about mental illness are usually made by trained professionals, guilty verdicts are handed down by carefully selected juries, and sentences are pronounced by judges with expertise in the legal field. Unfortunately, there is evidence to the contrary. A study of incarcerated mental patients (Farina et al., 1977) showed that unattractive patients received more severe diagnoses and remained hospitalized longer than physically attractive patients. In the legal arena, there is evidence that attractive defendants are acquitted more frequently than unattractive ones (Hatfield & Sprecher, 1986). Even if attractive defendants are found guilty, they receive lighter sentences (Solomon & Schopler, 1978).

Cute Boys and Girls Are Better People, Too

The attractiveness stereotype is by no means limited to adults' perceptions of other adults. Adults also discriminate in favor of attractive children. Clifford and Walster (1973) showed research participants academic records that ostensibly belonged to an attractive or a plain-looking fifth-grader. Cute boys and girls were perceived to be more intelligent and more likely to pursue and receive advanced degrees. Furthermore, research participants thought that the parents of the attractive child were more interested in their child's education than the parents of the plain-looking child. Not surprisingly, teachers are not exempt from this bias (Lerner & Lerner, 1977). In one particularly illustrative study (Ross & Salvia, 1975), elementary school teachers looked at files of an attractive or an unattractive 8-year-old boy or girl with an alleged IQ of 78. They were asked to make recommendations as to whether the child should be placed in a class for children with mental retardation. As one would expect, the unattractive child was more likely to be recommended for the special program than the attractive child, despite their identical records.

Differences in physical attractiveness also play a role in how punitive adults are toward children who make mistakes. Dion (1972) had male and female research participants observe an experimenter interact with a child who was made to appear either physically attractive or unattractive. Subsequently, research participants were asked to administer penalties to the child for incorrect responses on a picture-matching task (taking away one to five pennies for each error). The results indicated that the punitiveness of men was not influenced by the attractiveness of the child. Women, on the other hand, penalized the unattractive child more severely than the attractive child.

Children exhibit attractiveness biases just as much as adults do, even before they are completely out of their diapers. When presented with pictures of attractive and unattractive children, preschoolers as young as age 3 preferred to look at pictures of those high in attractiveness (Dion, 1977). Of course, this could be attributed to differences in the reward properties presented by looking at pictures of attractive versus unattractive children. After all, most adults and children alike probably prefer to look at "nice" pictures, whether they depict social (e.g., people) or nonsocial events (e.g., sunsets, landscapes). On the other hand, there is reason to suspect that these differences may, at least in part, be due to the operation of an attractiveness stereotype. One study (Dion, 1974) asked preschoolers ranging in age from 4 to 6 to indicate which of their classmates they liked and disliked and to nominate peers that displayed various types of social behavior. Not surprisingly, children's liking of their peers was primarily determined by their perceived physical attractiveness. Consistent with the attractiveness stereotype, unattractive children were more frequently nominated as displaying a variety of antisocial behaviors. Although this was particularly true for boys, attractive children of both sexes were rated to be more independent and self-sufficient than unattractive children.

These findings suggest that some aspects of the attractiveness stereotype are acquired at an early developmental stage. Experience does not seem to ameliorate reliance on the stereotype. Instead, the stereotype held by adults seems to be more complex in the sense that it includes more attributes than that of children. Additionally, compared to young adults, older people seem to hold a stronger stereotype about physical attractiveness (Adams & Huston, 1975).

Origins of the Attractiveness Stereotype

To attribute the pervasive biases in favor of physically attractive people to the operation of an underlying stereotype can hardly be considered the whole story. To do this is a little like observing a person drenched in water and concluding that he must have gotten wet. To fully explain his condition, we really need to know where the water came from in the first place. With regard to the origins of the attractiveness stereotype, there are at least two possibilities worth considering.

People Get What They Deserve

Many of us believe that, by and large, people get what they deserve and deserve what they get. This belief in a "just world" (Lerner, 1970) presumably enables us to view our environment as a safe and predictable place in which we can obtain desired outcomes and avoid undesired outcomes through ability and effort. Being confronted with someone else's misfortune threatens our belief in a just world by reminding us that it could happen to us, too. To deal with this threat, we tend to conclude that, whether innocent or not, the victim probably deserved his or her bad fate, perhaps because of some corresponding bad disposition. From this vantage point, our bias toward physically attractive people may stem from a complementary bias toward "winners": Because they are attractive, they must have better dispositions and deserve a better fate. Consistent with this idea, Dion (1977) found that research participants who were particularly strong believers in a just world held the attractiveness stereotype discovered by Dion, Berscheid, and Walter (1972) more strongly than those with a more tentative belief in a just world. However, although this was true for the perception of attractive men, it was not true for the perception of attractive women.

Attractive People Are Better People, Period

The idea that attractive people might be better people is both odd and obvious at the same time. It seems odd because we are at a loss to explain how their attractiveness would in fact make them better. It seems obvious in part because the research on our perceptions of physically attractive and unattractive people suggests that we have vastly different expectations for attractive people. From this vantage point, it may be that attractive people become better people by living up to our raised expectations, thus yielding real differences between those who are attractive and those who are unattractive.

People react toward attractive and unattractive others in very different ways and thus create a qualitatively superior reality for those who are good looking. For example, when physically attractive people need help, they are more likely to receive it than unattractive people (Benson, Karabenick, & Lerner, 1976), especially when the emergency is perceived to be severe (West & Brown, 1975). It was perhaps for this reason that a special insert into the owner's manual of a 1964 Studebaker contained the following instruction for women who found themselves faced with a flat tire: "Put on some fresh lipstick, fluff up your hairdo, stand in a safe spot off the road, wave and look helpless and feminine." Of course, it is not clear how receiving help would endow attractive people with better dispositions. At the same time, attractive people show an increased reluctance to seek help from others, especially when they expect to interact with the prospective helper in the future (Nadler, 1980). There may be a couple of reasons why this is happening. First, asking for help exposes people as needy and this may have adverse implications for their self-esteem. Second, coming across as needy may alter the otherwise favorable reactions that the prospective helper might display in response to the victim's physical attractiveness. Either one of these possibilities is somewhat diminished when help is received without solicitation. In such cases, victims might even convince themselves that they received help because they deserved it.

The social reality we create for attractive people through our behavior manifests itself in more subtle ways, as well. Reis and his colleagues (Reis, Nezlek, & Wheeler, 1980; Reis et al., 1982) asked male and female college seniors to keep track of their everyday social interactions over 15 days by completing the Rochester Interaction Record (Wheeler & Nezlek, 1977). Among other things, this measure asks research participants to indicate the frequency, level of intimacy, as well as the pleasantness of their interactions with members of the same and opposite sex. Research participants' physical attractiveness had been independently assessed based on a photograph. The analyses of research participants' records showed that physical attractiveness and gender strongly influenced many aspects of their social lives. For both men and women, physical attractiveness was positively related to the affective quality of their social experience. In other words, attractive research participants perceived same-sex interactions as well as opposite-sex interactions as more intimate and pleasant than did unattractive research participants. Attractive males tended to have more interactions with females and fewer interactions with males than unattractive males. No such effect was observed for females. Attractive males were more assertive in their interactions and lower in fear of rejection by the other sex than unattractive males. Interestingly, attractive females were less assertive and less trusting of the opposite sex than unattractive females.

These sex differences aside, it is apparent that attractive people's social reality is very different from that of people with lower levels of attractiveness. Of course, there is a chicken-and-egg problem here. To some extent, the different social realities are created by the attractiveness stereotype. At the same time, our stereotypes compel us to treat attractive people in better ways. As a consequence, they may acquire some of the positive characteristics with which we imbue them, leading to differences that no longer exist solely in our minds.

"Don't Hate Me Because I'm Beautiful": Some Ugly Truths about Attractiveness

The pervasiveness of the attractiveness stereotype could be taken to suggest that there is little hope for those of us with less-than-perfect physical appearances. However, some aspects of physical attractiveness may make reconstructive surgery or joining a health club premature.

Despite the seemingly overwhelming evidence for a pervasive bias toward attractive people, there are indications that the underlying stereotype is perhaps not as strong as one would expect. Two meta-analyses of virtually all published studies on the attractiveness stereotype (Eagly et al., 1991; Feingold, 1992) found the phenomenon to be most pronounced when investigators asked research participants to judge attractive versus unattractive people on dimensions related to their social competence (such as social skills). Judgments of intelligence and adjustment were less influenced by physical attractiveness, and there was no difference between attractive and unattractive targets on judgments of their honesty and concern for others. On the other hand, attractive targets are generally perceived to be less modest and more vain than their less attractive counterparts. These findings suggest that whether or not experimental investigations of research participants' perceptions of attractiveness and unattractiveness uncover differences depends to some extent on the nature of the questions that are asked. Along these lines, Dermer and Thiel (1975) showed research participants pictures of people of varying levels of attractiveness, just as Dion, Berscheid, and Walster (1972) had done. However, this time around, research participants were asked to judge the targets in terms of how materialistic, vain, and snobbish they were, along with questions about their commitment to their marriages and their level of sympathy toward oppressed people. As it turns out, research participants rated attractive targets less favorably on all these dimensions.

Even if one were willing to look at these findings as the exception to the rule, being physically attractive can sometimes be more a curse than a blessing. Just like everybody else, attractive people are aware of the prevailing stereotype and the corresponding reactions they receive from others. One consequence is that they have a harder time dealing with praise. When they receive praise for their performance on a task, they often cannot tell whether the evaluator is sincere

(Sigall & Michela, 1976), and thus frequently discount the praise they receive (Major, Carrington, & Carnevale, 1984). Furthermore, some of the advantages physically attractive people enjoy in dating relationships can be offset by several distinct disadvantages. They often have a harder time starting relationships because their attractiveness can scare people away. They sometimes have trouble maintaining relationships because knowing that they have many alternative choices may elicit feelings of jealousy (Hatfield & Sprecher, 1986). Finally, although attractive people, and women especially, have an edge when it comes to dating, they are often rejected as friends by their same-sex peers (Krebs & Adinolfi, 1975). Of course, difficulties like these are not likely to trigger a massive outbreak of sympathy for the plight of those who are good looking. All things considered, the advantages of physical attractiveness are many and the disadvantages are few.

Is the Attractiveness Stereotype Culturally Universal?

Until recently, the attractiveness stereotype has almost exclusively been demonstrated in Western cultures. Some (e.g., Dion, 1986) have argued that its prevalence is due to the individualistic nature of the cultures in which it has been studied. In individualistic cultures such as the United States, identity is primarily based on personal attributes. On the other hand, in more collectivistic cultures, such as Korea and China, identity is based more on family and group ties (Triandis, 1994). This raises the theoretical possibility that in cultures in which identity is based on something other than personal attributes (such as looks), the attractivness stereotype may be less pronounced or be absent entirely.

The evidence for this speculation is somewhat mixed. One study comparing Chinese and North American college students at a Canadian university found that Chinese students were less influenced by physical attractiveness in making inferences about the presence or absence of socially desirable personality traits. However, when it came to speculating about desirable life outcomes, such as getting a good job, the judgments of both Chinese and North American participants were equally influenced by the attractiveness stereotype. Other studies (Wheeler & Kim, 1997; Zebrowitz, Montepare, & Lee, 1993) found that the attractiveness stereotype is just as prevalent in Asian (i.e., collectivistic) cultures, although its content is somewhat different. However, it appears that in each culture, attractiveness is related to ascribing culturally valued characteristics. For example, Western participants perceive attractive targets as stronger, more assertive, and more dominant; Korean participants perceive them as more honest and higher in concern for others (Wheeler & Kim, 1997). Thus, it appears that the attractiveness stereotype is to some extent culturally universal.

Summary

Issues. The physical attractiveness of another appears to be of paramount importance for the initiation of intimate relationships. What are standards of attractiveness? How do they vary over time and across cultures? How do our dispositions and the context in which we perceive others influence our perceptions of how attractive they are? Why exactly is physical attractiveness so important?

Theories.   Although beauty seems to be a universally recognized value, its standards vary considerably over time and across cultures. Even within a given culture, perceptions of beauty are often influenced by the context (i.e., the presence or absence of attractive and unattractive others) as well as our moods and whether we are involved in a relationship. This puts beauty largely in the eye of the beholder. However, these differences aside, physical features indicative of youth in women and dominance in men appear to be consensually sought. Evolutionary theories explain this in terms of the reproductive implications of these characteristics. Features indicative of youth in a woman provide cues about her fertility and reproductive potential. Features indicative of dominance in a man provide cues about his ability to support offspring. Social psychological theories attribute the importance of physical attractiveness to a stereotype which holds that what is beautiful is good.

Research.   Evidence in favor of the evolutionary perspective comes from studies showing that beauty is universally important, although there is a fair amount of variation in different cultures in terms of what is considered to be beautiful. Recent experimental studies indicate that reproductive issues may not be the only consideration in dating choices. Instead, both men and women appear to approach dating with mixed motives (e.g., nurturance, sexual maturity, kindness, and approachability), and thus both genders appear to look for an optimal combination of neonate and mature features. There is much support for the social psychological view suggesting the operation of a stereotype of beauty. Attractive people are often judged as having better personalities, especially with regard to their social competence. They frequently have an edge when it comes to evaluating such things as the quality of their work and their deservedness for promotions at work. Men further benefit from the radiating effects of being with an attractive woman. Physically unattractive people are often at a disadvantage in terms of judgments of their mental health, their responsibility for transgressions, and corresponding recommendations for punishment.

Although attractiveness can sometimes result in more negative perceptions on some dimensions, the observation that very young children as well as older adults seem to discriminate in favor of physically attractive others attests to the pervasiveness of the stereotype. And while the phenomenon seems to have its origins in the more general belief that people get what they deserve, it may eventually contain a kernel of truth because of the different ways in which we respond to those high and low in physical attractiveness.

4

Psychological Attraction

WASHINGTON—To Hanako Ikeno, it didn't seem strange to pledge herself in marriage . . . to a foreign man she's known just a day in a football-field ceremony surrounded by 28,000 couples. More than 20 years ago, her mother and father's marriage also was arranged by Rev. and Mrs. Sun Myung Moon, founders of the Unification Church. The Moons picked Keichi Kaneko, 19, of Japan to be her husband. . . . Ranks of new brides and grooms took up two-thirds of the football field once used by the Washington Redskins.

—*Chicago Tribune,* November 30, 1997

The physical attractiveness of another person is certainly a strong basis for the initiation of intimate relationships, as the previous chapter has shown. At the same time, those of us with varying degrees of imperfections have reason to take heart. For one thing, physical attractiveness, while of paramount importance, is *not* the only thing that matters for romantic relationships, although most Westerners would probably frown at the idea that a third party would select their partner for them. For another, intimate relationships that are not romantic in nature, such as same-sex friendships, are frequently based on principles that have very little to do with one's physical appearance. Of course, the question is: What are these principles? What kinds of things might Mr. and Mrs. Moon have taken into account when they chose a husband for Hanako Ikeno? Over the years, psychologists have discovered a number of answers to this question. Some of these answers were obtained by extending general psychological theories to the issue of relationship initiation. Other answers were obtained by trying to make sense of seemingly odd and surprising relationship phenomena. This chapter looks at the kinds of answers generated by both sets of approaches.

Theory-Driven Approaches

The Classical and Operant Conditioning of Liking

Most people who are able to spell the word *psychology* have at some point heard the story of Ivan Pavlov, the Russian scientist who received a Nobel prize for his research on the workings of the digestive tract. His research endeavor included the study of the chemical composition of saliva. Toward that end, he extracted saliva from dogs that were confined to his laboratory for several months. The dogs were hooked up to a saliva-extracting device similar to the ones used in a dental office. And although his animals secreted saliva at varying rates throughout the day, they were especially prone to do so around mealtime when they could see and smell their food. Over the course of the study, one of Pavlov's lab assistants noticed an increase in the dogs' rate of salivation not when they were presented with the food, but just a little earlier, when he turned on the light. The unheralded lab assistant's discovery had a profound impact on Pavlov's life and changed the course of psychology forever.

What happened? Pavlov was so disturbed by this discovery that he set out to find some sort of explanation for it, thus discovering the principle of classical conditioning (Pavlov, 1927). He reasoned that salivation in response to food is something that neither animals nor humans can easily avoid. Rather, salivation is a reflex, an *unconditioned response* to an *unconditioned stimulus*. Because the light had been turned on repeatedly and predictably just prior to the presentation of food, Pavlov's dogs learned an association between these two events. The light became a *conditioned stimulus,* which, by itself, acquired the power to trigger salivation. Pavlov termed the light-induced salivation the *conditioned response.* Note that the unconditioned stimulus and the conditioned stimulus refer to different events—namely, the food and the light. The unconditioned and conditioned response, on the other hand, refer to the same event—namely, salivation. The major difference between the latter two lies in the strength of the respective responses. The conditioned response is generally somewhat weaker than the unconditioned response.

How does classical conditioning operate in how we become attracted to someone? Essentially, it suggests that we will come to like those with whom good things are associated. This principle has been succinctly expressed to mean "that liking for a person will result under those conditions in which an individual experiences reward in the presence of that person, regardless of the relationship between the other person and the rewarding event or state of affairs" (Lott & Lott, 1974, p. 172). Accordingly, we should like someone better if we meet the person on a sunny day, at the beach, or in an interesting class rather than on a rainy day, in a cramped study hall, or in a boring class. Supposedly, the positive feelings induced by one's surroundings become conditioned to the person in question, resulting in increased liking. This idea seems almost self-evident and thus it comes as no surprise that numerous experimental studies have mustered support in its favor (e.g., Byrne, 1971; Byrne & Rhamey, 1965; Clore & Byrne, 1974; Lott & Lott, 1974).

At the same time, there is evidence for the idea that we will come to dislike others whom we meet under adverse conditions (Gouaux, 1971; Griffit, 1969; Griffit & Veitch, 1971; Veitch & Griffit, 1976). In these kinds of experiments, research participants typically evaluate fictitious others while they are in lab rooms ranging from hot and crowded to comfortable and roomy (Griffit & Veitch, 1971). Consistent with predictions from the classical conditioning model, the fictitious strangers are evaluated less favorably as the conditions deteriorate. Again, it appears that the negative affect induced by the adverse situation becomes conditioned to the person being evaluated, leading to a decrease in liking.

One noteworthy feature of the studies on the conditioning of negative affect is their reliance on rating a fictitious rather than a real stranger. In the case of the Griffit and Veitch (1971) study, one might wonder what would have happened if the research participants had been asked to evaluate the other people who were in the room with them rather than the "bogus stranger." There is good reason to raise this question. In June of 1994, when the former WWII allies celebrated the 50th anniversary of the invasion of Normandy, newspapers carried stories about friendships that had been forged among soldiers who participated in the allied landing. In most cases, these were friendships that had survived the test of time and geographical separation. What is equally remarkable is the fact that they developed among people who met each other in a highly aversive environment. At least one laboratory study (Rotton et al., 1978) reports increased attraction among research participants who met in an environment polluted by ammonium sulfide.

These kinds of phenomena are not overly conducive to an explanation in terms of classical conditioning, as it would predict that the negative affect induced by being fired at or inhaling polluted air would somehow carry over to the others present in the situation. Then again, the research using the aversive conditioning paradigm shows this happening primarily for fictitious strangers. It seems safe to speculate that the soldiers on the Normandy beaches would have given less favorable ratings of their enemy's kindness or Ronald Reagan's acting ability had they been asked to do that. The people who share their fate are an entirely different matter. There is good reason to predict that adverse environmental conditions may actually lead to an increase in liking rather than a decrease, as predicted by classical conditioning. Remember that our need for affiliation (Schachter, 1959) is most pronounced when we are experiencing fear and uncertainty. The presence of others helps to reduce both, and this may explain why we find ourselves more attracted to people with whom we share adversity.

It is possible to make sense of the competing predictions for the influence of adversity on the liking of fictitious versus real strangers within the context of learning theory. Negative affect becomes associated with bogus strangers, just as classical conditioning would predict. Real strangers, however, have rewarding qualities because their mere presence can help us deal with whatever adverse conditions might be present. Our increased attraction to these people can be explained within *operant conditioning* as a result of *escape conditioning* (Kenrick & Johnson, 1979). In other words, we can come to like others because their presence can help us escape an aversive situation.

Of course, there is something unsettling about a set of theories that predict that we would be equally likely to be attracted to a stranger we meet at a bus stop on a balmy, sunny day (classical conditioning) or a cold, stormy day (operant conditioning). It appears that attraction will always increase unless the situation is neutral—that is, not perceived as either pleasant or unpleasant. It is hard to conceive of situations that are in fact truly neutral, and thus the predictive power of learning theories is diminished by virtue of explaining too much. This does not mean that pleasant or aversive situations cannot lead to increased attraction to a stranger. Instead, it means that the *reasons* for it may have to be explained in different ways. This is especially true given the nonconscious nature of classical and operant conditioning. They supposedly take place in the absence of insight or other higher mental processes.

Attraction as Misattribution of Arousal

If one accepts the prevailing view of humans as active information processors who try to explain their behavior in the context of the world around them (e.g., Fiske & Taylor, 1991), it becomes possible to reexamine why particularly pleasant as well as aversive situations might stimulate attraction to a stranger. If nothing else, being in either type of situation increases our level of *physiological arousal*—that is, our general level of activation. These increases can be subjectively experienced as positive or negative emotional states depending on what kinds of explanations or attributions we make for them (Schachter & Singer, 1962).

Inherent in this idea is the notion that increases in physiological arousal—such as increased heart rate, perspiration, and breathing—are initially somewhat unspecific, being characteristic of positive as well as negative emotions. What ultimately decides how we subjectively feel depends on the type of attributions we make for our arousal, which, in turn may be suggested by the situation. For example, if you notice an increase in arousal and realize that persistent ice storms have prevented you from playing tennis three days straight, you may explain your arousal in terms of the nasty weather and label it irritation. If, on the other hand, that same increase in arousal is coupled with the realization that spring has finally arrived, you may label it as happiness. The point is that arousal, by itself, is not specific to any emotion. Instead, the subjective emotional experience is determined by the kinds of cues in the situation as to the possible causes for our arousal (Schachter & Singer, 1962).

In many cases, the situational cues are unambiguous and readily available (such as whether it is sunny or rainy outside). Over the course of our lives, we also develop pretty good ideas about what kinds of things make us happy, irritated, and angry. Thus, the process of attributing or labeling our arousal is not exactly a big, mysterious task, proceeding instead with apparent ease and lack of awareness. On the other hand, there are situations in which such labels or explanations can be harder to come by. This is the case when the situation contains multiples cues about the origin of one's arousal. To return to the bus stop example, if we stand there by ourselves, any increase in arousal may be attributed to the fact that it is raining, or our realization that we are running late. If, on the other hand, we find ourselves in the presence of an attractive member of the opposite sex, things get a little more interesting, as the presence of the other person adds a novel cue to explain our arousal. Instead of feeling irritated, we my decide that we are madly in love!

The idea that attraction can be a result of misattributing one's arousal is not as farfetched as it may seem. Dutton and Aron (1974) conducted a field experiment on men who had just crossed either a shaky or a sturdy bridge. These men were approached by a male interviewer or an attractive female interviewer who asked them to fill out a short questionnaire and gave them the opportunity to contact her (or him) in the future if they had further questions. The differences between the two bridges, and thus the two experimental conditions, were fairly dramatic in terms of their respective fear-arousing qualities. The shaky (experimental) bridge was a 5-foot wide, 450-foot long suspension bridge constructed of wooden boards attached to wire cables, crossing a 230-foot deep canyon. It had a tendency to tilt, sway, and wobble. These characteristics, along with low handrails of wire cables gave the impression that one was about to fall over the side at any moment. The sturdy (control) bridge was 10 feet wide, ran only 10 feet above a shallow creek, and was constructed of heavy cedar, making it wider and firmer than the shaky bridge.

The experimenters were primarily interested in the number of research participants who accepted the interviewer's phone number and availed themselves of the opportunity to call. Consistent with their expectations, 9 out of 18 research participants who had crossed the shaky bridge ended up calling the attractive *female* experimenter. Of the research participants having crossed the sturdy bridge, only 2 out of 16 called. Hardly any of the research participants called the *male* experimenter, regardless of whether they had crossed the shaky (2 out of 7) or the sturdy bridge (1 out of 6). Evidently, research participants who had crossed the shaky bridge attributed any residual arousal to the presence of the attractive female interviewer. No such misattribution occurred when there was little arousal present to begin with, or when the interviewer was male and thus provided a relatively poor cue to research participants' arousal.

Dutton and Aron's (1974) finding that romantic attraction can be explained in terms of arousal brought on by external stimuli being attributed to a potential object of attraction has proven to be a fairly robust phenomenon. A number of experiments manipulating research participants' level of arousal have yielded similar results. For example, male research participants expecting a painful electric shock became more attracted to an attractive female confederate experimenter than research participants expecting to receive only a mild shock (Dutton & Aron, 1974; Experiment 3). Similar results were obtained in experiments that manipulated research participants' level of arousal through exposure to erotic material (Stephan, Berscheid, & Walster, 1971) or through unflattering feedback on a personality test (Jacobs, Berscheid, & Walster, 1971).

Perhaps the most revealing evidence for the notion that "adrenaline makes the heart grow fonder" comes from a study on young dating couples asked to rate (1) the extent of romantic love they felt for their partner and (2) the amount of parental interference to which their relationship was subjected (Driscoll, Davis, & Lipetz, 1972). Not surprisingly, from a misattribution view, the study found a positive relationship between the amount of love and the amount of parental interference. In other words, the more parental interference existed, the more couples felt they were in love. According to data reported by Rubin (1973), dating couples who came from different religious backgrounds reported more romantic love than couples with similar religious backgrounds. Presumably, in both instances the arousal produced by parental interference or the conflict with respect to different religious orientations was attributed to the partner, resulting in more subjectively experienced love.

Some (Kenrick & Cialdini, 1977) have argued that increased attraction resulting from increases in arousal may just as easily be explained in terms of operant conditioning. According to this argument, an increase in attraction may be due to the other person's fear-reducing qualities rather than a misattribution of the arousal produced by the fearful situation. This point is not without some validity. In order for arousal to be attributed to a stranger or a romantic partner, its source needs to be at least somewhat ambiguous (i.e., unexplainable). When the arousal can easily be explained as stemming from the anticipation of a painful electric shock, increased attraction to a stranger may in fact be a result of that person's propensity to reduce fear. When the source of the arousal is more ambiguous, increased attraction may be a result of misattribution (White & Kight, 1984).

So what explanation applies to the men on Dutton and Aron's (1974) shaky bridge? It appears that their heightened attraction to the attractive female confederate was a result of misattribution rather than operant conditioning for two reasons. First, the source of their arousal was probably at least somewhat ambiguous. It may have been due to the swaying and tilting of the bridge, but at the same time, research participants may have discounted this as a likely cause. After all, they are guys and thus not supposed to be scared by crossing a bridge that was open to the general public. If crossing it were truly life-threatening, it would be closed. Second, research participants' increased attraction was limited to the attractive female interviewer whose presence could constitute a reasonable source of arousal. If operant conditioning were all that mattered, research participants should have been just as attracted to the male interviewer, because his presence should have been just as fear reducing as the presence of the female interviewer.

The misattribution view on attraction has some clear-cut implications about how one might want to proceed in the early stages of dating. Rubin (1973) pointed out that courtship experts in Roman times advised men to take their would-be lovers to the arena to watch the gladiators. Supposedly, the generalized arousal initially created by watching the contests would eventually be misperceived as having its source in the woman's suitor and be labeled as love. Today, both men and women might similarly benefit from taking their dates to see a scary movie or a competitive athletic event.

Of course, it is entirely possible that neither the operant conditioning nor the misattribution perspective provides the most plausible or parsimonious account of arousal-attraction phenomena. Specifically, it has been suggested that arousal of any kind contributes to attraction by facilitating the dominant response (Allen et al., 1989). This *response facilitation* perspective assumes that liking is the dominant response to a same-sex person in an aversive environment and that romantic attraction is the dominant response to an attractive potential date. Arousal, regardless of whether its source is ambiguous or obvious, is said to facilitate these responses, thus accounting for increased liking of a same-sex other as well as increased romantic attraction to an opposite-sex other encountered in an aversive situation. Thus, response facilitation can explain findings generally understood in terms of a reinforcement-affect model as well as those generally interpreted as misattribution of arousal.

Characteristics of Others (Part I): The Gleam of Praise

To this point, the discussion of the psychological bases of attraction has been limited to situational variables. Clearly, whether we come to like another also depends in large part on the nature of that individual's behavior toward us. All else being equal, it is probably the case that we like those who act to reward us. Praise for our thoughts, emotions, and actions is one kind of reward that is specifically tied to others and may itself stem from a more general need for approval. From this point of view, it is probably fair to say that we like those more who praise us than those who derogate us or act indifferently toward us. Based on this simple principle, Dale Carnegie (1936) advised that heaping praise on someone is the most foolproof means to ascertain that person's friendship. In reality, the role of praise in interpersonal attraction is considerably more complicated than that. Several hundred years ago, Dutch philosopher Baruch Spinoza (1981) provided an important insight into this issue through proposition 44 of *The Ethics*:

> Hatred which is completely vanquished by love passes into love: and love is thereupon greater than if hatred had not preceded it. For he who begins to love a thing, which he has wont to hate or regard with pain, from the very fact of loving feels pleasure. To this pleasure involved in love is added the pleasure arising from aid given to the endeavor to remove the pain involved in hatred, accompanied by the idea of the former object of hatred as cause.

With respect to the role of praise in attraction, Spinoza's insight suggests that we would like others more who first derogate us and then subsequently praise us. Social psychologists have gathered evidence for this idea. Aronson and Linder (1965) created an experimental situation in which research participants overheard a confederate talk about them following several brief interactions. In one condition, the confederate consistently conveyed a positive impression of the subject (intelligent, good conversationalist, outstanding person). In another condition, the confederate consistently conveyed the opposite impression. Needless to say, there were marked differences in terms of how much research participants liked the confederate in either one of these conditions, as one would expect. Most interesting, however, were the outcomes in which the confederate started out conveying first a negative impression and then changed it to become more positive. Under these conditions, research participants liked the confederate even more than when she had been positive all along. Not surprisingly, when the confederate's evaluation went from initially positive to negative, research participants liked her even less than when she had consistently conveyed a negative impression.

Why would we like someone more who first thinks poorly of us and later becomes more favorable than someone who likes us all along? One reason is that we perceive the switch from negative to favorable evaluations as a relative gain, just as Spinoza (1981) had suggested. By the same token, we like someone less who switches from a positive evaluation to a negative one. Compared to people who have hated us all along, we perceive the switch as a relative loss, which then adds to our dislike of that person. To some extent, these gain-loss effects may be due to the kinds of things we do when we receive praise from others. We often engage in an attributional analysis to discern the other person's motives. Others may use praise to cull favors or gain approval from us. Not surprisingly, when we perceive praise as resulting from an ulterior motive, it leads to a decrease rather than an increase in attraction (Jones & Pittman, 1982; Jones & Wortman, 1973). Given these considerations, the realization that someone changed his or her mind about us in a positive direction may lend credibility to the praise and hence increase attraction. When this change occurs in the opposite direction, we may conclude that the initial praise was perhaps not sincere, and consequently attraction would decrease.

Dispositions on the part of those on the receiving end of praise further complicate the picture. Despite the appeal among laypeople and therapists (e.g., Rogers, 1961) that people are motivated by a need for approval, the idea has not figured very prominently in the psychological literature. In fact, when Murray (1938) proposed that there were 39 needs underlying human behavior, need for approval was not among them. It has been proposed that, rather than seeking approval, people seek feedback that is consistent with their self-conceptions, even if these self-conceptions are negative (Lecky, 1945). This striving for self-verification implies that people with positive self-concepts prefer positive feedback, including praise. On the other hand, people with negative self-concepts prefer negative feedback (Swann, 1983). Consistent with this idea, people with positive self-views tend to choose partners who evaluate them favorably, whereas people with negative self-views prefer partners who evaluate them unfavorably yet confirm their own views of themselves (Swann et al., 1990; Swann, Stein-Seroussi, & Giesler, 1992). Similarly, married couples report a higher level of commitment when they feel that their spouse really knows them, including their shortcomings and flaws (Swann, Hixon, & De La Ronde, 1992).

Characteristics of Others (Part II): Agreement Is Everything

On some level, praise may be a specific, if exaggerated, form of agreement. Someone who compliments us on our choice of wardrobe or political opinions essentially communicates agreement about these choices. Obviously, disagreement can be detrimental for the initiation and maintenance of close relationships. If two people cannot agree on what comprises a fun date, their relationship is not likely to develop much further. A couple whose relationship is marked by frequent disagreements over issues of more or lesser importance is likely to experience conflict, which can turn into dissatisfaction and to an eventual breakup.

Agreement, on the other hand, produces attraction, and attraction can produce agreement. This was first recognized by Heider (1958) and further elaborated on by Newcomb (1961) in their respective formulations of *balance theory*. According to this theory, to fully understand attraction in interpersonal relationships, one needs first to recognize that a relationship between two people involves sentiment relationships among three distinct units or elements. First, there is a relationship between a person (P) and another (O) characterized by mutual liking or disliking. Second, both P and O can have a relationship with regard to some issue (X), which could be an attitude, object, behavior, or personality trait. This unit relationship can take on many forms. It could involve perceptions of who is the best basketball player of all time (an attitude), a particular ice-cream flavor (an object), nose picking in public (a behavior), or honesty (a personality trait). The respective relationships could be marked by overt agreement (e.g., Michael Jordan is the greatest basketball player ever) or by mere association (e.g., the fact that P frequently picks his nose in public). These relationships among the elements of the P-O-X triad can be formally represented as triangles where a + denotes liking, agreement, or the presence of some attribute (see Figure 4.1).

By and large, people gravitate toward balanced triads. A triad is in a state of balance when "the perceived units and the experienced sentiments co-exist without stress" (Heider, 1958, p. 176). Formally, this is obtained when the multiplications of the signs result in a positive outcome, as is the case for Triad I, where two people like each other and evaluate something positively. Balance also exists for Triad II, where two people like each other and evaluate something negatively. In either case, the sentiment and unit relationships coexist in perfect harmony, and there is little reason for P and O to do anything other than to enjoy their relationship and reaffirm each other in their mutual dislike of some issue.

The story is different for Triad III. It is marked by a state of *imbalance* created by the fact that P and O have different sentiments about issue X. The resulting

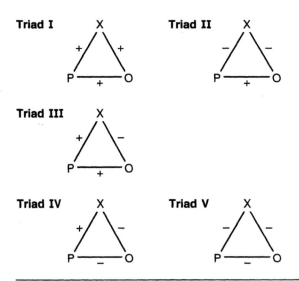

FIGURE 4.1 *States of Balance, Imbalance, and Unbalance among a Person (P), Another (O), and Sentiments toward an Issue, Object, or Person*

tension is hypothesized to motivate P to restore balance. This could be accomplished in a number of ways: (1) a change in P's attitude toward X, (2) a change in P's perception of O's attitude, (3) a reduction in the importance A assigns to X, (4) a reduction in the attraction of P for O, and (5) a reduction in the common relevance assigned to X by both P and O (Newcomb, 1961). Which of these paths is chosen depends to some extent on the nature of the relationship and the situation. A change in P's attitude toward X may be most likely when P is not heavily invested in X. On the other hand, if P has a strong and entrenched belief in X, a change in perception regarding O's attitude may more easily restore balance. However, people tend to avoid states of *unbalance*, marked by a mutual dislike between P and O (Triads IV and V), and thus a reduction in the attraction of P and O may be the least likely way to restore balance (Tashakorri & Insko, 1981). This appears to be especially true for relationships that are formed in the absence of free choice (such as relationships among coworkers and tenants, for example). In such situations, we even tend to increase our attraction for people whom we initially disliked (Tyler & Sears, 1977).

Speaking of people we dislike, balance theory can explain why we sometimes like those who dislike the same people we do. Remember that people gravitate toward balanced triads. Our enemy's (X) enemy (O) becomes our friend (Aronson & Cope, 1968) because in light of the shared dislike of X, balance can be obtained only by rendering the sign for the relationship between P and O positive (see Triad II). In a similar vein, balance principles can explain the unique experience of *Schadenfreude*, a German term for taking delight in another's misfortune. If Robert is poor and likes his neighbor who is rich, the relationship is imbalanced. Finding out that the neighbor lost her fortune in the stock market restores balance: The multiplication of the signs now results in a positive outcome, meaning that now Robert and his neighbor share a common fate.

Similarity: Do Birds of a Feather Flock Together?

The common observation that we like those who agree with us prompts the speculation that we might more generally be attracted to others who are similar to us in terms of their attitudes as well as their personal characteristics. In some ways, nothing could be more true. There is overwhelming evidence that we like others who are similar to us in age (Ellis, Rogoff, & Cramer, 1981), religion and race (Kandel, 1978), emotional experience (Rosenblatt & Greenberg, 1988), sense of humor (Murstein & Brust, 1985), intelligence (Lewak, Wakefield, & Briggs, 1985), performance and skill level (Tesser, Campbell, & Smith, 1984), and being a morning person versus an evening person (Watts, 1982). To some extent, similarity on such dimensions may promote the ease with which two people communicate and interact. Morning people and evening people may simply have a hard time coordinating their activities. On the other hand, superficial similarities may also be a cue to attitudinal similarity. For example, the proposition that "Led Zeppelin was the greatest heavy metal band ever" is more likely to be endorsed by, shall we say, "mature adults." Among people currently of college age this same proposition elicits condescending smiles at best and outright head shaking at worst.

The importance of attitude similarity for attraction was empirically established by Byrne and his colleagues (Byrne, 1971; Byrne & Nelson, 1965; Byrne & Rhamey, 1965; Clore & Byrne, 1974). In a nutshell, the research on attitude similarity and attraction shows that a stranger with similar attitudes is liked better than a stranger with dissimilar attitudes (Byrne, 1961). The degree of attraction is determined by the proportion of attitudes on which there is agreement rather than the total number of agreements. In other words, a stranger who is similar to us with regard to 5 out of 10 attitudes is liked just as much as a stranger who agrees with us 50 out of 100 times (Byrne & Nelson, 1965). The degree of attraction is further determined by the magnitude of similarity. In general, a stranger who is similar to us on attitudinal as well as personality dimensions is liked more than a stranger who is similar to us on only one dimension (Byrne & Rhamey, 1965). Finally, proportion and magnitude of similarity combine multiplicatively to produce the highest levels of attraction (Singh, 1993).

It is hard to disagree with the notion that, all else being equal, we will be more attracted to people who agree with us than people who disagree with us. At the same time, some research casts doubts on the pervasiveness of this phenomenon, and other research raises issues in terms of how the similarity-attraction relationship should be explained. Most of the experimental work in support of the importance of attitude similarity relies on paper-and-pencil measures of attraction. When behavioral measures of attraction are employed, a somewhat different picture emerges. In one study (Gormly, 1979), research participants' self-reports indicated that they liked attitudinally similar others more than attitudinally dissimilar others. However, when participants were asked to choose one of the two for a continued discussion, a whopping two-thirds selected the one whose attitudes were *dissimilar* to their own. A number of studies employing paper-and-pencil measures of attraction report findings that seem to qualify the similarity-attraction relationship in important ways. For example, similarity seems to matter primarily for people with favorable self-concepts (Leonard, 1975). In romantically tinged relationships, physical attractiveness is often more important than attitude similarity (Kleck & Rubenstein, 1975). When physical attractiveness is held constant, romantic settings can produce attraction to a dissimilar individual (Gold, Ryckman, & Mosly, 1984). Attitude dissimilarity leads to more attraction during the early stages of friendship formation than does attitude similarity, although established friends were most attracted to similar partners (McCarthy & Duck, 1976). In a similar vein, others (Sunnafrank, 1984) have argued that attitude similarity and attraction are mostly related in atypical communication settings, such as the psychological laboratory.

The atypical and inconsistent findings with regard to the similarity-attraction relationship may be considered as nothing more than exceptions to a general rule. On the other hand, the reason why this relationship exists has been subject to considerable debate. Presently, there are at least five distinct explanations for why attitude similarity should lead to an increase in attraction:

1. Byrne and his colleagues favor a *reinforcement-affect* explanation, which proposes that similarity and agreement are rewarding, or reinforcing, and therefore liked. We end up liking those who are similar to us because they are associated with these rewards.

2. A *balance* explanation may be less parsimonious than a reinforcement-affect explanation because of its theoretical necessity to invoke a motivational component (i.e., that imbalance is unpleasant), but at the same time it seems to allow for richer predictions regarding the dynamics in the P-O-X triad.

3. From the *impression management* point of view, it may be that the greater liking for a similar other is caused by a motive to create a good impression via the expression of liking. Consistent with this idea, when research participants are asked to create a negative impression, they prefer negative others (Jellison & Oliver, 1983).

4. The *uncertainty-reduction* explanation suggests that to the extent that we are often not sure about our views, agreement from another person provides consensual validation, whereas disagreement further increases our uncertainty (Goethals, 1986).

5. A *rewards-of-interaction* interpretation suggests that similarity is primarily important when similarity and dissimilarity have implications for the quality of an interaction with a stranger (Kandel, 1978).

Considering the many qualifications and interpretations for the seeming importance of similarity for attraction, some have argued that similarity is perhaps unrelated to attraction. According to this argument, people initially respond to strangers with liking. This initial liking turns into disliking, or repulsion, when dissimilarity begins to surface (Rosenbaum, 1986). In other words, we are not attracted to a select few who share our attitudes; rather, we are simply repulsed by those who disagree with us. To some extent, attraction for similar others results from the absence of repulsion. To make this point, Rosenbaum (1986) replicated Byrne's earlier work, except that he added a control condition in which no information indicating similarity of the other person was provided. As it turned out, this no-information condition produced levels of attraction similar to those obtained when the stranger was rendered as having similar attitudes. On the other hand, dissimilarity produced levels of attraction that were lower than the levels of attraction observed in the no-information condition, leading to the conclusion that it is dissimilarity rather than similarity that matters.

To conclude from these types of findings that similarity is irrelevant for attraction may be a little like throwing the baby out with the bathwater. The problem is with the meaning of the no-information condition on which Rosenbaum based his conclusion. By and large, people assume that their attitudes and opinions are shared by most, a phenomenon known as the *false consensus effect* (Marks & Miller, 1987; Ross, Greene, & House, 1977). This effect may very well come into play when research participants are confronted with a description of a stranger that is devoid of any information regarding attitudinal similarity or dissimilarity, as was the case in the no-information condition. In fact, under these conditions, research participants assume that the other person will agree with them at the rate of 73 percent (Singh & Tan, 1992). Given this high level of assumed similarity in the absence of specific information, it is unclear whether Rosenbaum really managed to create a true no-information condition (Byrne, Clore, & Smeaton, 1986). More importantly, it is unclear whether such a condition ever exists in real life. In light of these issues, the safest conclusion at this point seems to be that similarity and dissimilarity both matter in producing attraction and repulsion: Birds of a feather clearly seem to flock together as long as their feathers are attitudes.

Complementarity: Do Opposites Attract?

Given the widespread support for the importance of attitude similarity, it may seem pointless even to raise the issue of complementarity in attraction. However, every once in a while, we encounter instances that seem to fly in the face of the similarity hypothesis. One example of this was the much celebrated relationship between James Carville and Mary Matalin. What made this union so remarkable was that their courtship began when Carville ran Bill Clinton's campaign and Matalin ran George Bush's campaign during the 1992 presidential election. Carville and Matalin eventually tied the knot in 1994 and wrote a book about their experience, which became a best-seller in less time than it takes the average person to say "Republican National Committee." Of course, events like this may be nothing more than colorful exceptions to the more general rule that similarity leads to attraction. Moreover, although Carville and Matalin may be dissimilar in terms of their specific attitudes, they also had a lot in common, like similar occupations and a shared interest in politics.

One could make a case that complementarity is perhaps important when it comes to personality characteristics rather than attitudes. A person who is dominant might be better off with someone who is submissive, and a person who is nurturant might be better off with someone who is succorant, because of the complementarity in their respective needs. This general idea has some intuitive appeal and appears to have been supported by observations from family therapists (Kubie, 1956; Mittelman, 1956). To date, the most systematic and ambitious attempt to study the role of need complementarity comes from Winch (1958), who tried to reconcile the seeming importance of similarity with the seeming importance of complementarity. He reasoned that similarity was perhaps most important for meeting someone in the first place. Someone who spends every weekend playing softball is unlikely to meet someone who enjoys the theater. A devout churchgoer is unlikely to meet a Bohemian atheist. However, once two people have met on the basis of similar interests, whether their relationship succeeds depends in part on how they meet each other's needs.

Winch went to Murray's (1938) list of psychogenic needs and extracted those that he felt were most relevant to human mate selection: abasement (a tendency to yield dignity and prestige), achievement, approach, autonomy, deference, dominance, hostility, nurturance, succorance, recognition, status aspirations, and status strivings. In addition, Winch included the personality dimensions of anxiety, emotionality, and vicariousness. Two types of complementarity exist for these needs and traits. Type I complementarity exists when one partner is high on a need and the other partner is low. This would be the case when one person is high on dominance and the other is low. Type II complementarity exists when one partner is high on one need and the other partner is high on a different need. This would be the case when one person is high on hostility and the other is high on abasement.

To find out about the dimensions on which couples might be complementary, Winch (1958) selected 25 married couples who attended Northwestern University. He assessed their needs and personalities through a battery of objective tests, the outcomes of which he subjected to a number of statistical procedures. His conclusions were that the couples did indeed show complementarity, especially on such needs as achievement and passivity, nurturance and dependence, and dominance and deference. He further concluded that most of the marriages he studied could be classified by the degree of dominance and nurturance present in the husband and wife. This combination of dominance/submissiveness and nurturance/receptiveness yields four categories of marriages, as depicted in Figure 4.2.

A nurturant and dominant husband paired with a receptive and submissive wife results in *Ibsenian complementarity*, in which the husband is the protector and caregiver of his wife, who plays the role of the passive and somewhat incompetent role of a doll-child. In this type of marriage, the husband seeks to control and mold his wife into the kind of woman he wants her to be. The name for this type of marriage derives from Henrik Ibsen's play, "A Doll's House," which portrayed this very type of marriage. A nurturant and submissive husband paired with a receptive and dominant wife results in *Thurberian complementarity*, named after the artist James Thurber. In this type of marriage, the wife is a dominant, active woman, and the husband is a passive man who has a latent hostility that is only expressed under great provocation. This type of relationship is often considered to be somewhat comical, which perhaps explains why it frequently appears in cartoons. The relationship between the Peanuts comic-strip characters Charlie

| | **Nurturance–Receptiveness** | |
	Husband nurturant Wife receptive	Wife nurturant Husband receptive
Husband dominant **Wife submissive**	Ibsenian	Master- Servant Girl
Husband submissive **Wife dominant**	Thurberian	Mother-Son

FIGURE 4.2 *Dimensions and Types of Complementarity According to Winch (1958)*

Brown and Lucy is a case in point, as is the relationship between General Halftrack and his wife in Beetle Bailey as well as that of Mr. and Mrs. Dithers in Dagwood and Blondie. A receptive and dominant husband paired with a nurturant and submissive wife results in a *Master-Servant Girl complementarity*. In this type of marriage, the wife is more competent than the Ibsenian wife. The husband is the head of the house and the wife is the capable and worthy servant who is destined to become the mother of their children. On the surface, the husband is dominating and self-assured, but on a deeper level, he is also dependent on his wife's emotional support. A receptive and submissive husband paired with a nurturant and dominant wife results in *Mother-Son complementarity*. In this type of marriage the wife is nurturant and the husband seeks the kind of succorance he came to expect from his mother.

Winch conceded that his classification scheme was not exhaustive enough to account for all types of marriages. Furthermore, he acknowledged that his approach had other shortcomings, as well. For example, needs can exist on an overt, conscious level as well as on a covert, unconscious level. This could be problematic when overt and covert needs come into play simultaneously. A person might be dominant and self-assured on one level (perhaps because of role expectations) but might be dependent and seek succorance on another level. In such cases, it is unclear how to classify the person and the resulting relationships. Finally, Winch's sample of 25 couples was fairly small and perhaps atypical, given that the couples were comprised of married college students. Not surprisingly, subsequent tests of the complementarity model provided a mixed bag of evidence concerning the role of complementarity in close relationships. Some studies found support for Winch's ideas in the context of friendship choices (Schutz, 1958) and relationship development (Kerckhoff & Davis, 1962). Other studies found no evidence for complementarity in dating couples, newlyweds, and veteran couples (Bowerman & Day, 1956; Murstein, 1961). In light of such inconsistent findings, several reviews of the literature (Barry, 1970; Tharp, 1963; White & Hatcher, 1984) have concluded that, despite its appeal among laypeople and family therapists, the complementarity hypothesis simply lacked sufficient empirical support.

Given the strong evidence for the importance of similarity and the relatively weaker evidence for the importance of complementarity, are we to conclude that birds of a feather flock together and opposites don't attract? The answer is both "yes" and "no." On the one hand, the similarity hypothesis has withstood the test of time very well. On the other hand, much of the inconsistencies in the findings regarding complementarity stem from disagreements over how to measure needs in the first place. Projective tests, such as the Thematic Apperception Test, tend to tap into more covert needs, whereas objective, paper-and-pencil tests, such as the Edwards Personal Preference Scale, tend to tap into more overt needs.

Distinguishing between covert and overt needs may be important in ways that go beyond simple measurement issues. A person with a covert need for dominance may not seek submissive behaviors from others at all times and under all circumstances. Instead, whether a covert tendency toward dominance will lead to overt behavior eliciting submission may depend on the presence or absence of certain interpersonal goals. For example, Shawna may feel somewhat conflicted about her desire to dominate Tyrone, and may therefore camouflage her wish behaviorally. Alternatively, Tyrone's behavior may indicate that he does not wish to be submissive, which may lead Shawna to refrain from overt behaviors that would elicit such submissive behavior.

Based on such reasoning, Dryer and Horowitz (1997) argued that it is impossible to predict attraction from need complementarity without also taking into account differences in interpersonal style and interpersonal goals. From this perspective, interpersonal behaviors *invite* rather than evoke complementary responses. Because people can refuse such invitations, one would expect to find the most satisfactory relationships when the wish of one partner to dominate is met by the desire of the other to be submissive. To test this idea, Dryer and Horowitz had research participants, who had been classified as endorsing an either dominant or submissive interpersonal style, interact with a confederate who acted in either a dominant or submissive fashion. At the conclusion of the experiment, participants then rated their satisfaction with the interaction. As expected, participants who endorsed a dominant interpersonal style were happiest when the confederate had acted in a submissive fashion. And, analogously, participants who endorsed a submissive interpersonal style were happiest when the confederate had acted in a dominant fashion.

Among other things, findings such as this indicate that the relationship between complementarity and satisfaction is far more complicated than Winch (1958) had assumed. Specifically, it appears that when one looks beyond covert needs for dominance and submissiveness (e.g., by taking into account specific interpersonal and situational variables), the link between complementarity and satisfaction may be considerably stronger than it appeared to be in the past.

Phenomenon-Driven Approaches

To this point, discussion of the psychological underpinnings of attraction has focused on phenomena that could be explained by extending existing theories into the realm of attraction. The following section looks at research that was primarily driven by the existence of relationship phenomena in need of an explanation. Specifically, it will focus on proximity, the hard-to-get phenomenon, the allure of secret relationships, and fatal attractions.

Proximity: Marrying the Boy or Girl Next Door

That friendships, dating relationships, and marriages are not the result of random pairings was discovered long before psychologists embarked on systematically studying the psychological bases of attraction. As far back as the 1930s, there was evidence that people tended to marry those who lived in close physical proximity. For example, one study (Bossard, 1932) revealed that of the first 5,000 marriages formed in Philadelphia in 1931, one-third of the brides and grooms had lived within 5 blocks of one another, and slightly more than half had lived within 20 blocks. Studies of friendship formation in college dormitories (Lundberg & Beazley, 1948; Lundberg, Hertzler, & Dickson, 1949) as well as studies in housing projects (Festinger, Schachter, & Back, 1950; Nahemow & Lawton, 1975) showed that physical proximity was the most important predictor of who became friends with whom. Similar effects were even obtained when name place in the alphabet was used as measure of proximity among a group of state police trainees (Segal, 1974).

How can we explain the importance of a seemingly trivial factor such as proximity for the development of attraction? One answer might be that people who live in close proximity are perhaps similar on some important dimensions. This type of explanation could account for the marriage studies in the sense that neighborhoods are often defined in terms of ethnicity and socioeconomic status. On the other hand, dormitory assignments are for the most part random, and thus the resulting friendships with those who live close to each other cannot easily be cast in terms of similarity. A more likely explanation is that attraction to those close in physical proximity may result from an increase in mere exposure to those who are close. This idea has its roots in experimental demonstrations showing that people come to evaluate everything from a character in the Chinese alphabet to a political candidate more favorably the more they are exposed to it (Moreland & Zajonc, 1982; Zajonc, 1968). This mere exposure effect holds for attraction to other people, as well. In one study (Brockner & Swap, 1976), research participants were exposed to others who were either attitudinally similar or dissimilar at a rate of one, two, four, or eight times. Consistent with the mere exposure hypothesis, there was a tendency for the most frequently seen other to be rated more favorably. This effect was somewhat more pronounced when the other person was attitudinally similar, suggesting that mere exposure leads to more attraction primarily when the initial evaluation is positive or neutral (Grush, 1976).

Playing "Hard to Get": Do We Love Those We Cannot Have?

Throughout the ages, one of the cardinal rules of dating held that a person who appears hard to get is a more desirable catch than a person who seems overly anxious to forge a union. There are at least two sets of social psychological theories that would similarly predict an advantage for those who play hard to get. Dissonance theory (Festinger, 1956) as well as personal equity theory (Seta & Seta, 1982; Seta, Seta, & Martin, 1987) hold that when one has to expend a great deal of effort toward achieving a goal, the goal increases in value, perhaps in part to justify the effort (Aronson & Mills, 1959). Alternatively, frustrated efforts may result in increased physiological arousal, which then becomes misattributed as love or desire (Dutton & Aron, 1974).

Interestingly, experimental investigations have shown the hard-to-get phenomenon to be more elusive than one might expect. In five different studies that varied the ease with which women were available for dating, Walster and colleagues (1973) found no evidence for the idea that playing hard to get made the women more desirable dates. The reason for this became clear when the investigators looked at how the women were perceived. Both the easy-to-get woman and the hard-to-get woman were perceived to have interpersonal assets as well as liabilities. The easy-to-get woman was perceived as friendly, warm, flexible, yet unpopular and unselective. The hard-to-get woman was perceived as unfriendly, cold, rigid, yet popular and selective. Clearly, one woman's assets were the other woman's liabilities, and when research participants added them up, there was no difference in desirability. Interestingly, a sixth study showed that a woman who is selectively hard to get (relatively easy for the subject but hard for everybody else) was perceived to have no liabilities. She turned out to be the most desirable date because she was considered friendly, warm, flexible, selective, and popular. These findings suggest that playing hard to get is fraught with pitfalls, as it seems to work only when the game is played selectively. However, when playing hard to get is done properly, it can be a very powerful part of our toolbox of dating behaviors. Furthermore, the observation that members of established couples often keep their ex-partners as friends suggests that it may work even beyond the initial stages of dating.

The Allure of Secret Relationships

Frequently, an initial attraction for someone can be amplified by the need to keep it secret from others. This is often the case in settings that have institutional prohibitions against dating, such as universities and workplaces. When students fall in love with their teachers or when employees find themselves drawn to fellow employees, the resulting relationships may need to be hidden from others. At the same time, the allure of secrecy often renders the relationship more exciting than it would otherwise be.

Why would the need for secrecy increase attraction? There are two possible answers. First, keeping a relationship secret from others may produce additional arousal, which can be misattributed to the object of one's desires. Another answer can be found when one looks at the cognitive operations required to maintain a sense of secrecy. To hide a relationship from others requires that all thoughts about the other are banished from consciousness, especially in situations where one might be tempted to blabber about it. As it turns out, suppressing any kind of thought is more difficult than one might think. People may succeed for a time but usually at the expense of a massive rebound in which the suppressed thought returns with an even stronger force (Wegner et al., 1987). Moreover, the very attempt at suppressing a thought often renders it hyperaccessible to consciousness even during the suppression attempt, especially when attention needs to be allocated to other things (Wegner & Erber, 1992). Either way, suppressing thoughts about someone to whom we are attracted can well lead to a preoccupation with that person, resulting in increased attraction (Lane & Wegner, 1994).

This phenomenon is more than mere speculation, as the topic has been demonstrated in the psychological laboratory. In one study, for example (Wegner,

Lane, & Dimitri, 1994), mixed-sex pairs of research participants were asked to play a card game. One pair was asked to make foot contact under the table as a form of communication; the other pair received no such instructions. Furthermore, some research participants were told to keep the foot contact a secret from the other pair, whereas other research participants were not required to maintain secrecy. As one might expect, research participants who had been required to maintain foot contact in secrecy felt more attracted to their partners than any other group in the experiment. They were more likely to see themselves going out with their partner, to think that their partner would be a good romantic match, and to feel close to their partner. Furthermore, these same research participants reported to have more intrusive thoughts about their partner at the conclusion of the experiment. These results suggest that having to keep a relationship secret can indeed increase attraction, and this increase is produced by a preoccupation resulting from the need to keep the relationship a secret.

What Is So Lethal about Fatal Attractions?

For many of us, thinking about fatal attractions brings to mind the motion picture, *Fatal Attraction.* In this movie, the main character (played by Michael Douglas) has a brief and intense sexual encounter with a woman (played by Glen Close) while his wife (played by Ann Archer) takes the kids to the country for a weekend. After a few days of steamy sex, all hell breaks loose, resulting in one dead lover and one seriously boiled pet rabbit. One might conclude that fatal attractions are lethal because they inevitably result in someone's death. However, nothing could be further from the truth. Rather, in fatal attractions, individuals are drawn to a partner because of characteristics they find initially pleasing but they later dislike, thus leading to the death of the relationship (Felmlee, 1995; 1998a). In the movie, it was the woman's sexual aggressiveness that first attracted the man but then turned him off once his wife and kids were back in town.

For most of us, the characteristics that help produce fatal attractions are much more innocuous. For example, we might be attracted to someone because he is funny, only later to become bothered by his constant silliness. Alternatively, we may initially appreciate another's refreshing innocence, only later to be troubled by a complete lack of maturity (Felmlee, 1995). It appears that people are especially prone to fatal attractions when the characteristic they like in another is different from their own qualities, different from the average, or different from normative expectations (Felmlee, 1998b). Thus, a timid person might be attracted to someone who appears adventurous. Others, such as the character portrayed by Michael Douglas, may be attracted to someone because of her unusual sexual appetite.

What explains why such initial attractions eventually turn into repulsions? There are several possibilities. It may be that the characteristic to which we are drawn was carefully planted by another's self-presentation. As time goes by, it may become apparent that this very quality has many downsides, leading to eventual repulsion. This may be further exacerbated by our tendency to idealize others during the early stages of a relationship. Fading infatuation may gradually expose the liabilities of the other's qualities. In an attempt to please the other, we may reinforce his or her behavior to the point to which they perform it with troubling frequency. And finally, behavior that is different or novel may simply become old over time, ultimately rendering a partner's initially likeable qualities annoying.

Summary

Issues. Aside from physical attractiveness, what else leads us to become attracted to others? Is attraction akin to an acquired habit? What role do praise, agreement, similarity, and complementarity play in becoming attracted to another? Why does proximity matter? Do playing hard to get and keeping the relationship secret produce more attraction? If so, why? What renders some attractions "fatal"?

Theories. Classical conditioning explains attraction as stemming from associating a person with a pleasant context or event, and thus predicts that meeting others in pleasant surroundings would stimulate attraction. Operant conditioning looks at others in terms of their ability to reduce fear and uncertainty, and thus predicts heightened attraction when we meet someone in situations that are aversive. Misattribution theory provides an alternative account for this phenomenon. Balance theory stresses the importance of praise, agreement, and general similarity for attraction to occur.

Research. Support for the classical conditioning approach to attraction comes mostly from experimental studies in which research participants evaluate fictitious others under pleasant and aversive conditions, which raises some questions in terms of whether the findings would hold up for ratings of "real" others. Research findings showing increased attraction to real strangers in an aversive situation have been explained in terms of negative reinforcement. That is, the strangers' presence helped to alleviate the aversiveness of the situation. The misattribution view, which suggests that attraction to strangers in aversive situations may be due to a misattribution of the arousal produced by such situations, has received support by a number of studies using different methodological approaches. It appears that misattribution may be the explanation of choice for situations in which the source of the arousal is at least somewhat ambiguous. Praise produces attraction primarily when it cannot easily be attributed to ulterior motives, and it has particularly strong effects when it comes on the heels of derogation. Predictions from balance theory are borne out by studies showing that people avoid terminating relationships with others in light of disagreement and instead change their own attitude so as to create a balanced triad involving themselves, another, and an object, issue, or person.

Overwhelming evidence shows that similarity in terms of attitudes as well as more superficial characteristics leads to attraction. In fact, the level of attraction increases as the amount of similarity increases. Attempts to explain the importance of similarity in alternative ways have met with limited success. The primary evidence for the idea that we will become attracted to others who complement our needs comes from one extensive study of married undergraduates. However, a number of methodological problems raise questions about the validity and generality of the findings. Both laboratory studies and correlational studies suggest that secret relationships become particularly alluring because the pressure of keeping them a secret creates an intense preoccupation with the other, which contributes importantly to the level of attraction that is experienced.

5

Self-Presentation and Self-Disclosure

*The honeymoon was over quickly for a Wisconsin bride who spent her
wedding night in jail on charges that she tried to run down her husband
with their car. After being married Dec. 8, Kimberly Borrego . . . was
charged Dec. 9 with recklessly endangering her new spouse, Manuel
Borrego. . . . The couple had been on their way to Joliet, Ill., to tell Kimberly
Borrego's children about their marriage when they stopped at a bar. . . . Back
on the road, they argued when Kimberly Borrego repeatedly turned up the
volume on a country music station and her husband turned it down again. . .
. After Manuel Borrego stopped at a parking lot and got out, his wife got
behind the wheel and chased him with the car.*

—*Chicago Tribune*, March 2, 1998

Anybody who has ever had a crush on someone will agree that attraction of some
sort is a necessary but not sufficient cause for the initiation of an intimate relationship. Once two people's eyes have met across the room, they still face a gargantuan task on their way to forming a relationship. Through flirtation, people
communicate their interest in each other; through self-presentation, they communicate what they want the other to think of them; and through self-disclosure,
they reveal who they truly are. And all this is necessary just to get relationships
started! Evidently, the Borregos' courtship fell a little short in the self-disclosure
department, leading to disastrous consequences. In mature relationships there is a
continued need to communicate—everything from emotions to such seemingly
trivial matters as deciding who gets the kids ready for school in the morning.

Flirtation

Of all the phenomena in close relationships, flirtation is among the least understood. It is not uncommon to liken it to a game; however, unlike most games, flirtation does not appear to have a set of constitutive rules that define it (Sabini &
Silver, 1982). For example, the game of chess has a point, which is to move one's
pieces in such a way as to checkmate one's opponent. The larger purpose is to
beat one's opponent, win a championship, or make money. Pleasure is then derived from winning the match altogether or even from such intermediate steps as
exchanging a pawn for a bishop or turning around a seemingly lost game. The
point of flirtation is to stimulate sexual interest, but its purpose is not necessarily
to have sex. People flirt for all kinds of reasons. Sometimes they do it to communicate or stimulate sexual interest; on other occasions, they do it to pass the time or
to find out if they are still able to stir sexual interest in another. Consequently, the
pleasures derived from flirting can be manyfold and may be somewhat independent of whether sex is the ultimate outcome.

Assume for the moment that two people flirt with the explicit purpose of communicating and stimulating sexual interest. How do they go about doing it? It is generally considered uncool to blurt out, "I find you very attractive and want to have sex with you right here and now!" If anything, such a blunt communication is likely to put the other person off, and thus might well produce counterintentional results. As it turns out, people frequently employ more subtle, nonverbal cues when flirting with another. Among these nonverbal involvement cues are gaze, body posture, facial expressions, touch, and grooming gestures (Patterson, 1987). Some have argued that what sets these behaviors apart from other nonverbal behaviors, such as scratching and self-touching, are their propensity to signal submissiveness and affiliation (Eibl-Eibesfeldt, 1974; Givens, 1978).

Seeking and maintaining eye contact, maintaining an open body posture, smiling, brief touching, and picking a piece of hair off one's coat can all be interpreted as indicating attraction. Breaking eye contact, maintaining a closed body posture, and not smiling or touching, can indicate disinterest (McCormick & Jones, 1989). Of course, these nonverbal signals are saddled with considerable ambiguity. For example, prolonged eye contact can just as easily be interpreted as hostility or disbelief at the sight of someone who is wearing his hat backward. Similarly, a person who picks a dog hair off one's coat may just be compulsive or perhaps allergic to dog hair. On the other hand, the ambiguity of nonverbal behavior makes it a perfect tool for flirtation, especially early on. After all, people can never be sure that they will be able to stir up sexual interest; by using ways that somewhat veil the intention can save considerable embarrassment to the other as well as the self (Sabini & Silver, 1982).

Whether an ambiguous nonverbal signal is ultimately interpreted as a sign of attraction depends to some extent on the sender and the situation in which the particular behavior takes place. Few people would mistake the smile of their aunt during a Thanksgiving dinner as a sign of attraction. On the other hand, that same smile coming from a seemingly unattached member of the opposite sex may well be a sign of romantic interest. Prolonged eye contact from a fellow motorist whose car we just dented is likely to signal hostility. However, a gaze in a setting such as a bar or a club may indicate attraction, provided that we didn't just spill our drink on someone's leisure suit or otherwise behaved foolishly (Kleinke, 1986).

Although the exchange of nonverbal cues is a common tool in flirtation, it is by no means the only one. Frequently, flirtation is accomplished through a combination of verbal and nonverbal cues. For example, an unsolicited and unexpected compliment in a bar is likely to be interpreted as flirtation, especially when the delivery of the compliment involves a level of effort, such as crossing the room (Downy & Damhave, 1991). Opening lines are often crucial, with most people preferring innocuous or direct remarks to cute and flippant ones (Kleinke, Meeker, & Staneski, 1986).

It appears that men's and women's flirtatious behaviors follow a somewhat different path and time course. Women tend to use the full arsenal of gaze, touch, facial expressions, and grooming gestures, whereas men tend to rely more on touching. Furthermore, when women are not interested in pursuing a romantic encounter, they tend to deescalate their flirtatious behavior early during the interaction, whereas men deescalate later (McCormick & Jones, 1989). The origins of these gender differences are currently not well understood, but their prevalence, along with the considerable ambiguity of nonverbal behaviors, show that flirtation can be a fairly tricky process. Yet, despite the difficulty of interpretation, most people eventually manage to sort out whether there is mutual attraction, which could then become a basis for a subsequent relationship.

Self-Presentation

Once mutual attraction has been ascertained, people's focus tends to shift toward becoming acquainted. In this process, they may be initially motivated to create a favorable impression and to present a positive yet plausible image of the self. Of course, the ultimate goal of self-presentation is to elicit liking from another; therefore, self-presentation is more like creating a desired impression than a revelation of one's true self. This does not mean that self-presentation is necessarily deceitful in nature. Instead, as Goffman (1959) emphasized, it frequently involves the "over-communication of some facts and the under-communication of others." In this process, people employ one or more tactics, such as the following (Leary, 1995):

Self-descriptions	Describing oneself in ways that communicate a desired impression
Attitude expressions	Expressing attitudes to convey the presence or absence of certain characteristics
Attributional statements	Explaining past and present behavior in ways that elicit a desired image
Compliance with social norms	Acting in ways that are consistent with the prevailing norms of the situation
Social associations	Expressing associations with desirable others and disassociations with undesirable others
Changes in physical environment	Using and modifying aspects of one's physical environment to elicit a desired impression

Perhaps the simplest way to create a desired impression is to use verbal *self-descriptions* of such things as likes and dislikes, accomplishments, family background, and personality characteristics. Usually, this type of information is conveyed in face-to-face interactions, such as on a first date. However, it is just as easily conveyed in written form, which is perhaps why such self-descriptions are common in personal ads.

Given the importance of attitude similarity for close relationships, it is not surprising that people often volunteer information about their attitudes during the acquaintance process. Sometimes such *attitude expressions* are nothing more than self-descriptions (e.g., "I love basketball"). However, expressing attitudes often allows us to make further inferences about a person. For example, if we hear a person say that she is in favor of a law designed to reduce air pollution, we can safely infer that she is likely an environmentalist with generally liberal attitudes.

Sometimes people try to put past behavior in an appropriate context by complementing descriptions of their behavior with *attributional statements*. By and large, the types of attributions being volunteered are self-serving. Frequently, people try to convince others that a given behavior was due to positive motives (e.g., wanting to help someone) rather than ulterior motives (e.g., trying to look good in the eyes of others) (Doherty, Weingold, & Schlenker, in press). Similarly, people tend to take credit for success ("I got an A in my psychology class because I worked really hard") but refuse to accept blame for failure ("I flunked my physics course because the instructor hated my guts") (Miller & Ross, 1975). When such attributions are volunteered in an interpersonal context, they can promote a positive impression and deflect a negative impression. Of course, under some circumstances, the opposite may also be true. By refusing credit for success, one can come across as modest, and by accepting blame for failure, one can create the impression of being magnanimous (Miller & Schlenker, 1985).

To some extent, people use *compliance with social norms* to control the impression they attempt to generate. This can manifest itself in a number of ways. Showing up for a date well groomed and well dressed indicates that we are sane and serious about the occasion. Furthermore, it may allow inferences about our level of good taste and socioeconomic status. Of course, the more general rule may be to match our appearance to the situation. A suit and tie may elicit a good impression when they are worn for a dinner in an expensive restaurant, but when the same suit is worn while attending a college football game, the wearer is likely to be perceived as nerdy. In a similar fashion, we often try to match our emotional expressions to the situation. We express anger when someone tells us an upsetting story and delight when we hear about someone else's good fortune, primarily because we know that these types of reactions are expected.

At times, people manage the impressions they create by pointing to their *social associations*. People generally like to be associated with others who are popular, successful, and attractive if for no other reason than to bask in their reflected glory. This desire is so strong that it can sometimes be downright comical. For example, the wall behind a urinal in the men's room of a popular Chicago Little League ballpark holds a plaque bearing the inscription "Michael Jordan stood here, September 12, 1992." Surely, to have used the same urinal as Michael Jordan has given many a young athlete (and perhaps their fathers, as well) a much-needed boost in self-esteem. People frequently tell about their personal associations, real or imagined, by dropping names ("I once auditioned for a role opposite Robert DeNiro") in order to gain esteem in the eyes of others. Sometimes these associations can be of a more symbolic nature, such as basking in the reflected glory of an athletic team by wearing team-identifying apparel (Cialdini et al., 1976). Regardless of whether the associations we brag about are real, symbolic, or imagined, we tend to mention them in order to create a favorable impression.

Finally, people vary aspects of their *physical environment* in the service of self-presentation. To some extent, such seemingly rational choices as where and how to live may be partly influenced by self-presentational concerns. For instance, some people go to great lengths to avoid living in the suburbs, and would think nothing of passing up a bargain on a minivan because it would not fit the image they are trying to project. Similar self-presentational concerns may influence the choice of furnishings and coffee-table books. After all, our impressions of people who have Plato's *Republic* lying around the living room are likely to be quite different from those who keep stacks of *Organic Gardening*. The way people decorate their offices may be similarly influenced by self-presentational concerns. The professor whose office door is plastered with cartoons is perhaps not primarily interested in making her students and colleagues laugh. More likely, she wants to create the impression of a good-natured, likeable person.

Self-Presentation Norms

The extent to which any of these self-presentational tactics lead to the desired outcome of creating a favorable impression depends on how their application fits with a number of norms that guide self-presentation. First among these norms is *decorum* (Leary, 1995), referring to behaviors that conform to established standards of behavior. If nothing else, decorum may modify our emotional expressions. If, while sitting in a restaurant, our friend tells us a sad story about her life, we are likely to respond with an expression of sadness. At the same time, the setting prevents us from weeping uncontrollably. In fact, a complete emotional breakdown under these circumstances is likely to have counterintentional effects because of the norm violation it involves (Baumeister & Tice, 1990).

A general norm of *modesty* similarly constrains our choice of self-presentational tactics. It suggests, for example, that to avoid being perceived as bragging or showing off, name-dropping as a means to point out one's social associations should not be overdone. Similarly, modesty prescribes that one should not be overly self-aggrandizing in one's self-descriptions. A successful businessperson is generally better off saying that he makes a good living rather than revealing that he makes an obscenely huge amount of money. On the other hand, too much modesty has the potential to backfire. In general, slight modesty is more effective than extreme modesty. Doing well but downplaying the importance of one's performance ("Today I performed five brain surgeries, but it's no big deal") does not lead to more favorable impressions. Downplaying one's accomplishments is only effective when the other person is aware of them in the first place (Schlenker & Leary, 1982).

A norm of *behavioral matching* prescribes that two people's self-presentations should match somehow. If someone is boastful, we are to be boastful in return. If someone is modest, we should likewise be modest. Finally, the norm of self-presentational consistency dictates that people should behave in ways that are consistent with their expressed attitudes, and that this consistency manifests itself in a variety of situations and over time. People who say one thing one day and the opposite the next day tend to be perceived as weak, unreliable, and unpredictable.

Self-Presentation in the Heat of the Interaction

In many cases, self-presentational tactics are employed during a dyadic interaction such as a date. This poses some unique challenges for both the senders and the recipients of self-presentation. To the extent that self-presentation entails the undercommunication of certain facts, senders can find themselves forced to keep a tight lid on the kinds of things they want to conceal. As noted in the previous chapter, this can be a most daunting task, as it is notoriously difficult to suppress any kind of thought. People often succeed at keeping an unwanted thought out of consciousness for a period of time when they devote a considerable amount of effort to it. However, this usually happens at the expense of a massive rebound of the suppressed thought later on (Wegner et al., 1987). More important, when people's attentional focus is divided between suppressing a thought and another task, such as engaging in a conversation with another, attempting to suppress a thought can make that thought hyperaccessible to consciousness (Wegner, 1994; Wegner & Erber, 1992). As a result, people often cannot help but blurt out the very thing they are trying to suppress. In the context of self-presentation, this means that we may often end up communicating those things we are trying to hide.

Whereas the attentional demands placed on a self-presenter by virtue of interacting with another can be detrimental, these same demands on a recipient's attention can work to the sender's advantage. In some ways, the goal of creating a favorable impression is directed at eliciting attributions of positive personality traits (e.g., warm, honest, kind, witty, etc.). In listening to a self-presentation, the recipient's focus of attention is necessarily directed toward the sender. As research on impression formation has shown (e.g., Storms, 1973; Taylor & Fiske, 1975), focusing attention on a person (as opposed to the situation) in itself can lead to dispositional, or personality, attributions. Furthermore, it generally takes less effort to generate dispositional attributions than situational attributions. In forming impressions of others, we often rely on implicit personality theories that inform us about which traits and behaviors go together. Thus, when someone tells us that she went out of her way to save a neighbor's cat from drowning, we can instantly infer that the person is helpful as well as kind. Situational attributions are harder to make for two reasons. First, situational information is generally difficult to come by. Second, even if situational information is available, recipients may be preoccupied with self-presentational concerns of their own, thus depriving them of the attentional resources needed to take situational information properly into account (Gilbert, Pelham, & Krull, 1988).

Detecting Deceit in Self-Presentation

Two people who meet for the purpose of creating a favorable impression with one another find themselves in a somewhat paradoxical situation. While they are trying to generate favorable impressions of themselves, they are to some extent aware that this may be the other person's goal, as well. From this perspective, people may be motivated to find out just how truthful the other is in presenting himself or herself. This is often hard to figure out from verbal descriptions alone, unless they are particularly outrageous ("I used to date Mel Gibson but I got bored with him very quickly"). Instead, we often have to rely on nonverbal cues to detect whether someone is telling the truth or is lying to us. Nonverbal cues (e.g., facial expressions) are difficult to control, and thus people's thoughts and feelings may leak out despite their best efforts to conceal them (DePaulo, 1992). If anything, the higher the stakes, the more likely that leakage will occur (DePaulo, Lanier, & Davis, 1983). One way in which this manifests itself is through inconsistencies among different channels of nonverbal communication (DePaulo, Stone, & Lassiter, 1985). For example, a person may look us straight in the eye while telling us about his occupational accomplishments, thus conveying openness and honesty on his face. If, at the same time, the person shifts his body around nervously we can infer from the discrepancy between facial expressions and postural movements that he may be lying.

Furthermore, deceit is reflected in people's speech. The pitch of their voices tends to rise (Zuckerman et al., 1982) and they engage in more sentence repair (Stiff et al., 1989). Interestingly, the more motivated people are to lie about something, the more likely it is that their true thoughts and feelings will leak out through their nonverbal behavior (DePaulo, 1992). Of course, detecting deceit requires that we pay attention not only to what people say to us but also to their nonverbal behavior. Therefore, the successful detection of deceit may be impaired when we are preoccupied with our own self-presentation.

Models of Self-Disclosure

It probably goes without saying that relationships cannot survive very long on good impressions alone. In fact, self-presentational concerns may be an outright hinderance for the further development of a relationship. For example, if two romantically involved people refuse each other access to their homes out of fear that the decor may not match the image they worked so hard to convey, trouble is likely to ensue. The point is that relationship development is closely tied to changes in communication. We eventually have to go beyond merely coming across as likeable and instead reveal a sense of who we really are. This is accomplished through *self-disclosure*, a process that has been defined as "what individuals verbally reveal about themselves to others (including thoughts, feelings, and experiences" (Derlega et al., 1993, p.1). Self-disclosure in developing relationships follows a fairly predictable path, which has been captured by several theoretical models.

Self-Disclosure as Social Penetration

According to social penetration theory (Altman & Taylor, 1973), we can look at self-disclosure in terms of the number of topics that are covered (its breadth) as well as the personal significance of the topics (its depth). Early in a relationship, self-disclosure may be limited to a few superficial topics, often indicating simple preferences ("I like Lite beer"). As the relationship develops, self-disclosure becomes more intimate ("Sometimes I have too many Lite beers") to the point of being very intimate ("When I drink too many Lite beers, I go crazy"). At the same time, the number of topics covered in self-disclosure increases, too. To some extent, the course of self-disclosure resembles a wedge that becomes deeper through the increasing levels of intimacy and wider through the increasing number of topics covered, as illustrated in Figure 5.1.

Social penetration theory predicts that as a relationship develops, self-disclosure goes from narrow and shallow to broad and deep. This raises two important issues. First is the question of causality. One could argue that increasing self-disclosure causes a relationship to develop further. However, one could just as easily argue that self-disclosure is a result of relationship development. In other words, the closer two people become, the broader and deeper their self-disclosures will be. The solution to this apparent riddle is that both processes are possible, which has led some (Derlega et al., 1993) to propose that self-disclosure and relationships are *mutually transformative.* That is, self-disclosure increases as a relationship develops and relationships develop partly as a result of self-disclosure.

The second issue relates to what happens to self-disclosure over time. By virtue of employing the analogy of a wedge, social penetration theory implicitly suggests that the increase in self-disclosure over time is gradual and linear for some

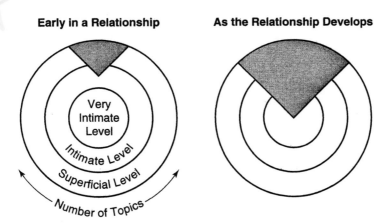

FIGURE 5.1   *The Social Penetration Model of Self-Disclosure*

Source: S. S. Brehm, *Intimate Relationships,* 2nd ed. (New York: McGraw-Hill, 1992). Reproduced with permission of The McGraw-Hill Companies.

time before eventually leveling off. However, this is not necessarily the case. Instead, the rate of change in breadth is not the same as the rate of change in depth. People tend to increase the number of topics they talk about before they increase the intimacy of their self-disclosures. Once the increase in topics levels off, intimacy increases sharply (Brehm, 1992). At the same time, couples on the verge of a breakup tend to decrease the number of topics on which they self-disclose but actually increase the intimacy of their self-disclosures (Tolstedt & Stokes, 1984).

Furthermore, no two relationships develop at the same rate. In some relationships, self-disclosure may increase gradually, but instead of leveling off, it might actually decrease. Research on couples who have been together for some time supports this idea. For example, Huston, McHale, and Crouter (1986) found that couples became less disclosing after just one year of marriage. At the same time, in relationships that fall under the general heading of "love at first sight," self-disclosure may develop almost immediately and increase sharply rather than gradually. In fact, couples who show this pattern of self-disclosure are more likely to stay together than couples who follow a more gradual pattern (Berg, 1984; Berg & Clark, 1986; Berg & McQuinn, 1986). Of course, one does not know whether the longevity of such relationships is due to the particular pattern of self-disclosure or something else. It appears, however, that couples self-disclose more rapidly when their relationship fits their ideal of a relationship fairly well (Berg & Clark, 1986).

Self-Disclosure Reciprocity

Whatever the exact time course of social penetration and depenetration, how do people manage their level of self-disclosure as couples? Unlike self-presentation, self-disclosure necessarily involves two people interacting with one another. From this perspective, people manage to increase or decrease their levels of self-disclosure through *self-disclosure reciprocity* (Berg & Archer, 1980, 1982). This strategy is akin to a tit-for-tat, whereby people tend to match the other's self-disclosure in terms of its intimacy and valence (Taylor & Belgrave, 1986). In other words, highly intimate self-disclosure is reciprocated with intimate self-disclosure, whereas self-disclosure that is low in intimacy is reciprocated with low-intimacy self-disclosure. Similarly, positive self-disclosures ("I'm thinking of getting a puppy") are reciprocated with positive self-disclosures ("I like dogs"), whereas negative self-disclosures ("My dog just died") are reciprocated with negative self-disclosures ("I once had a hamster that drowned"). Thus, one important function of the reciprocity norm is that it regulates how people go about disclosing to one another (Derlega, Harris, & Chaikin, 1973).

Additionally, there is evidence that responding to another's self-disclosure in kind is associated with attraction. Berg and Archer (1980) exposed research participants to a taped interaction that had allegedly taken place between two strangers. One of the strangers disclosed items that were either low or high in intimacy. The other stranger either responded in kind, responded to a highly intimate disclosure with a disclosure low in intimacy, or responded to a disclosure low in intimacy with a highly intimate disclosure. Research participants were asked to indicate how much they liked the stranger who responded to the initial self-disclosure. As it turns out, liking was strongly determined by the extent to which the responding stranger matched the other's initial level of self-disclosure. Similar results were reported by Chaikin and Derlega (1974).

These kinds of findings are important because they suggest that self-disclosure itself does not produce attraction. Rather, attraction appears to be a result of following a tit-for-tat type of strategy by which people match their levels of self-disclosure. Of course, people could pursue a matching strategy simply to follow a perceived norm of reciprocity. On the other hand, the extent to which someone matches or mismatches another person's level of self-disclosure itself conveys information.

According to Berg and Archer (1982), there are at least three different aspects to self-disclosure. Through *descriptive intimacy,* people convey factual information, which, among other things, can be used by the other to form an impression. Through *evaluative intimacy,* people express strong emotions and judgments, which can help in being liked by the other. Finally, and most importantly for the present purpose, through *topical reciprocity,* people convey that they are responsive and flexible. In other words, by sticking with the same topic in response to another's self-disclosure, one elicits positive attributions about one's personality, and this in turn can lead to an increase in attraction. Switching to a different topic, on the other hand, may lead to negative attributions and a resulting decrease in attraction. This makes a great deal of sense. Imagine, for example, that during the course of a first date, we reveal that we like animals. If our date responds by subtly switching the topic of conversation to the Chicago Bulls, Bears, and Cubs, we are likely to think of our date as unresponsive, inflexible, and self-centered.

Individual Differences in Self-Disclosure

Altman and Taylor's (1973) social penetration model as well as Berg and Archer's (1980, 1982) topical reciprocity model are to some extent idealizations of the self-disclosure process. Neither one takes into account important individual differences that can lead to considerable variations in how mutual self-disclosure unfolds.

Gender-Related Differences.   Men and women are not alike when it comes to self-disclosure. Although both sexes are similarly willing to disclose their emotions, women tend to be more willing to disclose about feelings of depression, anxiety, anger, and their greatest fears (Rubin et al., 1980; Snell, Miller, & Belk, 1988). This general tendency of women to disclose more information of a more intimate nature is somewhat attenuated when they expect to interact with the recipient of their disclosure. Under these circumstances, women's self-disclosures become less revealing and less intimate, whereas men's self-disclosures become more revealing and intimate (Shaffer & Ogden, 1986). It appears that women avoid self-disclosure primarily to avoid personal hurt. When men avoid self-disclosure they often do so strategically, that is to maintain control over their relationships (Rosenfeld, 1979).

Most of these sex differences are not so much related to gender per se, but more to differences in expectations of what constitutes proper behavior for men and women. The U.S. culture has assigned women the role of socioemotional specialists. As a result, men as well as women expect females to disclose more than males. In support of this contention, men and women alike tend to rate males who fail to disclose as better adjusted than males who disclose information about personal problems. The opposite is true for perceptions of women who either disclose information about personal problems or fail to disclose it (Derlega & Chaikin, 1976). Furthermore, men who are particularly high in masculinity are less willing to disclose intimate information, especially to other men, but men with a more feminine orientation generally disclose more intimate information, spend more time doing it, and expect intimate disclosures in return, particularly when they are disclosing to a woman (Winstead, Derlega, & Wong, 1984).

Self-Monitoring.   Regardless of gender, the degree to which people monitor their behavior in the context of a social situation has an impact on self-disclosure. In general, *high self-monitors* like to adapt their behavior to the demands of the current social situation. *Low self-monitors,* on the other hand, do relatively little in terms of modifying their behavior in light of situational constraints (Snyder, 1987; Snyder & Gangestead, 1986). As a result, high self-monitors tend to look for cues about appropriate behavior by inspecting the behavior of others, and they tend to act differently when in different situations and with different people. Low self-monitors are guided more by their "true" attitudes, beliefs, and feelings, and they would be reluctant to change the way they do things just to please another. Not surprisingly, when asked to disclose personal information to another, high self-monitors are more prone to reciprocate the intimacy, emotionality, and descriptive content of another's disclosure than low self-monitors are (Shaffer, Smith, & Tomarelli, 1982). Apparently, high self-monitors use the other's lead to decide on what constitutes the proper level of self-disclosure.

Shaffer, Smith, and Tomarelli's (1982) findings are certainly consistent with the generally hypothesized differences between low and high self-monitors. However, Ludwig, Franco, and Malloy (1986) found that low self-monitors followed the reciprocity norm more closely than high self-monitors, who always disclosed at a high level of intimacy regardless of their partner's behavior. How can this apparent mystery surrounding these contradictory findings be resolved? One possibility is that differences in the ways high and low self-monitors reciprocate another's self-disclosure may be influenced by whether they expect to interact with the other in the future. Remember that high self-monitors want to please others, perhaps with the ultimate goal of being liked. Thus, it may be that high self-monitors are particularly likely to reciprocate to another's self-disclosure when they expect to have contact with that person in the future. To test this idea, one study (Shaffer, Ogden, & Wu, 1987) varied the prospect of future interaction along with an initially high or low level of disclosure intimacy. Results showed that high self-monitors reciprocated to their partner's self-disclosure only when they expected to meet that person again. This difference was not observed when there was no prospect of future interaction. Under these circumstances, both low and high self-monitors followed the reciprocity rule equally.

Self-Consciousness. A concept that appears superficially related to self-monitoring is *self-consciousness*. It describes our tendency to focus our attention inward—toward our feelings, goals, and values (e.g., "I want to be a rocket scientist"). Once we focus our attention on ourselves, we compare them with our current state. If we discover a large enough discrepancy (e.g., "I flunked all my physics courses"), we are likely to adjust our behavior so as to bring our current state more in line with our goals and values. Self consciousness takes on two forms (Scheier & Carver, 1985). *Private self-consciousness* refers to our tendency to reflect on private aspects of ourselves—that is, the extent to which our behavior corresponds to how we would like to act. *Public self-consciousness* describes the extent to which we reflect on how we might appear in the eyes of others. Both types of self-consciousness can vary situationally. Seeing ourselves in the mirror or listening to a tape of our own voice generally raises our levels of both private and public self-consciousness. Additionally, there are chronic differences between people's level of self-consciousness in the absence of such devices. Either way, heightened self-consciousness is hypothesized to lead to an inspection of our behavior and a subsequent adjustment of that behavior if necessary.

To date, research has shown that self-consciousness can affect self-disclosure in a couple of ways. One study (Archer, Hormuth, & Berg, 1982) shows that research participants who were asked to disclose intimate information about themselves became more reluctant disclosers when they did the task while sitting in front of a mirror. Apparently, the increased public and private self-consciousness induced by the presence of the mirror made research participants watch more closely how their disclosures might compare with their own standards and the kind of impression they wanted to convey. With respect to reciprocity of self-disclosure, a slightly more complicated picture emerged from a study that looked at research participants who were either high or low on private and public self-consciousness (Shaffer & Tomarelli, 1989). Research participants who scored high on one aspect of self-consciousness and low on the other tended to reciprocate the level of intimacy of another's disclosure. Research participants who were uniformly low or high on both private and public self-consciousness did not follow the reciprocity norm to the same extent. Apparently, research participants who were concentrating on both aspects of the self had suffered from some sort of attentional overload that prevented them from paying attention to the level of intimacy of the other's self-disclosure.

Anxiety, Trust, and Machiavellianism. The number of personality dimensions on which people differ is almost endless. Consequently, a thorough treatment of how they might affect various aspects of the self-disclosure process might fill volumes. In the interest of brevity, the remaining discussion will focus on a few personality dimensions that are particularly obvious or particularly intriguing.

Not surprisingly, people who are highly anxious are concerned with self-protection. They feel vulnerable enough as it is and thus tend to disclose at a moderate rather than a high level of intimacy, regardless of whether the other person discloses information high or low in intimacy (Meleshko & Alden, 1993). On the other hand, people who have a high level of generalized trust and therefore approach others without the notion that they might get hurt tend to reveal more information, especially information of an intimate nature (Wheeless & Grotz, 1977). Of course, a high level of interpersonal trust may be detrimental when one discloses to another who uses self-disclosure as a means of manipulating others for the purpose of interpersonal control. Rather than presenting an honest and accurate image of themselves, people with such Machiavellian tendencies disclose strategically to control the behavior of the other and ultimately their relationship (O'Connor & Simms, 1990). Interestingly, some researchers have reported this type of strategic self-disclosure to be prevalent among women (O'Connor & Simms, 1990), yet others have shown it to be more prevalent among men (Dingler-Duhon & Brown, 1987), suggesting that it is perhaps more a question of personality rather than gender.

Context Influences on Self-Disclosure

At this point, there is probably little doubt that self-disclosure is important for the initiation of close relationships, particularly those that are intimate in nature. However, this is by no means the only context in which self-disclosure takes place. Absence of self-disclosure, either by choice or for lack of opportunity, is associated with loneliness (Berg & Peplau, 1982; Davis & Franzoi, 1986). Males and females alike suffer from loneliness in the absence of opportunities to self-disclose to members of the opposite sex. However, a lack of self-disclosure to same-sex friends is associated with loneliness among women (Solano, Batton, & Parish, 1982).

To the extent that self-disclosure to friends and peers can buffer the possible effects of lack of self-disclosure to intimate partners, one might ask if self-disclosure in these types of relationships would perhaps unfold in different ways. After all, self-disclosure in ongoing friendships, for example, does not serve the purpose of getting to know one another. Rather, it appears that self-disclosure is volunteered for social support and coping (Pennebaker, 1989, 1995). From this point of view, one would not expect reciprocity to matter much. Consistent with this idea, it appears that intimacy of disclosure is most closely associated with friendship. It is important to note that it is the psychological closeness rather than the physical closeness of friends that is responsible for this relationship. We generally disclose intimate information to those who are psychologically close to us, whereas we disclose nonintimate information to those who are close in terms of their proximity (Rubin & Shenker, 1978).

Intimate self-disclosure to an acquaintance or even a stranger is considered to be inappropriate, which is perhaps one reason why we generally avoid it. In fact, people who violate this implicit norm are frequently perceived as maladjusted (Chaikin & Derlega, 1974). This does not mean that we would never disclose intimate information to a stranger under any circumstance. If this were the case, most experimental studies of self-disclosure would have failed miserably and most daytime TV talk shows would have gone off the air long ago. Intimate self-disclosure to a stranger is more likely to occur when the stranger is physically attractive, especially in the absence of a strong need for approval (Brundage, Derlega, & Cash, 1977). Our transient moods further affect our willingness to disclose intimate information. People in good moods tend to be more willing to disclose intimate information, whereas people in bad moods are more reluctant to do so (Cunningham, 1988).

Finally, alcohol consumption seems to promote willingness to disclose personal information, especially for men. However, to some extent this is more due to how intoxicated people *believe* they are. In one study (Caudill, Wilson, & Abrams, 1987), men who believed that both they and their partner were drunk showed an increase in self-disclosure even when no alcohol was consumed. At the same time, women who believed they were drunk showed a decrease in self-disclosure. It may be that the women who believed they were drunk reminded themselves of their heightened vulnerability and thus decided to exercise caution.

Self-Disclosure in Mature Relationships

Advice columns in newspapers and magazines are filled with letters from spouses complaining that they and their partners do not talk anymore. Specifically, the common complaint is about the absence of intimate self-disclosure. The frequency with which such complaints are volunteered testifies to the importance of self-disclosure for marital satisfaction (Hendrick, 1981). However, that intimate self-disclosure would decrease with the length of relationship is not entirely surprising. After all, intimate self-disclosure is a means to get to know the other person. People in long-term relationships tend to know their partners fairly well, and thus in such relationships there may simply be less need for self-disclosure. Then again, if this is true, one would expect fewer complaints about the lack of intimate self-disclosure on the part of long-term husbands and wives.

Most intact long-term relationships are not entirely devoid of intimate self-disclosure. However, compared to self-disclosure to a prospective date, there is a shift in terms of the type of intimate information that is disclosed. Relative to strangers, spouses tend to reveal more descriptive intimacy but less evaluative intimacy, although this is more pronounced for husbands than for wives, who prefer disclosures high in evaluative intimacy (Morton, 1978). Contrary to popular belief, there is little difference in terms of the sheer amount of information that husbands and wives disclose to one another. For both, the amount of information disclosed becomes less with age and with length of relationship (Antill & Cotton, 1987). This does not mean that people will necessarily become unhappy with their relationship over time. Instead, there is evidence that marital happiness is determined by the perceived discrepancy in the partner's affective disclosure. Marital satisfaction decreases as this discrepancy increases (Davidson, Balswick, & Halverson, 1983). The intent and valence of self-disclosure are equally important for marital satisfaction. Honest and positive self-disclosures result in more happiness than disclosures aimed at gaining control of the relationship (Dickson-Markman, 1984).

The picture of a mature relationship marked by a decrease in self-disclosure and a preponderance of self-disclosures high in descriptive intimacy can change quickly and dramatically in response to stressful events. People who are distressed tend to be preoccupied with their problems to the point where their thinking becomes overwhelmed by them. This often triggers a need to confide in others, spouses included (McDaniel, Stiles, & McGaughey, 1981). Such confessions often make people feel better because by virtue of confiding in someone, they have transferred some aspects of their problem to the other person (Pennebaker, 1990). Because this need to confide does not depend on where the stress comes from in the first place, this perspective suggests that self-disclosure, especially the type high in evaluative intimacy, may be especially prevalent in relationships that are marked by turmoil. Once the relationship stabilizes, one can expect a return to lower levels of self-disclosure high in descriptive intimacy.

Summary

Issues. How do people communicate their mutual attraction to one another? What do they do to increase their chances that the other will maintain an interest in them? How do they get to know one another? How do mature couples manage self-disclosure?

Theories. Flirtation, and its inherent ambiguity, appears to be a safe way of communicating interest among people seeking an intimate relationship. Theories of self-presentation hold that people try to communicate a positive yet plausible image of themselves through a variety of tactics, including self-descriptions; attitude expressions; attributional statements; compliance with social norms, such as decorum, modesty, and behavioral matching; social associations; and changes in environment. Because presenting a positive yet plausible image of oneself often entails deemphasizing or omitting negative information, self-presentation can sometimes border on deceit, which can be hard to detect. Two models of self-disclosure focus on different aspects of the process of getting to know one another. The social penetration model emphasizes the importance of moving from superficial disclosure of a few topics to more intimate disclosures involving a variety of topics. The reciprocity model focuses on the importance of matching as well as the intimacy of another's disclosure.

Research.   People use many tactics in the service of creating a positive yet plausible impression. Appropriate explanations for our accomplishments tend to elicit the impression of general modesty, whereas inappropriate explanations can trigger less favorable impressions. Mentioning social associations capitalizes on our propensity to bask in the reflected glory of another, and complying with social norms guiding such situations as a date can elicit impression of interest, caring, and sincerity. Moreover, compliance with specific norms regulating self-presentation generally elicits favorable impressions, whereas norm violations can lead to negative impressions. Because self-presentation frequently takes place in the context of a social interaction, which may pose important constraints on one's ability to process information, successful self-presentation is not always an easy task. The same is true for our ability to detect deceit in another's self-presentation.

Research has modified the social penetration model of self-disclosure in important ways. Breadth and depth of disclosure appear to increase at a somewhat different rate, with the rate of breadth changing faster than the rate of depth, and there are substantial variations from one couple to the next. Research on the reciprocity model shows that reciprocating to another's self-disclosure within the same topic and with the same level of intimacy is particularly important because it connotes sensitivity and likeableness. Furthermore, as relationships mature, the intimacy of self-disclosure does not really appear to decrease. Instead, it seems that over time self-disclosure increases in descriptive intimacy while it decreases in evaluative intimacy. The predictions from both models are subject to a variety of individual differences, including gender, self-monitoring, self-consciousness, anxiety, trust, and Machiavellianism, as well as differences due to the context in which self-disclosure takes place.

6

Fairness and Equity

Season for Giving in Japan

Good manners, formalities, and carefully wrapped gifts are all integral components of Japanese Society. The social significance of giving presents is never more apparent than in July when TV commercials suddenly feature fancy gift boxes of the advertised product, be it coffee, beer or detergent. It's all part of the Ochugen *rush.* Ochugen *is not a holiday, but a season of gift-giving as an expression of gratitude. . . . The origin of* Ochugen *is somewhat hazy, but one theory says it originated ages ago with people who came to the cities to work. Before returning to their home villages for the summer remembrance of the deceased, they offered a gift to say thank you for any assistance they had received. The concept linking* Ochugen *with other forms of gift-giving is* giri—*the Japanese belief in obligation and reciprocity. Giri itself is tied to the idea of* wa, *or social harmony. The protocol includes the gift-giving itself, which usually must be reciprocated. In some situations when one receives a gift, proper acknowledgment means giving a gift of half-value in return. How do you figure out the value of the original gift? Study an* Ochugen *catalog and you will notice that the order code number on each gift subtly correlates to the price. While the thoughtfulness of Japanese gift-giving is impressive, obligations can weigh heavily on both giver and re-ceiver. The level of stress in the stores at the height of* Ochugen *is palpable*
—*think of a Marshall Field store as Christmas eve approaches. Givers, too, recognize they are not just offering a gift but presenting a social burden.*

—Michael Lev, *Chicago Tribune*, July 16, 1996

The kinds of interactions we have with close others can vary greatly from one re-lationship to another. The relationships we maintain with our friends are different from those we maintain with our romantic partners, and both are different from our relationships with our parents and family. Even within a single relationship, our interactions are prone to change over time. A dating relationship in its early stages is qualitatively different from an established-long term relationship in many ways, and the kinds of things we do with our friends will change as we move from adolescence to adulthood. Despite these differences, some (e.g., Levinger & Huesman, 1980) have argued that it is possible to view them all from one single theoretical viewpoint: social exchange theory. This viewpoint proposes that all human interactions can be construed in terms of exchanges of mutually rewarding activities. It assumes that, although the rewardingness of various ac-tivities will be different from person to person and on different occasions, people will conduct their relationships so as to maximize rewards and minimize costs.

The idea that close relationships can be conceptualized in terms of interper-sonal exchanges is at once compelling and controversial. It is *compelling* because of the simplicity of its assumptions that seem to be borne out by the relationship phenomena discussed in the previous chapters. Remember that people often desire others who match their level of attractiveness. From the perspective of exchange theory, what people are doing in this process is trading levels of attractiveness so as to gain a fair exchange. People who desire others with similar attitudes and beliefs may similarly be trading mutual agreement. The importance of a reciprocity norm during self-disclosure in its early stages further suggests the operation of exchange principles.

Exchange theory is *controversial* because it suggests that there is little difference in how we conduct our relationships with close others and strangers. In both cases, we attempt to maximize our gains and minimize our costs. Of course, to do this successfully we need to monitor closely what we put into a given relationship and compare our inputs to what we get out of it in return. Many find such a materialistic, tit-for-tat approach inappropriate to explain what happens between close and intimate others. Moreover, the story at the beginning of the chapter suggests that matters of exchange in intimate relationships can often become very complicated.

To appreciate fully both the strengths and shortcomings of exchange theory for the explanation of various processes in close relationships, it is necessary to examine the predictions it makes regarding what types of commodities people exchange, how they decide whether their relationship is fair and equitable, and how they react to inequities. As it turns out, there are several different perspectives, each looking at different aspects of the exchange.

The Nature of Resources Exchanged

Rewards and Costs

What is it that people in casual as well as close relationships exchange? On the most abstract level, people exchange rewards. By definition, a *reward* is anything a person values, and thus rewards can take on many forms, ranging from money to hugs. As a rule, people tend to place greater value on things they don't have than on things that are in ample supply. Finding a $20 bill in the laundromat will be more rewarding for a college student, for instance, than it would for a baseball player with a multiyear, multimillion-dollar contract. Similarly, a hug will mean more to someone deprived of physical affection than to someone who receives hugs and kisses all day long.

Of course, the flipside of rewards are *costs*. Giving another person any kind of reward is usually associated with a variety of costs. Because engaging in one activity usually precludes some alternative activity, opportunity costs are almost always incurred. For example, spending an evening talking about one's relationship can be quite rewarding, but it may come at the expense of not being able to go to a movie with friends. Of course, the cost of an activity is directly related to the desirability of the alternative activity. If the alternative to talking about one's relationship is to watch the grass grow, the costs for the activity are fairly low.

Apart from the unavoidable opportunity costs, most activities tend to become more costly as they are repeated over a period of time (Secord & Backman, 1964). Frequent exchanges of the same commodity may lead to fatigue in one person and satiation in the other. Remember that the value of a reward decreases once there is no shortage of it. This decrease in value, coupled with an incremental increase in the cost associated with the production of the reward, further increases the total cost of the activity. Because relationships change over time, new activities need to be substituted for older ones to avoid fatigue and satiation and to provide appropriate rewards.

Variety of Resources Exchanged

To talk about exchange exclusively in terms of reward and cost does not really tell us about the specific types of resources, or commodities, that people exchange. In both casual and close relationships, people can exchange a wide variety of resources that fall into six distinct classes: (1) love, (2) status, (3) information, (4) money, (5) goods, and (6) services (Turner, Foa, & Foa, 1971). These resource categories can be distinguished in terms of how concrete and particularistic they are, as illustrated in Figure 6.1.

Goods and services are more concrete than money, and all three are more concrete than love, status, and information, which are relatively more abstract. Furthermore, some resources are more particularistic; that is, their reward value depends on the person who is providing them. Love is perhaps the most particularistic of all resources, simply because finding love in all the wrong places is generally not very rewarding. Money, on the other hand, may be the least particularistic of all resources, because, by and large, its value is the same regardless of who gives it to us (not withstanding drug money or blatant bribes).

Given the differences in the nature of interpersonal resources, one can expect that different rules apply to the exchange in casual as opposed to close relationships. For one thing, it may be that different resources are exchanged. Just as

	Particularistic		
	More		*Less*
Abstract		Status Information	
	Love		Money
		Goods Services	
Concrete			

FIGURE 6.1   *A Classification of Interpersonal Resources by Concreteness and Particularism According to Turner, Foa, and Foa (1971)*

nobody would expect to find love at the hardware store, few would probably expect their loved ones to provide them with roofing nails. More importantly, exchanges among strangers are more constrained. The general expectation is that the exchange will involve resources from the same class or from proximal classes. The clerk at the grocery store can rightfully expect the appropriate amount of money in exchange for a packet of cream cheese. Likewise, the mechanic can expect the appropriate amount of money in exchange for repairing the brakes on our car. People in close relationships have a little more leeway in how they conduct their exchanges. They can trade resources from proximal as well as distal classes. For example, a friend may offer us money, a dinner, or a whole lot of praise in exchange for letting her tape our R.E.M albums. In light of the variability of exchanges possible in close relationships, some (e.g., Scanzoni, 1979) have gone so far as to propose that intimates spend a great deal of time negotiating the values and exchangeability of certain types of behaviors. Although it is not clear whether relationships can be entirely defined by that, it is clear that a certain amount of negotiation does at least occasionally take place.

Determining What Is Fair: Equity Theory

Assuming that people in close relationships find ways to decide on the types of resources they wish to exchange, the question becomes: How do they decide if they are getting what they deserve? Some (Homans, 1961) have phrased the answer simply in terms of interpersonal profit: "The open secret of human exchange is to give the other man behavior that is more valuable to him than it is costly to you and to get from him behavior that is more valuable to you than it is costly to him" (p. 62). This idea, then, proposes that two people will seek maximum gains at minimal cost. Others have argued that people will focus on fairness. Specifically, equity theory (Adams, 1965; Hatfield, Utne, & Traupmann, 1979; Walster, Berscheid, & Walster, 1973, Walster, Walster, & Berscheid, 1978) proposes that people scrutinize their outcomes relative to their inputs and then compare the result to their partner's inputs and outcomes by applying the following formula (Adams, 1965):

$$\frac{O_A - I_A}{I_A} = \frac{O_B - I_B}{I_B}$$

I_A and I_B represent the respective perceptions of the inputs from Person A and Person B. O_A and O_B represent the respective perceptions of the outcomes Person A and Person B are receiving. *Inputs* describe participants' contributions to the exchange that entitle them to rewards, and thus can be considered the costs of the relationships. *Outcomes* describe the positive or negative consequences participants perceive to have received as a result of the exchange. In principle, a relationship is considered to be *equitable* when the ratio of inputs to outcomes of Person A equals the ratio of inputs to outcomes of Person B. In other words, people feel like they are getting a fair shake out of their relationship when their partner puts in as much and receives as much as they do.

Establishing Whether There Is Equity

Of course, one might ask just how people go about determining the magnitude and value of their inputs as well as those of their partner. According to the theory, equity is in the eye of the beholder. In order for the formula to work, two people need to agree on how they assess one another's inputs and outcomes. This may be more easily said than done. *Inequity* can be fairly easily determined when there is a wide gap between two people's inputs. For example, if one person spends an hour cleaning the kitchen after dinner while the other person plays basketball for an hour, it is pretty clear who incurred more costs. It may be more difficult to make the same determination when one person washes the dishes while the other person takes out the garbage. One could argue that it may be more costly to do the dishes if it requires more time than taking out the garbage, creating a temporary sense of inequity. But if disposing of the garbage should involve going out in the rain or having to talk with one's least favorite neighbor, the equation is quickly thrown out of whack because of the increase in cost stemming from getting drenched or having to listen to deliberations about power tools.

Admittedly, the example of cleaning up after dinner is a mundane one. However, it illustrates the difficulties in assessing what is equitable. If it is hard to determine equity regarding two people's contributions to a simple task, it may be next to impossible to determine if one's relationship as a whole is equitable. For one thing, assessing equity requires people to scrutinize the many aspects of their relationship at any given point in time. For another, people need to keep track of their inputs and outcomes as well as those of their partner over long periods of time. Even if people were inclined to do that, and there is reason to believe that they frequently don't (Clark & Mills, 1979), there may still be a problem in terms of the value two people put on their respective inputs and outcomes (Hatfield, Utne, & Traupmann, 1979). A person who puts little stake in an impeccably clean house will likely place little value on his or her partner's painstaking clean-up efforts. Because of this, the gains provided by a clean house will be perceived as relatively low, and, as a result, the other's input tends to be devalued. Of course, the reverse is true for someone to whom a clean house is of paramount importance. Because the gains are fairly high, the other's input will increase in value.

Do People Really Seek Equity?

Given the many problems in deciding what is equitable, one might well ask if people do, in fact, apply an equity rule in determining what is fair in their relationships. One way to figure this out is to look at how well research supports this idea. According to Clark and Chrisman (1994), there is little research that directly examines the extent to which people in ongoing relationships apply an equity rule. However, there is research broadly concerned with the effects of equity on relationship satisfaction and stability, which allows an indirect evaluation of the idea that people would seek equity in a relationship (e.g., Lloyd, Cate, & Henton, 1982; Sabatelli & Cecil-Pigo, 1985; Sprecher, 1988).

To date, the evidence for the importance of equity is somewhat mixed. In one study (Sprecher, 1986), research participants who were involved in a dating relationship were asked to indicate whether they or their partner contributed more to the relationship and who seemed to be getting a better deal out of their relationship. Additionally, research participants were asked about their level of commitment to the relationship and the frequency with which they had experienced a variety of positive and negative emotions in their relationship during the past month. Consistent with predictions from equity theory, research participants who felt that they and their partner were getting an equally good deal out of the relationship and contributed to it equally reported a higher level of commitment and a preponderance of positive emotional experiences. Similarly, Sabatelli and Cecil-Pigo (1985) found that married couples who reported their relationship as equitable were more committed to their relationship than couples who felt their relationship was inequitable. Additionally, Lloyd, Cate, and Henton (1982) found that perceived equity was associated with higher relationship satisfaction among serious as well as casual daters.

Thus, there appears to be some evidence that perceived equity is related to happiness as well as relationship satisfaction and stability. However, to conclude from these studies that people may, in fact, apply an equity rule to evaluating the quality of their relationship would be premature. Virtually all of the studies in support of this idea used a global measure of equity (e.g., "Are you getting a better, worse, or equally good deal from your relationship as your partner?"). When dating couples are asked to rate the extent to which there is equity on *specific* dimensions of relationship inputs and outcomes, levels of equity no longer predict relationship satisfaction. Others (Clark & Mills, 1979) have even found that subscribing to a principle of equitable exchange can be downright harmful for the further development of a relationship. Specifically, people in close relationships who feel like they are being repaid for every benefit they award to the other end up being less attracted to that person. More importantly, and contrary to what equity theory predicts, people in a close relationship often avoid keeping track of their respective inputs (Clark, 1984; Clark, Mills, & Corcoran, 1989).

Reactions to Inequity

The preceding discussion of the difficulties inherent in deciding what is equitable suggests that people in close relationships may be less motivated to achieve and maintain equity at all times. At the same time, it is reasonable to expect that glaring inequities may not go unnoticed. Theoretically, a relationship can be marked by inequity in either one of two ways. A person may find herself underbenefitted. Her outcomes, relative to her inputs, may be lower than that of her partner. Another person may find himself overbenefitted. His outcome, relative to his inputs, exceed those of his partner. According to the theory, both situations should have negative emotional consequences. This is fairly obvious in the case of the person who finds herself underbenefitted. She is likely to feel exploited, unhappy, and angry, and her satisfaction with the relationship may be low. Contrary to what intuition might suggest, the person who finds himself overbenefitted is not much better off. If nothing else, the person should feel guilty about getting more than his fair share. Both types of inequity, along with their respective emotional consequences, should lead to attempts to make the relationship more equitable. This can be accomplished in a variety of ways. People might simply try to convince themselves and their partner that they are getting more or less out of the relationship than they actually do. Or they might try to convince themselves that their partner is getting more or less than he does.

Alternatively, people who find themselves in an inequitable relationship may attempt to restore equity behaviorally. An underbenefitted member of a couple may decide to decrease her inputs, whereas an overbenefitted member may increase his inputs. Or the couple may choose the somewhat more difficult option of asking each other to increase or decrease his or her inputs. Of course, symbolic attempts at restoring equity through changes in the perceptions of inputs may be more successful than actual behavioral attempts, as it is generally easier to change one's perceptions than one's actual behavior.

There is some evidence for some of the predictions equity theory makes about the emotional and behavioral consequences of inequity. Several studies have shown that being underbenefitted results in feelings of unhappiness and anger, whereas being overbenefitted results in feelings of guilt. Equity is generally associated with happiness and contentment (Hatfield, Utne, & Traupmann, 1979; Walster, Walster, & Traupmann, 1978). However, all these findings were obtained by asking research participants first about how equitable or inequitable their relationship was and then asking them to indicate how content, happy, angry, and guilty they felt. It is never clear just how much people's self-reports can be trusted (Nisbett & Wilson, 1977), and, in the case of these studies, some extra caution should be warranted, especially since no attempt was made to disguise their purpose. It may be that responding to the questions made salient norms about how one *ought* to feel in cases of inequity (e.g., "I get more out of this than my partner, so I had better feel guilty"); thus, the results may be partially due to the demands inherent in each study.

Empirical tests of the predictions made by equity theory about behavioral avenues toward the restoration of equity have not fared much better. Reasoning that underbenefitted members of couples may call in the chips in order to restore equity, one study (Hatfield, Utne, & Traupmann, 1979) hypothesized that dating couples in which the male partner is underbenefitted would have sex more frequently than couples in which the male partner is overbenefitted or couples who have an equitable relationship. The general idea is that there is a double standard suggesting that men are supposed to have sex and women are supposed to dispense it cautiously. Therefore, if a man finds himself shortchanged, equity can be restored by an increase in the frequency with which the couple has sex, because it requires an increase in the woman's input to the relationship, which should lead to an increase in the man's outcomes. At the same time, couples in which the man is overbenefitted should have sex less often, because women may now withhold sex to restore equity.

Those who find this line of reasoning less than compelling may be reaffirmed by the results of the study, which showed that couples who felt that their relationships were equitable had sex more frequently than any other set of couples. Although this finding is inconsistent with the specific predictions of the study, it does make a great deal of sense, perhaps even from an equity point of view. Remember, couples who feel that their relationship is equitable are generally happier than couples who feel there is inequity. And while happiness is not a prerequisite for sex, common sense suggests that it promotes its enjoyment.

To sum up, at some point, equity theory appeared to be a promising approach to finding out how two people may evaluate their relationship outcomes, including a seemingly easy-to-use formula. In its heyday, some (e.g., Hatfield, Utne, & Traupmann, 1979) felt that equity theory might some day become the foundation for a general theory of human behavior. However, support for its major predictions has been hard to come by. This, combined with a more general distaste for a theory that proposes people would keep track of relationship inputs and outcomes in an almost bean-counting fashion, has put equity theory's seeming promise in perspective.

Evaluating Relationship Outcomes: Comparison Levels

The difficulties with equity theory aside, it is probably fair to say that people will evaluate their relationship at least occasionally. Most people have a pretty good idea of how satisfied or dissatisfied they are in their relationship. Of course, if such evaluations are not based on rules of equity, one must ask just how people go about making these types of assessments.

The Thibaut and Kelley Model

One approach (Thibaut & Kelley, 1959) proposes that people evaluate their relationship against two standards. The first standard is a *comparison level (CL)* that summarizes what people expect to get or deserve from a relationship. This comparison level may be an idealized standard, such as perpetual romance, or it may be a more realistic standard comprised of past relationship experiences, cultural ideas, or social comparison to one's siblings or friends. From this latter perspective, comparison levels can change over time. A series of highly satisfying relationships is likely to increase one's CL, whereas a series of bad relationships is likely to decrease it. The extent to which people are satisfied with their relationship is then a function of their current outcomes compared to their expectations

(CL). When the outcomes exceed the CL, people will be satisfied with their relationship; when the outcomes fall below, people will be dissatisfied. The degree of satisfaction or dissatisfaction is determined by the magnitude of the discrepancy between outcomes and CL.

In Thibaut and Kelley's (1959) original proposal, the CL was considered a universal quantitative standard against which outcomes are compared. Thus, if Ashley expects five units of companionship and Derek provides eight units, she should be quite satisfied with her relationship. However, the issue becomes complicated when one takes into account people's mental models of relationships—that is, the kinds of things they idiosyncratically expect from their relationship. As it turns out, people vary widely in terms of the characteristics their ideal relationship should have (Rusbult, Onizuka, & Lipkus, 1993). On the surface, Ashley may be quite satisfied with the level of companionship Derek provides, but if she really values passion and intimacy and her outcomes on these dimensions fall below her CL, she will likely be somewhat unhappy. After all, even though companionship may be a good thing, it does not really compensate for a perceived lack of intimacy and passion. Thus, in order to determine whether someone is satisfied with a relationship, one needs to take into account both the quantity as well as the quality of what is received.

In addition to comparing relationship outcomes to a general comparison level, people use a *comparison level for alternatives (CLAlt)*. In this comparison, people contrast their current relationship outcomes with the outcomes they could obtain from a possible alternative relationship. If the current outcomes exceed the Cl_{Alt}, people are somewhat dependent on their partners and their relationship will be relatively stable. On the other hand, if the outcomes are lower than the CL_{Alt}, a person may decide to leave a current relationship in favor of the alternative. Of course, a person's CL_{Alt} may fluctuate, as its level depends on the availability of possible alternatives, which may vary over time and across situations.

The two comparison levels produce at least four different kinds of relationships, depending on how one's current outcomes stack up against the CL and the CL_{Alt}, as depicted in Table 6.1. Level 1 shows a person in a relationship marked by *attractive stability*. The person's outcomes from his current relationship exceed both his CL and his CL_{Alt}. He should be highly satisfied with his relationship, but also fairly dependent on it, because his outcomes from an alternative relationship

TABLE 6.1 *Different levels of satisfaction and dependence stemming from comparisons between relationship to a CL and CL_{Alt}*

Level 1	Level 2	Level 3	Level 4
0	CL_{Alt}	CL	CL_{Alt}
CL	0	0	CL
CL_{Alt}	CL	CL_{Alt}	0

would be much lower than his current outcomes. Level 2 shows a person in a relationship marked by *attractive instability*. The person's outcomes exceed her expectations, but she could do better by leaving the relationship in favor of the alternative possibility. Level 3 shows a person in a relationship marked by *unattractive stability*. The person is unhappy because he is getting less from his current relationship than what he expects, but by leaving it, he would be even worse off. Level 4 shows a person in a relationship marked by *unattractive instability*. What this individual gets from her current relationship falls below her expectations and what she could get from an alternative relationship. According to comparison level theory, it is a pretty safe bet that the relationship will end soon. In fact, there is ample research suggesting that, compared to individuals whose relationships persist, those whose relationships end often report lower satisfaction along with more attractive alternatives (Rusbult, 1983; Rusbult, Johnson, & Morrow, 1986; Sabatelli & Cecil-Pigo, 1985; Simpson, 1987).

Interestingly, our evaluations of possible alternatives appear to decrease as our commitment to a relationship increases. You may recall from Chapter 3 that people in exclusive dating relationships tend to perceive opposite-sex persons as less attractive than people who are dating more casually or not dating at all (Simpson, Gangestead, & Lerma, 1990). It turns out that this effect is not limited to perceptions of physical attractiveness, but instead extends to other characteristics, as well (Rusbult, 1983). This tendency to devalue possible alternatives is strongest among those who are committed to a relationship and are presented with an extremely appealing alternative. Furthermore, this devaluation is more closely related to commitment rather than satisfaction per se (Johnson & Rusbult, 1989).

The Investment Model

Of course, one might ask what creates commitment in the first place. This question has been addressed by a model that extends interdependence models in two ways. Specifically, the investment model (e.g., Agnew et al., 1998; Rusbult, 1983) suggests that attraction and dependence are to some extent influenced by the level of *investment* one has in a relationship. Lucinda becomes increasingly dependent on Michael to the extent that the relationship is rewarding, that there are few alternatives, and that she feels bound by the relationship (i.e., is highly invested in it). The confluence of these forces lead to relationships marked by increasing cognitive interdependence. As Lucinda and Michael become increasingly committed to continuing their relationship, foreseeing an extended future, they are likely to engage in more frequent relationship-relevant cognitive activity (e.g., Wegner, Erber, & Raymond, 1991), and the nature of their identity and self-presentation is likely to shift, as well (e.g., Aron & Aron, 1997). In other words, Lucinda will come to view herself as part of a unit. Interestingly, this link between commitment and interdependence is strongest in romantic relationships (Agnew et al., 1998), suggesting that it is a unique mechanism that sustains exclusivity—a relationship feature that is more important in romantic relationships than in friendships.

It is all too easy to construe commitment and investment in terms of extemporaneous markers such as marriage. However, they are also present to varying degrees in dating relationships (Rusbult, 1983) as well as gay and lesbian relationships where marriage is not an option (Duffy & Rusbult, 1986). In short, it appears from these observations that investment is a state of mind one brings to a relationship.

In conclusion, the research based on Thibaut and Kelley's (1959) theory does a good job of describing how people evaluate their relationships and in predicting the consequences of certain types of comparison outcomes. People are undoubtedly happy with their relationships if they exceed their expectations and people become dissatisfied when their relationships fall below their expectations. The theory suggests reasons why many people remain in relationships with which they are unhappy, and further suggests reasons why some people may walk out of what seem to be perfectly good relationships. Still, some scholars are bothered by the suggestion that people apply some sort of calculus involving a comparison of their relationship outcomes. After all, such a notion seems to imply that there is little difference in how we conduct ourselves in close relationships and casual relationships. The following section considers a somewhat radical proposal that emphasizes the differences in the norms guiding our relationships with close others and strangers.

Close Relationships as Communal Relationships

Some (Clark & Mills, 1979) have argued that our relationships with close others are fundamentally different from those we have with casual acquaintances or strangers. According to this view, for example, relationships with our employers and those who provide us with goods and services are based on exchange principles. We expect our employers to compensate us adequately for the amount of effort we put into our jobs. When we realize that we are getting less than we can reasonably expect, we become unhappy and, depending on the availability of alternatives, might decide to take our skills elsewhere. When we pay $50 for a concert ticket, we expect the band to show up, start on time, and play for more than 45 minutes. When we lend our chainsaw to a neighbor across the street, we often do it with the expectation that some day he will let us borrow his jumper cables. In all these examples, people exchange things with the expectation of getting something in return, either immediately or in the near future.

Other types of relationships are not as easily captured in terms of exchange. What is it, for example, that teachers and their students exchange? If it is a tradeoff between effort and grades, what are the teacher's contributions to the exchange? What is the nature of the exchange that takes place between parents and their children? Historically and culturally, children were often expected to provide for their parents once they reach old age. However, this type of exchange has in many cases given way to employer-sponsored retirement funds, social security, and nursing homes. Of course, one could argue that raising children has its own rewards. Then again, how many smiles and coos do we expect in return for changing one messy diaper?

Faced with such difficulties in conceptualizing a variety of relationships in terms of exchange principles, Clark and Mills (1979) proposed that close relationships may best be considered communal in nature. In communal relationships, giving and receiving benefits are guided by different norms and principles, which render them qualitatively different from exchange relationships.

Giving and Receiving Benefits

In exchange relationships, benefits are given either in exchange for past benefit or with the expectation of receiving benefits in the future. This is why we often feel compelled to return favors when we are dealing with relative strangers or casual acquaintances. Such considerations do not matter in close relationships. Instead, the giving of benefits is, or should be, guided by the other's needs or our desire to please the other (Clark & Mills, 1979). For example, in deciding on a wedding gift for a couple of friends, we carefully examine what they would like and need by consulting their registry and making a choice accordingly. It matters little what they have given us for our own wedding. Moreover, if we find that a close other responds to us by returning favors and assistance in a tit-for-tat fashion, we are likely to experience a measure of discomfort, and we may even like him or her less.

These assertions about a need-based norm regarding the giving and receiving of benefits in close relationships have received a fair amount of empirical support. One of the first investigations was designed to test the idea that in exchange relationships, benefits are given in exchange for receiving past benefits or with the expectation of future benefits. In communal relationships, on the other hand, benefits are given according to the other's needs, without consideration of past or future benefits (Clark & Mills, 1979). In this study, male research participants were led to believe that they could expect either an exchange or a communal relationship with a female confederate who posed as either married or new in town and thus anxious to meet people. Participants then worked on a task that required them to create as many words from a set of letters as they could for points from the experimenter. While doing the task, they were under the impression that the female confederate was in another room doing the same task but using fewer letters. Because that essentially made the confederate's task harder, the experimenter gave research participants the opportunity to send any extra letters to the confederate if she so requested through an elaborate message system. This manipulation allowed research participants to give benefits to another with whom they expected either an exchange or communal relationship. In addition, the confederate responded to research participants' benefits in one of two ways. She sent research participants a note, thanking them for the letter, and included a letter from her set in return. This essentially communicated that she was desiring an exchange relationship. Alternatively, she sent research participants a note containing a simple "Thank you" without returning the favor. At the end of the experiment, research participants were asked to indicate their liking for the confederate.

The results of the experiment were in line with what Clark and Mills (1979) had predicted. Research participants who expected an exchange relationship with the allegedly married confederate liked her most when she followed exchange-based norms—that is, when she returned research participants' favors. On the other hand, research participants who expected the possibility of a communal relationship with the single woman liked her most when she followed communal norms—that is, when she offered no repayment. Moreover, when the confederate violated the norms of the type of the expected relationship by either following communal norms in the exchange situation or exchange norms in the communal situation, research participants' liking of her decreased substantially.

There are several reasons that may lead to decreased liking for someone who violates our expectations about the rules in which people in exchange and communal relationships are to conduct themselves. In exchange relationships, *giving* a benefit comes with the expectation of repayment, ideally in the form of a comparable benefit. At the same time, *receiving* a benefit creates an obligation to respond with a comparable benefit. When this expectation is violated, people will feel shortchanged and exploited, just as equity theory would predict. However, this same expectation is not only absent in communal relationships but it may be downright absurd (e.g., Mills & Clark, 1994). In its strongest form, it would suggest that if Jennifer gives Jason a three-pack of Calvin Klein underwear for his birthday, Jason is to reply in kind. At the very least, this type of gift exchange is likely to leave Jennifer with a sense of bewilderment at Jason's lack of originality. Things do not become much better if Jason decides on a gift that simply costs as much as the underwear and is thus comparable in value. After all, it is considered tacky to leave the price tag on gifts (partly because it creates the impression that we expect future, comparable repayment).

Of course, the differences in the norms guiding the giving and receiving of benefits in exchange relationships, as opposed to communal relationships, should be reflected in terms of how much we like someone who either follows or violates the respective rules. Moreover, one would also expect to find differences in terms of how closely people keep track of their inputs in casual and close relationships. Specifically, one would expect people in casual relationships to monitor their inputs more closely than people in communal relationships would. This speculation was borne out in two studies (Clark, 1984) that looked at the communal-exchange distinction in two ways.

The first study was similar to the procedure used by Clark and Mills (1979). Pairs of strangers were led to believe that their partner desired either an exchange or communal relationship. All research participants then worked on a joint task for which they expected a reward. The task consisted of circling numbers that were arranged as a matrix; the reward would be given according to how well the pair (rather than the individuals) performed. To complete the task, research participants could choose pens that were the same color as or a different color from the one their partner used. As expected, research participants who considered the relationship with their partner as an exchange relationship chose the different color pens significantly more often (87.5 percent of the time) than what one would expect by chance. Apparently, their choice was motivated by a desire to keep track of each other's inputs in the service of dividing the joint reward proportionately. At the same time, research participants who desired a communal relationship chose the different color pens significantly less often than what one would expect by chance (12.5 percent of the time), presumably because they felt compelled to obscure any differences in the respective inputs. Similar results were obtained in the second study, when the behavior of friends, who should think of their relationship as communal in nature, was compared to the behavior of strangers, who should think of their relationship as an exchange relationship.

For the same reason that keeping track of inputs becomes unimportant for communal relationships, keeping track of the other's *needs* increases in importance. This should be true regardless of whether the other person has an opportunity to reciprocate for a benefit in kind. Instead, the giving of benefits in communal relationships should be exclusively guided by an orientation toward the other's needs. This should not be the case in exchange relationships, where reciprocation, expected or actual, should determine the willingness to give a benefit. These hypotheses were confirmed in a study (Clark, Mills, & Powell, 1986) that employed a paradigm similar to the one used by Clark and Mills (1979). The main difference was that instead of actually returning benefits, research participants had a chance to check on whether their partner needed help under conditions of reciprocation or no reciprocation. As it turned out, research participants who expected an exchange relationship checked more often when they knew the other might reciprocate, whereas for research participants who expected a communal relationship, the possibility for reciprocation did not influence the frequency with which they checked for calls for help. Another way to look at relationship orientation is in terms of stable individual differences. In other words, people chronically differ in the extent to which they approach relationships in an exchange or communal fashion. Toward that end, Mills and Clark (1994) developed a scale to measure these individual differences. It is depicted in Figure 6.2.

Controversies Surrounding the Communal-Exchange Distinction

Despite the impressive amount of research in its favor, the distinction between exchange and communal relationships is not without its critics. One frequent argument claims that the distinction is based on research conducted in somewhat artificial laboratory settings in which the type of relationship is experimentally manipulated. However, this argument is not particularly compelling in light of the fact that studies that looked at the behavior of friends (e.g., Clark, 1984; Clark, Mills, & Corcoran, 1989) have, by and large, obtained results that are consistent with those studies that manipulate the type of relationship experimentally.

A second issue relates to whether communal relationships are really exchange relationships with a fairly long time perspective. In other words, people in

FIGURE 6.2 *Items from the Communal and Exchange Orientation Scale*

The nature of a relationship influences which orientation (communal versus exchange) people adopt. In addition, communal-exchange orientation may also be viewed as an individual difference variable. Some people approach relationships with a communal orientation, whereas others approach them with an exchange orientation. Margaret Clark and her colleagues (e.g., Mills & Clark, 1994) have developed two scales to measure such individual differences. Below are some sample items from both scales. On a scale from 1 (not at all) to 5 (extremely), respondents rate the extent to which these statements characterize themselves.

Items from the Communal Orientation Scale

It bothers me when other people neglect my needs.

When making a decision, I take other people's feelings into account.

I believe people should go out their way to be helpful.

I expect people I know to be responsive to my needs and feelings.

When I have a need that others ignore, I'm hurt.

Items from the Exchange Orientation Scale

When I give something to another person, I generally expect something in return.

When someone buys me a gift, I try to buy that person a gift as comparable as possible.

When people receive benefits from others, they ought to repay those others right away.

It's best to make sure things are always kept "even" between two people in a relationship.

Source: J. Mills and M. S. Clark, "Communal and Exchange Relationships: Controversies and Research," in R. Erber and R. Gilmour (Eds.), *Theoretical Frameworks for Personal Relationships* (Hillsdale, NJ: Erlbaum, 1994). Reprinted by permission.

communal relationships may not expect repayment or reciprocation in the short run, but instead expect the giving and receiving of benefits to be equitable in the long run. However, this idea is not easily reconciled with the findings showing that people in communal relationships do not keep track of their inputs. Without such knowledge, it is unclear how they would determine what to expect in the future.

It appears, then, that the distinction between exchange and communal relationships is a meaningful one both in terms of its theoretical and empirical foundations. However, in certain ways, it describes a somewhat ideal world in which benefits are given solely on the basis of perceived needs. In real life, this may be more constrained than one might think. For example, one could argue that whether or not one responds to another's need may to some extent be determined by how legitimate the need is perceived to be. Most people, for example, are somewhat squeamish in accommodating their partner's need for "more space." Furthermore, some (Leventhal & Michaels, 1971) have argued that the giving of benefits is multiply determined by need, contributions, and various distributive norms. Finally, it may be that people for whom equity is highly salient, perhaps because they are deprived of it at work and elsewhere, might seek it in their close relationships in a compensatory fashion. None of these issues is likely to shatter the usefulness of the distinction between communal and exchange relationships. Instead, they highlight the need for further research.

Summary

Issues.   It is not uncommon to look at relationships in terms of exchanging interpersonal resources or in terms of their respective rewards and costs. If one adopts this view, what is the nature of the resources that are exchanged? How does it proceed? What are the consequences of inequity? How is all this related to attraction and relationship stability? Is it possible that close relationships operate on communal rather than exchange principles?

Theories.   Equity theory proposes that people strive for relationships in which the respective inputs and outcomes of one partner equal those of the other. It further predicts that people will closely monitor their own inputs as well as those of their partner. Inequity from being either underbenefitted or overbenefitted is said to result in attempts to restore equity via perceptual or behavioral means. Comparison level theory proposes that members of couples compare their relationship outcomes to a standard comprised of their expectations (CL) as well as a comparison level for alternatives (CL_{Alt}). Communal-exchange theory proposes that, although maintaining equity may be important for casual relationships, the giving and receiving of benefits in close relationships is primarily guided by perceived needs.

Research.   A great deal of research supports many of the predictions from equity theory. However, the results are frequently based on self-reports that may be subject to alternative explanations. Moreover, at least one study failed to provide support for a crucial prediction regarding attempts to restore equity. Comparison level theory has been supported by several studies showing that satisfaction in combination with dependence are important considerations in deciding to maintain or terminate a relationship. Furthermore, commitment appears to be an important mediator of perceptions regarding the attractiveness of alternatives. Research on the distinction between communal and exchange relationships has provided ample evidence showing that both types of relationships are guided by different principles when it comes to the giving and receiving of benefits. This evidence is based on studies that manipulated research participants' expectations for a communal versus exchange relationship as well as studies that compared pairs of research participants who either shared a communal relationship (friends) or an exchange relationship (strangers).

7

Love and Emotion

> *LAHORE, Pakistan—Saima Waheed, a conservative Muslim who has worn a veil outside the home since puberty, never thought she'd fall in love. She did though, and when she got married her parents took her to court. Monday, Pakistan's High Court ruled that Waheed can stay with her husband. However, the court made no ruling on whether women can marry for love, avoiding a decision on whether a woman can defy the strong Pakistani tradition of arranged marriage. . . . Waheed fell in love with Ershad Ahmed, and after a brief, secret courtship, he asked for her hand in marriage. Waheed's father refused. . . . Last year, in a show of independence that is rare in Pakistan, Waheed defied her father's wishes and married Ahmed.*
>
> *—Chicago Tribune, October 12, 1998*

If one were to name a relationship issue that has consistently fascinated people for a long time, it would probably be the topic of love. Songwriters, philosophers, poets, and even religious scholars have speculated on the antecedents, features, and consequences of love. Some have suggested that love is a many-splendored thing; others have offered that love stinks; and still others have focused on the nature of different types of love, such as platonic love, brotherly love, and Christian love. For most Westerners, love is considered a necessary, but not sufficient, condition for marriage, whereas other cultures award it a more secondary consideration. For Waheed's father, a marriage based on love is just as outrageous as the idea of a marriage arranged by one's parents is for most of us.

Psychologists, in general, and social psychologists, in particular, entered the scientific study of love at a relatively late stage. This is not entirely surprising, in light of the various paradigms that dominated the discipline at one point or another. Freud's seemingly obsessive preoccupation with sex as a major motivator of human behavior compelled him to define love as a compensatory mechanism that kicked in whenever the desire for a sexual union was blocked. Presumably, sexual frustration of this sort leads to idealization of the other person along with a feeling of falling in love (Freud, 1922). For the behaviorists, with their exclusive focus on stimulus-response connections, sex was important for the experience of love in a very different way. Specifically, Watson (1924) looked at it as an innate response elicited by the cutaneous stimulation of the erogenous zones. Finally, social psychologists of the 1950s and 1960s treated love as just another attitude that predisposes one to think, feel, and act toward another in certain ways (Rubin, 1970).

Presumably, if Jane thinks that John is a pretty neat guy, she will have positive feelings about him and will consequently entertain a proposal for a dinner date with some degree of seriousness. Such a sequence of events is suggested by one prominent view (e.g., Breckler, 1984; Eiser, 1986) that looks at attitudes as consisting of three components: (1) a *cognitive component*, which consists of everything we know and believe about an object or a person; (2) an *affective component*, which describes our feeling toward the object or person; and (3) a *behavioral* or *conative component*, which contains our behavioral intentions toward the object or person.

Thus, someone who has a favorable attitude about broccoli is likely to have favorable beliefs about it, along with positive feelings and an urge to consume it whenever the opportunity arises. Similarly, if Brian has favorable beliefs about Julie, then he is likely to have positive feelings about her, along with a tendency to seek out her company. Note that there is an underlying assumption of consistency here. Favorable or unfavorable beliefs about an object or a person usually fall in line with positive or negative feelings and their corresponding behavioral intentions. As it turns out, this assumption is more troublesome than one might suspect. Frequently, our beliefs about the healthiness of broccoli does not translate into liking, much less into a desire to eat it, and the same can hold for our *attitudes* about people (e.g., Tesser & Shaffer, 1990). As a result of such complications, research on attitudes became more preoccupied with resolving issues of consistency among its components than with delineating the nature of their affective components.

In defense of academic psychology, it is important to note that laypeople appear to be just as confused about the nature and meaning of love. Visitors to the United States are frequently struck by the effusiveness with which Americans express what appear to be simple preferences. We claim that we love (or hate) skiing, broccoli, and mai-tais when in fact we merely like (or dislike) them. This seems to imply that love is nothing other than a whole lot of liking. On the other hand, people often go to great lengths to assure us that they like us but not necessarily love us. The suggestion to "just be friends" is not really an indication that a reduction in love should ensue but instead implies that liking should be the predominant sentiment in the relationship.

Liking and Loving: A Conceptual Distinction

Given the profound implications of labeling one's feelings for another as "love" rather than "liking," psychologists were eventually forced to abandon the idea that love was nothing more than intense liking (Heider, 1958). Interestingly, the first crack at differentiating between the two types of sentiments came out of an attempt to develop attitude scales that would distinguish the extent to which a person *likes* another and the extent to which a person *loves* another. Specifically, Rubin (1970) developed two attitude scales to measure love and liking. A few samples follow:

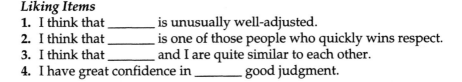

Liking Items
1. I think that _____ is unusually well-adjusted.
2. I think that _____ is one of those people who quickly wins respect.
3. I think that _____ and I are quite similar to each other.
4. I have great confidence in _____ good judgment.

Love Items
1. If I could never be with _____, I would be miserable.
2. I feel very possessive toward _____.
3. I would do almost anything for _____.
4. I feel I can confide in _____ about virtually everything.

A look at the items of both scales shows several things. First, liking appears to be a matter of favorable evaluation of the other (e.g., "I think that _____ is unusually well-adjusted"), respect for the other (e.g., "I think that _____ is one of those people who quickly wins respect"), and the perception of similarity (e.g., "I think that _____ and I are quite similar to each other"). Love, on the other hand, seems to consist of an affiliative and dependent need component (e.g., "If I could never be with _____, I would be miserable"), an exclusiveness and absorption component (e.g., "I feel very possessive toward _____"), and a predisposition to help (e.g., "I would do almost anything for _____").

To further explore the differences between liking and love, Rubin administered both scales to 158 dating couples and asked them to respond once with their dating partner in mind and once with a close same-sex friend in mind. The finding from this study corroborated many of Rubin's speculations about the difference between liking and love, although there were a few surprises, as well. First, the two scales were only moderately correlated, suggesting that although liking and love often go hand in hand, they are not the same thing. As we all know, we can like others without loving them and sometimes we may love others without really liking them all that much. Along these same lines, research participants liked their dating partners only slightly more than their same-sex friends, but they loved their dating partners much more than their friends. Somewhat surprisingly, scores on the love and liking scales were more highly correlated for men, suggesting that men are perhaps more confused about the true nature of their feelings, whereas women are prone to make more subtle distinctions. Finally, women tended to like their boyfriends more than they were liked in return. This difference was almost entirely due to differences in the ratings of task-related dimensions, such as good judgment, intelligence, and leadership potential. Keep in mind, however, that this study was conducted 30 years ago. It may be that in these days of increased equality among the genders, this type of finding may no longer be obtained.

The Prototype of Love

In thinking about the differences between love and liking, Rubin (1970) was initially inspired by the writings of anthropologists, psychologists, and sociologists. Their speculations about the nature of love became the basis for many of the items that subsequently formed the Love scale. In using this approach, Rubin ended up with a sample that was strongly biased in favor of highly educated academics who were perhaps marked by peculiar ways of thinking.

But what about people whose thinking has not been contaminated by years of intellectual immersion in an academic discipline? Would they think of love in the same way as a psychologist or an anthropologist? Maybe. Maybe not. To some extent, what love is in most people's minds may be an empirical question. Toward that end, all one would need to do is to ask a sufficient number of people to list the features of love as they see it and look for a consensus about which features are considered more or less central by most people. This would establish a proto-type of love; that is, the results would yield the features most commonly associated with love. Fehr (1988) took this very approach by first asking a large number of undergraduate research participants to list as many features of love as they could think of in three minutes. This procedure resulted in a list of 68 features that were listed by two or more people. Fehr then asked a second group of under-graduates to rate each item on the list in terms of how central this feature is to love, using an 8-point scale ranging from 1 ("extremely poor feature of love") to 8 ("extremely good feature of love"). The 10 most central and the 10 least central features are listed in Table 7.1.

The picture of love painted by this study is slightly different from that of Rubin. On the one hand, Rubin's predisposition to help seems to be reflected in "Concern for the other's well-being" and "Supportiveness." Similarly, Rubin's affiliative and dependent need appears to be reflected in "Want to be with the other" (not shown in Table 7.1). On the other hand, "Friendship" and "Respect," which were among Fehr's most central features of love, had been classified by Rubin as being part of liking. However, before we can brand academics as sadly misguided in their thinking, we need to acknowledge one possible flaw in Fehr's (1988) study. It may be that Fehr's research participants' responses were at least

TABLE 7.1   *The 10 Most Central and the 10 Most Peripheral Features of Love According to Fehr (1988)*

Most Central	Most Peripheral
1. Trust	1. Scary
2. Caring	2. Dependency
3. Honesty	3. Uncertainty
4. Friendship	4. Butterflies in stomach
5. Respect	5. See only other's good qualities
6. Concern for other's well-being	6. Gazing at the other
7. Loyalty	7. Euphoria
8. Commitment	8. Heart rate increases
9. Acceptance	9. Energy
10. Supportiveness	10. Thinking about the other all the time

Source: Fehr, 1988. Reprinted by permission.

partly influenced by their normative expectations regarding what love should be rather than what love is. This would also explain why "Sexual passion" (not shown in Table 7.1) was rated as a peripheral rather than a central characteristic of love.

The shortcomings of both studies aside, it is probably safe to conclude that for most people, love is a curious mixture of trusting, caring, helping, wanting, and commitment. With this in mind, we can now look at some theories that deal with the issue of how this peculiar emotion comes about in the first place.

Causal Theories of Love

Love as Misattribution of Arousal

In *The Cheyenne Social Club*, Henry Fonda and Jimmy Stewart played two aging gunfighters. At one point during the movie, Fonda asks Stewart if he had ever been in love. Stewart demurs, and then answers, "I thought I was in love once, but it turned out to be gas." Stewart's reply may sound silly to most, but it illustrates misattribution theory (Schachter & Singer, 1962), which was discussed at length in Chapter 4. As you may recall, within the framework of this theory, any emotion is a result of a change in the level of physiological arousal (e.g., increase in heart rate, perspiration, pupil dilation, etc.) that becomes labeled according to the cues available in the situation. And although no single study has explored the effects that misattribution of arousal may have for the specific experience of love, it is safe to speculate that any arousal-producing event or situation has the potential to at least intensify feelings of love. Trouble at work or school, parental or societal disapproval (e.g., Driscoll, Davis, & Lipetz, 1972), and the need to keep a relationship a secret (Lane & Wegner, 1994; Wegner, Lane, & Dimitri, 1994) are but a few possible extraneous sources of arousal. Within the dynamics of a relationship, such things as disagreement and sexual frustration may serve as sources of arousal with similar effects, as long as there is at least some ambiguity about the origin of the arousal in the first place.

Love as Preoccupation with the Other

The misattribution perspective on love primarily takes into account the importance of unexplained arousal, and it awards thinking a somewhat subsidiary status, as it limits its role to the task of explaining the arousal. However, it may be the case that thinking, particularly thinking about the other, may be an important component for the generation and subsequent intensification of subjective feelings of being in love. To outside observers, people who are in love often appear as though they have lost their minds. Not only do they go around with strange smiles on their faces but they also seem to have a hard time concentrating on the most elementary tasks of life, such as working and enjoying time with their friends.

There is, of course, a good reason for this. People in love simply cannot help thinking about the object of their love at practically all times. But given the pervasiveness of this preoccupation, it may be that thinking about the other has a causal effect on the experience of love. If nothing else, thinking about the other may intensify feelings of love in ways similar to how our evaluations of a variety of things seem to change the more we think about them. If, for example, we just left a movie theater with a sense of disappointment, further thinking is likely to increase our feelings. By the same token, if we liked the movie we saw, thinking about it more is prone to increase our initial liking. Presumably, continued preoccupation with the movie brings to mind thoughts that are largely congruent with our initial evaluation, and thus additional thinking is likely to further polarize them (Tesser, 1978).

That this type of reasoning may explain the intensification of love over time is suggested by the results of a study in which members of dating couples recorded how often they thought about their partner over a period of two weeks (Tesser & Paulhus, 1976). Additionally, research participants in this study also reported on how much they felt they were in love at the beginning and end of the two-week period, using the Love part of Rubin's Liking and Love scales, as well as the number of dates during that time. Finally, research participants were asked to keep track of any discoveries they made about the other that could give rise to decreased feelings of love (e.g., strange and intolerable personal habits). This measure served as an indication of the reality constraints within which research participants' thinking about the other took place. The general idea was that discovering that their partner is an alcoholic or an ax murderer might substantially alter the nature of research participants' thoughts about the partner and ultimately bring about a more or less drastic attenuation of love.

The results, as expected, showed that the frequency with which the members of the couples thought about each other was strongly correlated with their subjective experience of love. This manifested itself in a couple of ways. First, the frequency of thought at Time 1 (the beginning of the two-week period) was highly predictive of how much in love research participants felt at Time 2 (the end of the two-week period). At the same time, how much in love research participants felt at Time 1 predicted the frequency of thinking at Time 2. In other words, the more research participants felt in love, the more they subsequently thought about the other, with the ultimate outcome of intensified feelings of love. Not surprisingly, dating frequency and love were positively correlated, but encountering reality constraints was negatively correlated with love. This latter finding is important, for it suggests that love is not totally blind. Obsessive preoccupation with the other may to some extent border on idealization, but discovering things that we dislike about the other seems to impose an important constraint on this process. Furthermore, it suggests that obsessive thinking may have its most profound impact when we are lacking a lot of information about the other, perhaps because the relationship is in its very early stages and little self-disclosure has occurred, or perhaps because the lovers are kept apart by circumstances (Beach & Tesser, 1978).

Type Theories of Love

In some ways, causal theories of love focusing on the role of arousal and obsessive thinking are neat and tidy theories, as they isolate some of the factors that help translate attraction into love and lead to a further intensification of love. The tidiness of such mini-theories (Bentler & Huba, 1979), however, is not without its cost. For one thing, cynics might object to these theories as treating love as a "secondhand emotion," originating primarily from physiological arousal and obsessive thinking. For another, by focusing primarily on increases (or decreases) in the experience of love, these theories look at love mostly in terms of its *quantitative* aspects. At the same time, they devote little or no attention to the *qualitative* differences in the experience of love from one person to the next. Obviously, the kind of love we have for our siblings is different from the kind of love we feel for our romantic partners. Moreover, because relationships necessarily involve two people, we can expect differences in how love manifests itself for one person in different relationships of the same type that are not merely intensity related. For example, when people review their past intimate relationships, they often note such things as differences in infatuation, companionship, and the like rather than differences in terms of just how much they loved one another. That love has many manifestations, even in the context of intimate relationships, has been addressed by various theories stressing individual differences in love. Common to these approaches is the theme that there are different types of love that vary more or less systematically among people.

The Colors of Love

In many ways, the intellectual godfather of all individual difference approaches to love is Lee's (1973, 1988) typology of love as colors. By drawing on the color metaphor, Lee was able to come to some interesting assumptions about possible differences in love styles among people. First, just as we have different color preferences, we have idiosyncratic preferences for different love styles. Second, just as we prefer some different colors for our wardrobe and our home, we prefer different love styles for different people. Third, just as color preferences change over time, preferences for love styles as well may change as we get older, perhaps as a result of one's relationship history. Finally, just as primary colors can be mixed to produce new ones, primary love styles can be mixed to produce secondary ones.

Armed with this set of assumptions, Lee went on to examine everything that had been written about love by poets, philosophers, and social scientists throughout history. Using the conclusions from his readings as a framework from which to understand people's experiences, he collected structured accounts of how people experienced love. On the basis of his combined analysis, Lee (1973) initially identified 12 different love styles that characterized the way most people experience and think about love. Eventually, this initial classification was pared down to 6 different love styles, composed of 3 primary love styles and 3 secondary styles, which represented mixtures and compounds of the primary styles. In order to correspond to the different types of love described in the classical literature, Lee gave them Greek and Latin names rather than names of colors.

Primary Love Styles.   The first love style Lee identified was *Eros,* which describes the passionate love often caused by a strong attraction to the physical attributes of the other. Eros is love that is certainly not blind. Moreover, people characterized by this love style tend to think that finding the perfect mate is the most important thing in life. Once they have found their mate, the relationship is frequently characterized by a strong desire for abundant physical and verbal acknowledgments of their love. The polar opposite to Eros is *Storge,* a kind of companionate love style that develops out of friendship and interaction. It is most common in agrarian societies, where partner choice is limited by virtue of people's proclivity to stay in one place for most of their lives, and is less typical for societies with high mobility. Unlike Eros, overt expressions of love and passion are rare; instead, the focus in Storge is on commonly shared interests. In addition to Eros and Storge, there is *Ludus,* which describes a sort of playful love mostly for the short term. Ludus lacks a "falling in love with all its trimmings" as well as commitment in either time or exclusivity, and thus is characteristic of people who prefer to remain single.

Secondary Love Styles.   Mixing the proper amount of Eros and Ludus results in a love style Lee called *Mania,* the kind of dependent and possessive love characterized by obsessive preoccupation and intense jealousy. Similar to Eros, Mania requires constant and tangible assurances of love, but just like Ludus, there is no preference for any particular type of person. As the term implies, lovers characterized by Mania appear to have lost their senses as they vacillate between demonstrating their love and getting control of the relationship. As such, manic love has an element of pathology, which is further amplified by the tendency of manic lovers to project desired qualities onto their partner of choice.

Mixing Storge and Ludus results in the very different love style of *Pragma,* which describes a love style anchored around matters of logic and practicality. For pragmatic lovers, finding the compatible mate is first and foremost a practical problem that can be solved through effort and persistence. Just like Storge, Pragma tends to develop slowly, as pragmatic lovers are wary of warning signs. And, like Ludus lovers, pragmatic lovers are restrained about commitment and the future, at least until they find the right partner. Sexual compatibility is considered to be important, but it is perceived to be a matter of sharpening skills rather than chemistry. Not surprisingly, pragmatic lovers like to join organizations, such as singles clubs, to find a partner.

Finally, mixing Eros and Storge yields *Agape,* a form of love that is selfless, giving, and altruistic. Lovers characterized by Agape consider love as a duty to respond to the needs of the other, even if their love is not reciprocated. And while Agape is espoused in the New Testament as the ultimate form of love (1 Corinthians 13:4–7), it is perhaps the least common form of love in adult romantic relationships. Instead, it may be descriptive of the kind of love parents have for their children.

Research on Love Styles

Many readers of Lee's typology are initially struck by its seeming face validity, as most are able to sort themselves and their love styles into one his categories. Thus, it is not surprising that social scientists were quick to explore the utility of Lee's typology for a variety of relationships phenomena, including partner choice, relationship satisfaction, and relationship stability.

Much of this work was made possible by the development of the Love Attitude Scale (LAS), a 42-item measure that corresponds to Lee's distinctions among the various love styles (Hendrick & Hendrick, 1986). Using this measure, several studies reported generally positive correlations in the love styles of two partners, especially on Eros (Davis & Latty-Mann, 1987; Hendrick, Hendrick, & Adler, 1988). That is, erotic lovers were most likely to be paired with an erotic partner. However, although this finding may be suggestive of attempts on the part of both partners to be with someone who matches their erotic love style, there are other ways to look at it. The crucial issue is a chicken-and-egg-problem with the interpretation of the results. Are the matching love styles the basis of choice or do partners in a relationship simply come to share each other's views of that relationship? In other words, if one partner sees a lot of Eros in the relationship, the other partner may also come to see it as an erotic relationship. Thus, the positive correlations may be a result of shared and continued interaction rather than partner choice per se. Of course, it may be much harder for partners to share the view that their relationship should be marked by intense jealousy or a conspicuous lack of commitment, and thus correlations between Mania and Ludus tend to be low or even negative (Davis & Latty-Mann, 1987; Hendrick, Hendrick, & Adler, 1988).

Although the findings on the relationship between love styles and partner choice are somewhat difficult to interpret, the results of research on the relationship between love styles and relationship satisfaction are relatively straightforward. Eros and Agape are generally associated with various measures of relationship satisfaction, whereas Ludus and satisfaction tend to be negatively correlated (e.g., Bierhoff, 1991; Davis & Latty-Mann, 1987; Hendrick, Hendrick, & Adler, 1988; Levy & Davis, 1988). This is hardly surprising, in light of the importance people place on passion and altruism for relationships. Finally, matching levels of Eros and Agape, along with Pragma, seem to predict the stability of a relationship as well as the number of children a couple has (Bierhoff, 1991). But again, as with partner choice, there are some questions in terms of the proper interpretation of these findings. It is possible that matching love styles produce relationship outcomes, such as commitment and investment, which would predict relationship stability more directly. However, because such variables were not measured, this question remains an open one.

In some ways, the interpretational ambiguities inherent in much of the research on love styles are mirrored by a number of conceptual ambiguities surrounding the very concept itself. As some (Clark & Reis, 1988; Davis et al., 1994) have pointed out, Lee's theory is essentially a descriptive typology of relatively complex syndromes containing components that are not necessarily found together in ways that an ideal type would suggest. What is lacking is a sense of which of the various components are more or less central to the various love styles. For example, is wariness of warning signs more central to the Pragma love style than is achieving sexual compatibility through practice or joining an organization to find a compatible mate? The trouble is that without specifying which features of a given love style are more central and which ones are more peripheral, it becomes difficult to assess the degree to which any one person matches each style.

Lee's theory is also silent on the issue of how the different love styles evolve in the first place and how they change over time. Of course, it is always tempting to conclude that further research and theorizing will eventually work out the kinks. However, in this case, such expectations might be unduly optimistic because of the inductive way in which Lee generated the theory in the first place. Instead of making propositions based on one or more psychological frameworks, he essentially let the data (i.e., the literary accounts) speak to him without a clear idea of what to expect. Thus, the lack of theoretical guidance makes it difficult to modify the theory in the ways necessary to provide a maximally useful framework from which to understand just why and how "love is a many-splendored thing."

A Triangular Theory of Love

Whereas Lee's (1973, 1988) typology has a number of shortcomings, it has been influential in setting the stage for other typologies of love that, although still primarily descriptive in nature, avoid some of the problems inherent in Lee's theory. Working in a less inductive manner, Sternberg (1986) proposed that love consists of three basic ingredients: intimacy, passion, and decision/commitment. The *intimacy* component refers to feelings that promote closeness, bondedness, and connectedness, and includes such feelings as concern for the welfare of the other, subjectively experienced happiness, positive regard, sharing, support, mutual understanding, and intimate communication. The *passion* component refers to sources of arousal that promote the experience of passion, such as sexual needs, needs for self-esteem, affiliation, submission, dominance, and self-actualization. Finally, the *decision/commitment* component refers to the decision that one is in love with the other and the commitment to maintain that love.

Intimacy, passion, and commitment follow a unique time course as a relationship develops. In successful relationships, intimacy increases steadily, much in the way that self-disclosure increases. Dying relationships are characterized by a decrease in intimacy. Passion develops rapidly in the beginning of a relationship and is eventually replaced by habituation. However, drastic decreases or even a loss of passion may lead to a somewhat cyclical pattern by returning a relationship to its beginning. Of course, the larger question is: Where do increases and decreases in passion come from in the first place? One possibility is that passion is a function of intimacy. At the early stages of a relationship, passion will be high because of initial increases in intimacy (Baumeister & Bratslavsky, 1999). Simply put, learning about another, sharing experiences, and finding out that the other person cares about you are arousing and thus provide the basis for passion. By the same token, as two people reach the point where they feel they know everything about the other, have run out of new experiences to share, and feel they understand each other completely, passion decreases accordingly.

The temporal pattern of decision/commitment depends somewhat on the success of a relationship, which to some extent is influenced by the development of intimacy and passion. In successful relationships, with rapidly increasing passion along with gradually increasing intimacy, commitment initially develops somewhat slowly. Dramatic events, such as having sex for the first time or moving in together, generally mark a drastic increase in commitment. Once couples are established because they are married, own a home, and have children, commitment levels off primarily because it reaches a ceiling; that is, it cannot increase any further.

The three components of love are present in all close relationships to various degrees. Assuming that in any given relationship, intimacy, passion, and commitment can be either low or high, Sternberg (1986) came up with eight forms of love that are characteristic of qualitatively different relationships (see Table 7.2).

As the term implies, consummate love describes the kind of relationship for which many strive and that perhaps few achieve. Realistically, most romantic relationships may be lacking in one or more components. Romantic love, with its emphasis on intimacy and passion in the absence of strong commitment, is perhaps characteristic of couples in the early stages of dating. Fatuous love, or infatuation, with its emphasis on passion and commitment, seems to be marked by sex without intimacy. Companionate love, with its lack of passion, describes many mature relationships in which sexual drives have been supplanted by intimacy

TABLE 7.2 *Eight Types of Relationships and Their Characteristics According to Sternberg (1986)*

Types of Love	Components Present or High
Consummate love	Intimacy, passion, and commitment
Romantic love	Intimacy and passion
Infatuation	Passion
Fatuous love	Passion and commitment
Companionate love	Intimacy and commitment
Empty love	Commitment
Liking	Intimacy
Nonlove	———

and commitment. Empty love, with its almost exclusive focus on commitment in the absence of anything else, describes couples who are staying together for matters of convenience, child rearing, or tax purposes. Liking, with its exclusive emphasis on intimacy, describes relationships among close friends. Finally, although nonlove may seem to be an artifact of the classification (if everything can be high it can also be low), it does perhaps describe the kind of sentiment that exists among people whose relationship has ended.

Sternberg's (1986) typology is useful in understanding how different forms of love result in qualitatively different relationships. However, its utility depends to some extent on how well it explains relationship satisfaction and stability. At this point, there is little, if any, research on these issues. Nonetheless, several speculations are plausible. On the most basic level, one could argue that people will be happy with their relationship to the extent that it meets their mutual expectations. For example, two people may be quite satisfied with a relationship low on commitment as long as they both agree that commitment is not important. Mismatches in expectations regarding the importance of any of the components of love is likely to lead to conflicted relationships (and thus keep advice columnists in business). On the other hand, Sternberg felt that the three components of love were of equal importance in close relationships. From this perspective, one would expect relationships that contain equal parts of intimacy, passion, and commitment to be the most successful. By the same token, relationships that are heavily slanted toward one component may be under pressure to achieve a more balanced state.

Passionate Love and Companionate Love

The eight different types of relationships described by Sternberg (1986) represent the range of theoretical possibilities created by the varying levels of intimacy, passion, and commitment. By themselves, they give no indication of which ones are more likely to occur empirically. Some (Hatfield, 1988) have argued that most close relationships fall into one of two categories.

Passionate love is characterized by an intense longing for a complete union with the other and is represented by both the unadulterated passion of infatuation and the intimate passion of romantic love in Sternberg's typology. According to Hatfield, passionate love comes in two forms. Reciprocated passionate love creates a sense of fulfillment along with feelings of elation and perhaps even ecstasy on the part of both members of the couple. Unrequited passionate love often results in feelings of emptiness, anxiety, and despair on the part of those whose love is rejected. As it turns out, unrequited love is difficult for the would-be lover as well as the rejector. Would-be lovers often look back on the relationship with a mixture of positive and intensely negative emotions. They feel that the love had been mutual, that they had been led on, and that the rejection had not been communicated clearly. Contrary to what one might believe, rejectors are by no means better off. Looking back on the relationship elicits mostly negative emotions. And while rejectors feel morally innocent, they feel guilty over their inability or unwillingness to return the other's love. At the same time, however, they perceive any attempts on the part of the would-be lover to keep the relationship going as intrusive and annoying (Baumeister, Wotman, & Stillwell, 1993).

Hatfield (1988) proposed that passionate and companionate love have a lot in common with attitudes to the extent that they contain cognitive, emotional, and behavioral components. The *cognitive* component of passionate love, which is defined as a state of intense longing for a union with the other, includes intrusive thinking and a general preoccupation with the other, along with an idealization of the other and the relationship as well as a desire to know the other and be known. The *emotional* component includes attraction, especially of a sexual nature. Positive feelings prevail when the relationship goes well, but when things go awry, negative feelings will arise. Additionally, there is usually a longing for reciprocity, a desire for a complete and permanent union, and an abundance of physiological arousal. The *behavioral* component of passionate love brings with it actions toward determining the other's feeling, a proclivity to study the other person, and a desire to do things for him or her.

Companionate love lacks some of the aspects of longing that passionate love has, and instead describes the attraction we feel toward another person with whom our lives are deeply intertwined. Cognitively, it entails sharing information about one another, even if it is of an embarrassing nature. The emotional component of companionate love is characterized by the possession of intimacy rather than a longing for it. On a behavioral level, continued proximity creates a sense of comfort rather than arousal.

It is all too easy to look at close relationships as being either passionate or companionate. However, realistically, many successful relationships probably have elements of both in the sense that for many people their lover is also their best friend. Moreover, as relationships mature, they may undergo a transformation from being primarily passionate to being primarily companionate. After all, as Sternberg (1986) has argued, passion is subject to habituation, and the focus of a relationship may shift as a result of specific events.

Consistent with this idea, Tucker and Aron (1993) reported results from a study that measured the amount of passionate love couples experienced at three important transition points: before and after they got married, before and after they had their first child, and before and after the children were old enough to leave the house. The amount of passionate love declined steadily over time and from before and after the transitions, suggesting that the relationships took on a more companionate nature. However, these decreases were relatively small. Even couples who were contemplating or experiencing the "empty nest" still reported at least moderate amounts of passionate love.

If nothing else, this last finding indicates that passionate love is not reserved entirely for young adults. In fact, there is reason to believe that even very young children can experience feelings akin to passionate love. Hatfield and colleagues (1988) administered the Juvenile Love Scales, a children's version of the Passionate Love Scale to research participants ranging in age from 4 to 18 and found that 4-year-olds experienced just as much passionate love as 18-year-olds. The only exception to this pattern was the finding that boys around the age of 12 reported experiencing little in the ways of passionate love, perhaps because they are at an age where they tend to think of girls and perhaps everything female as gross. On the face of it, the finding that even young children can experience passionate love may be taken as an indication that Freud was perhaps correct in proposing that there is sexuality in childhood. However, there is a more likely explanation. Hatfield, Brenton, and Cornelius (1989) found that among children, passionate love was correlated with dispositional anxiety as assessed by the trait part of Spielberger's (1966) state-trait anxiety scale. Thus, it may be that in an attempt to explain anxiety-related arousal, highly anxious children imitate adult models by attributing it to passionate love.

How well does the distinction between passionate and companionate love explain differences in relationship satisfaction and stability? One could argue that the experience of passionate love is perhaps more rewarding in part because of the overwhelming experience of longing for a union with the other. One could further argue that companionate love may be more predictive of success in the long term because it lacks the emotional turmoil often created by the experience of passionate love. Unfortunately, there is little research that addresses these issues, although one study (Aron & Henkemeyer, 1995) reports that women who experienced a great deal of passionate love were happier, more satisfied with their relationship, and more excited about their relationship than women who experienced little passionate love. Interestingly, these same associations were not found for men, suggesting perhaps the existence of gender differences in love.

Individual Differences in Love

Gender

Whether the experience of love is different for men and women has been a matter of almost perpetual debate. Newspaper advice columns as well as talk shows are flooded with complaints from people who feel their partner does not love them. Frequently, such complaints are based on a perceived lack of companionship, intimacy, or sex. Keep in mind, however, that for every person who registers complaints about his or her love life, there are probably thousands who appear to have no problems in this regard. Not surprisingly, then, research on gender differences paints a somewhat sketchy and inconsistent picture. It appears that for every study that reports gender differences on such measures as Rubin's Love Scale (Black & Angelis, 1974; Dion & Dion, 1975), romanticism (e.g., Sprecher, 1989b), or passionate love (Aron & Henkemeyer, 1995), there is an equal number of studies that fail to find gender differences (cf. Cunningham & Antill, 1981; Hatfield & Rapson, 1987; Hatfield & Sprecher, 1986; Rubin, 1973). Thus, it appears that any effects of gender on the specific experience of love may be mediated by other variables.

Differences Due to Age and Relationship Duration

Age is one variable that may affect the experience of love among men and women. For example, one cross-sectional study comparing the experience of love among young adults, their parents, and their grandparents points to the influence of age specifically on a romantic view of life (Hieger & Troll, 1973). Whereas young adult women were more romantic than males, the exact opposite was found when the researchers looked at the entire sample. Furthermore, the grandparents in the sample were less romantic than the young adults.

This finding is interesting for a couple of reasons. For one thing, it appears that young couples are more inclined than older couples to engage in behaviors indicative of passion and romanticism, such as embracing and kissing in public and holding hands. For another, one theory (Berscheid, 1983) suggests that the experience of love and other emotions in relationships decrease over time. This is the case because of the kinds of things that bring about emotions in the first place. According to Simon (1967) and Mandler (1975), emotions result from interruptions of ongoing behavior. Many activities we perform throughout the day are either so well practiced (e.g., driving a car) or so engrossing (e.g., reading a novel) that performing them results in little or no emotion. However, when they are interrupted by external events, such as a fiery car crash in the next lane or the phone ringing in the kitchen, a variety of emotional reactions can occur.

Couples whose relationships have reached a state of maturity have usually found ways to handle the chores of everyday life, perhaps relying on a transactive memory or a more general division of labor. Furthermore, such chores as getting the kids ready for school, shopping for groceries, and preparing meals often require highly interdependent and sequential contributions from both adults. For example, Jane can load the kids in the van for the trip to school only after John has made sure that they are properly dressed; Bob may be able to fix dinner only if Ann made a stop at the grocery store on the way home from work. According to Berscheid (1983), there is little room or cause for strong emotions when things go smoothly. However, when these interdependent sequences of behaviors are interrupted because John sleeps through his alarm or Ann has to stay late at work, considerable emotion can result. And although these examples suggest a potential primarily for the experience of negative emotions, the theory predicts the occurrence of positive emotions, as well.

Moreover, the theory predicts a steady decrease of love over time. Basically, falling in love constitutes a major interruption in our lives and thus results in strong emotional experiences. As the focus of a relationship shifts toward raising children and making ends meet, the experience of love is somewhat diminished, although the potential is still there. It generally diminishes again once the kids leave the house and financial security has been achieved. Under these circumstances, people's lives become less intertwined, thus decreasing the potential that interruptions will lead to the experience of love and other emotions.

Several things are appealing about Berscheid's approach to love and emotion in close relationships. The theory appears to explain the data reported by Aron and Henkemeyer (1995) fairly well and it provides hope for those whose lives revolve around dirty diapers, night-time feedings, and providing taxi service to ballet lessons and basketball games. Equally important, it suggests that apparent decreases in love, passion, and romanticism may not be an inevitable outcome of age per se, but instead of relationship duration. This is important in part because there is little we can do about getting older yet we can arrange our relationships in a way that they can provide us with the experience of love over a lifetime.

Love over Time: Does It Get Better or Worse?

It is disheartening to think that the love two people have for one another would decrease as their relationship matures beyond its early tumultuous stages. Interestingly, Berscheid's theory is not the only one that makes precisely that prediction; it is implicit in at least one other theory. Aron and colleagues (e.g., Aron & Aron, 1986; Aron et al., 1991) conceptualized "falling in love" as a process by which the self is expanded to include another person. This means that forming a close relationship with another involves integrating the other's perspective, resources, and characteristics into the self, resulting in self-expansion. Of course, as people get to know each other more and more as their relationship matures, opportunities toward self-expansion may decrease at the same rate. To the extent that self-expansion and love are linked, reduced opportunities for self-expansion may be accompanied by decreases in love.

Fortunately, these somewhat dire predictions about decreases in love as relationships mature are not well supported by actual data, in part because the human mind seems to have found important mechanisms to keep one's love alive. One study in particular (Sprecher, 1999) asked members of 101 heterosexual dating couples two sets of questions at varying intervals over a four-year period of time. First, at each wave, couples were asked to report their perceptions about how their feelings of love, commitment, and satisfaction had changed since the last data collection. Second, couples also responded to "objective" measures of their current levels of love, commitment, and satisfaction. The results from those couples who were still together at the conclusion of the study (roughly 40 percent) showed an intriguing pattern. In terms of their *perceptions of change*, most couples reported *increases* in their feelings of love, commitment, and satisfaction. In addition, the *objective measures* yielded *no increases* over time. In other words, even though respondents were no more in love with their partner two, three, or four years after the relationship began, they felt as if they were!

Beyond Love: A Quick Look at Guilt

Love, in its many manifestations, is undoubtedly of paramount importance for close relationships. Feelings of increasing love are associated with the initiation of close relationships, whereas decreasing feelings of love are often precursors for their termination. Of course, continued feelings of love for the other also help maintain a relationship even in times of conflict and turmoil. However, it appears that guilt provides love with a powerful ally in this process. Just like shame, the experience of guilt is promoted by interpersonal contexts. Whereas shame mostly results from failure combined with a concern with others' evaluations, guilt usually stems from moral transgressions involving harm to others (Baumeister, Reis, & Delespaul, 1995; Tangney, 1992), especially valued partners in close relationships (Baumeister, Stillwell, & Heatherton, 1994). Thus, it is not surprising that guilt is commonly found in relationships that are communal in nature (Baumeister, Stillwell, & Heatherton, 1994), generally as a result of neglecting the other, skipping out on obligations, and selfish actions.

Interestingly, guilt is more than just the emotional price one partner pays for committing a variety of transgressions. Instead, it appears that guilt may be a powerful mechanism in the maintenance of close relationships, as it can help restore power among the powerless (i.e., the victims of transgression). In other words, guilt can pave the way toward influencing the behavior of the transgressor in terms of eliciting apologies and promises involving corrective behavior in the future. This perspective suggests that victims of interpersonal transgressions are not as poorly off as they may seem, as long as the perpetrators experience feelings of guilt over their transgression. And since guilt itself is caused by harming a close other in the first place, only the most cynical may be exempt from its experience.

So where does this all leave us? It seems that Senator Proxmire's admonition not to take the mystery and excitement out of love by subjecting it to scientific examination has become somewhat of a rallying cry for social scientists. Theorizing and research on love have proliferated ever since. Although a lot of it has in fact added to our understanding of the role of love in relationships, numerous questions remain unanswered. In light of this, many researchers have recently come to conceptualize love as a form of attachment, much like the attachment infants have to their caregivers. We will look at this perspective more closely in the next chapter.

Summary

Issues. What exactly is love and how can it be distinguished from other sentiments, such as liking? What brings about the experience of love? What forms or types of love are there? To what extent can typologies of love explain pertinent relationship phenomena like satisfaction and stability? What differences, if any, are there in how people of different genders and ages experience love? In what ways can guilt be harmful and beneficial for close relationships?

Theories. Rubin (1970, 1973) was among the first to propose a conceptual distinction between liking as a matter of favorable evaluations of the other, respect of the other, and perceptions of similarity, and loving as a matter of affiliation, dependency, and exclusiveness. Fehr (1988) further added to our understanding of love by specifying its prototypical features. Causal theories of love emphasize the importance of physiological arousal as well as cognitive preoccupation with the other for its experience and intensification. Type theories of love divide the pie in several ways. Lee (1973) identified six forms of love—Eros, Storge, Ludus, Mania, Pragma, and Agape—based primarily on an analysis of literary writings. Sternberg (1986) suggested that three components of love—intimacy, passion, and commitment—combined to form eight types of relationships. Hatfield (1988) elaborated specifically on the differences between passionate and companionate love. The research of Baumeister and colleagues sheds light on how guilt can work as an effective yet somewhat costly mechanism in the maintenance of a relationship.

Research.   By and large, research supports the idea that people distinguish between liking and love, that some features are more central to love than others, and that people experience love in vastly different ways, as suggested by the various typologies. Furthermore, there is evidence that the experience of physiological arousal and cognitive preoccupation with the other person are important causal factors for the experience of love. On the other hand, it is less clear how different types of love may influence relationship satisfaction and stability. Whereas many couples share similar love styles, it is unclear whether this influences partner selection or whether it is a result of adopting each other's views of love. Similar problems arise with the interpretation of findings that suggest that similarity in the levels of Eros and Agape are associated with higher levels of relationship satisfaction. Although some of the problems with the utility of love typologies stem from conceptual ambiguities, other problems are created by individual differences in the experience of love between the sexes and among people of varying ages. Research has shown that guilt may be important for the maintenance of close relationships once transgressions have occurred.

8

Attachment

Already, 13 percent of German couples conduct their relationships long-distance, and the number of the involuntarily separated is likely to increase as a result of the government's move from Bonn to Berlin. About half of Bonn's government employees will leave a partner behind. The list of adversarial consequences induced by living apart is long. In addition to the sheer cost of maintaining two residences, there are psychological costs. Many couples complain of exhaustion from the constant travel. Others complain that they don't feel at home in either place. Even though few admit to it publicly, many have nightmares about betrayal during the lonely nights they spend apart.

—*Der Spiegel*, September 27, 1999
(condensed and translated by the authors)

For many of us, falling in love triggers an almost inexplicable desire to spend most, if not all, of our time with the person toward whom our feelings are directed. When we are with those we love, the world seems like a safe and rewarding place. When we are without them, it seems cold and possibly dangerous, and we long for the moment when we are once again reunited with our loved one.

Admittedly, this description of some of the feelings that go along with being in love may not apply to everyone, and it is probably somewhat exaggerated. However, the truth of the matter is that some aspects of our adult romantic relationships bear an almost uncanny resemblance to the relationships we had with our caregivers when we were infants. In other words, the emotional bonds between adult romantic partners can be understood in terms of the nature and quality of the emotional attachment that exists between infants and their caregivers.

To understand the nature of adult attachment and its ramifications for individuals and their relationships, it is first necessary to take a closer look at what developmental psychologists have uncovered about the nature of children's attachments to their caregivers. Attachment research has its origins during World War II. As a result of the massive destruction and loss of life, many social service agencies began to wonder about the ramifications of the lack of maternal care. In 1950, the World Health Organization asked John Bowlby, a British psychiatrist, to undertake a study of the mental health problems of children who had been separated from their families and were cared for in hospitals, nurseries, and orphanages. His systematic observations of these children who had either lost their parents or were otherwise separated from them resulted in a general theory of attachment, which was published in three volumes over three decades (Bowlby, 1969, 1973, 1980).

Patterns of Attachment in Infancy

According to Bowlby's theory, all children develop an attachment to their caregivers. Bowlby characterized this attachment as an internal working model that children use as a standard to guide their interactions with their caregivers as well as other adults more generally. What differs from one child to the next is the extent to which the child is attached as well as the quality of his or her attachment. Children who are *securely* attached form a mental representation of their caregivers as a secure place from which to explore the world and as a source of comfort in times of distress. Children who are *anxiously* attached form a generalized expectation that their caregivers cannot be reliably counted on to provide comfort in times of distress. And children who are *avoidantly* attached do not think of their caregivers as a source of comfort at all.

To test Bowlby's speculations about the different forms of attachment, Mary Ainsworth and colleagues (Ainsworth, Bell, & Stayton, 1971; Ainsworth et al., 1978) devised the "Strange Situation," an experimental paradigm that allows for the observation of children's behavior in response to being separated from their mothers. A typical experiment contains the following sequence of events. Mother and her 12- to 18-month-old child arrive at the laboratory, set up as a playroom, and are initially greeted by a stranger. The stranger leaves and mother and child spend a period of time together, during which the child can play with a number of toys (i.e., explore the unfamiliar environment). Then, without warning, the mother leaves, the stranger reenters, and, after a short period of time, the mother returns. Because virtually all children below the age of 18 months show distress when their mother leaves suddenly and unannounced, researchers are able to observe a child's behavior while playing, when a stranger offers comfort, and when the mother returns.

Children's behavior under these circumstances falls into three categories that relate on to the different types of attachment Bowlby had initially proposed. A securely attached child plays comfortably with the toys as long as his or her mother is present. When the mother suddenly leaves, the child becomes visibly and vocally upset. He or she is unlikely to accept the stranger's invitation for comforting, but calms down quickly and resumes playing once the mother returns. About 65 percent of U.S. middle-class children show this pattern of attachment. An anxiously attached child is more reluctant to play and instead prefers to stay close to his or her mother at all times. When the mother leaves, the child becomes very upset and does not calm down when the mother returns. Instead, the child seeks renewed contact with the mother yet simultaneously resists her attempts at comforting. About 23 percent of U.S. middle-class children show this pattern of attachment. An avoidantly attached child resembles a securely attached child to the extent that he or she does not worry about where the mother sits while they are playing. The child may or may not cry when the mother leaves, but when the child does cry, he or she readily accepts the stranger's attempts at comforting. When the mother returns, the child might look or turn away from her instead of seeking closeness and comfort. About 12 percent of U.S. middle-class children show this pattern of attachment.

Causes of Different Attachment Patterns

How do these differences in attachment come about in the first place? It appears that they result from a complex interaction among specific characteristics of the mother (or, more generally, the caregiver), innate characteristics of the child, as well as the larger cultural context. In general, mothers of securely attached children tend to be more involved with their infants, more responsive to signs of distress and feeding needs, more appropriate in responsiveness, and more positive in their emotional expression (Isabella, 1993). Most of the research attempting to pinpoint the child's contribution to attachment has focused on the child's temperament. Granted, it is intuitively plausible that mothers would have a harder time responding appropriately and positively to children who are fearful or who get upset at the drop of a hat, but the evidence to date is somewhat inconclusive. Although some studies show an effect of temperament on subsequent attachment (Kiyake, Chen, & Campos, 1985), others fail to demonstrate it (Vaughn et al., 1989).

Finally, Ainsworth (1967, 1982) suggested that the distinct patterns of attachment are to some extent culturally universal, but there is also evidence that attachment patterns can be greatly influenced by the unique childrearing practices of a culture. For example, among Israeli children who grow up in kibbutzim, where they are cared for primarily by adults other than their parents, a smaller percentage of 14-month-olds were classified as securely attached (37 percent compared to 65 percent in the United States). One study of German children (Grossmann et al., 1985), found that a mere 33 percent of 1-year-olds could be classified as securely attached, whereas a whopping 49 percent tested as avoidantly attached. However, this should not be taken as evidence that half of German mothers are insensitive and uncaring. Instead, the large proportion of avoidantly attached infants may be the result of childrearing practices revolving around the idea that children, like clothing and kitchen floors, should be *pflegeleicht* (i.e., easy to care for). More specifically, it appears that avoidant attachment may result from the pursuit of creating independent, nonclingy infants who do not make too many demands on their parents.

Among children raised in traditional Japanese families, where the mother stays home to care for them, one finds a high proportion of anxiously attached infants but virtually no avoidantly attached infants. This pattern may be due to the fact that traditional Japanese mothers rarely leave their children in the care of anyone else, and instead raise them in ways that promote a sense of dependence. For example, it is not at all uncommon for children to sleep in their mother's bed until the time they start elementary school. Naturally, if such children are put into the "Strange Situation," they are more than likely to become extremely upset.

Adult Attachment

Developmental psychologists generally agree that acquired patterns of attachment—whether secure, anxious, or avoidant—are relatively stable over time (i.e., over a period of at least several months). This sounds like an awfully short amount of time. However, there is evidence that a secure attachment evident at ages 12 to 18 months can become less so, or even turn into an anxious attachment, as a result of external stressors, such as unemployment, prolonged illness, or conflict within the family (Lyons-Ruth et al., 1991; Main & Weston, 1981). Of course, the reverse is also true. As stressors that may have contributed to an anxious attachment are removed, attachment patterns are likely to become less anxious and even secure. The observation that attachment is somewhat malleable, however, should not be taken as an indication that it can fluctuate wildly throughout infancy and early childhood. Instead, because optimal attachment develops during a relatively short, sensitive period, shifts in attachment should primarily be observed if the presentation or removal of family stressors falls within that period.

If anything, attachment patterns are generally fairly stable and appear to be present through adulthood (Bowlby, 1982). Of course, in adulthood, the partner in a close, intimate relationship becomes a person's attachment figure, completing a period of transition in which the attachment figure is transferred from parent to peer (Kerns, 1994). In other words, the attachment styles that marked infants' relationships to their mothers should be evident in the sense that adults can be attached to their romantic partners in a secure, anxious, or avoidant way. Note that Bowlby had good reasons to advance this idea. After all, he conceived of attachment as "inner working models" of the self and social relationships. Not surprisingly, then, research that has looked at adult attachment has found ample support for Bowlby's (1982) notion and has provided important insights into the importance and ramifications of adult attachment patterns. Before jumping into a review of the relevant research, it is important to keep in mind that much of the research is, out of necessity, correlational in nature. Thus, any statement suggesting a causal relationship should be taken with a grain of salt.

In one of the first studies (Hazan & Shaver, 1987), over 1,200 adults (with an average age of 36) responded to a questionnaire that appeared in the *Rocky Mountain News*. It contained a total of "95 questions about your most important romance." The crucial question asked respondents to describe their feelings about relationships (see Figure 8.1). Respondents who indicated that they found it easy to get close to others, were comfortable depending on them, and did not fear abandonment were classified as securely attached. Those who indicated that they were reluctant to get close and worried about the other's love were classified as anxiously attached. And finally, those who reported that they were uncomfortable being close and felt that they had problems trusting their partner as well as reciprocating with their level of closeness were classified as avoidantly attached.

The nature and scope of this study revealed a wealth of data about the importance of attachment in romantic relationships. To begin with, the percentages of adults who displayed the three attachment styles were remarkably similar to the percentages usually obtained when one looks at the attachment styles of infants. Specifically, 56 percent were characterized by a secure attachment (compared to 65 percent of infants); 19 percent were characterized by an anxious attachment (compared to 23 percent of infants); and 25 percent were characterized

FIGURE 8.1   *Adult Attachment Styles According to Hazan and Shaver (1987)*

Secure: I find it relatively easy to get close to others and am comfortable depending on them and having them depend on me. I don't often worry about being abandoned or about someone getting too close to me.

Anxious: I find that others are reluctant to get as close as I would like. I often worry that my partner doesn't really love me or won't stay with me. I want to merge completely with another person, and this desire sometimes scares people away.

Avoidant: I am somewhat uncomfortable being close to others; I find it difficult to trust them completely, difficult to allow myself to depend on them. I am nervous when anyone gets too close, and often, love partners want me to be more intimate than I feel comfortable being.

by an avoidant attachment (compared to 12 percent of infants). Moreover, the different attachment styles were associated with markedly different experiences of love. Secure lovers characterized their most important relationship as happy, friendly, and trusting. They further emphasized that they were able to accept and support their partner unconditionally. Anxious lovers reported their experience of love as being marked by obsession, desire for reciprocation and union, emotional ups and downs, along with extreme sexual attraction and jealousy. Finally, avoidant lovers' most important relationship was characterized by fear of intimacy, emotional ups and downs, and jealousy (in the absence of sexual attraction). Given these qualitatively different experiences, it is not surprising that the duration of secure lovers' most important relationship was markedly longer (about 10 years) than those of anxious and avoidant lovers (six years and five years, respectively).

Finally, Bowlby's (1982) speculations about the transfer of attachment from the mother to the adult romantic partner received some support, as well. Of course, it would be impossible for most adults to recall the nature of the attachment they had with their caregivers at the tender age of 18 months. For that reason, respondents instead answered a series of questions about their parents' general behavior toward them during childhood as well as their parents' behavior toward each other. Compared to insecure respondents, secure respondents reported generally warmer relationships with both parents and between their parents. Anxious respondents recalled their fathers, in particular, as having been unfair, and avoidant respondents described their mothers as cold and rejecting.

From Infant Attachment to Adult Attachment: Models of Transition

In light of the close correspondence of infant and adult attachment, it is reasonable to ask about the mechanisms that might be responsible for this continuity. At this point, there are several tentative answers in the form of broad theoretical perspectives. One answer, rooted in the psychodynamic tradition known as *object relations*, proposes that early interactions between parents and children become the basis for more generalized expectations about the nature of close relationships. Moreover, these expectations incorporate both sides of the interaction (e.g., aggressor and victim; nurturance and succorance), thus providing the child with a repertoire for interactions with others in general (Osofsky, 1982). This perspective suggests that adult attachment incorporates both aspects of the infant attachment (i.e., child and parent) and thus can help explain why avoidant lovers, for example, would be both distrustful and fearful of another's attempts at being close.

A second perspective (Kerns, 1994) emphasizes the importance of infant attachment for interactions with peers throughout childhood, adolescence, and adulthood. Once children are able to interact with peers, the immediate importance of the parental attachment figure becomes somewhat diminished. At the same time, the various developmental stages carry with them different friendship goals that require different skills. It is with regard to these goals and skills that early attachment has its effects.

For very young children, establishing friendships with peers requires a sense of coordinated interaction based on responsiveness, communication, and the ability to resolve conflicts. Anyone who has been unfortunate enough to witness a birthday party for a 3-year-old has observed firsthand that coordinated interaction with minimal conflict is far from typical for this age group. Oftentimes, the youngsters engage in parallel play, appearing to take little notice of what everyone else is doing. On the occasion when two or more children want to play with the same toy, parental admonitions to share or take turns frequently fall on deaf ears. The trouble is that coordinated play as well as sharing and taking turns requires communication, responsiveness, and at least minimal conflict resolution skills. Securely attached children who, by definition, received more responsive caregiving are more likely than anxious or avoidant children to be responsive to others, thus providing them with an edge in developing and sustaining successful friendships during early childhood (Kerns, 1994; Park & Waters, 1989).

As children get older, their friendship goals shift toward developing stable peer relationships (sometimes called *chumships*) that provide them with companionship. For children to be able to form such relationships, they need to be sensitive as well as able to empathize with another (i.e., be able to take another's perspective). Securely attached children whose inner-working models of relationships include responsiveness and sensitivity, and who have earlier acquired superior skills in resolving conflicts, are more likely to develop chummy friendships with peers (Elicker, Englund, & Sroufe, 1992).

During adolescence, with its conflicting needs for autonomy as well as intimacy, peers become a prime source for emotional support. Of course, in order to gain emotional support, one has to engage in intimate self-disclosure and be able to place trust in its recipient. Although there is little research on friendship in adolescence, it seems reasonable to speculate that those who were securely attached as infants would once again have an edge. Because they tend to be more responsive, have superior conflict resolution skills, and have the ability to form friendships, they should have an easier time with open and intimate self-disclosure.

Finally, in late adolescence and adulthood, individuals face the task of developing relationships of depth with a specific other. These relationships become the primary source of intimacy and support, especially among men (Reis, Senchak, & Solomon, 1985), and the friendships augment these attachment bonds by serving a person's social and affiliative needs (Weiss, 1982). The formation of romantic and friendship-based relationships requires the identification of those who are potential sources of support and affiliative needs. Again, although there is little actual research, it is easy to predict that those who began life with a secure attachment to their caregivers would have an edge because of the unique nature of their inner-working models along with the superior relationship skills that they acquired along the way.

Kerns's (1994) model of attachment transition is intriguing primarily because it does not propose a direct link from infant to adult attachment. Instead, it focuses equally on the effects of attachment on subsequent developmental periods. Thus, the model suggests that the transition is not simply a matter of near-magical transference but rather a result of a snowballing of attachment effects over the course of development. In other words, adult attachment styles observed at age 21 did not become fixed at age 1. Instead, the level of continuity is determined jointly by interactions in infancy as well as interactions throughout the remainder of childhood and adolescence. Furthermore, there is evidence that during adulthood, attachment styles may continue to perpetuate themselves by influencing everyday social activities. Consistent with this idea, one study using a diary approach (Tidwell, Reis, & Shaver, 1996) found that avoidantly attached adults experienced lower levels of intimacy, less enjoyment, lower levels of positive emotions, and higher levels of negative emotions, particularly in opposite-sex interactions.

The self-perpetuation of attachment may come full circle when one considers the implications of different attachment styles for attitudes about and relationships with children. One study (Rholes, Simpson, & Blakeley, 1995) found that, compared to securely attached adults, avoidant college men and women were less certain about having children and whether they would be able to relate to young children. Anxiously attached men and women desired to have children but felt unsure about their parenting ability. Among those who had children, avoidantly attached mothers reported that they lacked a feeling of closeness toward their preschool children and they behaved less supportively toward them in a teaching task than did mothers who were securely attached.

Consequences of Adult Attachment Styles

Issues of continuity aside, Hazan and Shaver's (1987) seminal work on adult attachment has triggered a virtual avalanche of research looking into the consequences of different adult attachment styles on both the individual level as well as the relationship level.

Attachment Style and Emotional Control. To the extent that secure attachment comes with a predilection to look at one's partner as a source of comfort, one would expect the different attachment styles to be related to a more general ability for emotional self-control. In support of this reasoning, Feeney and Kirkpatrick (1996) found a marked difference in how secure, anxious, and avoidant individuals responded to stress when their partner was either present or absent. Compared to secure research participants, anxious and avoidant individuals showed increased levels of physiological arousal (indicative of anxiety) when they had to complete a stressful task (counting backward by 13 as quickly and accurately as possible) in the absence of their partner. Moreover, this increased level of anxiety persisted when they tried to do a similar task in the presence of their partner. These results suggest that secure attachment comes with a generalized anxiety-reducing tendency, whereas insecure attachments produce anxiety related to separation in a stressful situation. Moreover, the observation that the presence of one's partner does little to reduce the anxiety levels of insecure individuals in a stressful situation suggests an approach-avoidance conflict that is likely brought on by the generalized expectation that the other cannot be counted on as a source for emotional support (Carpenter & Kirkpatrick, 1996).

Studies that look at support seeking and support giving among individuals with different attachment styles lend further support to the idea that those who are securely attached are more likely to seek *and* receive support from their partner when confronted with an anxiety-provoking situation. Specifically, Simpson, Rholes, and Nelligan (1992) observed the behavior of heterosexual couples as the female partner was about to enter into an anxiety-provoking situation of an unspecified nature. As expected, securely attached women used their partner as a source of reassurance and comfort as their anxiety about the upcoming task increased. Avoidant women looked for emotional support from their partner when their anxiety level was low, and anxious women did not seek support from their partner, regardless of the level of anxiety they experienced. Presumably, this lack of support seeking among anxious women may be due to an internal conflict with regard to proximity needs. Although they might need and desire comfort and reassurance, they also know that their partner is not consistently available to provide it. Thus, the need for proximity becomes associated with anger and resentment, which is likely to add to the level of stress already experienced. Not surprisingly, then, when the researchers looked at the behavior of the male partners, they found that secure men offered greater reassurance, comfort, and support than anxious and avoidant men.

Of course, findings like these should not be taken as an indication that individuals with insecure attachment styles are unable to control emotions such as fear and anxiety. Instead, it appears that such individuals may have an edge in the self-control of such emotions because they have learned that their partner cannot be relied on as a source of comfort and reassurance. Consistent with this idea, one study (Feeney, 1995) found that a proclivity for emotional self-control was most pronounced among couples in which both partners endorsed insecure attachment styles.

Attachment Style and Partner Choice.   In light of the observation that the seeds for adult attachment are sown as far back as infancy, one might ask whether adults choose partners with similar attachment styles. At least two answers are possible. On the one hand, based on the importance of similarity for attraction, one might argue that individuals would seek others with similar attachment styles. Consequently, if one drew a random sample of couples, one would expect to find secure-secure attachments, somewhat reflective of the base rates. On the other hand, one could argue that a secure attachment is something of an ideal type of a relationship that everyone would seek regardless of his or her attachment style. From this perspective, the same random sample might yield a relatively higher number of couples in which a secure partner is paired with either an anxious or an avoidant partner.

Not surprisingly, the evidence appears to come down in favor of the similarity hypothesis. One study (Frazier et al., 1996) independently looked at participants' attachment styles in relation to the attachment styles of those they were presently dating as well as their preference for partners with different attachment styles. The results on both measures were overwhelmingly in favor of the similarity hypothesis. Secure individuals tended to date and prefer partners who were also secure, whereas anxious and avoidant participants tended to date partners with similar attachment styles.

Another study that looked at the specific dimensions underlying the different types of attachment provided similar results (Collins & Read, 1990). Participants who reported that they were comfortable getting close were more likely to be with a partner who was equally comfortable with closeness. Those who felt they could depend on others tended to be dating a partner who felt similarly. Furthermore, participants who were comfortable with closeness tended to be dating partners who felt they could depend on others and were much less likely to be dating partners who worried about abandonment. However, there was no evidence that those who worried about abandonment were with partners who shared their anxiety in this regard. Among other things, this latter finding suggests that couples in which both partners have an anxious attachment style may be empirically rare.

Perhaps there are good reasons why one would not find many couples in which *both* partners are anxiously attached. Although the individuals may initially be drawn to one another on the basis of similarity, the reality of their relationship would likely render it highly unstable. Remember that on an individual level, Hazan and Shaver (1987) described anxious attachment as a preoccupying and painful struggle to find union with the other. This may be difficult when the union is sought with a securely attached other and next to impossible when it is sought with someone who is similarly preoccupied with obtaining love and holding on to it. At the same time, an anxious person concerned with dependability and commitment may find that an avoidant partner who is concerned about too much intimacy and commitment displays a relationship orientation consistent with his or her expectations. Likewise, for an avoidant person, the distrust and demands for intimacy by an anxious partner may confirm his or her relationship expectations. It is perhaps for these reasons that several studies found anxious women who were dating avoidant men, and anxious men who were dating either anxious or avoidant women (Collins & Read, 1990; Simpson, 1990).

Attachment Styles, Relationship Satisfaction, and Stability.   To some extent, these speculations are supported by studies that looked at the quality of people's ongoing relationships (as opposed to one's "most important relationship," as Hazan and Shaver had done). Several studies report that, compared to people with secure attachment styles, those with anxious and avoidant attachment styles tend to have relationships marked by less trust, commitment, and satisfaction. Interestingly, lack of commitment and interdependence are particularly descriptive of avoidant attachment styles, whereas lack of trust is more descriptive of anxious attachment styles (Collins & Read, 1990; Feeney & Noller, 1990; Simpson, 1990). Moreover, people with anxious and avoidant attachment styles report their relationship as a source of more frequent negative emotions and less frequent positive emotions; the reverse is true for those with secure attachment styles (Fuller & Fincham, 1995; Simpson, 1990). Not surprisingly, both partners in a relationship tend to be particularly dissatisfied when either partner suffers high anxiety over abandonment (anxious attachment) or low comfort with closeness (avoidant attachment) (Jones & Cunningham, 1996).

Given the implications of different attachment styles for relationship satisfaction, one might suspect that attachment styles also have at least indirect implications for the stability of a relationship. Specifically, one might expect relationships characterized by secure attachments to be relatively more enduring, especially when both partners are securely attached, than relationships in which one or both partners are anxiously or avoidantly attached. Establishing theoretical and empirical links between attachment styles and relationship stability is important, as it may help shed light on the more general relationship between relationship satisfaction and stability. As discussed in Chapter 6, Thibaut and Kelley (1959) suggested that the two are somewhat independent of one another. Whereas satisfaction is determined by a comparison of one's outcomes to one's expectations, stability is determined by a comparison of one's outcomes to the possible alternatives.

Consistent with this idea, there is evidence that not all couples that stay together are in fact happy and not all unhappy couples break up (e.g., Rands, Levinger, & Mellinger, 1981). This suggests the intriguing possibility that attachment styles may help predict why some relationships persist even though they appeared to be doomed when one applies the yardstick of satisfaction. Similarly, attachment styles may help predict why relationships marked by relatively high degrees of satisfaction might nonetheless break apart. For example, an anxious individual's preoccupation with reciprocation of affection along with a concern about abandonment may motivate special efforts to maintain the relationship even though it may fall well short of expectations. Avoidant individuals, on the other hand, may be compelled to break up out of a fear of becoming overly dependent, even though the relationship goes swimmingly.

There is evidence in favor of both sets of speculations. Remember that in Hazan and Shaver's (1987) study, secure respondents reported that their current relationship had lasted longer (10 years) than those of anxious (6 years) and avoidant respondents (5 years). Additionally, secure respondents were less likely to be divorced (6 percent) than anxious (10 percent) and avoidant respondents (12 percent). That these differences may be due to the different qualitative nature of relationships based on various attachment styles is suggested by a study that tracked couples over a four-month period (Keelan, Dion, & Dion, 1994). In this particular sample, secure individuals reported consistent levels of relationship satisfaction, relationship costs, commitment, and trust. Anxious and avoidant individuals, on the other hand, evidenced decreasing levels of satisfaction, commitment, and trust, along with increasing relationship costs.

However, the results of at least one study (Kirkpatrick & Davis, 1994), which tracked well over 300 heterosexual dating couples over a period of three years, suggest that the relationship among attachment, relationship satisfaction, and relationship stability might be more complex. Specifically, it appears that the effects of some attachment styles on satisfaction depend to some extent on gender. Whereas securely attached individuals displayed high levels of satisfaction and stability, anxious and avoidant attachment styles had some interesting effects. In couples in which the *woman* was *anxiously attached,* both partners tended to be unhappy with their relationship. In couples in which the *man* was *avoidantly attached,* the men (but not the women) rated their relationship negatively. At the same time, however, the relationships of avoidant men and anxious women were remarkably stable over time. Interestingly, even though the sample of couples was large, there were no couples in which both partners were anxiously or avoidantly attached.

Among other things, these findings seem to preclude any generalizations about which attachment styles might be superior or inferior for a relationship. Instead, it seems that what impact attachment styles may have on relationships in general depends on the particular relationship stage as well as gender. This appears to be especially true for couples in which at least one partner's attachment is insecure. Because of the nature of their working models of relationships, anxious individuals expect their partners to avoid intimacy, withdraw, and be rejecting. Thus, choosing an avoidant other confirms anxious people's expectations about the nature of relationship. Avoidant individuals expect others to be demanding and clingy, and thus choosing an anxious other confirms their expectations in a similar fashion. By the same logic, a partner with a similar insecure attachment style violates one's expectations, thus helping explain why it is hard to find anxious-anxious and avoidant-avoidant couples.

But why would relationships between anxious women and avoidant men be just as stable as those of secure men and women? The answer to this question may be related to the unique gender stereotypes in U.S. culture. Women are generally expected to seek and maintain intimacy and to be the general caretakers of relationships. It may be that anxious women, for whom the possibility of abandonment is a central concern, are more motivated to initiate processes that would hold the relationship together, thus accounting for the relatively high temporal stability in their relationships with avoidant men. This process may further be aided by the relatively low expectations that avoidant men have for their partners and their relationships.

Of course, the observation that relationships between anxious women and avoidant men can be surprisingly stable should not be taken as an indication that they are marked by happiness and bliss. Instead, it appears that they are lacking in trust, which, according to some (Holmes & Rempel, 1989), is one of the most sought-after qualities of close relationships. Trust in one's partner is one of the cornerstones for the development of intimacy (Sternberg, 1986) and it is necessary for the development of commitment and feelings of security (Holmes & Rempel, 1989). It appears that securely attached individuals may have an edge when it comes to trusting their partners. In one study using a diary technique (Mikulincer, 1998), securely attached partners remembered more relationship episodes marked by trust and reported adopting more constructive coping techniques in response to violations of trust (e.g., talking to their partner) than their anxious and avoidant counterparts. Not surprisingly, anxious and avoidant individuals remembered fewer relationships marked by trust. Further, anxious individuals tended to respond to violations of trust with rumination and worry; avoidant individuals responded with attempts to distance themselves from their partner. Interestingly, whereas achieving intimacy was considered important by everyone, regardless of attachment style, anxious individuals were struggling to attain a sense of security and avoidant individuals were attempting to gain control over their relationship.

Summary

Issues. What are the manifestations of attachment in infancy and early childhood? How do they come about? To what extent can attachment to one's romantic partner mirror earlier attachment patterns? How does infant attachment get transformed into adult attachment? What are the ramifications of different adult attachment styles for the individual, partner choice, and relationship quality?

Theories. Developmental theories stress the importance of mother-infant interactions for the development of different attachment patterns. Transitional models focus on the importance of attachment for the various developmental tasks individuals confront over the course of development. Adult attachment styles have predictable effects on individuals' ability for emotional control and partner choice. Further, attachment-related partner choice has both predictable and surprising effects on relationship satisfaction and relationship stability.

Research. To date, a great deal of research has shown that attachment styles depend on the nature of the interactions between infants and their caregivers. Even though secure, anxious, and avoidant styles are universally represented, there is a great deal of variation due to cultural influences. Further, attachment styles continue to be malleable throughout the early stages of life. Changes in the nature of the interactions between infants and their caregivers can lead to changes in attachment patterns for the better or the worse. Evidence shows that attachment influences peer interactions throughout childhood, thus contributing to the transformation of infant attachment into adult attachment. Securely attached adults are better at emotional control than those who are anxiously attached. Although many gravitate toward partners evidencing signs of secure attachment, many anxiously attached individuals (especially women) seek avoidant partners. This can be explained in terms of avoidant partners meeting the expectations of anxious individuals. Even though the relationships between anxious and avoidant partners may not be highly satisfying, they nonetheless tend to persist over time.

9

Sexuality

An angry Ellen DeGeneres is threatening to quit her ABC comedy because of battles over how to present gay-themed scripts and an "adult content warning" placed on Wednesday's show. At the start of the "Ellen" episode in which DeGeneres' character . . . kissed a female costar, ABC flashed this sentence: "Due to adult content, parental discretion is advised."

—*Chicago Tribune*, October 10, 1997

In the minds of many, love and sex are often closely connected. In fact, studies that explore people's attitudes about the role of sex in a dating relationship find that affection for the partner is the most frequently cited reason for having sex (e.g., Robinson & Jedlicka, 1982; Sherwin & Corbett, 1985), especially for women (Michael et al., 1994). This is hardly surprising in light of the fact that sexuality is perhaps the one feature that sets romantic relationships apart from other close relationships (Scanzoni et al., 1989). We can share intimate details with our friends and be strongly committed to our relationships with family members, but sex is something that is supposed to be shared specifically with the one we love in a romantic way.

Attitudes about Sex: A Brief History

Despite its ubiquity in intimate relationships, sex is something that Americans have historically approached with a sense of ambivalence. Many cultures consider sex a fact of life like eating and drinking (Mead, 1963), but in the American way, it is best done in a climate marked by darkness, drawn curtains, and hushed silence. In many ways, our collective squeamishness about sex can be traced to our Puritan and Victorian heritage. In line with their dualistic view on the mind and the body, as espoused by the Apostle Paul, the Puritans felt that sex was primarily a matter of the spirit succumbing to the flesh. Consequently, in the eighteenth century, many colonial settlements had strict prohibitions against public exchanges of affection such as kissing and holding hands, even for married couples. The attitudes of many Anglo-Saxon settlers of the late nineteenth century were epitomized by the advice English mothers allegedly gave their daughters on the eve of their wedding night: "Close your eyes and think of England."

Much of our Puritan and Victorian heritage continued to permeate attitudes about sex well into the twentieth century. As late as the 1950s, the motion picture industry worked with a set of self-imposed restrictions that prohibited showing actors in bed together. Even married couples on the screen were depicted as sleeping in separate beds, and in the rare occasions that they were shown in a double bed together, both actors were required to keep one leg out from under the covers during filming. Occasionally, some directors found imaginative ways to work around these restrictions in order to convey their point to the audience. For example, in the movie *North by Northwest*, Alfred Hitchcock managed to show that the male and female leads had entered into a sexual relationship through a series of cuts combined with appropriate symbolism. In the closing sequence of the movie, Cary Grant saves Eva-Marie Saint from falling off Mt. Rushmore. The camera then cuts to a sleeping compartment in a train where we see him pull her up to his bunk. Next, the train enters a tunnel before the closing credits appear on the screen.

Even the liberalization of sexual attitudes brought on by the much talked-about sexual revolution of the 1960s had limited effects when it ran up against stalwarts of conservative morality. Prior to performing their hit single "Let's Spend the Night Together" on *The Ed Sullivan Show* on January 15, 1967, the Rolling Stones agreed, under some pressure from the show's producer, to change the lyric to "Let's spend some *time* together." And as recently as 1994, the version of the song "Laid" (by the singer known simply as James) that played on radio stations in Alabama was electronically altered to say "She only *sings* when she's on top" instead of "She only *comes* when she's on top."

A Brief History of Research on Sex

Alfred Kinsey: What We Do When the Lights Are Out

In light of our longstanding cultural ambivalence toward sex, it is not surprising that research on sexual matters was slow in developing. Initially, the field was left to dubious characters such as Wilhelm Reich, a German immigrant and self-proclaimed psychiatrist who speculated that engaging in sex released a substance called the "orgone," which he considered to be the source not only of all pleasure but also of life in general. Much of his research efforts were devoted to harnessing the orgone by asking research volunteers to engage in sex in shielded tanks. Little is known about the outcomes of this type of research, as all his efforts came to a crashing halt when he was committed to an insane asylum, where he died soon after.

That we know a little more about sex than we did during the days of Wilhelm Reich is almost serendipitous. Some time in the 1940s, a professor at Indiana University who taught a course on human sexuality had to leave town on the day he was scheduled to lecture on the biology of sexual behavior. Instead of canceling class altogether, he recruited a faculty member from the biology department who he felt was qualified because of his expertise in the sexual behavior of the gall wasp. His name was Alfred Kinsey, and the rest, as they say, is history. Kinsey just happened to think that it was not appropriate to deliver a lecture on the gall wasp to students in a course on human sexuality. Thus, like every conscientious scholar, he went to the library to prepare for his lecture. He soon came across an abundance of research on the sexual behavior of all sorts of animals. However, he found virtually no research that was specific to the biology of *human* sexual behavior, and thus he decided to start his own research. He began by distributing questionnaires about sexual behavior to students in his classes as well as students in classes taught by supportive and friendly colleagues. He eventually expanded his efforts to include fraternities, Parent-Teacher Associations, and just about any group willing to support his efforts. Several years and roughly 18,000 respondents later, Kinsey published his findings in a book titled *Sexual Behavior in the Human Male* (Kinsey, Pomeroy, & Martin, 1948). Five years later, he published a follow-up titled *Sexual Behavior in the Human Female* (Kinsey et al., 1953). Together, both volumes have become widely known as "The Kinsey Report."

In compiling his data, Kinsey took some liberties with regard to generally accepted conventions of sampling. Rather than defining a random sample of respondents that gave every one in the United States an equal chance to be selected, he simply collected responses from anyone who was willing to provide them. Kinsey was quite aware of this shortcoming in his sampling technique, but he felt that the sheer size of his sample made up for the lack of true randomness. Moreover, his two volumes provided such a provocative look into what goes on in the bedrooms across the United States that they became the major compendium of everything we always wanted to know about sex. Despite its widespread popularity, however, Kinsey's work was not without its detractors. Many felt uncomfortable with the Kinsey Report's primary message that sex was perfectly natural—a response that is not entirely surprising given the prevailing attitudes about sex at the time. But even those who might have accommodated themselves with the idea that sex was indeed a natural thing had a hard time dealing with the real or alleged ramifications of some more specific results. For example, the finding that 50 percent of all men reported to have had extramarital affairs was taken as a hint that the breakdown of the moral order was just around the corner. Moreover, there was widespread fear that the publication of such findings would further contribute to this breakdown. After all, reading about the prevalence of extramarital affairs might give men the idea that it is perfectly normal, and thus drive even the most devoted suburban husband into infidelity.

Another finding created an even bigger stir: Kinsey reported in 1953 that 50 percent of all women were not virgins when they married. At the time, the United States was engaged in a war in Korea. How, the argument went, could our boys overseas fight the enemy when they had to worry about whether their sweethearts back home would still be virgins when they returned? Finally, many objections were raised against Kinsey's finding that 10 percent of all males were exclusively homosexual, as it was considered to be an exaggerated estimate. This is ironic given that many advocacy groups today consider it to be an underestimation of the true number of homosexual men.

Masters and Johnson: The Physiology of Sex

A few years before Kinsey began collecting the data that became the empirical foundation for the Kinsey Report, the outbreak of World War II forced William Masters, a young graduate of Hamilton College, to abandon his plans to study in

Cambridge in preparation for a career as an English teacher. He instead enrolled at the University of Rochester Medical School in pursuit of a medical degree. By the time he graduated in 1942, he had decided that he wanted to conduct research on sex. However, his mentor advised him that conducting research on such a taboo topic before being well established at a major university would be akin to professional suicide. Thus, in his early days at Washington University , which had hired him as an assistant professor of obstetrics and gynecology, Masters spent most of his time doing research on female infertility and hormone replacement therapy for postmenopausal women while also distinguishing himself as a gynecological surgeon.

In 1954, Masters decided that it was time to pursue his life's dream to study the physiological aspects of sex. Because of the sexually repressive nature of the times, he felt uneasy about recruiting research participants from among the student body or placing ads in the local paper. Instead, he began his work with prostitutes, who he believed might be more willing than the mainstream population to come into his lab for research purposes. And although this was true, the use of prostitutes was accompanied by a myriad of other problems that basically foiled his early research attempts. However, the experience taught him a valuable lesson: If he wanted to conduct sex research with female volunteers, he had better hire a woman to work with him. Consequently, he placed an ad in the university's newspaper for a lab assistant in medical research. The ad was soon answered by Virginia Johnson, a recent divorcée and former big-band singer who needed a job to support her two children. Together, and with funding from the university as well as local clergy, they launched their major study on sex. Much to their surprise, getting research participants was much easier than Masters had imagined (in part because fraternities were more than willing to volunteer their pledges). Within a period of 10 years, Masters and Johnson collected data from 700 male and 700 female research volunteers who were observed masturbating or having intercourse. By one estimate, the two researchers observed a total of 10,000 orgasms.

Masters and Johnson repeatedly tried to publish their findings, only to have their articles rejected by the major medical journals. Thus, in 1966, they compiled the results of their research into a book titled *Human Sexual Response*. Although the book was deliberately written as a hard-to-read medical text, its first printing sold out in one day, and it remained on the best-seller list for more than six months. One of the reasons for the book's instant popularity was that it dispelled many myths about female sexuality for a public whose desire to follow the sexual revolution was hampered by an almost total lack of direction (i.e., awareness of what happens physiologically during sex). Among many other things, *Human Sexual Response* revealed that orgasms unfold in four phases and that women are capable of experiencing multiple orgasms. But perhaps the most intriguing finding was the observation that there was no difference in the physiological responses that accompany orgasms brought on by clitoral versus vaginal stimulation. This finding is noteworthy because it flies in the face of Freudian theorizing that had proclaimed that clitoral orgasms were immature and neurotic whereas vaginal orgasms were mature and superior.

The public embraced Masters and Johnson's work to the point that many of their findings have by now become common knowledge, but it also drew widespread criticism. Scientists were quick to point to methodological flaws, suggesting, among other things, that by relying on research volunteers, sex maniacs may have been overrepresented among their research participants. Conservative opinion leaders felt Masters and Johnson's book was nothing more than thinly veiled pornography destined to lead the nation farther down the path of moral decay. The federal government felt that the work was of a nature that did not deserve to be funded with tax dollars.

Having most of their funding for their research taken away, Masters and Johnson turned toward applying their findings to help people with a variety of sexual problems. In the process, they launched sex therapy as an entirely new discipline. Their approach focused on the couple as the therapeutic unit rather than the individual, and it used a two-week program rather than the customary once-a-week therapy over several years. Masters and Johnson reported success rates of 80 percent for such common problems as premature ejaculation among men and difficulty achieving orgasm among women. Their program was consequently emulated by many practitioners interested in treating sexual dysfunction.

In their later years, Masters and Johnson shifted their research attention toward issues related to homosexuality and AIDS. Their 1979 book, *Homosexuality in Perspective*, made the point that sexual functioning in homosexuals is no different from that of heterosexuals. Furthermore, it treated homosexuality as a learned behavior rather than a disease. Unfortunately, their model of homosexuality implied that it was something that could be remedied through therapy, which drew the ire of many gay rights groups. However, the biggest controversy was yet to come. When they reported in 1988 that (1) the government underestimated the number of AIDS cases by at least 50 percent and (2) AIDS could be spread through heterosexual as well as homosexual sex, a public outcry followed that culminated in the Surgeon General publicly admonishing them for a lack of scholarship. And although they were soon vindicated by the facts, in 1991, they decided to dissolve their collaboration of 35 years and their marriage of 22 years and both retreated into private life.

Sex in the United States Today

Have the dire predictions of those who felt the publication of the works by Kinsey and Masters and Johnson would result in widespread permissiveness and a breakdown of the moral order come true? The answer appears to be no. The results of a national survey (Michael et al., 1994) suggest that the sexual landscape of the United States has not changed much from the days of Kinsey. Perhaps our sexual behavior is less repressed than it was 40 or 50 years ago, but it is relatively conventional, bearing no resemblance to the portrayals rendered in daytime soap operas. The results of the survey are based on face-to-face interviews with a representative national sample of 3,500 adults. Initially, the researchers planned to interview a total of 20,000 respondents. They were forced to go with a smaller sample, however, because federal granting agencies refused to provide the funding necessary for such a large-scale study; thus they had to rely on smaller grants from private foundations. The results are nonetheless representative and therefore generalizable to the population as a whole because it used a national probability sample to select the respondents.

The conclusion that our sexual behavior is relatively tame and conventional is based on a number of specific findings. According to the survey by Michael and colleagues (1994), we tend to have sex with people who are similar to us in terms of race, age, education, and religious beliefs. Of course, this is not entirely surprising, since our attraction to others is profoundly determined by similarity on these dimensions in the first place. The majority of people meet their eventual sexual partners at school, work, private parties, and church or are introduced to them by friends, colleagues, and family members. Only 15 percent of the respondents indicated that they had met their partners in bars, on vacations, or through personal ads.

Compared to 30 years ago, the average age at which Americans first have intercourse has dropped by about 9 months, although there are variations depending on gender and race. The smallest drop was observed for white males (from 17.9 to 17.4 years old) and the largest drop was found among white females (from 18.9 to 17.5 years old). However, this general decrease is most likely due to an earlier onset of sexual maturity (perhaps brought on by improved nutrition and health habits) than to increased permissiveness. A seeming lack of permissiveness is also evident when one looks at the average number of sex partners Americans have. Some 94 percent of the survey respondents who were married had been faithful to their spouses during the year prior to the survey. Even among single people, 61 percent had sex with just one partner if they had sex at all. Only 4.1 percent of the men and 1.6 percent of the women reported having sex with more than five partners during the relevant time period. Similarly, a look at the frequency with which people in the survey reported to have sex suggests that they are less than fiendish about it. As Table 9.1 shows, more than two-thirds of U.S. men and women reported to have sex from a few times a month to two to three times a week. There is a higher percentage of people who never have sex than people who have sex more than four times a week!

Having shown that the publication of Kinsey's (Kinsey, Pomeroy, & Martin, 1948; Kinsey et al., 1953) work has not led to a large-scale outbreak of permissiveness, we can now look at the possible long-term impact of Masters and Johnson's

TABLE 9.1   *Frequency of Sex among U.S. Men and Women According to Michael and Colleagues (1994)*

	Not at All	*Few Times a Year*	*Few Times a Month*	*2–3 Times a Week*	*More than 4 Times a Week*
Men	14%	16%	37%	26%	8%
Women	10%	18%	36%	30%	7%

(1966) research by examining respondents' reports about how they experience sex. Somewhat surprisingly, it seems that many of the problems couples had in the 1950s and 1960s persist to this very day. For example, 40 percent of men and women reported feelings of extreme physical pleasure and emotional satisfaction, yet only 29 percent of the women reported to always experience orgasms as a result of intercourse, compared to 75 percent of the men. Moreover, as was the case when Masters and Johnson devised their sex therapy, the most frequently cited "sexual problem" is still premature ejaculation for men and lack of interest for women. One possibility for this discrepancy may be a continued insistence on vaginal intercourse as the preferred sex act.

Sexual Interactions

The research on sex discussed thus far is largely descriptive in nature. Although it is informative with respect to many factual aspects of sex (frequency, satisfaction, etc.), it tells us little about how people go about having sex. To raise this issue may at first sound silly because the answer seems so obvious. However, a closer look reveals that sexual encounters can entail a set of rather complicated issues.

Sexual Communication

Consider a scene from the movie *The Big Chill*, in which a number of former college friends come together for a weekend to attend a funeral. During the course of the weekend, many rekindle past feelings and relationships to the point where the character played by Jeff Goldblum (who is forced to sleep in the nursery by himself) wakes up one morning to exclaim that he can feel sex happening. In many ways, Jeff Goldblum could not have been more wrong. Simply put, sex is not something that just happens like a change in the weather. Instead, a more realistic way to think about it is in terms of interactions between two people that take place in a social context.

From this perspective, we can look at sex as something that two people negotiate with the help of their sexual communication system. A sizeable part of this system is verbal in nature (Victor, 1980). Talking about past sexual experiences and simply voicing sexual interest can often suffice to initiate a sexual encounter. Expressing sexual preferences and fantasies as well as voicing sexual pleasure can shape the experience in important ways. However, such verbal expressions are often preceded or accompanied by a number of nonverbal signals, such as reducing interpersonal distance and increasing eye contact and touch (McCormick, 1979; Perper & Weis, 1987). During the early part of a relationship, men and women alike tend to rely heavily on nonverbal signals, ostensibly to fend off the possibility of rejection or its potential impact (Perper & Weis, 1987). At the same time, men and women often interpret the meaning of such symbols in vastly different ways. Men tend to think of women who reduce interpersonal distance, maintain eye contact, and touch them as sexy, seductive, and promiscuous, and men thus experience a heightened level of sexual attraction. The same is not true for how women perceive the corresponding behaviors in males (Abbey & Melby, 1986).

In light of the observation that men tend to overperceive sexual intent on the part of women, it is perhaps not surprising that men are also more likely to initiate sex. This appears to be true for marital and cohabiting relationships (Brown & Auerback, 1981; Byers & Heinlein, 1989) as well as dating relationships (DeLamater & MacCorquodale, 1979), although there is evidence that women become more comfortable about initiating sex as a relationship matures (Brown & Auerback, 1981). Of course, the existence of sex differences in the likelihood to initiate sex raises an interesting question in terms of how the initiation of sex proceeds among homosexual couples. Although little is known about such encounters, it appears that the partner who is more emotionally expressive is the one who usually initiates sex in both gay and lesbian couples (Blumstein & Schwartz, 1983).

Whereas men are, by and large, more likely to initiate sex, women often find themselves in a position to have to resist sexual advances. Although this may sound like a stereotype, research shows that, compared to men, women are both more *comfortable* saying no (Grauerholz & Serpe, 1985) and more *likely* to say no to a partner who wants sex (Clark, 1990; Clark & Hatfield, 1989). How do people go about telling their partners that they don't want to have sex? One study (Perper & Weis, 1987) found two general categories of rejection strategies. A strategy aimed at *avoiding proceptivity* entails avoiding or ignoring an unwelcome sexual advance. By using a strategy aimed at *incomplete rejection*, a woman may indicate that she is not ready to reciprocate at this time because it is too early in the day or the relationship, for example.

The preponderance of these two strategies illustrates that rejecting another's sexual advances is not an easy thing to do. People who find themselves in such a position are often motivated to avoid hurting another's feelings by directly rejecting attempts at initiating sex, although it appears that direct rejection is both more common and more acceptable in long-term relationships (Byers & Heinlein, 1989; Cupach & Metts, 1991). In married or cohabiting relationships, there is always tomorrow, and thus rejection, even when it is direct, is less threatening to both partners than it might be in more casual dating relationships. Of course, the use of an indirect rejection strategy is not without its downside. Because of their indirectness, such strategies can often be misinterpreted by the recipient for something other than rejection, and thus result in conflicted sexual interactions. We will return to this issue later.

Sex and the Dating Couple: Sexual Pathways

For dating couples, the initiation of sex is often more than just a matter of negotiation via the sexual communication system. The first time a couple has sex often has special meaning and significance. For one thing, it is usually accompanied by strong emotions and thus remembered in vivid detail for a long time. For another, the first time marks a significant turning point, as it generally results in an increase in commitment (Baxter & Bullis, 1986). Consequently, couples tend to give consideration to several factors before deciding to have sex. Using an Inventory of Sexual Decision-Making Factors, one study (Christopher & Cates, 1984) found that couples' reasons for engaging in sex for the first time could be classified into four dimensions.

The *positive affection/communication* dimension contains reasons for having sex that are primarily characterized by feelings of love for one's partner. *Arousal/receptivity* relates to the level of sexual arousal both partners experienced prior to intercourse. *Obligation and pressure* refers to the partners' pressure to have intercourse, and the *circumstantial* dimension refers to disinhibiting factors in the situation prior to having intercourse. The relative independence of these four dimensions does not imply that a couple necessarily relies on just one set of reasons to have sex. Instead, combinations of reasons, such as love and arousal or arousal and disinhibition, may often be responsible for the initiation of sex. Moreover, there are some marked differences in the kinds of reasons, depending on gender and relationship duration. For example, women, more than men, tend to cite affection for their partner as an important reason for having sex—a finding that was also reported by Michael and colleagues (1994). The same is true for sexually inexperienced couples, whereas arousal-related factors are more important for sexually experienced couples.

In addition to identifying differences in the reasons couples cited for having sex, especially for the first time, Christopher and Cates (1984, 1985) also found differences in the timing of couples' first intercourse. *Rapid involvement couples* (roughly 7 percent of the sample) had sex very early in the relationship, often on their first date. *Gradual involvement couples* (31 percent) reported a gradual increase in sexual behavior (from kissing to petting to intercourse) as their relationship developed from the first date to casual dating to considering becoming a couple and finally perceiving themselves as a couple. The single largest group in Christopher and Cates's sample were *delayed involvement couples* (44 percent) who postponed sexual involvement of any kind until they perceived themselves as a couple. Only a small percentage (17 percent) could be classified as *low involvement couples,* who were still not very sexually active even though they perceived themselves as a couple. Other typologies rely less on stages of relationship development and more on timing in a chronological sense. For example, Peplau, Rubin, and Hill (1977) distinguished among early-sex couples (41 percent of their sample), who have sex within the first month of dating, later-sex couples (41 percent), who postponed sex until they had been dating for at least a month, and abstaining couples (18 percent), who continued to abstain from sex despite having been together for several months.

Regardless of how one looks at the relationship between dating and sex, it is clear that being sexually active is a common reality in dating. On the other hand, it appears that there is no set way by which couples decide on when the time has come. Instead, the decision to have sex depends in large part on whether a couple feels that the time is right, which itself is likely based on one's perception of "couplehood."

Sex and the Married Couple: How Often Is Enough?

A number of surveys (Kinsey, Pomeroy, & Martin, 1948; Kinsey et al., 1953; Michael et al., 1994) indicate that married couples in their 20s have sex at the highest frequency, although several studies suggest that young cohabiting couples may be the one group who has sex most frequently (Blumstein & Schwartz, 1983; Risman et al., 1981). Does this mean that marriage and cohabitation are necessarily accompanied by perpetual bliss? On the surface, the answer appears to be yes, as several studies show a positive relationship between sexual frequency (as well as sexual satisfaction) and relationship satisfaction (e.g., Blumstein & Schwartz, 1983). However, due to the correlational nature of the results, the causal direction in the link between sexual frequency and relationship satisfaction is open to at least two interpretations. It could be that increases in sexual frequency lead to increases in relationship satisfaction. Alternatively, it could be that couples who are happy with their relationship for any reason have sex more often. It is difficult to tease these explanations apart, primarily because it is not easy to test their veracity in tightly controlled laboratory studies. Nonetheless, it is perhaps safe to arrive at the same conclusion as Blumstein and Schwartz (1983): The more external problems infringe on people's sex lives, the less likely they will want to have sex together. The resulting decrease in the frequency of sex could then, in itself, become a source of dissatisfaction.

But even if one assumes that sexual frequency can lead to relationship satisfaction, marital bliss as a result of frequent sex is by no means guaranteed. One problem is that men, by and large, wish they could have sex more often (Levinger, 1966). This was poignantly illustrated in the scene of the movie *Annie Hall*, where actors Woody Allen and Diane Keaton lament about their sex lives to their respective therapists. Although both reported to have sex about three times a week, Woody felt they rarely had sex and Diane felt that they had sex all the time. Further complicating matters is the well-documented observation that the frequency of sex declines over time (e.g., Blumstein & Schwartz, 1983; Greenblatt, 1983; James, 1980). It may be tempting to conclude that this decline is perhaps due to decreases in vitality and virility as a function of age alone. However, increases in other life commitments (Greenblatt, 1983) as well as pregnancy, childrearing, and job demands (Call, Sprecher, & Schwartz, 1992) may affect sexual frequency even more profoundly.

The single-most important reason for the decline of sexual frequency over time probably has to do with the decreasing novelty of the activity itself along with an increasing familiarity with one's partner. It is perhaps a psychological truism that any continuously repetitive activity will eventually become boring, and sex does not appear to be exempt from this. Specifically, Berscheid's (1983) theory of emotion in mature relationships predicts that the positive emotional fallout from having sex will diminish over time. As novelty wears off and familiarity grows, the behavioral sequences necessary to initiate and experience sex become intermeshed to the point where less and less emotion will result. Of course, by the same token, anything that increases novelty and thus helps interrupt intermeshed sequences of behavior may result in an increase in the emotional concomitants of sex. This is precisely why popular sex therapists such as Ruth Westheimer (Dr. Ruth) continually admonish couples to change the time and location for sex and not to adopt one routine way to have sex.

Extradyadic Sex

One reason for Dr. Ruth's success and popularity is that her advice, geared toward introducing novelty into couples' sex lives, usually works. Moreover, it is generally preferable to the alternative of seeking novelty by having sex with partners outside of one's relationship. New partners are inherently exciting and thus can prompt an increase in sexual desire. This has been called the *Coolidge Effect* in light of a story that has been ascribed to President Calvin Coolidge. According to the story, the President and his wife once toured a chicken farm. When they came upon a rooster, their guide pointed out that the rooster's only purpose in life was to have sex all day long. When Mrs. Coolidge heard that, she asked the guide to convey this message to Mr. Coolidge, whose desire for sex ostensibly had been diminished by the burden of his office. When the guide continued to explain that the rooster had sex with not just one but all the chickens on the farm, Mr. Coolidge was quick to ask the guide to convey that fact to Mrs. Coolidge.

Many might be tempted to look for a quick fix for sexual boredom within a relationship by having sex with a novel partner, although it is not entirely clear how prevalent extradyadic relationships are. Some studies estimate the rate as high as 50 percent for married men and 26 percent for married women (Kinsey, Pomeroy, & Martin, 1948; Kinsey et al., 1953); a more recent study, using a representative national sample (Greeley, 1991), puts the rates as low as 11 percent and 9 percent, respectively. Moreover, the frequency of extradyadic affairs seems to depend in part on the type of relationship. For example, Blumstein and Schwartz (1983) estimated the prevalence of extradyadic affairs at 33 percent for male cohabitors, 30 percent for female cohabitors, 82 percent for gay men, and 28 percent for lesbians. Although these data were obviously collected before AIDS became an epidemic and may therefore overestimate the current rate of extradyadic involvement in general and gay men in particular, it does appear that men are more prone to extradyadic affairs than women. This suspicion is borne out by a study that compared the characteristics of men's and women's extradyadic affairs (Glass & Wright, 1985). It appears that men have extramarital affairs primarily for sexual reasons, even when they are otherwise satisfied with their marriage. This does not mean that women do not have extramarital affairs. However, they engage in them primarily with the purpose of seeking emotional satisfaction and when they are deeply dissatisfied with their existing relationship.

Men and women who have extramarital affairs for both sexual and emotional reasons tend to be the ones who are most dissatisfied with their existing relationship. Again, this can be interpreted in one of two ways. One could argue that it is a deep-seated unhappiness with one's relationship that leads people to seek sexual and emotional satisfaction elsewhere. On the other hand, extradyadic affairs can come with a rather steep price tag. Even if the partner is kept in the dark about an extramarital affair, feelings of guilt and shame on the part of the perpetrator may further complicate matters for the relationship. Mutual knowledge about an extramarital relationship is likely to induce conflict and thus may further increase existing levels of dissatisfaction. In many cases, couples will eventually find ways to solve the problem, but in other cases, the conflict may put a greater strain on the couple and may even result in the dissolution of the relationship.

Sexual Orientation

Until recently, conventional wisdom held that most humans were naturally predisposed to be heterosexual, and that anything different was a matter of (poor) choice, a flaw of character, or both. As noted earlier, until 1974, psychologists subscribed to these kinds of beliefs by considering homosexuality as a psychological disorder that could be prevented and cured. More recently, the tide has turned somewhat in light of alternative approaches to understanding how people develop sexual preferences. At this time, there are three viewpoints on sexual orientation that differ vastly from the medical model.

The Social Construction of Sexual Orientation

Social constructionists propose that the concept of sexual orientation is a culture-bound invention designed to categorize people (e.g., DeCecco & Elia, 1993). In favor of this notion, they cite historical evidence showing that the very concept of homosexuality and the way we think about it has changed dramatically over the course of the past 100 or so years. Interestingly enough, the term *homosexuality* did not appear in our language until the end of the nineteenth century. Prior to that, there were two kinds of people: normal people and sexual inverts. Of course, "normal people" were masculine men and feminine women with heterosexual preferences. "Sexual inverts" were comprised of feminine men, masculine women, cross-dressers, people with same-sex partners, and, interestingly enough, suffragists (i.e., those in favor of awarding women the right to vote) (Bem, 1996).

This classification eventually gave way to dichotomizing sexual orientation into heterosexuality and homosexuality. The simple typology was soon deconstructed by Kinsey, Pomeroy, and Martin (1948), who proposed that sexual orientation was more appropriately construed in terms of a continuum ranging from exclusive homosexuality through bisexuality to exclusive heterosexuality. How people were placed along this continuum depended both on their overt sexual behavior and their sexual fantasies. For example, people whose sexual behavior and sexual fantasies were limited to opposite-sex partners were considered exclusively heterosexual. People who reported a mixture of heterosexual behavior and homosexual fantasies were placed closer to the bisexual point of the continuum of the scale. Although the continuum model of sexual orientation made some intuitive sense, others (e.g., McWirther, Sanders, & Reinisch, 1990; Shively & DeCecco, 1977) pointed out that heterosexuality and homosexuality are really distinct components of sexual orientation (i.e., heteroeroticism and homoeroticsm) that should not be merged into a single, bipolar continuum. Instead, they (e.g., Bem, 1974; Spence & Helmreich, 1978) proposed that sexual orientation be classified as heterosexual, homosexual, and asexual, depending on the intensity of an indivdual's homoerotic or heteroerotic responsiveness.

Whether homosexuality and heterosexuality are two sides of the same coin or whether they are conceptually distinct components of sexual orientation is likely to be subject to continued debate. However, from the social constructionist point of view, it is less important which perspective will eventually dominate. Instead, social constructionists conclude on the basis of this continued debate that sexual orientation is a culturally bound notion.

Biological Essentialism

Some who feel that sexual orientation is more than an arbitrary and culture-bound notion to distinguish among types of people have looked for biological mechanisms that might bring about heterosexual and homosexual preferences. To date, they have provided evidence that sexual orientation may be coded genetically, or determined by prenatal hormones and brain neuroanatomy. The most compelling evidence for the idea that homosexuality is inherited comes from a couple of studies that compared the incidence of homosexuality among monozygotice and dizygotic twins. One study of gay men (Bailey & Pillard, 1991) found that 52 percent of monozygotic twin brothers were gay, compared to only 22 percent of dizygotic twin brothers. In a comparable study of lesbian women (Bailey et al., 1993) 48 percent of monozygotic twin sisters were gay, compared to only 16 percent of dizygotic twin sisters. Although these studies fall short of pointing to a genetic marker for homosexuality, they nonetheless point to a genetic influence. After all, monozygotic and dizygotic twins share the same environment and learning experiences, but monozygotic twins also share the same genetic makeup.

Hormonal influences were among the earliest biological variables implicated in the development of sexual orientation. One of the oldest hypotheses held that gay men had too little and lesbian women had too much testosterone. However, this does not appear to be true for adult men and women (Gartrell, 1982). Instead, it appears that prenatal exposure to unusually high or low levels of androgens can masculinize or feminize the brain, which may then lead to homosexual preferences. However, this conclusion has been demonstrated only with rats and only with regard to their mating postures. Thus, the idea that human males prenatally exposed to unusually low levels of testosterone and human females prenatally exposed to unusually high levels of testosterone will develop homosexual preferences is somewhat speculative (Ellis & Ames, 1987).

Neuroanatomical differences in the brains of gay and heterosexual men constitute a third set of biological variables that have been implicated in the development of homosexuality. For example, some have pointed to differences in the hypothalamic structures of gay and heterosexual men (LeVay, 1991), whereas others have found differences in the anterior commisure (Allen & Gorski, 1992) and in the size of the suprachiasmatic nucleus (Swaab & Hoffman, 1990). However, before we start looking in our biology books for maps to locate these particular brain structures, we have to keep in mind the correlational nature of this evidence. It may be possible that these differences developed prenatally or during the early years of life and subsequently led to homosexuality. However, it is equally possible that these differences came about as a result of being homosexual to begin with.

The Exotic Becomes Erotic: The EBE Theory of Sexual Orientation

The most intriguing theory on the development of sexual orientation is one that takes into account both biological and experiential factors (Bem, 1996). It proposes a temporal sequence in which biological factors exert an indirect influence on sexual orientation:

> Biological variables ⟶ Childhood temperament ⟶ Sex-typical/atypical activity and playmate preferences ⟶ Feelings of similarity/dissimilarity with same/opposite-sex peers ⟶ Nonspecific arousal to same/opposite-sex peers ⟶ Erotic attraction to same/opposite-sex persons

Specifically, exotic becomes erotic (EBE) suggests that biological variables, such as genes and prenatal hormones, may not determine sexual orientation per se but instead influence childhood temperaments, such as aggression and activity level, which then predisposes children toward sex-typical or sex-atypical activities. Some children will be gender conforming by virtue of preferring sex-typical activities (e.g., boys enjoying rough-and-tumble play) with same-sex peers enjoying similar types of activities. Others will be gender nonconforming by virtue of preferring sex-atypical activities (e.g., girls enjoying rough-and-tumble play) most likely with peers of the opposite sex. Gender-conforming children will feel different from their opposite-sex peers, perceiving them as dissimilar, unfamiliar, and perhaps even exotic. However, gender-nonconforming children will feel different from their same-sex peers, and consequently perceive them as dissimilar, unfamiliar, and exotic.

Some evidence exists that gender conformity and noncomformity in childhood are indeed fairly good predictors of sexual orientation. Specifically, a study from the Kinsey Institute (Bell, Weinberg, & Hammersmith, 1981) indicates that, compared to their heterosexual counterparts, homosexual adult men and women did not enjoy sex-typical activities as children and instead preferred sex-atypical activities by an average margin of about 4:1. Of course, because these types of data are retrospective self-reports, they may not necessarily reflect accurate self-assessments but instead be the result of distortions, perhaps in the service of trying to explain one's sexual orientation. However, if we assume for the sake of the argument that the results of this study have some veridicality, we need to figure out how these early feelings of similarity and dissimilarity become transformed into later heteroeroticism and homoeroticism.

Although Bem (1996) does not supply any direct evidence for how this might occur, he speculates about several psychological mechanisms that might bring about the transformation in question. At the core of all these speculations is the well-documented idea that novelty and unfamiliarity produce heightened physiological arousal (Mook, 1987). This increased arousal may produce attraction to members of the same or opposite sex in a number of ways. For instance, it may simply be a result of labeling arousal in appropriate ways, as suggested by Schachter and Singer (1962). In childhood, dissimilarity may be experienced largely in negative ways, as evidenced by such exclamations as "Girls are yucky" and "Boys are weird." However, as we grow older and learn to associate arousal with attraction, the story changes dramatically. For those who have been gender conforming, the presence of an opposite-sex other may produce the arousal necessary for the experience of attraction, whereas for those who have been gender nonconforming, the presence of a same-sex other may do the same thing.

Of course, there is at least one problem in applying this approach to the development of heteroeroticism and homoeroticism. Recall from Chapter 3 that in virtually all of the studies showing a link between arousal and attraction, the arousal came from an external source (e.g., having to cross a shaky bridge). It is not clear if such a misattribution of arousal would occur when the source of the arousal was clearly related to the other person.

In light of these and other difficulties in accounting for why the exotic becomes the erotic via a labeling of arousal approach, it is worthwhile to consider an alternative perspective on emotion. Some time ago, Solomon and Corbitt (1974) proposed a homoestatic theory of affect in which our nervous system is set up to counteract the prolonged experience of strong negative as well as positive emotions by producing the opposite emotion. Among other things, opponent process mechanisms help explain why most people's emotional lives tend to be balanced when examined over long periods of time. It also explains why, among parachutists, the initial terror experienced at the thought of jumping out of a plane is eventually replaced by euphoria and why experienced runners report a "runner's high" rather than the pains and aches that most casual runners experience. In the present context, *opponent process theory* predicts that among heterosexuals, prolonged negative affect brought on by the perception that the other sex is either yucky or weird would eventually be replaced by more positive affect, such as feelings of attraction. And, of course, the same would be true for those who spend a considerable part of their childhood being turned off by members of their own sex.

Regardless of the precise mechanisms that transform the exotic into the erotic, EBE theory is a promising approach to understanding how sexual orientation develops. Although many of its propositions still await empirical scrutiny, it helps explain why gays and lesbians would seek partners with sex-typical characteristics (Bailey et al., 1997). EBE theory is also appealing because it suggests that heteroeroticism and homoeroticism are not caused by one single mechanism but are instead the result of a complex process in which hereditary and environmental variables interact in interesting yet predictable ways.

Homophobia

Have the increased advances in our understanding of the causes of homoeroticism resulted in creating better lives for gays and lesbians? The answer to this question contains both good and bad news. On the one hand, the 1990s practice of "coming out" appears to suggest a higher acceptance of homosexual lifestyles. Moreover, a number of municipalities, including Chicago and San Francisco, enacted "domestic partner laws" under which partners of gay and lesbian employees are entitled to the same benefits as married partners of heterosexual employees. Gay rights advocates have mounted legal challenges aimed at affording gay and lesbians the right to become legally married in several states.

On the other hand, despite these and other advances in the treatment of gays and lesbians, there are many indications that this population is still confronted with deep-seated prejudice. For example, although ABC allowed the main character in its TV show *Ellen* to "come out" to sky-high ratings, it subsequently canceled the show on the grounds that there was little entertainment value in depicting the daily life of a lesbian character. In real life, many spectators at annual Gay and Lesbian Pride parades seem to attend with the singular purpose of voicing their disapproval. Instances of job and housing discrimination abound. But perhaps nothing exemplifies the extent of our prejudice more than the cases of Alan Schindler and Matthew Shepard. A gay sailor in the United States Navy, Schindler was savagely beaten to death by two of his shipmates in a public restroom in Sasebo, Japan, in October 1992, apparently for no other reason than his sexual orientation. Shepard, a gay student at the University of Wyoming, was abducted by two men and a woman in the winter of 1998. After pistol-whipping him and burning his genitalia, they tied him to a fence in subfreezing weather and left him to die.

Instances such as these prompt the question as to why prejudice against gays and lesbians is so widespread and deeply rooted, and why it can sometimes take on such violent forms. Interestingly, one answer is provided by the psychodynamic proposal that homophobia is an anxiety-based phenomenon. Specifically, the proposal suggests that homophobia may be the result of repressed homosexual urges or, more precisely, a reaction to latent homosexual tendencies. When placed in a situation that threatens to excite their repressed or latent homesexuality, homophobics tend to react with panic, anger, and hostility as a means to avert or deny the threat (West, 1977). To the extent that this is true, homophobics should be more sexually aroused by homosexual cues than non-homophobics.

This idea was tested in a study (Adams, Wright, & Lohr, 1996) in which self-identified heterosexual men who were classified as homophobics or nonhomo-phobics based on their responses to a number of questionnaires watched several sexually explicit videos. One video portrayed a heterosexual couple, a second depicted a male homosexual couple, and a third showed a lesbian couple. The researchers measured the men's objective sexual arousal using a measure of erection as well as their self-rated levels of erection and sexual arousal. Virtually all of the men were sexually aroused by the heterosexual and lesbian videos, regardless of their level of homophobia. However, far more of the homophobic men became aroused while watching the male homosexual video, as indicated by the objective measure of erection. Interestingly, the self-reports of arousal among these men did not correspond to their objective levels of arousal, suggesting that they somehow tried to deny that the homosexual video excited them.

Of course, although these data suggest a powerful mechanism responsible for the development of homophobia, antihomosexual prejudice is too widespread to be accounted for solely as a defense mechanism typical for homophobic men. Such things as false conceptions about the origins and manifestations of homosexuality, along with moral objections perhaps rooted in religious beliefs, are likely to contribute to the pervasiveness of prejudice against homosexuals. To the extent that false notions about the characteristic of any group can often be dispelled by getting to know individual members, one would expect that prejudice would decrease among those who either know someone who is homosexual or who otherwise have interpersonal contact with homosexuals. The results of a national telephone survey (Herek & Capitanio, 1996) in which 583 adults responded twice over the period of 12 months suggest just that. Those who reported having various forms of interpersonal contact with homosexual individuals had more favorable attitudes about homosexuality in general than those who had little or no contact.

These results suggest that disclosure of one's sexual orientation may, in the long run, lead to a decrease in antihomosexual prejudice. Interestingly, it appears that the benefits of "coming out" do not end here. Instead, research indicates that, compared to those who conceal their homosexual orientation, those who reveal it to others can decrease their risk for cancer and a number of common infectious diseases (Cole et al., 1996).

Summary

Issues.   Early approaches to the study of sexuality have focused on describing patterns of sexual behavior and sexual functioning. More recently, research has focused on sex as a form of social interaction requiring communication of intent as well as rejection. Other issues revolve around how couples decide to have sex and the link between sexual satisfaction and relationship satisfaction. More recently, explanations of the origins of homsexuality and the causes of homophobia have taken center stage.

Theories.   Theories aimed at explaining the interactive nature of sex have focused on the importance of verbal and nonverbal signals in the communication of sexual intent. Couples' decisions to engage in sex have been linked to relationship development and duration, but it is less clear how sexual frequency and satisfaction are related to general relationship satisfaction. Whereas early theories about the origins of homosexuality treated it as a disease that can be cured, more recent theories focus on the role of biological and social factors as well as its interactions. Homophobia appears to be a complex phenomenon that can be explained partly by reference to unique psychodynamic processes as well as more general perceptual processes.

Research.   By and large, the descriptive research on patterns of sexual behavior shows that the sex life of most Americans is relatively conventional and has changed little over the past 40 years. People appear to have sex with similar others at a moderate frequency and a high level of exclusivity. Couples generally increase their sexual behavior gradually as their relationship develops, and most decide to have sex within one month of dating or when they feel that they are a couple. For most couples, sexual frequency and relationship satisfaction are related, but the correlational nature of the data complicates a causal interpretation of this relationship. At this time, there is tentative support for the idea that homosexuality is caused by a complex interaction between biological and social processes. Whereas homophobia appears to be caused in part by repressed and latent homosexual urges, it is also caused by false conceptions about the origins and manifestations of homosexuality. Evidence suggests that interpersonal contact goes a long way toward dispelling common myths, and there are indications that disclosure of one's sexual orientation has direct benefits for one's physical health.

10

Communication and Relationship Management

Saying they were moved by the tearful testimony of the victim, Cook County Criminal Court jurors took less than two hours . . . to convict Kevin Phelps of heinous battery and aggravated kidnapping for setting a 15-year-old girl on fire two years ago. However, the jury members acquitted Phelps, a paraplegic, of attempted first-degree murder because they believed he was trying to scare the teen, Pleasure Heard, not kill her. . . . The testimonies of Heard and Phelps were strikingly different, including how each characterized their relationship. Heard testified that Phelps was "just a friend [whom she] would help with chores and errands." However, Phelps called Heard his "girlfriend." Both claimed to have known each other for about nine months before the attack.

—*Chicago Tribune,* September 21, 1999

Few things better define the social spirit of the 1990s than the proliferation of popular books on improving close relationships, particularly those between men and women. One could argue that the trend represented an improvement over the 1980s, when much of the book-buying public rushed to get hold of the latest recipe promising self-improvement in 12 steps or less. After all, the shift away from self-improvement toward improving relationships with close others could be taken as a sign that the "me decade" had finally and mercifully come to an end. Whether this happened because we all became perfect and fulfilled or because we simply gave up on the whole idea is of little relevance. What matters is that the self-help shelves of the 1980s have become increasingly occupied by books promising to hold the ingredients necessary for improving relationships between men and women.

A look at the titles of some of the most successful books on relationships gives us an idea about what many popular writers perceived to be the root cause of all relationship problems. Deborah Tannen's (1990) *You Just Don't Understand: Women and Men in Conversation* and *Talking from 9 to 5—Women in the Workplace: Language, Sex, and Power* (1994a) clearly suggest that improving communication between men and women might be the key to healthy and mutually rewarding relationships. John Gray's (1992) wildly successful *Men Are from Mars, Women Are from Venus,* along with its equally successful sequels, did not mean to propose that the battle of the sexes had turned into intergalactic warfare. Rather, he echoed in a much amplified voice what researchers in psychology have known for some time. First, there are relatively stable differences in the ways men and women communicate. Second, these gender differences have traceable origins. Third, gender-based communication differences are at the heart of most relationship problems.

Sex Differences in Communication

Men and women differ on numerous dimensions in the ways they communicate. Some of these dimensions have less to do with *what* they say to each other but with *how* they do it. To illustrate some of these differences, consider the following scenarios.

As Norm enters his favorite sports bar after work, he notices that his friend Cliff is already seated on his favorite bar stool—the one closest to the TV that shows the baseball game. Norm sits down alongside him. They are both fixated on the TV screen, although their bodies are turned toward each other ever so slightly in order to have equal access to the bowl of Beernuts that sits between them on the bar. The following conversation begins to unfold:

Norm: Man, I'd like to have your job. How do you manage to get out of work so early every day?

Cliff: Hey, I'm in my cubicle by seven in the morning, so come 4:30, I bolt.

Norm: What's the score?

Cliff: Cubs up by two, bottom of the eighth.

Norm: Sosa hit any homeruns?

Cliff: No, but Lieber's got a two-hitter going.

Norm: Hey, I've been thinking about buying a truck.

Cliff: Hmm. A guy at work just got one of those SUVs. Says he loves it but the thing guzzles gas like there's no tomorrow.

Norm: Did you notice how much gas prices have gone up? If this keeps up I'm gonna have to take out a second mortgage just so I can drive to work.

Cliff: C'mon how can that be a strike? That pitch wasn't even in the same zip code as the plate!

Norm: You know, I remember when a gallon of gas was like 50 cents.

Cliff: Yeah, back when Fergie Jenkins still played for the Cubs.

Norm: Fergie Jenkins. Those were the days.

Cliff: And Ditka. They just don't make them like that anymore.

Meanwhile, in a quiet corner of the same bar, Oni and Susan find a small table at which to sit. They pull up the chairs so they can face each other as they catch up on what's been happening in their lives.

Oni: How have you been? It's been almost a week since I last saw you.

Susan: I've been trying to shake this awful cold.

Oni: You do look like you're a little under the weather.

Susan: Under the weather? I've been sniffling and sneezing almost the entire winter. Everybody at work's been doing the same thing, so I'm sure that doesn't help.

Oni: I've been lucky so far. Do you take vitamins or any kind of supplements? I've been doing that and I think it's been helping me this year.

Susan: Well, I take a multiple vitamin and some extra Vitamin C on occasion. But I don't know about that other stuff, like Echinacea and stuff. I sometimes wonder if they do more harm than good.

Oni: I see your point. It's probably a good idea to stay away from stuff that's not FDA approved. How are things at work?

Susan: All right, I guess. There's this new guy in accounting who's been acting kind of weird. I mean he is nice and real easy on the eyes, but he keeps dropping sexual innuendos all the time. That really makes me feel kind of yucky.

Oni: We had a guy like that, too, a few years ago. He probably thought he was funny, but some people didn't and filed a sexual harassment complaint against him. I don't exactly know what came out of it, but one day I came to work and he was gone.

Susan: I wish my company had a policy against sexual harassment. I mean, I don't like what's going on, but I don't think I want to file a lawsuit and stuff.

Oni: Well, who would? It costs an arm and a leg and it's probably hell to prove. So what are you going to do?

Susan: I don't know, I just wonder why guys have to be like that.

Oni: Weird creatures, I'm telling you. Just look at those two over at the bar (pointing to Norm and Cliff). I wonder what they're hatching.

Susan: Whatever it is, I'm not sure I want to know.

Admittedly, some aspects of these fictitious conversations reflect popular stereotypes more than anything else. There is no research evidence to indicate that men are more likely to talk about sports and pickup trucks than do women. And there is little to suggest that women talk more than men (James & Drakich, 1993). However, there is evidence that the sexes approach the job of talking to one another in very different ways. By looking at the conversational styles evident when men talked to each other and when women talked to each other, Tannen (1994) found several differences. By and large, men prefer side-by-side interactions, whereas women prefer their bodily alignment to be oriented toward each other. Consequently, Norm and Cliff prefer to sit at the bar, whereas Susan and

Oni sit at a table. But even though the preference for a side-by-side alignment prevents men from gazing at each other, their conversations are not necessarily less engaged than those of women. Rather, their engagement proceeds as if on parallel tracks. Not surprisingly, there is evidence that the different alignment preferences may be related to differences in the kind of activities men and women enjoy (Caldwell & Peplau, 1982). Specifically, it appears that men prefer activities that can be done in parallel (e.g., going fishing), whereas women prefer activities that promote talking (e.g., having lunch together).

Compared to men, women establish topics for their conversations quickly and talk in depth about a small number of them for an extended period of time. Men, on the other hand, show less topical cohesion, preferring instead to cover a lot of topics for a shorter period of time. Interestingly, these differences in alignment and topical cohesion appear to manifest themselves at an early age. In Tannen's (1994) study, differences were equally present among 6-year-olds as well as 25-year-olds. Before we look at possible explanations for these differences, let us look at another feature of mixed-sex conversations: interruptions.

Interruptions: Let Me Finish, Please!

It is easy to see that the different conversational styles might clash once men and women talk to each other rather than among themselves. Men might become impatient with women's proclivities to talk about one topic at length. Women might take men's tendency to jump from one topic to the next with trailblazing speed to indicate a lack of attention and caring. Moreover, one might speculate that men would be tempted to interrupt women more during a conversation. Preferring to jump from one subject to the next quickly, men might cut women off as they are talking in depth about a single topic. Moreover, interruptions can be interpreted as a means by which men reassert control and dominance in an interaction (e.g., Mishler & Waxler, 1968; West & Zimmerman, 1983; Zimmerman & West, 1975). Researchers who work within this framework look at interruptions as violating normal conversational rules, as being negative or undesirable behavior, and as constituting an attempt to exercise power and to dominate and control the interaction through control of the floor and of the topic of conversation.

So, are interruptions more common in mixed-sex conversations? In other words, are men more likely to interrupt women than they would other men? Are women less likely to interrupt a speaker of either sex? An early study that recorded naturally ocurring conversations in public places (Zimmerman & West, 1975) seems to suggest that the answer is a resounding yes. In this study, 31 conversations were recorded in such places as coffee shops and drugstores. A total of 10 conversations took place between men, another 10 between women, and the remaining 11 between mixed-sex pairs. Interruptions were operationally defined as simultaneous speech that penetrated into the structure of the speaker's utterances more than two syllables from completion. The results indicated that when men talk to men and when women talk to women, interruptions are about equally divided between the two speakers. However, in mixed-sex dyads, a whopping 96 percent of interruptions were initiated by men.

Many took these findings as proof for the asymmetrical pattern of interruptions predicted by both the topical coherence perspective as well as the reasserting dominance perspective. However, as Aries (1996) has pointed out, such a conclusion may be more in line with wishful thinking than the actual data. The main problem is that the number of interruptions observed by Zimmerman and West (1975) was very low to begin with. A mere 7 interruptions took place in the 20 same-sex conversations and they occurred in only 3 of the 20 conversations (leaving 17 conversations that took place without any interruptions whatsoever). This is an awfully small database on which to base the somewhat sweeping conclusion that interruptions in same-sex conversations are about even. In the mixed-sex conversations, a full quarter of all interruptions came from a single man who repeatedly interrupted a female teaching assistant as she was trying to explain something to him. Once again, given the small sample size, the behavior of this single outlier may have skewed the data to the point that the conclusions might be at least somewhat erroneous. The reason this particular man interrupted so frequently may have been less rooted in his desire to dominate the female than in his wish to fully understand the concepts she was explaining.

Of course, based on a close look at just one study, one should be reluctant to reject the popular notion that men interrupt women more. However, a comprehensive review of all relevant studies between 1965 and 1991 suggests that reports of sex differences in interruptions may have been greatly exaggerated (James & Clarke, 1993). Only 6 of 20 studies on interruptions in mixed-sex dyads find a higher frequency of interruptions by men. More than twice as many studies (13) report no differences in the frequency of interruptions by men and women, and 2 even find that women are the interrupting sex!

Empirical considerations aside, there is reason to believe that researchers have historically defined interruptions too narrowly. In other words, interruptions are not necessarily evil devices employed in the service of dominance and control. Instead, some interruptions may be made for the purpose of clarification or simply to express agreement. Interruptions of this nature have been termed *confirmation* interruptions (Kennedy & Camden, 1983). They are very different from *rejection* interruptions, such as the expression of disagreement. They are further different from *disconfirmation* interruptions, including those that show awareness of the speaker's statement but make light of them (tangentialization) and those that are made with the ultimate goal of changing the subject.

When one looks at interruptions from this perspective, a very different picture emerges with regard to sex differences. One study looking at interruptions in naturally occurring mixed-sex graduate seminars (Kennedy & Camden, 1983) found that in this context, women actually interrupted more than men. Interestingly, almost half of the interruptions were confirmation interruptions (indicating agreement and asking for clarification). Of course, one might argue that the nature of the setting (graduate seminars) did not easily lend itself to interruptions based on power and dominance. On the other hand, a study that looked at interruptions during conversations between pairs of unacquainted men and women (Dindia, 1987) found that the majority of interruptions by both males and females expressed agreement.

The bottom line on interruptions in mixed-sex conversations seems to be that the popular belief regarding men interrupting women more than vice versa has very little support. This is not to say that men never interrupt women in the service of asserting or maintaining dominance. Rather, the conclusion should be that interruptions serve many functions (Aries, 1996) that may be invoked by men and women alike.

Language Use and Conversation Management

Interruptions to express agreement or to ask for clarification can serve as important tools for managing conversations. Even though it appears that there is little difference in the ways men and women use interruptions, the literature on gender and communication is replete with claims about scores of sex differences.

Politeness. One popular claim holds that women's speech is marked by politeness. For example, compared to men, women are more likely to use the words *please, might, may,* and *could* when making a request (Lakoff, 1973, 1975, 1977). Women are also more likely to avoid directives and imperatives (Brown & Levinson, 1978). In other words, a man working on his car's engine is likely to request a tool by uttering, "Get me a half-inch wrench!" whereas a women would request the same tool by politely asking, "Could you please get me a half-inch wrench?" Again, this claim appears to have some face validity. Furthermore, questionnaire studies in which men and women were asked to respond to hypothetical scenarios revealed such differences quite clearly (e.g., Baxter, 1984). However, there is reason to believe that a number of variables modify the extent to which men and women use more or less polite forms in making requests. Specifically, it has been suggested that the balance of power may play an important role (Sagrestano, 1992). A man might be more likely than a woman to use a directive when requesting the wrench from his adolescent son than his neighbor, who happens to be an expert in car repair as well as the owner of the wrench. And, of course, when the need for a wrench arises while motor oil is gushing from the engine, it may matter little whether the person making the repair is male or female.

Tag Questions. Another communication difference, first proposed by Lakoff (1973, 1975, 1977), has to do with the use of tag questions by men and women. The claim is that women often add a short question to the end of a sentence to express hesitancy and uncertainty ("We're eating out tonight, *aren't we?*"). However, there is conflicting empirical evidence regarding this claim. Some studies find support, others find the exact opposite (i.e., men asking more tag questions), and still others find no difference (Aries, 1996). One way to resolve the conflicting findings is to look at the functions that tag questions serve. As was the case with interruptions, not all tag questions are the same (Holmes, 1984). Some may be uttered to convey *uncertainty*, whereas others can serve to express *solidarity* and ask the person to join a conversation ("Still bummed out about your divorce, are you?"). Yet other tag questions may be used to soften a directive or a negatively toned speech act, thus adding a measure of *politeness* ("You're not going to play golf again, are you?").

One study that examined tags (Holmes, 1984) found a number of interesting sex differences, in terms of sheer frequency and in terms of how they are used. By and large, women use tags slightly more often than men. More importantly, the majority of women's tags were used in the service of expressing solidarity, and women used these types of tags far more frequently than men. Somewhat surprisingly, in light of Lakoff's claims, men used almost twice as many tags to express uncertainty than did women. Thus, it appears that women use tags primarily to promote conversation, whereas men use tags primarily to express uncertainty (as in, "We are having sex tonight, aren't we?").

Qualifiers and Hedges. Lakoff (1973, 1975, 1977) claimed that women expressed uncertainty and hesitancy by virtue of using more qualifiers and hedges, such as *I guess, I think, Sort of, I mean,* and *You know.* Among all of Lakoff's claims, this has been one of the most difficult to study empirically. Part of the problem is that many different meanings are attached to what Lakoff considered qualifiers. Take, for example, the use of "you know." Its precise meaning depends on both its position in a sentence as well as the speaker's intonation (Aries, 1996; Holmes, 1984). At the beginning of a sentence, it may simply be a call for attention and indicate *certainty* ("You know, we really need to clean up the kitchen"). At the end of a sentence, preceded or followed by a pause, it may serve as an invitation to provide feedback to the speaker and indicate a level *uncertainty*. For example, "It's nice out, you know" may prompt the other to ask, "Do you want to play tennis?" It is not clear if the same thing would happen if the phrase *you know* had been omitted.

By analyzing men's and women's formal and informal speech, Holmes (1984) found no overall sex differences in the use of the phrase *you know*. However, as one might expect, it seems to occur primarily in informal conversations. As was the case with tag questions, men use *you know* primarily to express uncertainty, whereas women use it to express certainty. Moreover, women use it more often than men to boost the strength of a statement ("You just bought a new car last year, you know") and to express certainty about the validity of a proposition ("They thought I was stupid, you know"). To boost the strength of a statement by means of the phrase *you know* generally entails falling intonation, whereas the expression of certainty entails rising intonation. In any event, there is little research to suggest that phrases such as *you know* are expressions of uncertainty by women. Nor does it seem to be the case that women use the phrase more frequently than men. In studies that find such a difference, "you know" is primarily used as a device to secure a conversation topic (e.g., Fishman, 1980).

Back-Channeling. Our discussion of the laundry list of sex differences in communication concludes with some considerations of Duncan's (1974) observations about back-channeling. Back-channeling includes a variety of verbal and nonverbal responses to another's utterances, such as sentence completions, brief restatements, head nodding and head shaking, and minimal responses of the *Hmm,* *Yeah,* and *Right* variety. Many studies indicate that women use back-channeling to a higher degree than do men, although it appears that an equal number of studies show the opposite or find no difference (cf. Aries, 1996). Back-channeling serves a variety of purposes; for example, minimal responses inserted during another's speech may indicate agreement and encouragement, whereas the same responses after a delay may be attempts to discourage further conversation about the topic. Interestingly, Fishman (1980) found that women use back-channeling more to express agreement, whereas men tend to use it primarily to signal lack of interest.

The mixed bag of evidence regarding Lakoff's claims about differences in men's and women's language use triggers at least two questions. First, why is there such a discrepancy between Lakoff's claims and the evidence? One problem is methodological in nature. In arriving at her conclusions, Lakoff relied primarily on inspections of her own speech and that of acquaintances, using introspection and intuition. If nothing else, it may be that this relatively severe sampling bias was ultimately responsible for her conclusions. Had she included a more representative sample of women, Lakoff may well have found what others did in the process of debunking her claims. The second question is more difficult to answer: Why, as a society, have we rushed to embrace Lakoff's findings so willingly and with little hesitation? The answer may lie in our deep-seated desire to find differences between the sexes. We all know perfectly well that men and women are different, but we are much less certain on exactly how they differ. In addition, Lakoff's observations about differences in politeness, use of tag questions, and qualifiers resonate well with our stereotypes about men and women in conversation.

Emotionality and Support

Our discussion of sex differences in communication has so far focused primarily on differences in the conversational *style* preferred by women and men. However, there is another area to investigate. Much literature seems to support the notion that women are more emotionally sensitive and expressive than men. Put a slightly different way, women approach talk with an *affective orientation*, whereas men approach it with an *instrumental orientation* (e.g., Ballswick, 1988; Gilligan, 1982; Vaux, 1985). Support for this idea comes from research on sex differences in self-disclosure, discussed in Chapter 5. In addition, much of its thrust comes from research that looks at sex differences in emotional support. Research consistently finds women to be more likely than men to do the following:

- Inquire about an upsetting situation (Mickelson, Helgeson, & Weiner, 1995)
- Provide emotional support (Trobst, Collins, & Embree, 1994)

- Seek emotional support from others (Ashton & Fuehrer, 1993)
- Feel confident about their ability to provide support (Clark, 1993)
- Place a high value on skills related to giving support (Burleson et al., 1996)
- Employ supportive strategies directed at emotions (Derlega, Barbee, & Winstead, 1994)

Even though some of the reported sex differences are relatively small, as is the case in differences regarding self-disclosure, the cumulative evidence suggests that sex differences in emotionality and emotional support are fairly pervasive. Thus, it is difficult to argue that these findings may be artifacts due to methodological shortcomings, as was the case with some of the purported sex differences in communication style. Accounting for these differences theoretically is an entirely different matter. We examine the prevailing view next.

Men and Women: Different Cultures, Different Planets?

Even though numerous explanations have been offered to account for a variety of sex differences in communication, by far the most prevailing and popular view is that women and men form different cultures (Wood, 1994). This perspective holds that the sexes are socialized into different cultures, with each sex developing vastly different but equally valid and effective ways of communicating, including expressions of emotional intimacy and support. This idea is not without appeal. For one thing, it seems to be a step up from biological accounts (e.g., Fausto-Sterling, 1985) that essentially proclaim biology to be destiny. For another, it seems to make intuitive sense. After all, everybody knows that girls and boys are raised differently. Little girls are encouraged to express their emotions and to be concerned about the feelings of others. Little boys, on the other hand, are encouraged to keep their feelings under wraps, especially when it comes to expressing emotions such as sadness and distress. Is it any wonder, then, that men and women will come to inhabit different speech communities (Wood, 1997), emotional cultures (Wood, 1994), or planets (Gray, 1992)? Is it any wonder that the different cultures view has become so widely accepted that it is taught like the gospel?

Unfortunately, the different cultures view has some rather profound implications for theory, research, and teaching (Kunkel & Burleson, 1998) that justify a more critical examination. For example, if women and men constitute different cultures, it may be necessary to develop separate theories of close relationships to account for the different things men and women seek in a relationship as well as the different ways in which they develop and maintain them. Further, if women and men are from different cultures, it may be necessary to develop culturally sensitive methods for our research. Finally, if men and women are from different cultures, it may be necessary to develop educational programs designed to respect and appreciate the differences in each other's culture. In other words, in order to get along with each other, men and women need diversity training (Kunkel & Burleson, 1998)!

So what's wrong with this picture? It is not entirely clear who belongs to the different cultures (Burleson, 1997). Many researchers assign membership according to biological sex (Maltz & Borker, 1982; Noller, 1993; Tannen, 1990); others, most notably Wood (1997), base assignment on psychological gender. This approach, then, suggests that the different cultures thesis does not necessarily apply to males and females per se, but instead to masculine and feminine speech communities. But how does one find out to which culture or community any given person belongs? Seemingly, the answer is that one examines the person's speech style: Those who use the feminine style are members of the feminine community, and those who use the masculine style are members of the masculine community (Wood, 1997).

There is something deeply troubling about assigning people to speech communities or even cultures based on their style of speech. For one thing, it is inherently circular. For another, it makes it unclear how the different cultures thesis could be tested empirically. In order to ascertain if we are dealing with different *cultures*, we need to provide data that go beyond simply showing that there are sex differences in communication. In light of this consideration, Burleson (1997) suggested that tests of the different cultures hypothesis should take into account differences that one would generally expect for different cultures, such as meanings, values, and preferences. In other words, if men and women form different cultures beyond communication styles, one would expect them to differ also in terms of the meaning they associate with important relationship concepts (e.g., intimacy, sex), the values they place on such things as emotional support, and general preferences regarding the way things ought to be done.

Interestingly, when one throws meanings, values, and preferences into the mix, there is surprisingly little support for the different cultures hypothesis. With respect to meanings, Monsour (1992) looked at sex differences in the meaning assigned to intimacy in friendships and found them to be very small. Men and women alike listed self-disclosure as the most common meaning of intimacy. Even though women did so more often than men (87 percent vs. 56 percent), the important thing is that the majority of both sexes appeared to feel the same way. Moreover, roughly even numbers of men and women listed emotional expressiveness as the second most common meaning of intimacy. Sharing activities was mentioned relatively infrequently by most sexes (0 percent of women and 9 percent of men). Many other studies show very similar results (Helgeson, Shaver, & Dyer, 1987; Parks & Floyd, 1996; Reis, 1990).

Research on the values men and women place on different communication skills is equally unsupportive of the different cultures thesis. In one study, male and female research participants rated the importance of various communication skills in friendships and romantic relationships (Burleson et al., 1996). The list included affectively oriented skills such as comforting (e.g., "Can really cheer me up when I'm feeling down") and ego support (e.g., "Makes me feel like I'm a good person") as well as instrumental skills such as persuasion (e.g., "Is able to get me to go along with what he/she wants to do") and narration (e.g., "Often comes up with witty remarks in conversation").

Women considered the affective skills of their partner as slightly more important than men regardless of relationship type. Men, on the other hand, viewed the instrumental skills of their partner as important. However, contrary to the different cultures thesis, both men and women placed a much higher value on the affectively oriented skills of their partner. Of course, in light of such findings, one might ask why women often report more problems in their long-term romantic relationships than do men. It appears that it is not a matter of differences in the standards or values that men and women deem important. Rather, it is that the perception of problems stems from discrepancies in the extent that the standards are fulfilled (Vangelisti & Daly, 1997) in the relationship.

Finally, the idea that men and women would prefer to interact with a member of their own culture has little support. It really does not make too much sense to begin with. Heterosexual men and women generally prefer to have sexual interactions with members of the opposite sex (a.k.a. the different culture). But even when it comes to seeking emotional support, men and women do not gravitate toward members of their own sex. Instead, both sexes prefer to look for emotional support from women (Clark, 1994; Kunkel, 1995). Even the more general hypothesis that men and women find cross-sex interactions less rewarding than interactions with members of their own sex because of the "clash of conversational styles" (Tannen, 1990) has virtually no support (e.g., Goldsmith, McDermott, & Hawkins, 1996). If anything, evidence shows that members of both sexes find interactions with females to be more intimate and meaningful than interactions with men (Reis, Senchak, & Solomon, 1985; Wheeler, Reis, & Nezlek, 1983).

Different Cultures or Different Skills?

The differences in the communication styles of men and women, as profound as they may be, do not appear to justify claims of representing different cultures. Instead, it may be that the differences in men's and women's socialization lead to predictable communication deficits. In other words, men and women are part of one culture in which differences in socialization foster the development of emotional support skills among girls but discourage them among boys. The result is a *skill specialization* among women and a *skill deficit* among men with respect to support and comforting (Kunkel & Burleson, 1999). It is this difference in comforting skills that leads both men and women to turn to women for comfort and support during times of stress and emotional upheaval (Clark, 1994; Kunkel, 1995). The skill specialization account proposes a number of additional hypotheses that contrast maximally with the different cultures account, as shown in Table 10.1.

Several things are appealing about the skill specialization account of the sex differences in emotional support. First, unlike the different cultures view, skill specialization takes into account similarities between the sexes along with differences. Second, this viewpoint represents a much more parsimonious explanation than the different cultures account. Third, it is more soundly supported by the

TABLE 10.1 *Some Differences in Comforting Preferences Predicted by Two Theoretical Accounts*

Different Cultures Account	Skill Specialization Account
—Men and women live in different emotional cultures.	—Men and women live in the same emotional culture.
—Men and women have different but equally effective ways of dealing with emotional experience.	—Women have more effective ways of dealing with emotional experience than do men.
—Men and women will turn to their own sex for support.	—Men and women will turn to women for support.
—Men and women will feel more supported by members of their own sex.	—Men and women will feel more supported by women.

Source: Adapted from Kunkel and Burleson (1999).

data (Kunkel & Burleson, 1999). Fourth, and perhaps most important, skill specialization suggests a unique and perhaps simple solution to communication problems between men and women. As we said earlier, the different cultures account more or less suggests diversity training as the only solution to avoiding culture clashes between the sexes. The skill specialization account suggests that effective communication can be learned. Men may be able to learn women's communication skills by way of the three Ps involved in acquiring any skill: Practice, Practice, Practice.

Managing Relationships

One important aspect of close relationships is often overlooked when viewed through the different cultures lens. On a daily basis, most couples actually manage the mundane aspects of their relationships quite well. Communication is frequently not a problem when it comes to such tasks as paying the bills, taking out the garbage, getting dinner, and taking the kids to baseball practice. How do couples manage to get these and other chores done?

Transactive Memory in Close Relationships

If one took an exhaustive look at the sheer number of tasks that couples need to complete, living together may seem like a gargantuan task. Moreover, remembering who does what appears to be an equally tall order. However, most couples have little trouble assigning chores to one another and getting them done.

One of the reasons for the apparent ease with which couples manage the numerous chores imposed by everyday life is that they develop a *transactive memory* structure, a shared system for encoding, storing, and retrieving information (Wegner, 1986; Wegner, Giuliano, & Hertel, 1985). Transactive memory not only informs partners about what they themselves need to remember but also what the other person will remember. These assignments can be based on a number of principles. Gender and, more generally, sex roles can provide simple cues to what the other might know and can thus serve as default options. For example, men may be more likely to remember who won the 1984 World Series, and women might have an easier time recalling all the movies in which Mel Gibson starred. Thus, when questions about baseball or Mel Gibson come up, the members of a couple can turn to each other for answers without first ascertaining whether or not they might know them. From this perspective, memory assignments frequently follow the general division of labor among couples (Atkinson & Huston, 1984). Alternatively, memory assignments can be negotiated based on suspected expertise or on who has accepted responsibility for a task in the past.

The existence and importance of transactive memory among couples was demonstrated in a study in which couples who had been together for at least 3 months completed a memory task (Wegner, Erber, & Raymond, 1991). The memory task consisted of remembering items belonging to seven distinct categories. For example, the sentence *Midori is a Japanese melon liqueur* represented the category "Alcohol." The sentence *Yeasts reproduce by budding* represented the category "Science." Research participants could complete the memory task in one of two ways: by assigning categories to each other based on their relative expertise or through an arbitrary assignment provided by the experimenter. As expected, couples who used their relative expertise in assigning the memory tasks remembered more items than couples who had to complete the task according to the experimenter's scheme, which supposedly interfered with the way couples ordinarily remember things. How long the couples had been together did not influence their performance. Couples who had been dating for three months did just as well as those who had been together for years, as long as they could rely on their transactive memory. It is important to note that transactive memory does not operate by some sort of magic. Rather, intimate couples often use a variety of nonverbal cues, like eye contact, to ascertain who might know what, especially when they are confronted with novel memory tasks (Hollingshead, 1998).

These findings are important for a number of reasons. They suggest that couples develop a way of assigning memory tasks to each other, including knowing what the other knows (as opposed to knowing and remembering everything themselves). It seems that couples develop such a transactive memory early in their relationship, as evidenced by the absence of any effect due to the length of a relationship. Further, transactive memory retrieval works best when members of couples interact face to face. Finally, breaking up may be hard to do in part because it entails the loss of one's transactive memory. When a relationship ends, reassignment of expertise frequently occurs at great expense. The individual needs to become an expert in a number of topics that used to be a part of the other's domain. New information relating to the previous partner's areas of expertise may be handled poorly at first and perhaps for some time. The resulting confusion may lead to items in one's own domains to be mishandled, as well. Even if a new partner is eventually found, it will likely take time and effort for the new couple to know what the old couple took for granted.

Frequently, we lose partners not because of a breakup or death, but because they move away. Ours is a highly mobile society in which college choices and employment issues often put couples thousands of miles apart, forcing them to conduct long-distance relationships.

Long-Distance Relationships

For couples who either choose or are forced to conduct long-distance relationships, transactive memory retrieval in the absence of face-to-face interactions is probably the least of their problems. Even though there is little indication that "absence makes the heart grow fonder," there is reason to believe that the trials and tribulations of conducting an intimate relationship over a long distance may be less traumatic than one might expect. One study that examined how couples in long-distance and proximal relationships fare in terms of satisfaction, trust, and relationship progress found that proximal relationships were in no way superior to long-distance relationships (Guldner & Swenson, 1995). Not surprisingly, compared to couples in proximal relationships, those in long-distance relationships report a decrease in descriptive self-disclosure and companionship. However, they were comparable to proximal couples in their evaluative self-disclosure and level of affection for their partner (Van Horn et al., 1998). Of course, there is a reason for this seeming lack of profound decrements in long-distance relationships. Couples who are apart often find ways to cope with their physical separation. It appears that how frequently they visit each other and how often they communicate otherwise, via the phone or the Internet, contribute to their level of satisfaction (Holt & Stone, 1997). Coping in such ways may further explain why long-distance couples are no more likely to break up than proximal couples, at least in the short run (Van Horn et al., 1998).

It is reasonable to speculate about sex differences in adjusting to physical separation. Recall that both men and women alike gravitate toward women when it comes to seeking emotional support (Clark, 1994; Kunkel, 1995) and that both sexes find interactions with women more meaningful and rewarding (Reis et al., 1985; Wheeler et al., 1983). Based on these findings, one might expect that any negative ramifications of physical separation should be more pronounced for the male partner in a long-distance relationship. Some have even argued that women might be better off as a result of physical separation because it eases the burden of giving emotional support without receiving similar levels from their partners (Helgeson, 1994).

Creating and Maintaining Satisfying Relationships

The observation that women are less adversely affected by a breakup should not be taken as indication that they might be relieved when a relationship ends. Nor does it mean that women are necessarily more unhappy in intimate relationships than men. Instead, several interpersonal processes contribute to the level of satisfaction in intimate relationships.

Idealization.   Intimates can create and maintain a high level of satisfaction with their relationship as long as they look at their partners in an idealistic rather than realistic way (Murray, Holmes, & Griffin, 1996a, 1996b). This may strike some as counterintuitive. After all, idealization is characteristic of the early stages of relationship development, when the novelty of one's partner seems to short-circuit any type of rational thought. However, ample evidence shows that maintaining positive illusions, especially after experiencing adversity, has beneficial effects on one's mental and physical health (Taylor & Brown, 1988). There are two studies suggesting that maintaining positive illusions about one's partner is beneficial for intimate relationships. One study (Murray et al., 1996a) asked members of married and dating couples to rate themselves and their partner on a number of interpersonal attributes reflecting virtues (e.g., patience, understanding), faults (e.g., complaining, moodiness), and social commodities (e.g., self-assured, witty). The complete list of items is depicted in Table 10.2. You may want to take a moment to rate yourself and your partner, keeping in mind that the scientific way to assess levels of idealization is somewhat more complicated.

A number of interesting findings resulted from this study. First, intimates saw their partners in a more positive light than their partners saw themselves, suggesting somewhat idealized constructions of the other. Moreover, idealization was correlated with relationship satisfaction. Those who most idealized their partner were happiest with their relationship. Not surprisingly, in light of these findings, idealization also appears to have a number of self-fulfilling mechanisms that add to the stability of relationships. Specifically, relationships are most likely to persist, even in the face of conflicts and doubts, when intimates idealize each other the most (Murray et al., 1996b). However, once a conflict arises, idealization by itself is not likely to prevent escalation. Instead, it may be one among many variables that contributes to the extent to which a partner inhibits the temptation to respond destructively to a partner's transgression and instead chooses constructive ways to deal with the resulting conflict (e.g., Arriaga & Rusbult, 1998; Rusbult et al., 1991). We will discuss these and other issues in Chapter 13.

Attributions.   The extent to which we idealize our partners may ultimately be related to how we explain their behavior, especially when the behavior in question is detrimental for the relationship. In general, satisfied partners generate attributions that attenuate the impact of negative relationship events. Dissatisfied partners, on the other hand, tend to generate attributions that accentuate the impact of negative events and diminish the impact of positive events (e.g., Bradbury & Fincham, 1989). For example, Happy Harold may attribute his partner's disinterest in going dancing to his or her preoccupation with final exams. Sad Sally, on the other hand, may interpret the same behavior to indicate a lack of love and consideration. Of course, the extent to which a person chooses negative attributions has consequences for subsequent behavior. Negative attributions for a partner's

TABLE 10.2 *Interpersonal Qualities Scale*

	Self	Partner

Virtues
Kind and affectionate
Open and disclosing
Patient
Understanding
Responsive to my needs
Tolerant and accepting
Critical and judgmental

Faults
Lazy
Controlling and dominant
Emotional
Moody
Thoughtless
Irrational
Distant
Complaining
Childish

Social Commodities
Self-assured
Sociable
Intelligent
Witty
Traditional

Note: Assign a number from 1 ("Not at All Characteristic") to 9 ("Extremely Characteristic") for your-self and your partner. You are idealizing whenever the number for your partner is higher, except for attributes that are negatively worded. In these cases, negative discrepancies indicate idealization.

Source: Based on Murray, Holmes, and Griffin (1996a).

behavior tend to trigger negative behavior. If the partner responds to this situation in the same fashion (i.e., with negative attributions and negative behaviors), and if this pattern persists over a period of time, the couple will likely be enveloped by massive unhappiness. As will be discussed in detail in Chapter 13, this cyclical pattern of behavior and attributions is common in distressed couples (Bradbury & Fincham, 1992). It may be that idealizing one's partner acts as an important buffer in this cycle of events. If we have exaggerated views of our partner's personality, we may simply be less likely to attribute his or her behavior to a negative disposition.

Expectations. Finally, it is reasonable to suspect that partners' expectations regarding their relationship would be related to satisfaction. If two people expect their relationship to be marked by open self-disclosure and interaction resulting in identity affirmation, they will be happy if that occurs and unhappy if it does not (e.g., Hackel & Ruble, 1992). One situation in which expectations have been shown to be of paramount importance is the transition to parenthood. The birth of the first child represents an important transition and is frequently marked by a decrease in relationship satisfaction, especially for mothers (Belsky, Rovine, & Fish, 1989; Cowan & Cowan, 1988). This is not entirely surprising for a society that leaves providing and securing child care primarily in the hands of mothers. However, there is also evidence that the decline in relationship satisfaction after the first baby is born is neither universal nor inevitable. Some (e.g., Ruble et al., 1988) have found that the overall level of relationship satisfaction among parents remains at higher than average levels or does not differ very much at all from nonparents. How can one account for such conflicting results? It appears that whether relationship satisfaction takes a turn for the worse as a result of the transition from couplehood to parenthood depends in important ways on the extent to which the experience of childrearing confirms or disconfirms prepartum expectations.

Consistent with the idea that expectations are important, Hackel and Ruble (1992) found that mothers are not necessarily dissatisfied when they find out that they are left with the majority of chores related to childrearing. They are only dissatisfied if they previously had strong expectations regarding an equal and fair division of labor. Interestingly, women with traditional attitudes about the roles of women and men in society showed the opposite effect. They were actually happier with their relationship after they found out that their partners were going to contribute less than an equal amount of work. On the surface, this finding looks as though it is somewhat inconsistent with the idea that expectancy disconfirmation leads to negative affect. However, although having to do the bulk of the chores may have violated the mothers' expectations for the relationship, it confirmed their expectations regarding their role. Consequently, being primarily in charge of caring for the baby increased their happiness with their relationship. Of course, the larger implication here is that happiness is less determined by the number of diapers one changes than by one's *expectations* regarding how many diapers one will change.

To conclude, effective and rewarding communication is clearly important for the success of intimate relationships; however, they do not guarantee it. The extent to which intimate partners are happy with their relationship further depends on their ability and willingness to idealize the other and to generate benevolent attributions for negative relationship events, and their more general expectations regarding the nature of their relationship.

Summary

Issues. Men and women differ fundamentally in the ways in which they communicate. Compared to men, women tend to face each other during conversations, they tend to dwell on a topic, and they tend to provide more supportive interruptions. Some researchers claim that women and men differ in the ways they manage conversations through politeness, and their use of tag questions, qualifiers, and back-channeling. Although these claims regarding conversation management are somewhat controversial, there is widespread agreement that men and women differ in terms of emotional expressiveness and emotional support. Even though sex differences in communication might be expected to adversely affect how intimate couples manage their relationships, many couples manage their day-to-day interactions fairly well. Moreover, it appears that couples have a variety of tools to help them have proximal and long-distance relationships that are satisfying and rewarding.

Theories. Even though several different theories have been proposed to account for the sex differences in communication, the one most widely embraced suggests that men and women form different cultures. The popularity of this theory is not matched by empirical support, however. Instead, it appears that differences in socialization, rather than leading to the creation of different cultures, create diverse communication skills in men and women. One reason why couples often manage their relationships fairly well has to do with establishing a transactive memory that, in addition to one's own knowledge, contains information about the expertise of one's partner. Theories on relationship satisfaction emphasize the importance of idealizations, attributions, and expectancies for successful and happy relationships.

Research. Although some of the reported sex differences in communication are fairly robust (alignment, topical cohesion, emotionality), research documenting differences in communication management suffers from methodological shortcomings. Not surprisingly, evidence shows that, if anything, men rather than women use more tag questions, qualifiers, and back-channeling. But even the more reliable sex differences regarding alignment, topical cohesion, and emotionality are difficult to account for in terms of reflecting different cultures. Instead, because men and women share meanings, values, and preferences for interaction partners, it appears that the skill specialization account provides a better way to conceptualize these differences. Research on transactive memory supports the notion that couples establish a memory system that helps them navigate the many chores of their daily lives. Although this, in itself, is not related to relationship satisfaction, there is evidence that idealizing one's partner is of paramount importance. Relationship satisfaction is further influenced by the types of attributions individuals make for their partner's transgression along with the extent to which the relationship confirms their expectations.

11

Fidelity and Jealousy

NEW BRAUNFELS, Texas—Former Air Force Academy cadet David Graham, once an honor student and aspiring fighter pilot, was found guilty . . . of capital murder for killing a teenage girl to prove his love for a jealous fiancée [Diane Zamora].

Graham was convicted of killing 16-year-old Adrianne Jones by bludgeoning her and firing two bullets from a 9 mm pistol into her head early on Dec. 4, 1995, in a rural area near Ft. Worth.

In a confession to police, Graham said Zamora flew into a jealous rage when he told her he had sex with Jones after a high school track meet. She ordered him to kill Jones to prove his love, he said.

—*Chicago Tribune*, July 25, 1998

When asked to comment on the statement, "If you really love me, you'd be jealous," most people disagree vehemently with it and challenge its soundness. Some quite forcefully argue that jealousy is a selfish reaction to perceived threat and loss, indicative of poor self-esteem, possessiveness, and a lack of trust rather than a sign of true love. Yet, despite this widespread belief, who among us can honestly say that we have never experienced the bitter sting of jealousy? And if the statement above is reversed, can it be possible (or desirable) to truly love someone and *not* experience any jealousy at all? Why does it seem difficult, even impossible, to eliminate jealous feelings? On the other hand, would we really want to? Perhaps a better question would be: Why do we even question the validity of our jealousy in the first place?

Fidelity and Jealousy across Time and Cultures

Fidelity

Jealousy, along with anger and hate, are emotions that reflect the darker side of human nature. In fact, our current and largely negative reactions to jealousy may be rooted in the prevailing societal emphasis on political correctness, individualism, and sexual freedom (Mullen, 1991). In any case, the idea that cultural norms might be influencing our current intolerance of jealousy suggests that under other conditions, in another place and time, we might find jealousy less reprehensible— even acceptable. The fact that jealousy is the yin to fidelity's yang may clarify this notion, and thus leads us to the next question: Are there periods in history or differences among cultures in which *fidelity* is also more or less valued?

If we step back into the United States of the not-so-distant past, we see how the sexual revolution of the 1960s changed previously held beliefs about sexual behaviors, including fidelity, chastity, and sexual permissiveness. "Free love" was espoused by many disillusioned youths who turned on and dropped out. The country experienced an explosion of different sexual practices, especially among the middle- and upper-middle-class youths of the time: multiple partners, one-night stands, open marriages, and communal/group living and loving. Sex literally came out of the bedroom and the backseat of Chevies and into the open.

During this explosion of sexual experimentation, one can only imagine how fidelity and commitment fared. Marriage rates dropped and divorce rates increased (Cherlin, 1992). This climate of sexual permissiveness continued unabated over the next two decades (popular portrayals of which can be found in movies such as *Looking for Mr. Goodbar, Saturday Night Fever,* and, more recently, *Boogie Nights*). Indeed, although the idealism and political activism of the 1960s faded, the sexual revolution grew to include the gay community. Cruising as well as voluminous, anonymous, and casual sex were practiced, and not only by gays. Sexually transmitted diseases, such as herpes, threw a big scare into the revelers, but did little to stop the party. It was not until sexual gratification had the potential to kill that the benefits and value of fidelity, commitment, and chastity were allowed to resurface. The knowledge that indiscriminate sex could be fatal or leave one with a life-threatening disease chased many people "back to the fold." Monogamy and long-term commitment became respected conventions again, and those practicing chastity and fidelity were less likely to be viewed as "squares" or as old-fashioned.

The degree of fidelity and (its conceptual kin) monogamy practiced by romantic partners varies with time and place (see Chapter 9). And so it goes with jealousy, too; like fidelity and bell-bottomed pants, jealousy is in vogue one century and out the next. However, upon closer examination, there are (at least for our purposes) two levels of understanding fidelity and jealousy: from a personal, emotional level and from a societal, value-oriented level.

A Brief History of Jealousy

From a personal, emotional perspective, jealousy has always been recognized as a potentially destructive and embarrassing emotion. However, our conceptualization of jealousy, like our understanding of emotions, has undergone quite an evolution. For example, Homer viewed jealousy and other passions as external to the individual. Love, like a wound from Cupid's arrow or an infection from a cold virus, invades its victim from without rather than originating from within. Further, although jealousy and other passions might be harmful, the experience of Homer's jealousy was connected to commonly held social beliefs and moral norms dictating when and how to express these emotions. For example, jealousy would have been the appropriate response in cases where one's honor had been compromised by a spouse's infidelity. Thus, jealousy had a distinct social and moral role in the social order of the 1300s, and the individual experience and expression of jealousy was in complete accord with its social definition (Mullen, 1991).

Interestingly, fourteenth-century philosophers and lovers recognized in jealousy a broader, more encompassing emotional reaction. That is, instead of being simply the reaction to the loss of a romantic partner to another lover, it also embodied the eagerness, devotion, and zealousness of love (Mullen, 1991). St. Augustine (likely the originator of the question posed at the beginning of this chapter) believed that "qui non zealat non amat" ("he who is not jealous does not love"). In light of the more positive undertones of jealousy in the fourteenth century, perhaps this statement refers more to the excitement and ardor of love, rather than to possessiveness, ownership, and loss (Mullen, 1991).

Philosophers and writers in the seventeenth century believed that two forces motivated action: passion and reason, with reason, of course, being the superior of the two. Actions motivated by passion were described as uncontrolled, irregular, and erratic; whereas behaviors stemming from reason were just the opposite. Given this premise, the obvious best course of action would be to work toward controlling our emotions with reasoned action. In fact, it was thought best to deny passion of any type and, instead, to rely solely on reason as a guide. This view is reflected in many of our current thoughts on our darker emotions. For example, Brehm (1992), along with many others, exhorts us to "react rationally to jealousy."

Not surprisingly, a countervailing notion cropped up in the eighteenth century. As represented by Hume, passion regained primacy on the motivational hierarchy, and reason became its slave. In a complete turnabout, passions such as jealousy were no longer viewed as external to its sufferers nor as inhabiting spheres separate from reason. Passions were construed as the result of individual characteristics and specific situations; their expression was influenced by reason. Thus, it was no longer criminal or a sign of weakness to demonstrate or experience passion; rather, what was judged unacceptable were misdirected passions and inappropriate expression and demonstration of emotions. In other words, we have the dual notions of jealousy that is justifiable and jealous reactions that are either appropriate or inappropriate. In sum, although jealousy then, as now, was clearly the reaction to the loss of a loved one to a rival, it also had the potential to occur within socially acceptable bounds (e.g., as an objection to the violation of an exclusive relationship and as the defense of one's honor).

Subsequent centuries saw even more changes in the social evaluation of jealousy. These changes were predicated by the radical changes in courtship practices and marriage. In previous centuries, love was often sought in relationships outside of the marriage union, and marriage was viewed more as an economic undertaking, with wives contributing value as possessions (i.e., the property of their husbands). Recent history saw this part of our social order overturned as love prior to rather than following marriage became the norm. Romantic love became the prerequisite, the foundation, for modern marriage. All told, the shift from an economic to a romantic basis for marriage, coupled with the growing independence of women, had rippling effects that changed the way we view fidelity and jealousy.

One of the outcomes of these changes was a subtle but inexorable shift in our view of jealousy as a personal reaction governed by social norms and moral conventions to jealousy as a purely personal reaction occurring outside of societal strictures. Social philosophers saw jealousy stripped of all its positive connotations (i.e., enthusiastic, ardent love) and social function. In other words, in the dawn of twenty-first–century western culture, jealousy is no longer considered a valid, socially sanctioned way to defend one's honor or to protest a partner's infidelity. Jealousy has become a uniquely individual expression of rage. It has lost its place as a socially validated participant in the love process. In fact, current cultural norms suggest that jealousy is a sign of irrationality, immaturity, and even pathology (Mullen, 1991).

Jealousy and Fidelity across Cultures

Cross-cultural examples also support this historical pattern of social relativity as well as demonstrate the link between fidelity and jealousy. Without getting into an anthropological dissertation, researchers have found that cultures that value fidelity and partner exclusivity demonstrate higher levels of jealous expression, whereas cultures or subgroups (e.g, Tahiti, swingers) in which partner exclusivity is less important suggest far lower rates of sexual jealousy (Hupka, 1991; DeSteno & Salovey, 1996). In fact, partners often engage in strategies to reduce jealousy through weakening the link between sex and love (Buunk, 1991).

A certain amount of relativity is inherent in how we evaluate and feel about fidelity and jealousy. However, is jealousy a purely cultural construct (i.e., if society doesn't believe in it, it doesn't exist), or do feelings of jealousy exist regardless of the cultural and historical prevailing winds? Let us examine jealousy with the tools of modern scientific analysis and remove it from philosophical and literary analyses. We will start with an examination of what defines jealousy.

Defining Jealousy

What Is It and Who Has It?

One of the first questions we might ask is whether jealousy is a distinct emotion or an emotional hybrid of other feelings blended together in a cauldron of pain. Given its ability to torment and impart such intense anguish in its sufferers, one would feel justified in concluding that jealousy, like anger, is one of our basic emotions. Leading theorists on emotions, however, propose that there are from 8 to 10 primary emotions; the number varies depending on the theorist and the model (cf. Tomkins, 1991; Izard, 1991; Plutchik, 1994). These basic or fundamental emotions represent the building blocks of our emotional lives and are supposedly "hardwired" into our systems. Thus, according to this theory, these emotions are present at birth and universally recognizable. Although differing in some respects, six emotions are common across models: fear, anger, enjoyment, disgust, interest, and surprise. A seventh emotion, sadness, is also common to many of the models.

The English language includes more than 2,000 words describing emotions, which is to say we experience many more emotions than the seven listed here.

Theorists suggest that the other 1,993 emotions, such as jealousy, are produced either through a blending of the primary emotions (Izard, 1991) and/or through variations in intensity of the primary 8 to 10 emotions (Plutchik, 1994). Interestingly, relative to the primary emotions, there is more cultural variability in the expression and recognition of secondary emotions.

The prototype model of emotions (Shaver et al., 1987), like the preceding models, proposes that there are five or six basic emotions (anger, fear, joy, love, sadness, and perhaps surprise) and that all other emotions are subtypes of these basic six (see Figure 11.1). Loneliness, then, represents a subtype of sadness, whereas joy is the parent of ecstasy. And, according to the prototype model of emotions, jealousy is a subtype of anger.

Other emotion researchers suggest that, just as primary colors are mixed together to form secondary colors, our broad range of emotional experiences can be constructed through a blending of the primary emotions (Izard, 1991; Sharpsteen, 1991). According to this emotional blend approach, then, loneliness is a blend of

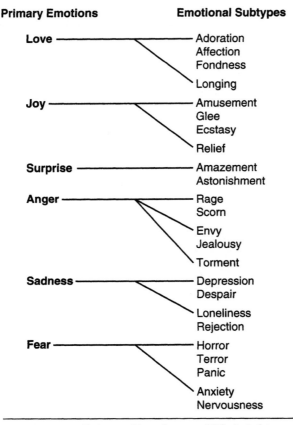

FIGURE 11.1 *Primary Emotions and Their Subtypes*

Source: Shaver, Schwartz, Kirson, and O'Connor (1987). Reprinted by permission.

sadness and fear, and ecstasy is a mixture of joy and love. Here, then, jealousy is defined as more than just a subtype of anger; rather, it is a blend of anger, sadness, and fear (Sharpsteen, 1991).

Whether a subtype or a blend, jealousy is a *bona fide* emotion (Parrott, 1991). In his cognitive appraisal approach to emotions, Parrott maintains that jealousy is an emotional episode comprised of feelings of anxiety, insecurity, anger, and sadness. In a slightly more intricate dissection of jealousy, Parrot suggests that the exact complexion of the jealous episode (e.g., anger versus sadness, betrayal versus loneliness) depends on the situation and focus of the individual. Similarly, Hupka (1984) found slightly different manifestations of jealousy, depending on features of the jealousy-provoking situation. In one set of studies (Hupka, 1984), participants were presented with scenarios describing people in different jealousy-evoking situations. Depending on which features of the situation were emphasized, participants believed that the people in the stories were feeling either sad, angry, or fearful. We will discuss this particular notion later in the chapter.

In sum, it is more or less widely accepted that although jealousy is an emotion, it is *not* one of our basic, "primary" emotions. One implication of this view is that jealousy, as either an emotional subtype or a blend, may be more amenable to cultural and social influences. As such, we cannot confidently proclaim its universality across time and cultures. However, much of our discussion of the social construction of jealousy throughout history alludes not to the personal emotional experience of jealousy, but to its evaluation by society and its acceptance or rejection of jealousy as a valid part of the romantic experience. Thus, our interpretation of our feelings and the degree to which we exhibit them may be culturally determined; however, the experience of a jealous emotional reaction may be more universal.

In fact, researchers have found support for the belief that jealousy is a universal human experience (Daly, Wilson, & Weghorst, 1982; Salovey & Rodin, 1985). A survey of over 25,000 *Psychology Today* readers confirmed the prevalence of jealousy across class, gender, and race (Salovey & Rodin, 1985). In other words, it appears as though cultures may vary in their acceptance of jealousy, the sanctioned ways of its expression, and the degree of appropriate emotional display, but the existence of feelings of jealousy has nonetheless been confirmed in people in almost all cultures.

Thus, despite the fact that some cultures may appear, on the surface, to be free of jealousy, the emotion exists, perhaps simply hidden beneath a veneer of social compliance (Daly, Wilson, & Weghorst, 1982). For example, although jealousy is currently maligned in U.S. romance, lovers, whether they admit it or not, still experience jealousy! A survey of marriage counselors revealed that over one-third of their clients sought help for problems related to romantic jealousy (Mullen, 1991). Furthermore, a casual glance at newspaper and magazine articles (see, for example, the story at the beginning of this chapter) reveals countless stories of tragedies stemming from jealousy.

In sum, few if any of us are spared jealousy's grip. And although there are differences throughout history and among cultures in how we evaluate jealousy, there is little doubt that we all have had at least the affective experience of jealousy. However, the question of how jealousy is expressed and how acceptable its expression is is more context dependent. Some cultures and periods in history find us embracing jealousy; whereas other cultures view jealous expressions as untoward and uncouth. Indeed, perhaps due to cases such as O. J. Simpson and other celebrated cases of stalkers-turned-murderers, jealousy today is viewed as a pathology rather than as a sign of love. Although jealousy is widespread, it is not to be confused with envy. What is the difference between the two?

Jealousy and Envy: I Want What I Cannot Have

Some researchers have suggested that envy and jealousy are the same emotion, differing only in intensity (Salovey & Rodin, 1986). However, whereas both envy and jealousy are negative reactions to desiring that which we cannot or do not have, there are subtle differences between them. *Envy* explains the way we feel when we "covet thy neighbor's" possessions (material or immaterial). It is about wanting to have that Pearl Jam compact disc collection that your classmate has, the good grades of your lab partner, the wealth of your affluent acquaintances, your cousin's sports utility vehicle, and the privileges and access of the powerful. Thus, envy is a triadic relationship among the person (A) who wishes to possess an object (C) (i.e., person, commodity, or thing both tangible and intangible) that belongs to another person (B).

Jealousy, on the other hand, stems from fidelity and is an affective reaction to perceived threats to a monogamous relationship. It is the desire to possess a cherished other and the angst we experience when we perceive a threat, real or imagined, to that relationship. In geometric terms, jealousy also can be represented by a triadic relationship among a person (A) who has a romantic relationship with person (B), wherein this relationship is threatened by loss of B to intruder (C).

Thus, if Fred and Linda are lovers, Fred might be envious of Linda's vast collection of old comics. If his mother had not thrown out his boxes of comics, his collection would rival Linda's. On the other hand, Fred might experience jealousy when, at a party, he sees Greg flirting with Linda, and Linda actually seems to be enjoying the attention.

Likewise, threats to Fred's security in the relationship might arise in the following situation. Linda, unlike Fred, enjoys the theater, which she attends regularly with her best friend, Eva. Linda and Eva often engage in long conversations of life and art as well as share many other interests and feelings. Fred feels uneasy about their closeness. Is Fred envious of Linda's relationship with Eva or is it jealousy? Is Fred suffering from some sort of pathology that throws him into agony over any diminution of Linda's attention to him? Better definitions of both envy and jealousy should help answer these questions.

Depending on the model, envy and jealousy are either very similar or dissimilar. Some of the scientific ambiguity is also shared by the general public, as the two terms *envy* and *jealousy* are sometimes used interchangeably (Parrott & Smith, 1993). This confusion might be explained by models, such as Shaver and colleagues' (1987) prototype model, in which both jealousy and envy are subtypes of anger. Similar to emotional intensity models (e.g., Plutchik, 1994), earlier research by Salovey and Rodin (1986) suggested that jealousy is simply a more intense form of envy. However, inasmuch as jealousy is unquestionably and quite frequently a more intense emotional experience than envy, perhaps it is this intensity that clouds the finer qualitative differences between the two (Parrott & Smith, 1993). Consistent with this notion, cognitive approaches to emotions and emotional blend models have found strong evidence that jealousy and envy are in fact two separate emotional experiences. Envy, researchers have found, is characterized by feelings of inferiority, longing, and disapproval; jealousy is constructed from a blend of anger, distrust, anxiety, and fear of loss or rejection (Parrott & Smith, 1993).

Apart from its emotional components, jealousy is commonly defined as the fear of loss of a relationship. But what separates jealousy from sadness or mourning (as well as from envy)? The defining element of jealousy lies in the presence of a *rival*. Romantic rivals are not the only sources of jealousy, however (Parrott, 1991). A woman might feel jealous of the time her husband spends with his parents, a man might feel jealous of his best buddy's new girlfriend, or siblings might experience jealousy over each one's relationship with their parents. Indeed, rivals need not even be human: Fred can be jealous of the extra time Linda has been spending at her new job (Parrott, 1991).

How can a rival's presence be so threatening? A rival's attention to a loved one (or a loved one's attention to something else) can be very devastating because it results in the loss to the jealous person (A) of the "formative attention" (Tov-Ruach, 1980) from the beloved (B). *Formative attention* refers to the type of self-concept–shaping validation and self-verifying feedback we receive from loved ones. Once this attention is lost, we are struck to the core of our identities and suffer this loss grievously.

Further, Parrott (1991) has identified two different types of jealousy: suspicious jealousy and *fait accompli* jealousy. *Suspicious jealousy* arises when a person suspects that formative attention is being deprived them and given to others. The jealous reaction to this threat includes feeling anxious and insecure. *Fait accompli jealousy* occurs when suspicion has turned to certainty; the disappointed partner has lost to the rival. There are three types of reactions to *fait accompli* jealousy. If the jilted partner focuses on the loss of the relationship, feelings of sadness will predominate. If, on the other hand, the person focuses on being alone, anxiety will creep in. And finally, if the person focuses on the betrayal, anger is sure to abound. As mentioned earlier, Hupka's (1984) research revealed very similar results.

These are some of the guises of jealousy. To define it is to know it, but only partially. The following sections investigate the sources of jealousy as well as discuss other indispensable and highly delectable information about this green-eyed monster.

Sources of Jealousy: Theories, Models, and Variables

Various theoretical approaches locate the causes for jealousy in different sources. Culture may again be cited as playing a role in the experience and course of jealousy. Fred might belong to a culture that values passionate lovers and hot-blooded possessiveness. Or, we might ask whether Fred is suffering some sort of pathology. Did he have trouble resolving the Oedipal stage of his development? Is he insecure and possessive? Perhaps it is not Fred so much as the relationship that is causing the problem—perhaps Linda is not holding up her end of the relationship bargain. Is jealousy then rooted in unstable relationships? Perhaps jealousy is the result of both individuals' unique reactions to elements in their relationship, an interaction between the individual and the relationship.

A careful dissection of jealousy-evoking situations reveals the following elements in the emotional equation: the jealous person, his or her partner, their relationship, the rival, the specific incident, and the perception and interpretation of threat. As we shall see, different theories and models have included various combinations of these elements in their explanations of jealousy.

The Jealous Person

> *Dear Abby: Some people may think my problem is silly, but they don't realize how serious it is to me—it's making my life miserable. . . . My problem is jealousy. I am jealous of all other females, and it has made my life pure hell. I am 37 years old and the mother of two children. I have a good husband, if he can manage to live with me. My family and friends, my husband, even my children think I am way overboard with my feelings of jealousy. . . . Please help me. This is not a joke. Jealousy is ruining my life.*
> (Signed) Jealous Julia in Ohio
>
> —"Dear Abby," *Chicago Tribune,* July 7, 1998

Most of us can recall at least one former girlfriend or boyfriend whom we thought insanely jealous and who caused us to vow never again to date someone so clingy and volatile! Does jealousy, like a cancerous defect, lie in the psyche of the individual? Before we explore individual characteristics that may lead to jealousy, it might be helpful to differentiate between chronic and situational (or relational) jealousy (White, 1981). *Chronic jealousy* applies to an individual trait—something inherent to the person that is a long-standing and established way of responding to situations and events. *Situational jealousy,* on the other hand, refers to situations that have the power to evoke jealousy in all of us. The following example of situational jealousy should make the point: If Fred found Linda in the middle of a room full of New Year's Eve revelers, giving passionate kisses away to Greg (before midnight) and in full view of other guests, Fred would not need to be high in dispositional jealousy to be upset. Thus, certain situations can elicit reactions (in this case, jealousy), even in the most dispassionate person.

One tantalizing piece of evidence that supports a dispositional explanation of jealousy comes from Lee's (1988) work on the "colors of love." Researchers have discovered people approach and engage in romantic relationships in six different ways or styles (see Chapter 7). One of these styles is called Mania. This love style is characterized by possessiveness, whereby the manic partner feels desperate and conflicted about love. The manic's intense desire for love is coupled with equally intense feelings of pain, insecurity, and jealousy when lovers are separated (Lee, 1988; Hendrick & Hendrick, 1993). Interestingly, roughly 2 percent of respondents in one study depicted their relationships as consistent with mania (Hendrick & Hendrick, 1993). This occurrence might also suggest a personality type or individual disposition dictating that one falls in love in a particular fashion—one that fosters the experience of pain and jealousy.

Another common cause of jealousy is low self-esteem. This is hardly surprising, as self-esteem has been and continues to be implicated in almost every behavioral explanation from success in school to violent criminal assault in teens, to weight gain and loss, to success in romantic relationships. But what have the data shown? Research on jealousy hints at an interesting relationship between jealousy and self-esteem in which low self-esteem may precede the experience of jealous feelings (e.g., Mullen & Martin, 1994; Salovey & Rodin, 1991; White, 1981) as well as be an outcome or result of jealous experiences (e.g., Bringle, 1991; Mathes, Adams, & Davies, 1985; Peretti & Pudowski, 1997).

With regard to self-esteem as a predisposing condition, many researchers have confirmed the existence of a strong correlation between lowered self-esteem and increased jealousy. For example, data collected from participants in New Zealand revealed that heavy drinkers and those with psychiatric problems (i.e., those who may have low self-esteem) were much more likely than others to experience jealousy in intimate relationships (Mullen & Martin, 1994). Furthermore, surveys collected from readers of a national magazine confirmed the correlation between low global self-esteem in feelings of jealousy (Salovey & Rodin, 1991).

Although many researchers have found support for the relationship between a poor self-image and jealousy, others have not found as strong or convincing support for this thesis (e.g., Buunk, 1982). One problem has to do with the correlational nature of these studies. And in fact, the role of self-esteem in breeding jealousy may be more complex. Buunk, for example, found only a weak correlation between self-esteem and anticipated jealousy in women, and no relationship between these variables for men. Hence, there is obviously much more to explore in painting the picture of jealousy.

Upon reading "Jealous Julia's" complaint in the earlier excerpt, one might wonder whether, in addition to Julia's feelings of personal inadequacy, her "good husband" may inadvertently be adding to her emotional turmoil. Researchers have found that jealousy is correlated to feelings of insecurity about one's relationship (White, 1991). That is, even though we may have great self-esteem and feel that we are highly capable and likeable people, if we doubt the solidity of our relationship, we, too, can be prone to jealousy. Additionally, we have all known people who seem to derive their self-worth from their romantic relationships, and who, in the absence of a romantic relationship, are adrift and desperate. Dependency on our relationships for defining our self-worth makes us especially vulnerable to the threat of loss (Bringle & Buunk, 1986).

Although it is useful to identify personality and relationship characteristics that can lead to jealousy, it tells only part of the story. For example, these types of approaches, separately, are inadequate to describe the dynamics of what happens in different types of relationships composed of different types of partners. We might ask: Would two chronically jealous partners be better than one? What happens to jealous individuals in different situations (e.g., jealousy-provoking versus a neutral situation)? The following models attempt to complete the tale.

Transactional Theory: Considering Person, Relationship, and Situation

The transactional theory of jealousy (Bringle, 1991) provides a more comprehensive account of the jealous experience and goes beyond a simple delineation of how personality and relationship variables can be separately responsible for jealousy. Specifically, it examines how three variables—arousability, commitment, and insecurity—moderate the jealous experience. First, individual differences in jealousy are determined by individual differences in levels of physiological *arousability*. That is, variation in arousal levels translates directly into the intensity and duration of the experience of jealousy. Individuals who are easily aroused have more intense jealous reactions than those lower in physiological arousal. In fact, Bringle and colleagues (Bringle et al., 1979) were among several different researchers who developed rating scales to assess individuals' propensity toward jealousy and its related constructs. (See Figure 11.2 for an example of a measure of chronic jealousy.)

Researchers using the Self-Report Jealousy Scale have not only confirmed chronic, individual differences in jealousy but they have also found that highly jealous individuals have lower self-esteem, lower life satisfaction, greater negativity toward the world, and an external locus of control, and they are more dogmatic and more reactive to threatening events (Bringle, 1991).

The second component of the transactional model, *commitment*, refers to the degree of involvement a person has in the relationship (Bringle, 1991). Clearly, the more involved we are in a relationship, the greater the threat of loss and therefore the greater the jealousy. *Insecurity*, the third element of the model, refers to the level of commitment on the part of our partner. If we perceive our partner to be less involved in the relationship than ourselves, then we should feel insecure. Thus, these three elements combine at three levels—the individual, the relationship, and the situation—to determine the intensity of jealousy experienced. However, according to this view, the individual's dispositional jealousy is of primary

FIGURE 11.2   *Multidimensional Jealousy Scale*

Cognitive component: How frequently do you have the following thoughts?
1. I suspect that X is secretly seeing someone of the opposite sex.
2. I am worried that some member of the opposite sex may be chasing after X.
3. I suspect that X may be attracted to someone else.
4. I suspect that X may be physically intimate with another member of the opposite sex behind my back.
5. I think that some members of the opposite sex may be romantically interested in X.
6. I am worried that someone of the opposite sex is trying to seduce X.
7. I think that X is secretly developing an intimate relationship with someone of the opposite sex.
8. I suspect that X is crazy about members of the opposite sex.

Emotional component: How would you react emotionally to the following?
1. X comments to you on how great looking a particular member of the opposite sex is.
2. X shows a great deal of interest or excitement in talking to someone of the opposite sex.
3. X smiles in a very friendly manner to someone of the opposite sex.
4. A member of the opposite sex is trying to get close to X all the time.
5. X is flirting with someone of the opposite sex.
6. Someone of the opposite sex is dating X.
7. X hugs and kisses someone of the opposite sex.
8. X works very closely with a member of the opposite sex (in school or office).

Behavioral component: How often do you do the following?
1. I look through X's drawers, handbag, or pockets.
2. I call X unexpectedly, just to see if he or she is there.
3. I question X about previous or present romantic relationships.
4. I say something nasty about someone of the opposite sex if X shows an interest in that person.
5. I question X about his or her telephone calls.
6. I question X about his or her whereabouts.
7. I join in whenever I see X talking to a member of the opposite sex.
8. I pay X a surprise visit just to see who is with him or her.

Source: Adapted from S. M. Pfeiffer and P. T. P. Wong, *Journal of Social and Personal Relationships,* 6 (pp. 181–196). Copyright © 1989 by Sage Publications Ltd. Used by permission.

importance. That is, despite considerations of situational influences, the individual's disposition is always weighted most heavily.

Situational influences, then, are important insofar as they moderate the degree to which a particular trait (in this case, jealousy) is expressed or exhibited. For example, comparing the jealous reactions of a single person, across situations, would reveal variations in the degree of jealousy from one situation to the next. Thus, the situation mediates jealous reactions. On the other hand, a comparison of

jealous reactions, across persons, should show that individuals high in dispositional jealousy will always be more jealous, situation by situation, than those
lower in dispositional jealousy. Disposition always reigns supreme over the situation. In fact, Bringle and colleagues (Bringle et al., 1983) found empirical support
for these predictions. However, despite the fact that this might be the perfect profile of one of our jealous romantic partners, situational factors also play a role in
moderating jealousy. And although the transactional model of jealousy incorporates the situation into its explanation, it does so only as a secondary influence to
that of disposition. Let us examine other models of jealousy that address these
other factors more directly.

Cognitive Motivational Approaches to Jealousy

Another paradigm to understanding jealousy is presented by cognitive motivational approaches. These models focus on how the jealous individual perceives
and interprets jealousy-provoking situations and take a more interactionist approach to understanding jealousy. For example, White (1981) suggested that we
can understand jealousy better by investigating people's expectations and beliefs.
Expectations and beliefs are important insofar as they can lead us to interpret the
same situation in a variety of ways. That is, depending on the schema or framework that has been activated, different interpretations can be made. For instance,
returning to our example, if the "helping an acquaintance" schema has been
evoked, Fred would not be jealous of Greg's attention to Linda. If, however, the
"attractive rival" schema is called into play, Fred will feel very threatened by the
same interaction between Linda and Greg. Thus, for White, jealousy describes a
complex process wherein emotions, cognitions, and behaviors are simultaneously
and inextricably involved.

White's (1981) cognitive motivational approach suggests that the interplay
between the individual's disposition and the individual's interpretations of his or
her partner's behavior leads to different types of jealous reactions. White (1981)
developed the Chronic Jealousy Scale (CJS) to assess dispositional variability in
jealousy. The CJS was designed to take global measures of jealousy, gauging the
frequency and intensity of romantic jealousy at the individual level. Thus, this
model suggests individuals differ in reactions to jealousy-evoking situations, with
some people reacting to a broader range of situations with greater magnitudes of
jealousy. That is, people high in dispositional jealousy are more likely to have
more intense experiences of jealousy, to have more frequent jealous reactions, and
to interpret many more situations as jealousy evoking.

Furthermore, individual reactions alone do not explain jealousy; dispositions interact with beliefs. Romantic hopefuls inquire, "Am I good enough to satisfy my partner?" "Am I a good lover?" "Is my partner's love for me as great as
mine?" Thus, jealousy also hinges on whether a person feels inadequate as a romantic partner and/or believes his or her partner does not share the same intensity of love and affection. Thus, if Fred believes that he is not a suitable partner for
Linda and that Linda doesn't love him with the same intensity that he loves her,

then Fred will be liable to experience a great deal of uneasiness, threat, and hence, jealousy.

Similar to the assumptions made by other cognitive motivational theorists, Sharpsteen (Sharpsteen & Kirkpatrick, 1997; Sharpsteen, 1995) proposed that explaining jealousy requires an understanding not only of the individuals but also of their goals and underlying motivations. A person motivated to a maintain a long-term relationship will react to a jealousy-provoking situation very differently from someone whose primary goal is to have a sexual fling over spring break. Once motivation has been established, Sharpsteen (1995) suggested that jealousy results from perceived threat to either the person's self-esteem or to the relationship.

In one study, Sharpsteen (1995) asked participants to imagine themselves in four different jealousy-arousing scenarios. Scenarios differed with regard to two dimensions: whether the characters experienced low or high threats to their self-esteem and whether there was a little or a great deal of threat to the relationship. Sharpsteen found that high levels of both types of threat lead to predictions of higher levels of anticipated jealousy. Indeed, we know that the quality of the romantic relationship can also act as an attributional filter, a lens through which information is screened and interpreted in a variety of ways. In other words, the degree of security and trust we have in the strength and validity of our relationship influence how secure or insecure, and hence how safe or threatened, we feel. In this manner, our feelings about our relationship, not surprisingly, directly affect the degree of threat we perceive, and therefore the intensity of jealousy we experience.

Thus far, we have reviewed theories of jealousy that attribute its source to some or all of the following: the jealous person's disposition, his or her partner, their relationship, and the perceived threat to all of the above. None of the dispositional or cognitive models, however, accounts for the fact that the specific, idiosyncratic characteristics of our rival might also influence the degree of jealousy we experience. Going back to the case of Fred and Linda, we might find that Fred experiences intense jealousy when Greg flirts with Linda, but he has no such feelings when Walter or Ed interact with her. Thus, we turn now to an explanation that includes the third and perhaps most essential angle in the jealousy triad—the rival and the particular threat that different rivals present to the jealous person and his or her relationship.

The "Other" Lover: Rival Characteristics and Jealousy

DeSteno and Salovey (1996) have proposed that jealousy is a type of Self-Evaluation Maintenance (SEM) process in which an integral part of its focus is the characteristics of the rival. Before exploring this approach to jealousy, let us briefly summarize the mechanics of Tesser's SEM model (Tesser, 1988; Erber & Tesser, 1994; Beach et al., 1998). According to Tesser and colleagues, self-evaluation is not equivalent to self-esteem; rather, it is a temporary and specific state of self-estimation—one that fluctuates with changes in the environment and situation. SEM is a social comparison process in which we conduct a self-evaluation, using, as our yardstick, how we stack up to someone else. Tesser (Erber & Tesser, 1994) suggested that we experience threats to our self-evaluation when, compared to close others, we perform more poorly. For example, we would feel the worst if our best friend outscored us on the intimate relationships midterm; however, we would not experience as much angst if a total stranger aced the exam. That is, our self-comparisons take on a different tone when we use close others (e.g., siblings, friends, lovers) as our measure of success.

Furthermore, it is not just any unfavorable comparison that has the capacity to destroy our self-evaluation, but it is unfavorable comparison on dimensions that are personally relevant and meaningful to us that hurt us the most. For example, suppose Fred is the intellectual type. Suppose, further, that his best friend, Chuck, surpasses him in rugby skill, but not at Trivial Pursuit. This would not threaten Fred much (if at all); however, Chuck's superiority at chess would pose a greater threat to Fred's self-evaluation. Thus, activities that are not personally meaningful or relevant do not engage the same type of comparison and do not hold the same kind of peril for our self-appraisal. Being outdone by a close other in a significant arena can lead to feelings of jeopardy, embarrassment, and loss of esteem. In sum, if it is important for Fred to be considered knowledgeable about Trivial Pursuit, then he would most likely be threatened by close friend, Chuck, campus Jeopardy champ. The threat to Fred's self-evaluation would be lessened if (1) he decided that being an expert at Trivial Pursuit is not as important as dressing well, (2) he discovered that Chuck was not such a good friend, or (3) if he found out that Chuck was actually cheating at Trivial Pursuit (stacking the deck to get the easy questions).

Recent work on the SEM model has successfully extended it to include comparisons made in close and romantic relationships (Beach et al., 1998). More than applying this model to close relationships, DeSteno and Salovey (1996) extended it even further to incorporate the jealousy triad. Here, the relevant comparison is between the jealous person and a rival. The comparison has to do with characteristics that are either self-relevant (i.e., the things that make the jealous person feel special and loveable) or qualities that are important to the relationship (i.e., the things that his or her partner admires and finds attractive). In this arena, SEM can predict which rivals will elicit feelings of threat in the jealous person.

To test the SEM model of jealousy, DeSteno and Salovey (1996) asked female and male students to complete a jealousy questionnaire. The questionnaire included a scenario in which participants were asked to imagine that their romantic partner was flirting with someone else at a university party. Participants were then presented with the descriptions of three different rivals whose profiles were varied so that each one excelled in a different domain (e.g., intelligence, athleticism, and popularity). The researchers hypothesized that the most intense jealousy would occur when rivals outshone participants on self-relevant dimensions.

As predicted, the intensity of participants' feelings of jealousy were dependent on their rivals' characteristics; rivals who were superior on self-relevant dimensions were much more threatening than those who were superior on nonrelevant ones. Returning to our example of Fred, SEM can predict which rival (Walter or Ed) is the most intimidating to Fred and his relationship with Linda. We can hypothesize that if Fred's self-concept were reliant on his being viewed as intelligent, then (when it comes to Linda) he would be most threatened by the amorous advances of Walter, the rocket scientist, and less so by the intentions of Ed, the star fullback.

One alternative explanation for DeSteno's and Salovey's (1996) findings might be that the participants were not jealous, but instead were competitive with rivals similar on key attributes. This contention was disproved by likeableness ratings. When evaluated outside the jealousy scenario, participants indicated the greatest degree of liking for rather than competition against the similar rivals. Thus, DeSteno and Salovey concluded that it is the jealousy-provoking situation and not social comparison alone that was responsible for the intense negative emotional experiences.

It seems, then, that an explanation of jealousy needs to include all critical elements (i.e., the person and situation, threat to self or relationship, characteristics of partner and rival) in order to account accurately for the rise and fall of this troublesome emotion. The SEM model of jealousy extends our understanding of jealousy to include the rival in addition to the person and situation. Before we discuss ways of coping with jealousy, one more dimension of romantic jealousy needs to be addressed. Another source of jealousy, an individual one, has recently received much attention in the literature: gender. What is it about men and women that causes them to find different elements of a situation threatening, and why do they react differently to that threat?

Gender Differences in Jealousy

As is true of many psychological phenomena, gender differences in jealousy can be explained at many different levels. As stated elsewhere in this book, the origins of gender-related differences are hard to pin down. Are gender differences biologically, physiologically, and hormonally determined? Or do they stem from cultural and parental differences in upbringing? Although this probably sounds like a middle-of-the-road compromise (perhaps even a cop-out), gender differences are most probably due to a complex interaction and interplay among all these variables and more.

The epigenetic view of development suggests that what we see as the outcome of human development is the result of a complete and ongoing interaction between nature and nurture. Who we are is completely determined by our physiology and just as completely determined by our environment. It is the transforming interaction between both these factors that leads to our growth and evolution. Let us keep this in mind as we explore the sources of gender differences in romantic jealousy.

Gender and Reactions to Infidelity

Oddly enough, although our admonishment to recognize the validity of multiple levels of explanation seems sound and reasonable beyond question, researchers investigating gender differences in reactions to infidelity have been skirmishing over the bragging rights to this area of scholarship. The gender difference in question involves reactions to different types of infidelity: emotional versus sexual misconduct. Generally, men tend to experience greater jealousy when their partner has engaged in sexual rather than emotional infidelity. Women, on the other hand, tend to be more jealous when their partner has been emotionally rather than sexually untrue (Buss et al., 1992). The debate over the source of this difference has pitted factions that believe gender differences are caused by genetic pressures handed down to us by our forebears against those who propose that gender differences are bestowed on us by the society in which we live. We will present three different approaches to understanding gender differences in romantic jealousy, starting with distal theories and concluding with a review of proximal explanations.

Evolutionary psychologists have fueled a burgeoning of alternative explanations that are exciting and challenging. According to this perspective, different evolutionary pressures on men (low investment, sperm providers) and women (high investment, baby producers and primary caregivers) translate into different behavioral goals. The vestiges of these drives have in turn trickled down to create the gender differences we see in our current social behavior (Buss et al., 1992; Buunk et al., 1996). Thus, let us see how this perspective explains gender differences in reactions to infidelity.

At least three suppositions lay the groundwork for the evolutionary explanation: (1) We are motivated to perpetuate our gene pools through procreation, (2) men and women have different degrees of investment in intimate relationships, and (3) with regard to parental certainty, women, as childbearers, have maternal certainty, whereas men experience varying degrees of paternal *uncertainty*. These factors are responsible for the different evolutionary pressures on men and women. Because men cannot be sure that they actually fathered their wives' babies, sexual fidelity is of primary importance. That is, only through sexual monogamy can men guarantee that the child is theirs.

Women, on the other hand, know that no matter whose sperm, half the genetic material in their offspring will be theirs. However, although genetic certainty is guaranteed, women have a higher investment in the entire childbearing process. Not only is bearing offspring more physically challenging for women (e.g., they're out of the mating, dating, procreating cycle for at least a year) but also the early years of childrearing are labor and energy intensive. Women are especially vulnerable during this time and need the assurance of male support in terms of economic as well as emotional investment.

These differences in how men and women approach romantic relationships lead to obvious differences in what men and women find important. Paternal uncertainty, for example, leads to the demand for female sexual fidelity wherein men jealously guard their chances of fathering *their* child. On the other hand, for men, sexual fidelity, though expected, is not expected to the same degree. One of the reasons may be that sexual infidelity has greater payoffs for men than for women: The more partners a man has, the greater the probability that he will sire many and more genetically diverse offspring. For women, the one-shot nature of getting pregnant and the long-term investment in childbearing and childrearing cause them to value emotional fidelity. Emotional commitment and loyalty will ensure them support through the difficult months of childbearing and child-rearing.

Buss and colleagues (e.g., Buss et al., 1992; Buunk et al, 1996) have conducted several tests of these predictions. In a forced-choice paradigm, participants were asked to imagine that their romantic partner had lost interest in their relationship and had started a relationship with someone else. Participants were then asked to indicate whether they would be more upset by imagining their partner developing a close emotional bond with someone else or by imagining their partner engaging in a passionate sexual encounter with their rival. Consistent with evolutionary predictions, men more so than women indicated that they were most distressed by imagining their partner having wild, unfettered sex with another guy. Women, on the other hand, were more distressed by the possibility of emotional infidelity on the part of their mates.

The evolutionary perspective provides a compelling explanation for social behaviors; however, it is difficult to rule out alternative explanations completely. For example, when the authors present the Buss scenario to their students, invariably, one or two sheepishly but resolutely protest that both types of infidelity would be equally disturbing to them. Thus, perhaps one alternative explanation might be that the forced-choice component of the research paradigm leads to the differential responses by men and women. Further, although evolutionary pressures may be at work in the jealousy process, they are by no means the only ones. Other researchers have uncovered more proximal explanations—explanations that have their antecedents in the psychological and cultural origins of gender differences. One of these hypotheses, for example, suggests that some gender differences originate in men's and women's socialization in their approaches or orientations toward sexual behaviors.

Generally, men more so than women have an unrestricted sociosexual orientation wherein sexual encounters are largely independent of emotional commitment or intimacy (Simpson & Gangestad, 1992). Conversely, women are more likely to maintain a restricted sociosexual orientation in which sexual interactions occur more exclusively as an expression of love, emotional closeness, and intimacy. These divergent sociosexual orientations lead to different prerequisites and interpretations of sexual encounters. That is, men can engage in sex without love, whereas women can be in love without engaging in sex (Harris & Christenfeld, 1996). One of the implications of this pattern of socialization into different sociosexual orientations is that men and women may find different types of infidelities more or less threatening.

This is precisely what many researchers have found (DeSteno & Salovey, 1996; Harris & Christenfeld, 1996). That is, the difference in gender orientation toward sex leads to different attributions for infidelity: Men and women interpret the meaning of unfaithfulness differently. As Harris and Christenfeld suggested in their "double-shot" hypothesis, certain types of infidelity are more troublesome than others because they signify a double-shot of unfaithfulness. Furthermore, this double-shot of infidelity has different implications for men and women. Supposedly, men are supremely bedeviled by women's sexual infidelity because sexual unfaithfulness in women necessarily implies emotional infidelity. Conversely for men, who engage in intercourse without love, having sex with other women represents just one type of infidelity—sexual. However, men's emotional unfaithfulness is likely to signal that not only is he in love but he is also sexually untrue: a double dose of infidelity.

In a survey of college students, Harris and Christenfeld (1996) first asked participants to respond to the usual Buss queries with regard to sexual and emotional infidelity. However, they also asked their participants to indicate the degree to which they believed one type of infidelity inferred the other. As predicted, women believed that, for men, love was very likely to imply sex, whereas sex was less likely to involve love. The pattern was largely reversed for men; they believed that sex, for their girlfriends, was more likely to imply love, but not the opposite (see Table 11.1).

Thus, several levels of explanation exist for the phenomenon of gender differences in fidelity. It does not seem that one would preclude the other; however, there also does not seem, at the current time, to be any clear way of integrating the two explanations presented here. Nonetheless, research on the perceptions and interpretations of infidelity continue to push our understanding of relationships and social behavior in new and exciting directions. Let us explore other gender differences in response to jealousy.

TABLE 11.1   *Mean Ratings of Participants' Beliefs about the Degree to Which One Type of Infidelity Implies Another for Members of the Opposite Sex*

Participant Gender	*Sex Implies Love for Members of Opposite Sex*	*Love Implies Sex for Members of Opposite Sex*
Females	2.70	3.75
Males	3.43	3.32

Note: Scores were obtained from a 5-point Likert scale, from 1 ("Not at all") to 5 ("Very much").

Source: C. R. Harris and N. Christenfeld, "Gender, Jealousy, and Reason," *Psychological Science, 7* (pp. 364–366). Copyright © 1996 by Blackwell Publishers. Reprinted by permission.

Gender and Perceptions of Threat

Researchers have found that not only do the genders have divergent perceptions and interpretations of infidelity but also that men and women differ in what they find threatening about a potential rival (DeSteno & Salovey, 1996; Nadler & Dotan, 1992). Indeed, it seems that among other things, men's jealousy is driven by their concern to protect their egos, whereas women's focus is on protecting their relationships (Nadler & Dotan, 1992). DeSteno and Salovey (1996) found very similar effects in their work on the SEM model of jealousy (discussed earlier). Men, as you may recall, were most imperiled by rivals who were exceptional on dimensions important to their self-definitions. In our example, Fred, for whom intelligence is vital to his self-definition, would feel threatened by Walter, who is as intellectually aggressive as Fred. Women, on the other hand, were found to be most threatened by rivals in whom they perceived characteristics important to their partners. Thus, although athleticism might be important to Linda with respect to her own self-concept, she would not feel threatened by rival Kathy's superior athleticism nor by rival Lei's popularity. Instead, Linda would feel most imperiled by Naomi's extraordinary intellectual abilities—abilities she believes Fred desires in a romantic partner.

Evolutionary psychologists might attribute these differences to evolutionary pressures. Men's desire to gain paternity certainty would drive them to be concerned about their status relative to their rivals, thereby propelling them to be the most dominant and attractive choice to guarantee sexual access. Women's motivation, according to this view, would be to keep their mate's affection and therefore support. In order to be successful in doing so, women must be highly attuned to what their mate finds pleasing and desirable in a wife. These explanations may make sense, but they are also disturbingly *post hoc*. Indeed, the exegesis presented here represents our deduction based on evolutionary assumptions.

Another explication for men's and women's response to threat lies in gender differences in self-esteem. Josephs, Markus, and Tafarodi (1992) have found that male self-esteem, as dictated by our socialization, is connected to achievement orientation. Males gain personal stature and esteem through individuating themselves and attaining success in culturally dictated pursuits. Female self-esteem, through socialization, is built through attachment and making connections with others. It follows, then, that just as self-esteem is derived from different spheres, what is threatening to one person is not as threatening to another. Hence, we have the divergent focus on rival characteristics.

Gender and Reactions to Jealousy

We know that some of the reactions to jealousy are anxiety, loneliness, sadness, and anger. However, the passage of time has altered our acceptance and expression of jealousy. Perhaps this transformation in our view of jealousy also corresponds to a change in how we react to it. In 1978, Shettel-Neuber, Bryson, and Young showed men and women videotaped episodes of a jealousy-provoking situation. Men viewed a videotape in which a male attempted to steal a female away from another male. Women saw a video with a similar scenario, except with a female playing the part of the interloper. The researchers asked participants to put themselves in the place of the person whose relationship was jeopardized by the rival and then to indicate how they would feel.

Shettel-Neuber, Bryson, and Young (1978) found several gender differences in reactions to the videotapes. Men were more likely than women to express anger, especially with themselves. Further, they claimed that they would get drunk or high and verbally threaten the intruder. Yet, at the same time, men said that they would feel flattered by their rivals' attention to their partner and would be aroused by their partner. Conversely, women were more likely than men to be depressed and engage in self-blame. They indicated that they would cry when alone, but then try to put on their best face in public. That is, they would try to make themselves more attractive to their partner and attempt to appear insouciant about the rival.

A slightly different picture arises from de Weerth's and Kalma's (1993) research (see Figure 11.3). They found that Dutch women more than Dutch men experience stronger feelings of anger in response to sexual jealousy. Further, women were also more likely to react to the threat of betrayal aggressively. In fact, women were more likely to respond to threat by reciprocating with verbal and physical aggression. Interestingly, similar to their 1970s counterparts, men in the 1990s indicated that they would be more likely to react to jealousy and threat by getting drunk. Indeed, another recent study involving U.S. men and women yielded very similar results to that of the Dutch sample: Women reacted with greater anger than did men to scenarios of sexual jealousy (Strachan & Dutton,

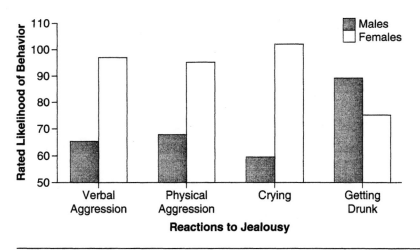

FIGURE 11.3 *Sex Differences in Reactions to Jealousy*
Source: Based on de Weerth and Kalma (1993).

1992). Although it is difficult to draw direct and reliable comparisons between these studies, they hint at the tantalizing possibility of longitudinal changes in reactions to jealousy.

Coping with the Green-Eyed Monster

Dear Jealous Julia: Jealousy is no laughing matter—it can make you and those around you miserable. . . . Until you learn to feel more secure about yourself, you will probably continue to have these feelings. Short-term therapy, focused specifically on this issue, will help you recognize that your feelings are not based in reality, and will give you useful tools to manage them. You may have to work hard to conquer this, as any counselor will tell you, but it can be done. (Signed) Abigail Van Buren
—*Chicago Tribune,* July 27, 1998

Logically speaking, discerning the source of jealousy would be one of the most effective ways of dealing with it. And, as we have seen, there are several potential sources and combinations of variables that may lead to jealousy: threats to the person, to his or her partner, and/or to their relationship, and characteristics of the rival or the situation. Many, like Abigail Van Buren, counsel us to repair our self-esteem. Brehm (1992), for example, suggested that jealousy represents selfishness and self-centeredness rather than love for and dependence on our partner. Hence, we should reduce jealousy by increasing our own self-worth rather than by relying on our relationships for self-value. Yet, even though these admonitions sound practical and attractive in their simplicity, they overlook the intricate web that is jealousy—the ambiguity of its emotional and social dimensions, and the way that relationships become entwined, enmeshed, codependent, and qualitatively changed.

In fact, clinicians, recognizing the volatile and multifarious nature of jealousy, suggest that participants in jealous triads are much more intertwined than one might at first suspect (Pam & Pearson, 1994). Helping a jealous person cope with his or her feelings might include, if one were to take a systems approach, a full consideration of the psychological state, needs, and motivations of not only the client but also of the (perhaps) cheating partner and the invading rival. The dynamic between these three participants can be extremely complex and equally resistant to change, enmeshed inextricably with one another.

Pam and Pearson (1994) offered clinical examples of couples who, even after the termination of their relationships, were unable to completely rid themselves of their former partners or their ties to the relationship. Although at least the psychological presence of the ex-partner and rival are necessary for closure and an eventual healing, the third wheel is not so easily discarded. In one example, a man left his wife for his mistress. After several years, the former mistress pleaded with the man's former wife to take him back. (She refused.) Incredibly enough, the man believed the women were still fighting over him, not quite realizing that they were now fighting to get rid of him (Pam & Pearson, 1994).

However, to exhort us to cast off jealousy entirely assumes that it is an utterly useless, unwanted, and undesirable emotion. This, of course, although consistent with the current societal stance to deny jealous impulses and avoid these types of situations rather than to confront them (Stearns, 1989), goes against what we know about the emotional complexity of jealousy. How, then, should we handle this problematic emotion? A blanket recommendation suggesting that jealousy should be banished from our relationships and our hearts is clearly inadequate. More useful advise might be extracted from our understanding of the different types of jealousy.

Individuals, such as "Jealous Julia," who suffer from chronic jealousy would definitely benefit from Abby's advice and other strategies to help them to become self-reliant (Salovey & Rodin, 1988). It would serve these types of chronic, insanely jealous individuals well to gain self-confidence and independence, and to realize that they can survive and flourish with or without a romantic relationship. These types of individuals should be helped to recognize their uniqueness, worth, and value as human beings.

On the other hand, this strategy would not work for individuals caught in the glare of jealousy-provoking situations, nor for those who are trapped (perhaps unknowingly) in a bad relationship. In fact, if your partner is cheating on you, isn't jealousy an appropriate reaction to this violation of your trust, the betrayal of your love? Furthermore, wouldn't the absence of jealousy, under this scenario, be more "abnormal" than its manifestation? For to discover a lover's infidelity and to experience no threat or fear of loss might beg St. Augustine's question: He who is not jealous does not love. Thus, increasing one's feelings of self-reliance and worth may help in recovering from jealousy, but this strategy shouldn't be used as a bandage to obscure the truth about either an unworthy partner or a doomed relationship. Just as pain serves as an indication that we have suffered physical harm, perhaps we should accept jealousy's role as an indication that a deeper ailment may be afflicting the relationship. Finally, denying our jealous feelings may backfire on us, for, according to work by Wegner and colleagues (e.g., Wegner & Erber, 1992), suppression can actually lead to a magnification of the unwanted thought. Further, together with Pennebaker's (1990) work on communication, we should strive to acknowledge our feelings of jealousy, find a helpful friend or counselor who cares to listen to our problems, and take positive strides to address the source of the jealousy.

An Attachment Approach to Jealousy

One more theory must be addressed in order to understand fully how to cope with jealousy. According to recent research (Sharpsteen & Kirkpatrick, 1997), our experience of jealousy, and therefore our reactions to jealous episodes, differ according to our attachment style. The attachment model has been applied to adult relationships (discussed elsewhere in this text) and is offered here as an approach to integrating data on how we experience and react to a threatening interloper.

Sharpsteen and Kirkpatrick (1997) suggested that both jealousy and attachment systems are mechanisms for maintaining relationships. Just as the attachment system is activated by separation from one's primary caregiver, jealousy is triggered by the threat of the loss of a romantic partner to an intruder. Thus, if romantic partners are viewed as attachment figures, we should find the activation of the attachment system foretelling jealous reactions. Furthermore, the types of jealous experiences that we have differ fundamentally depending on whether we are securely or insecurely attached.

Sharpsteen and Kirkpatrick (1997) found that attachment style predicted the intensity and frequency of jealous reactions as well as the cognitive and behavioral responses to jealousy. In their study, Sharpsteen and Kirkpatrick asked men and women to describe how they usually reacted to jealousy experiences in general as well as to recall and evaluate two specific jealous episodes. Participants also completed Hazan and Shaver's (1987) attachment style questionnaire and White's (1981) Chronic Jealousy Scale. The investigators found that the jealousy experience of anxiously attached men and women was dominated by feelings of fear and sadness. Further, anxious lovers felt inferior and, although angry, were careful to suppress expression of their anger. This pattern of emotions fits the anxious person's world and self-view. These are the types of romantic partners who view themselves as inadequate and unworthy. Their poor self-image leads anxiously attached lovers to harbor intense fears of abandonment and rejection.

In a similar vein, because avoidantly attached people expect rejection by close others, they approach relationships with hesitation and strive to maintain psychological and physical distance from romantic partners. Likewise, the jealousy episodes of avoidant lovers should be colored by their expectation that their relationships will fail. In essence, the emotional distance favored by avoidant lovers almost guarantees the failure of reconciliation, and thus jealousy-provoking situations should lead to feelings of doubt and sadness. Sharpsteen and Kirkpatrick confirmed these predictions, finding the avoidant experience of jealousy to be dominated by sadness.

Finally, because securely attached lovers approach their relationships with confidence and expect them to endure, their experience of jealousy should also reflect this orientation. Indeed, the jealous experiences of secure lovers reflected the least of amount of sadness and was dominated by feelings of anger and betrayal. Unlike anxiously attached individuals, secure lovers did not experience feelings of inferiority or self-doubt.

Reactions to jealousy situations were also consistent with attachment style. Securely attached individuals directed their considerable anger directly toward their partner and worked to maintain and improve their relationship. Avoidants, on the other hand, directed their anger and blame toward their rival. They also seemed to lend more importance to maintaining their self-esteem. Finally, anxiously attached individuals reacted to jealousy-provoking situations by focusing their anger inward and blaming themselves. However, unlike the avoidant lovers, anxiously attached participants did not show concerns about self-esteem maintenance.

In sum, Sharpsteen and Kirkpatrick's (1997) attachment approach to jealousy provides us with an organized way of predicting the intensity and frequency of jealous reactions based on attachment type, the type of cognitive and emotional experience these different types of lovers will have, and how they will react behaviorally to the intrusion. This knowledge is not only theoretically exciting but it can also be a powerful clinical tool.

Summary

Issues. One of the primary issues in jealousy research as well as in our everyday experience of it has to do with social evaluation of this emotion. We have seen how the relevance, significance, and acceptance of both fidelity as well as jealousy have fluctuated over time and across cultures. Further, as adherence to fidelity increases, so too does jealousy.

We fine-tuned our definition of jealousy, differentiated jealousy from envy, and identified different types of jealousy (e.g., suspicious and *fait accompli* jealousy). Further, researchers also suggest that we consider the emotional composition of jealousy as well as the difference between chronic and relational jealousy.

In addition to our consideration of the source or causes of jealousy, researchers have found many gender differences in the experience and expression of jealousy. Among the areas of dissimilarity are reactions to infidelity, the type of rival that men and women find threatening, and reactions to jealousy. Finally, we examined suggestions for how to cope with jealousy. Some of the issues inherent in coping go back to our earlier discussion of the social acceptability of jealousy and the place of passion and reason in our lives.

Theory. Several different models of emotions explore the nature of jealousy. Shaver and colleagues' prototype model suggests that jealousy is a subtype of anger, whereas others propose jealousy is a blend of emotions. Cognitive appraisal approaches contend that jealousy is a *bona fide* emotion and map the nuances of the jealous experience.

Different theories of jealousy locate its source in a variety of causes. Bringle's (1991) transactional theory of jealousy proposes that jealousy arises from the interplay between the individual and the situation. Cognitive motivational approaches, on the other hand, emphasize the types of attributions we make in jealousy-provoking situations. DeSteno and Salovey's (1996) SEM approach to jealousy focuses not on the deficiencies of the individual or the relationship, but on the interaction between rival characteristics and the jealous person's self-evaluation. Finally, a more controversial approach to examining jealousy comes from evolutionary approaches. We saw how the evolutionary perspective explains gender differences in sexual infidelity. Harris and Christenfeld provide a more proximal explanation for these differences in their double-shot hypothesis.

Finally, we end this chapter with a discussion of Sharpsteen and Kirkpatrick's attachment model of jealousy. Its power and elegance lies in its ability to predict, based on attachment style, the intensity and frequency of jealousy reactions as well as the nuances in the different types of reactions to jealousy-provoking situations.

Research.   Several experiments clarified the source and causes of jealousy. First, Salovey and Rodin (1985) surveyed over 25,000 readers of a national magazine to determine the prevalence of jealousy. Sharpsteen (1995) asked participants to imagine how characters in a story would feel about a romantic rival in order to determine the causes of jealousy: threats to their self-esteem and threats to their relationship. Jealous reactions to rival characteristics were uncovered by DeSteno and Salovey's (1996) examination of participants' responses to imagining their partners with rivals differing in competence.

Studies investigating reactions to jealousy revealed that men and women have different reactions to jealousy situations (Shettel-Neuber, Bryson, & Young, 1978). Finally, Sharpsteen and Kirkpatrick (1997) showed how different attachment styles lead to differences in how we react to threats to romantic relationships. Their studies provide us with a fresh understanding of the dynamics of attachment and jealousy.

12

Relationship Violence and Abuse

Michael Jones was shot in the face as he slept in his Bloomingdale home in February. When he recovered, he filed for divorce from his alleged assailant, Ann, his wife of 29 years. Police said that early Sunday Ann Jones used a more powerful handgun, and this time her estranged husband did not survive. . . . The first shooting took place . . . in the family home. . . . Four days earlier, the couple had discussed a divorce, according to Michael Jones' attorney. . . . After spending several days in the hospital, Michael Jones filed for divorce and obtained an order of protection. In his testimony seeking the order of protection, Michael Jones said he believed his wife was going to kill him and (his son) and burn their home. He also predicted that once Ann Jones learned about the protection order he was seeking, she would become "enraged and become physically abusive and try to kill me again."

—Chicago Tribune, August 25, 1998

When we think of violence and victimization, many of us believe that it is something that happens among strangers or acquaintances in faraway places. Upon entering the new millenium, the mugging in a dark alley, the high school massacre, and the gang-related drive-by shooting have become the prototypes of violence in our culture. However, there is mounting evidence that, for women at least, the most dangerous place is the home, and her most likely assailant is her domestic partner. Estimates based on representative samples suggest that up to 4 million women are *severely* assaulted (punched, kicked, beaten, threatened with a gun or knife) by their male partners each year (Straus & Gelles, 1990; Straus, Gelles, & Steinmetz, 1980). Between 21 and 34 percent of all women will be physically assaulted by an intimate male during their lifetime (Browne, 1993). One survey (Straus & Gelles, 1990) revealed that one-eighth of the husbands who had been interviewed admitted to having carried out one or more acts of violence against their spouse just during the 12 months prior to the survey. More than half of all women murdured between 1980 and 1985 were the victims of their domestic partners (Browne & Williams, 1989). Estimates based on shelter populations, hospitals, and court records paint an even more dramatic picture of the scope of the problem. For example, the National Crime Survey for the period between 1973 and 1975 indicates that 97 percent of assaults in the family were assaults on wives.

Needless to say, relationship violence is not a uniquely American issue. Instead, judging from recent data collected in a number of countries around the world, violence against women (by their male partners) seems to be a universal problem. For example, in 1996, Boris Yeltsin's advisor on women's issues announced that 14,000 women in Russia are killed each year by their domestic partners (Horne, 1999). In Japan, where relationships between spouses are extremely traditional, a convenience sample of roughly 800 women revealed a stunning 59 percent who had experienced some type of physical violence (Kozu, 1999). Moreover, because the majority of Japanese wives are financially dependent, they tend to stay in abusive marriages and endure physical violence over a long period of time (Nihon Bengoshi Rengokai, 1996). Somewhat closer to home, a random sample of women in Nicaragua revealed that 52 percent had experienced some form of relationship violence (Ellsberg et al., 1999).

These prevalence numbers are startling, and, if anything, they may underestimate the scope of the problem. Even though many studies conducted in the United States derive their estimates from probability samples, others rely on convenience samples in which women of color, the very poor, the homeless, and those who do not speak English are underrepresented. But even true probability samples ultimately gather their data from those who are home when the interviewers call, who are willing to talk to them, and, perhaps most importantly, who are willing to report having been assaulted. Regardless of what the actual numbers may be, physical assault against women perpetrated by their partners represents the most dramatic and perhaps most dangerous form of relationship violence. It is one type of abuse that also includes neglect, verbal put-downs, intense criticism, intimidation, restraint of normal activities and freedoms, and denial of access to resources (e.g., Pagelow, 1984; Walker, 1979). And although it can be directed at anyone in the relationship, including children and the elderly, domestic partners are its most common victims. Of course, any discussion of domestic violence should necessarily include sexual aggression, as well, including sexual harassment, along with date rape and marital rape, even though researchers interested in studying the causes and consequences of physical assault have rarely included sexual aggression.

Relationship Violence: Its Definition and Measurement

At first glance, to define relationship violence seems like a silly endeavor. After all, physical acts such as punching, shoving, kicking, and so on seem like obvious signs of violence and abuse. However, if we chose a number of women or children at random and asked them if they had been subjected to violent behavior from their partners or parents, few would probably say yes, even though several of them may have been subjected to some form of physical abuse.

The problem is that violent behavior can be interpreted in many ways. Those on the giving end may believe that a slap in the face is a form of disciplining, and those on the receiving end may interpret a shove as an expression of nothing more than temporary frustration. The presence or absence of physical injury is fraught with a set of different problems. Some victims may be subjected to consistent and prolonged violence at levels that never result in bruises or visits to emergency rooms. Others may be subjected to occasional yet extremely violent behavior resulting in severe physical injury. The bottom line is that we cannot define domestic violence through intent to harm, frequency, or severity of injury. Instead, whether or not it occurs in a relationship is a matter of what actual physical acts are or have been committed.

Some researchers maintain that relationship violence comes in two distinct forms (Johnson, 1995). One form of violence stems form patriarchical traditions that give men the right to control their wives. In families marked by such *patriarchical terrorism* (Johnson, 1995), violence occurs, on average, more than once a week and escalates in seriousness over time. The violence is almost exclusively initiated by the male partner, whose main motivation is a desire to exercise general control over his female partner. Patriarchical terrorism is not limited to physical violence; men who wish to control their partners have a large number of options that they can use either by themselves or in combination with others (Pence & Paymar, 1993). A graphic representation of these options is depicted in Figure 12.1. Even though many of these tactics do not contain elements of physical violence, the patriarchical terror they create is nonetheless violent.

A second form of relationship violence is not so much the product of patriarchy. Instead, *common couple violence* (Johnson, 1995) refers to the less gendered processes by which conflict escalates into occasional violence. Unlike the violence inherent in patriarchical terrorism, common couple violence rarely escalates over time and generally does not have life-threatening outcomes for its victims.

The most frequently used measures to assess relationship violence are primarily designed to tap into common couple violence. The Conflict Tactics Scale (CTS) (Gelles, 1979; Straus & Gelles, 1986), which we will discuss in more detail in Chapter 13, contains a subscale for physical violence. Five items (throwing something, pushing, grabbing, shoving, and slapping) are considered indications of *minor* violence. Seven items (kicking, biting or hitting with a fist, hitting with an object, beating up, threatening with a weapon, using a weapon, and choking) comprise the *severe* violence subscale.

In general, the CTS does a good job of determining whether violence has occured in a relationship; however, it also has a number of shortcomings. Because it was initially designed to be a measure of how people respond to conflict, it asks respondents to indicate the extent to which the behaviors occurred as a result of a conflictual situation. Consequently, it may do a less-than-adequate job measuring violence that is not a result of conflict, such as patriarchical terrorism. Conflict is a sufficient cause for violence but it is by no means a necessary one. In other words, violence can come about for many reasons. Thus, by tying the measure to conflict, instances of violence caused by something other than conflict may go unreported. Furthermore, the CTS gives little consideration to the seemingly obvious fact that violent acts committed by men against women often have different implications than acts of violence committed by women against men. On average, men tend to be larger and stronger than women, and consequently the same violent act may be more or less severe. In other words, a man's shove may be just as severe as a woman's kick.

To remedy these and other problems with measuring physical violence in a relationship, Marshall (1992a, 1992b) developed separate measures to assess the violence against women and men. The Severity of Violence Against Women Scale (SVAWS) measures male-to-female violence on four dimensions: symbolic violence, threats of mild violence, threats of moderate violence, and threats of severe violence. In the Severity of Violence Against Men Scale (SVAMS), symbolic violence is not a separate dimension, and the assignment of behaviors to the various

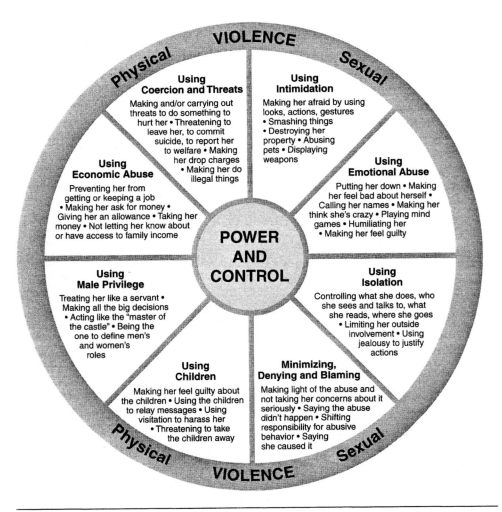

FIGURE 12.1 *The Power and Control Wheel*

Source: Michael P. Johnson, "Patriarchal Terrorism and Common Couple Violence: Two Forms of Violence against Women," *Journal of Marriage and the Family, 57* (2). Copyrighted 1995 by the National Council on Family Relations, 3989 Central Ave. NE, Suite 550, Minneapolis, MN 55421. Reprinted by permission.

classifications of violence is different to give due consideration to the unique ways in which women can be violent against their male partners. Unfortunately, even though the SVAWS and the SVAMS have some advantages over the CTS, they are too recent to have been used in research. Regardless of how one measures relationship violence and abuse, however, their prevalence gives rise to at least three important questions: What are the consequences of relationship violence on its victims, perpetrators, and the relationship itself? What causes violence in relationships? What, if anything, can be done to reduce the level of relationship violence?

Consequences of Relationship Violence

Violent victimization has numerous and often grave physical and psychological consequences. Obviously, being subjected to even mild forms of violence can result in *direct* physical injury. Typical injuries range from bruises, cuts, black eyes, concussions, and broken bones, to permanent injuries such as damage to joints, scars, and loss of hearing or vision. In some cases, the injuries sustained may not be limited to the victimized woman. The 1985 National Family Violence Survey revealed that one-third of victimized women had been physically assaulted while they were pregnant (Gelles, 1988). In addition, there are indications that violent victimization may also have *indirect* physical consequences. Extrapolating from rape victims, those subjected to violence report more symptoms of illness and visit their physicians twice as often as women who were not victimized (Browne & Williams, 1989). Furthermore, victims of relationship violence are likely to engage in a number of negative health behaviors, such as smoking, alcohol use, and failure to use seat belts (Koss, 1993).

Not surprisingly, physical violence causes a great deal of psychological harm to its victims. Growing evidence shows that victims of violence suffer from posttraumatic stress disorder (PTSD), a clinical diagnosis initially reserved for survivors of military combat and natural disasters (Browne, 1993; Koss, 1993). Like combat veterans, survivors of relationship violence often suffer from any or all of the following: fear and terror, flashbacks of the traumatic event, denial and avoidance, loss of memory for the traumatic episode, constricted affect, chronic anxiety and hypervigilance, insomnia, and nightmares (Browne, 1993; Dutton, 1992). Despite these similarities, there is one important difference between combat veterans and battered women. In the case of combat veterans, the traumatic event leading up to PTSD is generally known, thus facilitating the appropriate diagnosis. However, battered women do not receive a Purple Heart, and mental health professionals rarely screen for relationship violence. As a result, symptoms are often treated without considering the underlying cause. And although prescribing tranquilizers for a woman who complains about sleeplessness may take care of the immediate symptoms of insomnia, tranquilizers do little in terms of alleviating the conditions that brought on the sleeplessness in the first place (Browne, 1993; Herman, 1992).

Causes of Relationship Violence

The extraordinarily high prevalence of relationship violence and the realization of the grave consequences for its victims has resulted in several important initiatives. In the early 1990s, the American Psychological Association established a task force to conduct research on possible intervention strategies aimed at decreasing relationship violence of any kind. In 1993, the U.S. Senate passed legislation that treats violence against women as civil rights violations, thus rendering it equivalent to hate crimes based on gender. Of course, any attempts to resolve the problem of relationship violence ultimately hinge on finding its underlying cause. In other words, if we are to find ways to get men to abstain from subjecting women to violence, we have to understand what compels them to do this in the first place.

Common Beliefs and Realities

Speculations about the underlying causes of violence against women have been around for some time. They can be found in the psychological literature as well as in advice columns, daytime talk shows, and made-for-TV movies. Depictions of relationship violence in these media revolve around a number of more or less interrelated themes. Many people believe that violence is something that happens to other people, mostly those with a lower socioeconomic standing. Very little evidence supports such a claim, however. In fact, one study that looked at relationship violence in families of varying incomes (Makepeace, 1987) found that violence occurred just as frequently in high-income families as it did in low-income families. According to Marshall and Vitanza (1994), one reason for our perception that relationship violence is more likely to occur in low-income families has to do with differences in the living conditions between those with and without wealth. A neighbor is more likely to respond to violence when it occurs on the other side of an apartment wall than when it occurs in a home that is several hundred feet away. Thus, rather than reflecting true population differences, any variations in relationship violence among families of diverse income levels is likely the result of a reporting bias.

A related belief about relationship violence holds that its victims enable their abusers by not telling anyone about the violence. However, several studies of dating relationships among undergraduate students (e.g., Olday & Wesley, 1988; Pirog-Good & Stets, 1989) indicate that they tell others about dating violence quite openly. Nationally, the picture looks a little bleaker. One study indicates that women, not surprisingly, tell others (friend, family member, police) about being victimized at a higher rate than men, but the percentages were only 13.4 and 9.4, respectively.

Conventional wisdom holds that relationship violence is something committed primarily by men. But as the newspaper story at the beginning of this chapter illustrates, both men and women inflict and sustain violence. The results of several studies further corroborate this fact. In Straus and Gelles's (1986) national sample of married couples, 11 percent of respondents reported at least one act of husband-to-wife violence, whereas 12 percent reported at least one act of wife-to-husband violence. Similar results were obtained in studies looking at violence in dating relationships (Marshall & Rose, 1987; Pipes & LeBov-Keeler, 1997). Even though the frequency estimates vary widely depending on the question that is asked (e.g., threatened violence versus actual violence), men and women generally inflict violence at a similar rate. Of course, in light of such data, one might ask why there are few, if any, shelters for battered men. One of the reasons has to do with the different ways in which men and women express violence. With the exception of lethal violence, men generally cause more harm to their victims than women. As a result, female victims of relationship violence are generally in more need for places that allow them to avoid violence from their partner.

Much has been made about the role of violence in the family of origin to account for why people would become both physically abusive and endure abuse. Social learning theory (e.g., Bandura, 1965) teaches us that we learn our own behavior from observing relevant models. When it comes to modeling close relationship behavior, our own parents can play an important role. Assuming they stay together, they are the most prevalent and enduring relationship models available to us. Accordingly, watching Dad physically abusing Mom might give little boys the idea that the infliction of violence is part of the male relationship role. By the same token, little girls might come to believe that enduring violence from one's partner is part of their role.

Despite the intuitive appeal of this general hypothesis, there is actually little research that confirms it (Marshall & Vitanza, 1994). This may be due to several things. First, social learning via modeling works best when the model is rewarded for his or her behavior. Although violence may be perceived as leading to positive outcomes for the perpetrator (e.g., getting one's way, asserting dominance), the ramifications for the victim also show its obvious downside, thus clouding the rewarding nature of relationship violence. Second, violence of this nature is often not limited to domestic partners. Frequently, the abuse does not stop with one's partner but instead extends to children, as well, thus providing immediate experiences with the aversive outcomes of relationship violence. Similarly, when women stay in relationships in which they are physically abused, they may not be doing so because it is the type of behavior modeled by their mothers. Rather, this seeming passivity is usually the result of an acquired belief that no matter what one does, it will not affect one's situation for the better (Walker, 1979).

Another popular conception related to violence in relationships is that the occurrence of violence is somewhat cyclical. Walker (1984) described this cycle as consisting of several components. During a period of rising tension, the woman withdraws to avoid any behavior that could anger her partner. This generally does not lead to the desired outcome, but instead to an acute incident of battery in which the batterer unleashes a barrage of physical and verbal violence. Then, after the dust settles, the batterer engages in loving contrition, complete with profuse apologies, affirmations of remorse, acts of kindness, as well as gifts and compliments. Even though the idea of a cycle of violence seems to have some face validity, it may not be a good description of what actually happens. One problem is that Walker's (1984) hypothesis is based on a small sample of women in therapy. Another problem has to do with the intepretation of the seeming cyclical events. Even in the most abusive relationship, violence does not occur on a constant basis. Instead, abusive episodes may be interspersed with periods marked by relative normalcy and even signs of kindness and affection. Consequently, the perceived cycle of violence may simply be a result of such fluctuations in the interactions between the abuser and the abused.

Alcohol and Relationship Violence

The use of alcohol is often implicated as a contributor to relationship violence, partly because there is overwhelming evidence that alcohol can increase all forms of human aggression (Bushman & Cooper, 1990; Ito, Miller, & Pollock, 1996). Alcohol has disinhibiting effects, and thus its consumption by an already hostile partner may loosen any existing constraints on exerting violence. Additionally, alcohol has been shown to lead to myopia (Critchlow, 1983), a condition in which the range of behaviors deemed appropriate in a given situation is narrowed. During periods marked by tension, resentment, and anger, alcohol myopia may restrict the perception of means of resolution other than inflicting violence. Interestingly, little evidence exists for such a straightforward link between alcohol use and relationship violence. Several studies of batterers (Eberle, 1982; Fagan, Barnett, & Patton, 1988) report that alcohol is involved in only about one-third of battering incidents.

Does this mean that alcohol is not responsible for relationship violence? Of course not. To conclude this would be just as mistaken as to conclude that alcohol is not responsible for traffic accidents because the majority of them do not involve driving while intoxicated. Instead, the available data suggest that the relationship between alcohol use and relationship violence is a complex one. Specifically, it appears that alcoholics prone to relationship violence differ from their nonviolent counterparts in several important respects.

First, violent alcoholics tend to become alcoholics at an earlier age than nonviolent alcoholics. They also tend to have a history of antisocial behavior, are more likely to have been arrested, and generally experience a variety of problems associated with drinking. Second, it appears that this type of alcoholism, known as *Type II Alcoholism Syndrome,* is inherited primarily by males (Gondolf & Foster, 1991). Thus, relationship violence is most common among male alcoholics who fit this particular profile (Murphy & O'Farrell, 1994, 1996). Furthermore, unstable drinking *patterns* rather than drinking per se are causally related to relationship violence. Specifically, binge-drinking alcoholics have higher rates of relationship violence than steady-drinking alcoholics, even though steady drinkers may consume more alcohol in the long run (Murphy & O'Farrell, 1994).

In addition to differences in the nature of the alcohol problem and the pattern of alcohol consumption, violent and nonviolent alcoholics also differ in their beliefs about the effects of alcohol. Violent alcoholics and their partners tend to believe that alcohol causes marital problems. At the same time, violent alcoholics believe that they cannot weather interpersonal conflict without drinking (Murphy & O'Farrell, 1994). Interestingly, when alcoholics who are prone to relationship violence are asked to discuss problems under sober conditions with their spouses, they tend to display higher levels of hostility and defensiveness than their nonviolent counterparts.

The bottom line about alcohol and relationship violence is that alcoholics who abuse their partners differ in important ways from alcoholics who are not violent. The pattern of risk for relationship violence appears to hinge on the nature of the alcohol problem, consumption patterns, beliefs about alcohol's ability to cause harm to a relationship, and relationship-specific communication patterns. Furthermore, the findings discussed thus far suggest that relationship violence is multicausal. No single set of factors can explain why violence occurs in relationships, and consequently it is difficult to come up with a magic wand that would make the problem go away.

Looking at the issue more broadly, it appears that whether violence and abuse find their way into a relationship may depend on three sets of variables. There are person and relationship variables of the kind just discussed. Also, since relationships do not exist in a vacuum, how people conduct themselves is to some extent influenced by the macrocontext in which their relationships exist (Levinger, 1994). Additionally, broad individual dispositions also influence people's behavior in a variety of situations. We consider these next.

The Macrocontext of Relationship Violence

In the summer of 1998, White Sox slugger Albert Belle was accused of battery by his live-in partner. In reporting the story, local news interviewed a couple of fans who attended the ball game the day the allegations had been made. Both fans were quick to point out that although Belle's actions, if true, were regrettable, what he does in his home was ultimately his own business. The fan reaction to Belle's alleged (the charges against him were later dismissed) abusive behavior may be symptomatic of our society's general attitude toward relationship violence and abuse. Rather than being regarded the same as assault among strangers, subject to enforcement by law, it is often treated as a "domestic" issue to be dealt with by the parties involved. Perhaps this is one of the reasons why the United States has far more shelters for animals than shelters for abused women (Biden, 1993).

Law enforcement has traditionally been reluctant to make arrests for domestic violence unless the victim demands it or the suspect insults or assaults the officer (Sherman, 1980). To be sure, this reluctance is not borne out of callousness. Rather, it represents the response of police officers to the different options demanded by different groups. For instance, women's advocacy groups might recommend that the officer protect the victim, whereas colleagues and trainers might recommend forced separation or mediation as a short-term solution to the problem at hand.

Considering that relationship violence continues to be a problem, one might ask what would happen if violent offenders were to be arrested rather than talked to or forcibly separated from their victims. This question was first addressed in a field study conducted with the help of the Minneapolis Police Department (Sherman & Berk, 1984). Some 33 police officers stationed in the two precincts with the highest rate of domestic violence agreed to respond to calls of misdemeanor domestic assault by (1) arresting the offender, (2) separating the offender and victim for at least eight hours, or (3) dispensing advice, including mediation. In order for the experiment to have the highest possible internal validity, how officers responded to calls was not left within their control. Rather, their responses were designated by a prearranged random assignment plan. Over a 17-month period, this plan of action produced 98 cases in which an offender was arrested, 114 cases in which officers separated the offender and the victim, and 108 cases in which officers responded by dispensing advice. To check for the effectiveness of the different responses (i.e., the likelihood that the offender refrained from violence), additional data were collected in the form of police reports as well as interviews of the victims within six months of the initial incident.

The results strongly suggested that arrest, compared to separation and advice, acted as a deterrent to further relationship violence, at least over a period of six months. Of all three experimental groups, offenders who had been arrested were least likely to commit another domestic assault. Those who had been separated were most likely to assault their partners again, and those who had received advice or mediation fell somewhere in between. Based on these findings, 15 states passed laws that made arrest mandatory for all cases of domestic violence. However, the results of several subsequent replications of the originial Minneapolis experiment suggest that such legislation may have been premature, and further calls into question the generalizability of the Minneapolis findings (Sherman et al., 1992). Although replications in Colorado Springs and Dade County found a deterrent effect of arrest in line with what the Minneapolis study had found, replications in Omaha, Charlotte, and Milwaukee not only failed to find a *deterrent* effect, but they found an *escalating* effect of arrest. In other words, rather than reducing future domestic violence, getting arrested made an offender more likely to become violent again.

If nothing else, this example should teach us not to devise public policy on the basis of the outcome of one single study. An important question remains, however: Why did what seemed to have worked in Minneapolis fail so miserably in other places? The answer seems not to have anything to do with geography at all. Rather, it appears that punishment, such as being arrested for domestic assault, affects different people in different ways. Specifically, arrest works best as a deterrent for those who have a lot to lose. For people who have a job or are married, the stakes are particularly high, as repeated arrests could adversely affect their occupational and marital status. Together, these stakes constitute important forms of informal control to work in conjunction with the formal control of the law. From this perspective, it is not surprising to learn that those individuals with jobs and marriages were deterred from future violence by being arrested, compared to their counterparts who received advice or were separated from their victims.

Quite a different picture emerges for those people for whom the stakes are relatively low. Offenders who were unemployed or unmarried and who were arrested for domestic assault became more likely to become violent again in the future. Several reasons are possible for why this may have happened. The initial arrest may instill in the offenders the belief that they are deviant, and thus they change their identities accordingly. Repeated punishment may have further led to the discovery that the legal threat is overstated and relatively tolerable. In support of this point, in the Milwaukee experiment, only 1 percent of arrested offenders were eventually convicted. Finally, repeated punishment may have led to anger and resentment against the victim, the law, or society, resulting in future aggression and violence.

Thus, to some extent, the prevalence of relationship violence may be due to the vestiges of a system that has traditionally considered women to be possessions of their male partners. Changes in laws governing relationship conduct can contribute to a decrease in the prevalance of relationship violence, but only within limits. For one thing, as we have seen, laws and their enforcement affect different people in different ways. Consider further the draconian laws against drugs enacted during the 1980s and 1990s. They did little, if anything, to decrease drug-related violence. To make laws against domestic violence work, it will ultimately take a collective reorientation in terms of how society looks at the nature of domestic relationships.

The Microcontext of Relationship Violence: Individual Dispositions

Any union between two people ultimately involves two individuals who bring a multitude of characteristics, traits, and dispositions that uniquely affect the nature and quality of their relationship. For example, we have already seen how love styles and attachment styles of individuals can affect their relationships with others. What individual disposition could lead people to become violent and abusive? Many lay theories hold that violence and abuse are somehow related to power. *Power* has been defined by some as the ability to elicit compliance from others (Weber, 1976). Others have defined it as a general concern for (1) having an impact on others, (2) arousing strong emotions in others, and (3) maintaining a reputation and sense of prestige (Winter, 1988). However one looks at power, force can be a means of establishing, maintaining, or restoring the balance of power in a relationship.

The Need for Power. The balance of power in a relationship can be based on many things, including differences in socioeconomic resources. An alternative way of understanding power is to look at it as a social motive. In other words, just as people have needs for affiliation, belonging, achievement, and so forth, they also have needs for power. And, as is the case with all social motives, there is considerable variation among people in their need for power. In the majority of cases, relationship violence in heterosexual couples is initiated by the male partner; therefore, one might suspect to find the root cause of the problem in men's higher need for power. However, as intuitive as this idea may be, research has shown it to be wrong, at least in this simple form.

In a now classic study, Winter (1988) measured the need for power (referred to as n(pow)) in a sample of college women and men by having them create stories to describe what was happening in drawings of ambiguous situations. This projective test, known as the Thematic Apperception Test (TAT), is predicated on the assumption that people's needs will manifest themselves in their fantasies. A research participant who responds to a series of pictures with power-related themes ("He is telling her what to do," "He is demanding an explanation") would be considered to be high in n(pow), compared to someone who responds to the same pictures without reference to power-related themes ("He's telling her about a movie he just saw," "He's asking how her kids are doing").

Not surprisingly, the study found that people varied greatly in terms of their need for power. However, men and women did not differ in the nature and level of n(pow). In other words, n(pow) is equally present (or absent) in both sexes. What differed between the sexes were the actions associated with a high need for power. On the extreme end, men high in n(pow) had proclivities for alcohol and drug use, physical and verbal aggression, gambling, and precocious and exploitative sex (including a liking for magazines such as *Hustler*). In addition, or perhaps because of these proclivities, men high in n(pow) were found to have difficult and less stable intimate relationships and they tended to oppress women in general, both economically and psychologically. Such psychological oppression can manifest itself in a variety of ways, such as cutting a woman off during a conversation or touching her in nonsexual yet nonetheless inappropriate ways.

This pattern of profligate impulsivity was not obtained for the women who were high in need for power. Instead, it appeared that they expressed their need for power primarily in socially responsible ways. Women high in n(pow) tended to hold office in student government or attained high visibility by other means, such as writing letters to the editor of the student newspaper. In addition, they had a proclivity to acquire possessions associated with high prestige, such as televisions, stereos, and framed pictures (remember, this is a study of college students). Finally, women high in n(pow) indicated that they were planning to have careers, especially power-related careers, in such fields as teaching, therapy, journalism, business management, and the clergy. For those readers who are wondering how owning framed pictures and wanting to be a teacher or a minister is related to a need for power, remember that the definition of power emphasizes concerns with having an impact on others as well as maintaining a sense of prestige. Because teachers, journalists, therapists, and clergy have the ability to affect the lives of others in substantial ways (for better and worse), aspiring to these types of careers is considered related to a need for power. Similarly, posters of Monet's water lilies or Michael Jordan dunking a basketball are just that; however, in a frame, they become pieces of art.

It is one thing to demonstrate meaningful and reliable gender differences; explaining their origins is an altogether different matter. One might argue that gender differences, including those in the expression of need for power, are innate. But such an attempt would still fall short of pinpointing the origins of such differences, unless one could find something akin to a genetic marker. However, the observation that gender differences related to power are not so much a matter of differences in the need for power, but instead in the ways in which this need is expressed, suggests that their origins may be social in nature.

In several studies, Winter (1988) managed to trace the differences in how men and women express their need for power to differences in how males and females are socialized. Specifically, women are socialized to express their need for power in socially responsible ways, because throughout their upbringing they receive more responsibility training than their male counterparts. For example, girls are more likely to be asked to help in the care of younger siblings than are boys. Consistent with this speculation, the highest level of responsible nurturance was observed among women who had grown up with younger siblings. Moreover, more profligate impulsivity was found among women who did not have younger siblings and thus had been deprived of relevant opportunities toward social responsibility training. Put a slightly different way, women express a high need for power in socially responsible ways to the extent that they had opportunities for social responsibility training during childhood and adolescence. In the absence of such opportunities, they are very much like their male counterparts who are high in need for power.

Does this mean that men high in n(pow), especially those without younger siblings, are condemned to a life of substance use and gambling? Not necessarily. When all our rowdy friends are settling down, it is often because they have children of their own. It appears that being a parent can provide the social responsibility training that may have been missing from one's earlier years. Although parenthood may do little to change one's need for power, it can substantially alter the way it is expressed.

Power and Abuse.   How is need for power tied to relationship violence and abuse? One might suspect that profligate impulsivity could be at the core of the problem. From this perspective, both men *and* women who are high in need for power and who lacked opportunities for social responsibility training might be predisposed toward violence. However, not every person who fits this pattern will become violent. Thus, we need to look at other variables that might play a role in the connection of power and abuse.

One such attempt was made in a study that looked at a number of personality characteristics to predict the occurrence of relationship violence (Mason & Blankenship, 1987). Along with the need for power, the researchers measured the need for affiliation, activity inhibition, and stress, through appropriate tests. In addition, the researchers kept track of the length of relationships. The general idea was that the occurrence of relationship violence could be predicted by unique combinations of these variables. For example, it might be the case that violence will be inflicted primarily by those high in need for power, low in need for affiliation, and low in their ability to resist their violent impulses. Moreover, it might be that different combinations predict whether men and women will become violent.

The results suggest that relationship violence does in fact have multiple causes and that the nature of the causes is somewhat different for men and women. High need for power was significantly correlated with the infliction of abuse among men but not women, suggesting that profligate impulsivity stemming from a high need for power is the major reason men become violent. For women, the story is considerably more complex. Need for power did not predict the infliction of violence, as one might suspect. Instead, need for affiliation and level of activity inhibition moderated the effects that stress had on the infliction of abuse. In other words, women who were under a lot of stress, high in need for affiliation, and low in activity inhibition were most likely to inflict abuse. Of course, given the correlational nature of the study, the opposite is also true. Women who were under a lot of stress but were low in need for affiliation or high in activity inhibition were not particularly likely to inflict abuse.

Inflicting violence on one's partner has different consequences for the sexes. Men, by and large, get away with it; women who strike their partners get struck back. Interestingly, relationship violence most often occurs in mature, committed relationships. This finding is of some interest, as it begs two questions: Why do commited members of a couple resort to violence and abuse? Why do the victims of such violence remain in the abusive relationship? Psychologists have traditionally tried to address the second question yet have paid scant attention to the first. Cynics might argue that this is due to a bias that puts the onus on women for a pattern of behavior for which men are behaviorally and morally responsible. A more benevolent interpretation would suggest that any bias may be the result of a primary concern with the victims of relationship violence rather than the perpetrators.

If we look at the issue from a couple perspective we can identify several reasons why committed people, in particular, might be mired in abusive and violent relationships. As a relationship matures over time, the investment individuals have in it increases, as well. Thus, abused partners may find themselves engaged in some calculus that balances the costs of staying against the costs of leaving. Furthermore, over time, the number of alternatives may decrease, as well. This may ultimately lead to a lowered comparison level for alternatives (CL_{Alt}) (Thibaut & Kelley, 1959), thus increasing one's dependency on the relationship. Finally, as relationships mature, the number of material and psychological barriers in general increase to the point where leaving even an abusive relationship may be difficult. We will address these and other issues in the next chapter. For now, let us turn our attention to sexual violence and its relationship to power.

Sexual Violence

We can think of sexual violence as manifested in two ways. *Sexual harassment* refers to unwanted sexual advances between strangers or acquaintances. Incidences are often found in such settings as the workplace and school. Even though sexual harassment does not generally occur between intimates, the harasser often desires some sort of intimacy with the victim, and thus it is included in this discussion.

Coercive sex refers to sexual encounters without the consent of one partner. It can occur between strangers, acquaintances (date rape), as well as intimates. Sexual harassment and coercive sex have profound implications for their victims. The psychological and physical scars they leave are often just as severe as the scars resulting from the type of abuse we have discussed.

Sexual Harassment

During the televised U.S. Senate Judiciary Committee hearings on the nomination of Judge Clarence Thomas, Anita Hill, a college professor at the University of Oklahoma, testified that she had been sexually harassed by Judge Thomas while she was employed by him 10 years earlier. Although only about 25 percent of the general population believed her allegations (Eisenman, 1993), the case helped increase public awareness of sexual harassment issues to the point that it is now recognized as "a social problem of enormous proportions" (Fitzgerald, 1993, p. 1070).

However, sexual harassment did not begin with Judge Thomas making lewd remarks and issuing sexual invitations to Anita Hill. Instead, the earliest published accounts go as far back as the 1730s, when a group of domestic servants publicly expressed a concern that their employers "may do tender women mischief" (Foner, 1947, p. 6). Despite its long history, sexual harassment was not illegal until the passage of the Civil Rights Act of 1964, and a legal definition of what constitutes sexual harassment was not issued until 1980, when the Equal Employment Opportunity Commission outlined two broad categories of prohibited behavior. *Quid pro quo harassment* refers to attempts to extort sexual cooperation by means of subtle or explicit threats of job-related consequences. *Hostile environment harassment* refers to pervasive sex-related verbal or physical conduct that is unwelcome or offensive, even when not accompanied by threats of job-related consequences. In light of these guidelines, sexual harassment is now generally understood as "any deliberate or repeated sexual behavior that is unwelcome to its recipients, as well as other behaviors that are hostile, offensive, or degrading" (Fitzgerald, 1993, p. 1070).

That sexual harassment can be quite severe and even hostile has been documented in a number of high-profile court cases. For example, in *Meritor Savings Bank* v. *Vinson* (1986), Michele Vinson, an employee at Meritor Savings Bank, testified that her boss had repeatedly raped and fondled her and followed her into the restroom at her place of employment. In *Robinson* v. *Jacksonville Shipyards* (1991), Lois Robinson went to court after company officials had repeatedly ignored her complaints regarding the widespread display of pornographic pictures and sexually degrading graffiti in her workplace. However, the vast majority of sexual harassment is not quite so dramatic but instead consists of intrusive and unwanted sexual attention from superiors and coworkers. In one study of several thousand female government employees (U.S. Merit System Protection Board, 1981), 33 percent of the respondents reported having been subjected to repeated sexual remarks, 26 percent had been subjected to physical touching, and 15 percent had been pressured for dates.

In light of the pervasiveness of sexual harassment in the workplace, it is important to find out why it occurs. It should be noted that, although men and women both may be perpetrators as well as victims of sexual harassment, most cases involve the sexual harassment of women by men. This observation has given rise to several theoretical accounts. According to one hypothesis, sexual harassment of women at work is the result of *sex-role spillover*, which is defined as the carryover of gender-based expectations for behavior into the workplace (Gutek & Morasch, 1982). Sexual harassment due to sex-role spillover is most likely to occur when the sex ratio at work is skewed toward males. In these settings, women take on the status of "role deviates" and are treated differently from male workers. In other words, in male-dominated settings, men tend to treat women based on gender-based expectations that are largely irrelevant to the work setting but might be appropriate in other settings. From this perspective, whether a behavior is considered sexually harassing depends in large part on the context. For example, a request for a date may be perfectly reasonable when it is issued at a party but it becomes an issue of harassment when it is issued in the workplace.

The notion of sexual harassment resulting from sex-role spillover is not without empirical support (Gutek & Morasch, 1982; Sheffey & Tindale, 1992), and it helps explain why it often occurs in work settings that are dominated by males, such as the military (Pryor, 1995), medical training (Komaromy et al., 1993), and firefighting (Rosell, Miller, & Barber, 1995). On the other hand, although some forms of sexual harassment, such as asking for a date or complimenting a woman about her appearance, might be the result of applying behaviors based on gender expectations in the wrong setting, the sexual spillover hypothesis has a harder time accounting for a number of phenomena related to sexual harassment.

For one thing, not all men are equally likely to sexually harass women in the workplace. Instead, it appears that men vary in their proclivity to sexually harass. But even those with a high proclivity may not display harassing behaviors. Whether sexual harassment occurs tends to be a function of a predisposition on the part of men as well as cues in the situation that either permit or prohibit harassing behavior. To test this idea, Pryor, Giedd, and Williams (1995) recruited males, who had previously completed a measure indicating their likelihood to sexually harass, to participate in a study on employee training. The participants' job ostensibly was to instruct female participants in some basic office skills. Prior to conducting the training session, participants saw one of two short videos in which a model demonstrated how this was to be done. In one video, the male model complimented the female model on her appearance and touched her frequently while describing the task. In the other video, any sexually harassing behaviors were omitted.

Consistent with the hypothesis, male participants who scored high in the likelihood to sexually harass *and* who had seen a model get away with sexually harassing behaviors were most likely to sexually harass the woman they were supposed to train. Interestingly, men with a high likelihood to sexually harass who were exposed to a nonharassing model were just as likely (or unlikely) to harass their "trainee" as men who were low in the likelihood to sexually harass.

From a practical point of view, Pryor, Giedd, and Williams's (1995) study suggests that the incidence of sexual harassment, even from the most determined harassers, might be lowered by workplace policies that do not permit or even punish sexual harassment. From a theoretical point of view, the study prompts a more complete account of the kinds of things that make some men more likely to sexually harass than others. At this point, it appears that the behavior of men who sexually harass is strongly motivated by a need for power and dominance, particularly when it comes to interacting with women (Bargh & Raymond, 1995). Moreover, men who are likely to sexually harass appear to have a mental association that links power with sex. Thus, when the power end of this association is activated (e.g., by virtue of someone's position in the workplace), the sex end will be automatically activated, as well (Pryor & Stoller, 1994). As a consequence of the activation of this power-sex association, female coworkers are often perceived as more attractive, which can then bring about sexually harassing behaviors (Bargh et al., 1995). Of course, whether sexually harassing behavior will ultimately ensue may in part depend on additional signals indicating that the setting will either permit or prohibit it, as indicated by the Pryor, Giedd, and Williams (1995) study.

Sexual harassment necessarily involves a perpetrator and a victim. So far, we have concentrated on illuminating the reasons why some men sexually harass women at work. But how does sexual harassment affect its victims? Obviously, severe and violent sexual harassment (e.g., *Meritor Savings Bank* v. *Vinson*, *Robinson* v. *Jacksonville Shipyards*) is likely to have devastating consequences for its victims. But even harassment that does not include an overt form of sexual coercion affects women profoundly. One study of 10,000 working military women found that those who had been subjected to sexual harassment (59 percent) displayed lower productivity, negative attitudes about their workplace, and negative emotional reactions and problems with relationships in the family (Pryor, 1995). On the other hand, only a small minority of women ever report sexual harassment (Komaromy et al., 1993).

The underreporting of sexual harassment may occur for several reasons. Quid pro quo sexual harassment is likely to increase the possibility of losing one's job; thus, women subjected to this form of harassment may fail to take action primarily out of fear. But this is not the whole story. Sexual harassment is often surrounded by a great deal of ambiguity due to differences in men's and women's lay definitions of what constitutes sexual harassment in the first place. In general, men's definitions tend to be narrower and less inclusive than those of women (Fitzgerald, 1993). In other words, whereas a woman may think of a touch or a verbal comment as a form of sexual harassment, men often interpret such actions as an expression of mere friendliness. In light of these divergent perceptions, the legal system has supplemented the burden of proof on the part of the victim with a "reasonable woman standard," which holds the victim responsible for responding appropriately (Fitzgerald, Swan, & Fisher, 1995; Gutek & O'Connor, 1995). Although these legal hurdles protect the accused (as intended by the legal system), they make many women wonder if they would find justice as a result of filing a complaint (Rudman, Borgida, & Robertson, 1995). Consequently, women are often compelled to suffer in silence, especially when the harassment is not severe, when it does not come from a supervisor, and when the workplace lacks adequate policies on sexual harassment (Gruber & Smith, 1995).

Coercive Sex

The observation that coercive sex can occur as sexual harassment in the workplace goes against the long-held notion that rape is something that happens between strangers in a dark alley. As it turns out, most incidences of rape—legally defined as the nonconsensual oral, anal, or vaginal penetration, obtained by force, by threat of bodily harm, or when the victim is incapable of giving consent (Searles & Berger, 1987)—occur between people who know each other. In fact, several studies indicate that a woman is far more likely to be raped by her husband than by a stranger (Greeley, 1991; Russell, 1982). Other studies suggest that coercive sex may be even most common among acquaintances and dating couples. In one study of over 3,000 female college students, 54 percent reported that they had been subjected to some form of coerced sexual contact, and roughly half of those cases occurred on dates (Koss, Gidyzc, & Wisniewsky, 1987).

In some ways, it is not surprising that a woman would be more likely to be raped by a close other than a stranger. After all, husbands, cohabitors, and dating partners have frequent contact with their partners and the rape can be commited in relative privacy (Browne, 1993). At the same time, sexual coercion among intimates appears to be incompatible with the characteristics of a close relationship, and thus requires explanations for its occurrence. One way to account for this phenomenon is to attribute rape to sexual communication gone awry. In line with data from Abbey and Melby (1986), a man may be compelled to rape because he interprets a woman's flirtatious behavior as indicating sexual intent. However, rape frequently occurs and continues even after a woman has clearly indicated that she does not wish to have sex. Thus, overperception of sexual intent tells only part of the story. Additionally, men who commit rape approach women with the general notion that women's communications about sex and romance cannot be trusted, and these men fail to recognize negative reactions from others apppropriately (Malamuth & Brown, 1994). These characteristics themselves appear to be part of a larger problem. Sexually aggressive men tend to subscribe to the myth that deep down women like to be handled roughly (Burt, 1980). Furthermore, these men tend to endorse interpersonal violence and generally hold adversarial sexual beliefs, often thinking of sex as a conquest or a battle (Malamuth & Brown, 1994).

A more controversial account for the occurrence of coercive sex proposes that men's proclivity to rape is an outcome of an evolutionary adaptation to procreation (Thornhill & Thornhill, 1992). In other words, men are biologically predisposed toward rape because it has been adaptive to the different mating strategies employed by men and women. As we discussed at length in Chapter 3, in most mammalian species, a male's primary reproductive goal is to mate early and often so as to ensure the survival of his genes in future generations. Females, on the other hand, are primarily interested in ascertaining this genetic survival once conception has occurred, and thus they restrict sexual interactions to males who they perceive to be maximally capable of providing resources necessary for childrearing. From this perspective, rape is adaptive to males because it helps subvert females' gate-keeping tendencies, thus increasing the chances of meeting their reproductive goals.

This evolutionary approach is controversial for several reasons. With regard to its implications, many object that explaining rape in terms of its adaptive value merely justifies the status quo and absolves men from any responsibility. But even if a case could be made that these implications were unintended or even false, the evolutionary approach to rape has a couple of rough theoretical edges that undermine its explanatory power. For one thing, rape may have benefits for males, but it has substantial costs for females, and thus it is not clear how rape is an adaptive mechanism on the level of the species as a whole. For another, the evolutionary approach has difficulty explaining why rape is so frequent among married couples, where the certainty that mating will take place is fairly high.

Why men feel compelled to rape is likely to be subject to continued theoretical debate among behavioral scientists. This debate is important because in order to generate prescriptions aimed at the prevention of rape, we need to have a clear theoretical understanding of why it occurs in the first place. On the surface, approaches that treat rape as inevitable for evolutionary reasons may seem less than helpful in terms of generating practical solutions. However, such approaches may ultimately make an important contribution by provoking the formulation of alternative theoretical perspectives.

Summary

Issues. Violence among intimates is somewhat antithetical to the spirit on which close relationships are founded. Nonetheless, it surfaces with alarming frequency in the United States and abroad, often with severe consequences for its victims. Understanding relationship violence is complicated by controversies surrounding how it should be measured and defined. Although speculations about the origins of relationship violence abound, many appear to have little basis in fact. It may be best understood from a multicausal perspective that takes into account individual dispositions along with the macrocontext in which it occurs. Specific forms of sexual violence, including sexual harassment and coercive sex, are important issues to understand, particularly in light of their profound consequences for its victims.

Theories. Popular theories about the causes of relationship violence emphasize the importance of several variables. They suggest that relationship violence occurs primarily in low-income families, is hidden by the victim and abuser alike, is mostly committed by men, is related to patterns of abuse in the family of origin, takes on a cyclical nature, and is frequently promoted by alcohol use. Macrolevel theories propose that relationship violence is promoted by the lack of social and legal consequences for its perpetrators. Individual difference theories focus on the importance of power as a psychogenic need in eliciting violent behavior. Recent theories concerned with explaining the incidence of sexual harassment have attempted to explain it in terms of sex-role spillover and the existence of a mental association between power and sex on the part of the harasser. Theories trying to explain the incidence of rape among intimates have focused on individual characteristics of the rapist as well as the possibility that rape can be understood as an adaptive mechanism.

Research.   Descriptive research on the prevalence of relationship violence suggests that it is a universal problem. Furthermore, it appears that relationship violence takes on two basic forms: patriarchical terrorism, stemming from traditions that give men the right to control their partners, and common couple violence, in which conflict escalates into violence. There is little to indicate that popular notions regarding the causes of relationship violence provide an adequate understanding of either form of violence.

Community-based interventions increasing penalties for relationship violence have somewhat mixed results. They appear to work primarily for perpetrators for whom a lot is at stake. Need for power predicts why men would become violent in a straightforward way. However, the story for women is more complicated. Specifically, it appears that whether women become violent depends on a complex interaction among need for affiliation, impulse control, and stress. There is some evidence for the sex-role spillover theory of sexual harassment from studies that look at sexually harassing behaviors in settings with varied gender ratios. The importance of a mental association between power and sex has been demonstrated in studies that surreptitiously prime power in men and look at its effect on the perceived attractiveness of female coworkers. Those who attempt to explain rape in evolutionary terms support their case by citing evidence regarding the pervasive nature of coercive sexual behavior among all mammalian species. Other studies have found that rape is particularly likely to be committed by men who subscribe to the rape myth, endorse interpersonal violence, and hold adversarial sexual beliefs.

13

Conflict

Richard J. Thomas says he has tried just about everything to convince his wife to quit smoking, from hanging scare stories from Ann Landers's column on the refrigerator to trying to hold reasoned discussions with her about the latest health warnings.

In a last-ditch attempt to force her to stop, Thomas, 69, a retired Army colonel . . . , sued her Thursday in Federal court. . . . The lawsuit contends that secondhand smoke is a toxic pollutant under the Clean Air Act and should be forbidden in homes.

Thomas' wife, reached by phone at her home, declined to comment, but her husband acknowledges she is none too pleased about his legal action.

—Chicago Tribune, August 22, 1997

Not only is conflict a part of romantic liaisons but it is a part of all social relationships, from family relations to the closest friendships to workplace interactions. Indeed, an important part of socialization and maturation includes coping with conflict. Further, and perhaps partly because of its prevalence, these ordeals are sometimes euphemistically called "growth experiences." Even the most loving of couples are not immune to the occasional (or not so occasional) spat or fight. How do *you* handle conflict in *your* relationship—with cold silence, an argument, a glare, or perhaps, like Mr. Thomas, with a lawsuit?

If we're so in love, why must we disagree? This, of course, is just one of the many exquisite mysteries of intimate relationships. And not surprisingly, it is just one of the challenging questions that researchers in the area of conflict have attempted to address. Although it is fairly easy to spot an argument and identify conflicts, other aspects of conflicts are much more elusive. For example, how do conflicts start, where do they come from, how do we solve them, and why do we engage in them in the first place?

Conflict between Lovers versus Strangers

Before addressing these issues, let us take a few steps back. How, some readers might be wondering, does conflict in romantic relationships differ from conflict in general? In other words, do we really need to study conflict in intimate relationships apart from the study of conflict in general? The story of Mr. Thomas's legal recourse to persuade his wife to stop smoking is newsworthy because, although settling conflicts in court is not unusual, settling interpersonal problems in a courtroom is. Further, many of us can give personal examples to support the idea that there is a difference between conflict with a loved one as opposed to conflict with a coworker. Likewise, research supports this idea, as well (e.g., Dunn et al., 1995; Maccoby, 1996). Children, for example, demonstrate more affective and behavioral control and temper their confrontations with peers to a much greater extent than they do with family members.

An additional difference between the two types of conflict situations has to do with how the nature of the interactions themselves directly affects the conflict. Intimate relationships necessarily involve people who are in long-term relationships, who know one another well, and who are in forced proximity to one another (as opposed to disputants who have only a nominal acquaintanceship, hardly know one another, and can remove themselves easily from the situation). These elements in and of themselves change the complexion of disagreements, their magnitude, and the consequences of disharmony.

In a similar vein, Altman and Taylor's (1973) theory of social penetration provides an analogous picture of how communication patterns change as intimate relationships deteriorate. Generally, couples in intimate relationships talk about a wide variety of topics and communicate with each other at a deep, intimate level. However, as intimate relationships begin to deteriorate, the breadth of conversational topics becomes constricted while the depth of communication and intimacy remains or becomes even deeper. Thus, conversations about politics, philosophy, and movies dwindle while hurtful exchanges about each other's supposed weaknesses, shortcomings, and wrongdoings increase. Conversations become centered on issues of contention—real, imagined, or exaggerated. Altman and Taylor (1973) aptly characterized this communication pattern as a social dagger. In essence, the intimacy developed throughout the course of a close interpersonal relationship turns conflict into a deeper, more hurtful affair than would, say, an argument between coworkers or strangers.

A final reason why we should study conflicts in intimate relationships has to do with the outcomes of the conflicts. Stalking, property damage, partner violence, battering, and murder are just some of the dramatic outcomes of conflicts experienced between lovers. We will discuss some of these issues later in the chapter. Thus, there are some obvious reasons why we should strive to understand the nature of discord in romantic relationships and some less obvious but even more compelling reasons to do so. Let us begin our examination of the topic by looking at a couple of views on the very nature of conflict itself.

The Nature of Conflict in Intimate Relationships: The Good, the Bad, and the Ugly

The courtship and inexorable path toward Rosanne Barr and Tom Arnold's divorce were played out before a national audience. Not only were we witness to their provocative and sometimes distasteful displays of affection but we also looked on in horror as their turbulent relationship degenerated into an ugly public spectacle.

Ironically (or fittingly), the study of conflicts is not itself free from dispute. Conflict researchers have operated under a couple of different assumptions regarding the nature of conflicts. One of the earliest approaches viewed conflicts as largely negative events; that is, conflicts were regarded as destructive and completely negative forces (Coser, 1956). This belief is supported by news accounts of abusive relationships and murder-for-hire horror stories. For example, in celluloid Hollywood "reality," Kathleen Turner and Michael Douglas literally fought to the death in *The War of the Roses*. Thus, according to the conflict-as-destructive perspective, conflict engagement and involvement are signs of problems or weaknesses in the relationship. People should therefore strive to avoid and/or resolve conflicts at all costs.

More recently, however, the pendulum has swung, and researchers now take a more sophisticated view of conflicts. At the same time that it recognizes the destructiveness of conflicts, this "transformational" perspective also emphasizes the positive features of conflict—that is, conflict as the creative impetus underlying social change (e.g., Gottman, 1993; Peterson, 1983; Rausch et al., 1974; Rubin, Pruitt, & Kim, 1994). According to proponents of this perspective, conflict can be characterized as either constructive or destructive (e.g., Coser, 1967; Deutsch, 1969; Simmel, 1955). *Constructive* conflict is the force for change and growth in a relationship. It is through conflict and conflict resolution that we achieve group and dyadic unity. In fact, Gottman and Krokoff (1989) find that expression of disagreement and anger are predictive of long-term satisfaction and improvement of marital relationships. *Destructive conflict*, as the term implies, leads to the termination of relationships. It is painful, harmful, and damaging to its participants. It can be characterized by hurtful communications and the use of conflict escalation tactics.

For those of us who have been (or are) involved in bitter confrontations with a loved one, this idea sounds positively encouraging. And although this idea of conflict as growth may be a revelation to many of us, the roots of this perspective are not new. We can look to the philosophies of Freud, Darwin, and Marx to find identical assumptions, all of whom consider conflict (i.e., psychodynamic conflict, survival of the fittest, dialectical philosophy respectively) to be not only a necessary component of change but also the crux of growth (Rubin, Pruitt, & Kim, 1994).

A current more elaborate understanding of the role of conflict in relationships addresses how conflict adds balance to the often opposing needs that partners have, and may therefore contribute to relationship happiness (Gottman, 1993). Specifically, conflict may provide the balance among the competing and necessary needs of intimacy and privacy, openness and closedness, and expressiveness and privateness. That is, a relationship characterized by complete positivity may be as unstable as one that is totally negative.

The gain-loss hypothesis (Aronson & Linder, 1965) also corresponds with this notion. It predicts that a relationship totally lacking in negativity and comprised exclusively of positive events and affect can lead to boredom and even the diminishment or devaluing of the positive events themselves. These results suggest that honest, open communication (of both positive and negative information) will lead to the highest degree of relationship satisfaction. Thus, conflict consists not only of the bad and the ugly but the positive and beneficial outcomes, as well.

In sum, each of the theories regarding the nature of conflicts includes its own unique set of assumptions, predictions, and implications. According to the conflict-as-undesirable stance, discord is a sign of a serious rift in the system or relationship. On the other hand, transformational theorists acknowledge the pervasiveness of conflict and would actually counsel us to embrace *constructive* conflict and express discontent. Finally, recent accounts of conflict suggest that it has an even more complex relationship to happiness through its role in mediating the balance of needs in a relationship.

Defining Conflict

Now that we have a pretty good picture of the nature of conflict, let us consider some of the ways researchers have attempted to define and operationalize it. Peterson (1983) defines *conflict* as the "interpersonal process that occurs whenever the actions of one person interfere with the actions of another" (p. 365). Though indisputable, this definition provides a very broad interpretation that can be applied to conflicts between any two individuals or groups. Other typologies attempt to identify the different kinds of conflicts that have been observed—conflicts that range from orderly debates between strangers to impassioned and chaotic quarrels between lovers.

Brickman (1974), in just such a categorization, differentiates between conflict types based on the degree to which they are predictable and adhere to certain "rules of engagement." Similar to the earlier work of Rapoport (1960), Brickman suggests that there are four different types of conflicts: fully structured, partially structured, unstructured, and revolutionary. Debates are an example of *fully structured conflicts*, and are typified by exchanges that are norm bound, rule governed, and often moral. *Partially structured conflicts*, or games (Rapoport, 1960), include intense competition and bargaining, but are still largely rule bound. In *unstructured conflict*, on the other hand, there are no rules or constraints. This is conceptually akin to Rapoport's (1960) category of fights. Finally, *revolutionary conflict* can be considered "metaconflict," or conflict over the very rules of conflict.

From Order to Disorder: Self-Interest, Disorder, Ambiguity, and Confusion

Much has been said about the norms and rules that guide conflicts; much less attention has been focused on the disorder, ambiguity, and confusion inherent in these emotional exchanges. Further, although conflicts in intimate relationships occupy each of the four previously mentioned categories, severe conflicts are more likely to occur outside of rational, rule-bound communications (Sillars & Weisberg, 1987). That is, instead of being orderly and predictable, these exchanges often defy any sense of logic. Whereas mild conflicts follow a predictable pattern of communication, rules are often disregarded in serious conflicts. Self-interest motives take priority and disputants disregard established rules of communication such as being relevant, clear, complete, and truthful. Not surprisingly, severe conflicts tend to be intense, chaotic, less controllable, and highly confusing (Sillars & Weisberg, 1987).

In addition to self-interest motives and an inattention to the rules of normal communication, a further source of ambiguity in intense conflicts stems from both the breadth of topics over which a couple can disagree and the fact that problems can exist at various levels of abstraction (Sillars & Weisberg, 1987). The number and variety of disputable issues can lead to confusion because each person can focus on a different issue. For her, it's his displeasure with her posture, but for him, it's her indifference to his concern for their joint health and physical fitness.

Similar to Freud's notion that dreams are comprised of manifest (a cigar is a source of smoking pleasure) and latent content (i.e., the underlying, unconscious symbolic meaning; a cigar as a representation of a phallus), conflicts may involve surface, straightforward issues as well as those that go deeper to the core of the relationship. The difficulty, however, is in identifying which argument is about what type of issue. For example, seemingly superficial spats about "she doesn't wear enough make-up" or "his raincoat looks like a mortician's overcoat" may reflect deeper misgivings and in fact have their origins in more profound, basic issues of compatibility. Thus, arguments over what appear to be rather trivial matters may actually have to do with whether partners like each other for who they really are!

In sum, conflicts range from the predictable to the chaotic. And a large majority of serious conflicts in romantic relationships are comprised of the latter. This is not surprising, since conflicts, especially intense ones, are "hot" and drenched in chaos, ambiguity, and disorder. Now that we have a better idea of what conflict is, let us examine the origins of conflicts.

Sources of Conflict: "I Said . . . , You Said . . ."

We all know that anything can start a fight—from the little "It's the way you said it" and "Why don't you put the cap back on the toothpaste?" to the more serious "Your family comes before our relationship" and "Don't tell me what to do." So far, we have discussed some of the more general sources of conflict. Let us now examine its more specific origins and antecedents. Generally, conflict can arise from within the relationship (i.e., individual qualities or qualities of the pair) as well as from sources external to it (i.e., children, family, friends, jobs, economics, etc.).

Brickman (1974) suggests that one internal source is the allocation and sharing of resources. That is, simply through sharing and allocating resources, participants increase their likelihood of experiencing goal interference. Other internal sources of conflict and threats to relationship stability are the amount of time spent together, racial dissimilarity, quality of communication, and length of the relationship. Additionally, Rausch and colleagues (1974) propose that internal sources of conflict might also include issues stemming from friction between the needs of the one and the needs of the couple. That is, conflicts arise from the opposition among the most basic needs of the individual and those of the couple: intimacy and isolation, unity and individuality, separateness and connectedness, and openness and privacy. Finally, some external sources of conflict might be the availability of social support and alternative relationships as well as low income (Felmlee, Sprecher, & Bassin, 1990; Levinger, 1976; Thibaut & Kelley, 1959).

In a similar though more nuanced approach, Fincham and Bradbury (1987, 1988) suggest that the complexity of relationships can be traced to the multiple levels along which they occur (Bradbury & Fincham, 1990, 1992). Each level of the relationship—the individual, the dyad, and the social context—gives rise to its own source of conflict. In keeping with this, the researchers propose a more comprehensive categorization of the different sources of conflict: the self, the partner, the relationship, the external environment, and fate.

Dimensions of the self include gender, whereas age might be considered both a component of the self and the relationship (i.e., life stage and length of the relationship). Although much of this is self-explanatory, let's take a closer look at gender and age as sources of conflict.

Gender and Conflict: "He Said . . . , She Said . . ."

To some extent, conflicts arising from gender differences (i.e., in heterosexual relationships) can result from the very fact that "women are from Paris and men are from Newark." In other words, they occur because men and women differ along several important dimensions. And when individuals differing in some very fundamental ways are asked to live in close proximity and with a surfeit of contact, conflict is often the result and may very well be inevitable.

Whereas researchers of sex differences (e.g., Hoyenga & Hoyenga, 1981) insist that there are not even a handful of enduring and universal sex differences, this has not stopped the rest of us from pursuing an ever-expanding search for behavioral explanations based in gender. It seems almost a given that the competing needs of men and women automatically put partners at odds with one another. Research on dating couples reveals that the source of many conflicts lie in partners' preferences for different activities (Surra & Longstreth, 1990). Men, for example, are more likely to prefer physical pursuits, such as sexual activity; whereas women prefer intimacy, sharing, and relationship building to a greater degree.

Various widely accepted gender differences can lead to friction. For example, one consistent gender difference has to do with the conversational styles preferred by men and women (Tannen, 1994a), discussed in Chapter 10. Men prefer side-by-side interactions, such as bowling, fishing, or sitting at the bar and watching a ballgame on TV. Women, on the other hand, favor face-to-face interactions, such as having lunch with friends or sitting at a table in the corner of the bar and talking things out. If one adds to that the sex differences in how many topics are broached and the depth in which they are discussed, it is easy to see how these interaction patterns can lead to problems. A topic is introduced to the conversation; Bob offers his opinion; Sally replies, adds another nuance to the issue, elaborates on her thoughts, and awaits further discussion. In the meantime, Bob's eyes begin to glaze over; his thoughts are already on the next topic. Sally becomes upset because Bob is not listening her (and doesn't care?), and a disagreement along the lines of "you never listen to me" ensues.

In yet other gender difference investigations, researchers find that women tend to approach conflicts more constructively than do men (Levenson & Gottman, 1985; Rusbult et al., 1991; Tannen, 1990). This is consistent with women's greater preference to engage in activities that strengthen and maintain relationships (Surra & Longstreth, 1990) and men's relative difficulty in discussing their feelings (Levenson & Gottman, 1985; Tannen, 1990).

However, Rusbult and colleagues suggest that what might be more important than biological sex is *psychological* orientation (Rusbult, Zembrodt, & Iwaniszek, 1986; Rusbult et al., 1991). That is, a more reliable predictor of differences in how partners approach conflict may lie in psychological rather than biological gender orientation. For example, Rusbult found, regardless of gender, a relationship between psychological femininity and the tendency either to try to improve relationship problems or to wait until they improve. On the other hand, a weak but tantalizing relationship exists between psychological masculinity and the tendency to leave the situation or to passively allow the problem to worsen.

Insofar as biological gender is correlated with psychosexual orientation, this pattern means double trouble for couples in which both partners retain a psychologically masculine approach. On the other hand, couples in which both partners retain a feminine psychological orientation are most likely to work constructively to change conflict into positive outcomes for the good of the relationship. Thus, what seems to matter is not biological gender but psychological orientation.

These findings hold some interesting implications for disputes in homosexual couples. On the surface, it seems that couples of the same gender should avoid conflicts that arise due simply to the friction caused by gender differences in priorities and communication styles. However, research by Rusbult and colleagues (1991) suggests that although problems due to gender differences may be reduced, homosexual couples generally experience similar difficulties in conflict resolution. In other words, because psychological orientation is only loosely correlated with biological orientation, homosexual couples will most likely encounter the same differences in constructive versus avoidance reactions to conflict.

Age and Conflict

At first blush, one would expect increasing levels of conflict in older couples. Indeed, stereotypes of the elderly support this notion. Empirically, researchers have suggested that as couples age, the good fit that brought them together decreases, opening the door to more sources of conflict.

Time mediates the source and occurrence of conflicts in several ways. The aging of a relationship naturally leads to an evolution of "hot" issues: Couples who have been together for a longer period of time have dealt with and resolved many of the issues that are central to conflicts in "newer" couples and relationships. Research on long-term marriages supports this notion (Levenson, Carstensen, & Gottman, 1993, 1994). Thus, relative to younger couples, older couples experience fewer conflicts.

Another effect of time has to do with the changes that occur within each of us as we grow older. For example, different issues are important to younger individuals than to older individuals, regardless of the intimacy or tenure of the relationship. Another difference between new and old relationships is that as we age (or mature), we experience fewer extremes in emotions in all aspects of our lives (Costa et al., 1987). Indeed, research on conflicts supports this: Older couples experience lower levels of physiological arousal during marital interactions than do middle-aged couples (Levenson, Carstensen, & Gottman, 1994). Thus, although the goodness of the fit between partners may deteriorate over time, perhaps the concurrent reduction in emotional extremes may take the edge off the increasing number of differences between the couple.

Furthermore, this "leveling" of affect has direct implications for how we experience conflict. Specifically, because affective reactions to problems are modulated, interactions are less negative and more patterned. However, not only are older couples less likely to experience volatile and destructive conflicts and more likely to resolve them with less negativity but they are also more likely to demonstrate greater affection toward one another while resolving their grievances (Carstensen, Gottman, & Levensen, 1995).

Further bolstering this positive portrait of senior marriages is the fact that, relative to middle-aged couples, older couples experience greater common sources of pleasure. The reduction of gender differences with age may be one of the contributing factors to the greater correspondence in pleasurable activities (Levenson, Carstensen, & Gottman, 1993). It is noteworthy, however, that another effect of time may be at work here. That is, the sample of older couples may be a somewhat biased one: Unhappy couples with poor conflict strategies are unlikely to be included in this group due to separation or divorce. All in all, although not a heavily investigated area, research on older marriages supports a positive picture of love in the twilight years. Sources of conflict change with age, and our affective reactions to conflict diminishes—for the good of the couple.

Attribution and Conflict

Another source of conflict that transcends categories has nothing to do with what our partners have or haven't done; rather, it has everything to do with our perceptions of *why* our partners did what they did.

Soap operas succeed on the communication skills (or the lack thereof) of their characters. Angst, intrigue, and torment are perpetuated through misinformation, lack of information, and misattribution of causes: "I saw you smile at him across the room. I knew you loved him more than me—I couldn't stand the thought of you with him and so I wandered around Montana for the past five years." So, conflict arises not so much because of what we do, but because of the reasons or the perceived reasons for what we do. Perhaps it is not surprising that not only is attributional activity common in relationships (for aren't we constantly striving to determine the motives and reasons for each other's behaviors?) but it actually increases during conflicts and disagreements (Harvey, 1987).

Exactly what types of attributions do we make? Generally, attributions can be internal or external, stable or unstable. When we make *internal attributions* for behaviors, we attempt to explain the behavior by referring to internal, personal attributes, such as abilities, skills, and traits inherent in the individual (e.g., "Scott got upset when I went out with my girlfriends because he's jealous, controlling, and unreasonable"). *External attributions,* on the other hand, locate the cause of behavior in elements in the person's environment, such as weather, other people, fate, luck, and so on (e.g., "Scott got upset when I went out with my girlfriends because he's under a lot of pressure at work and had to stay overtime"). Further, these attributions can be stable or unstable. *Stable attributions* are fixed and constant (e.g., IQ, traits, ability, environmental causes, etc.), whereas unstable attributions are more variable and changeable (e.g., mood, fate, luck, etc.).

How do we make these attributions? Do we go about this process objectively and diligently? Are we like detectives or scientists when it comes to determining why others behave as they do? Or are we more irrational and subjective with our attributions? Generally, researchers find that westerners are more likely to make external attributions for their own behaviors and internal attributions for the behaviors of others (Jones & Nisbett, 1972). How do these findings fit into conflict management in our intimate relationships?

The work of Fincham and Bradbury (1987, 1988; Bradbury & Fincham, 1990, 1992; Lussier, Sabourin, & Wright, 1993) focuses on the role of attributions in intimate relationships and encompasses the complexity and subtleties of both the attribution process as well as the entire conflict process. In a study of married couples, Fincham and Bradbury (1987) found that both causal attributions and judgments of responsibility are key to determining blame and therefore to predicting conflict engagement. These results support the entailment model (Fincham & Jaspers, 1980), which posits the following relationship: Causal judgments lead to responsibility judgments lead to blame judgments. In other words, not only is the source of the conflict important (internal, external, stable, or global) but responsibility decisions are also key in determining blame. Further, responsibility judgments are comprised of elements, such as whether the action was freely chosen, and determinations of the actor's motivation and intent. Once responsibility has been determined, blame is assessed and a reaction is set into motion.

Going back to our earlier example, we can see how both types of attributions might lead to different types of blame judgments. In the first case (internal), we would blame Scott for being an imperfect mate with little tolerance for independent behaviors. We may feel our dignity and rights being trampled upon, and thus begin the battle. In the second instance (external), we might blame Scott for being too caught up in his work or too sensitive to workplace issues. In this instance, we might ignore his remarks and wait for a better time to interact with him.

In sum, although just about anything can lead to a disagreement, researchers have been able to identify different classes of causal factors. However, recent research reveals that it is not the topic of the dispute so much as our attributions for the behavior that is at the root of conflicts in intimate relationships.

Reactions to Conflict

Regardless of the source of a disagreement or the context of a dispute, we know that individuals react to and deal with conflict in a variety of ways: from all-out slugfests and yelling matches to icy walls of silence (or even lawsuits). We will review research on the affective reactions to conflict before delving into behavioral reactions.

As in all else scientific, several different models attempt to explain our behavioral reactions to conflict. In this portion of the chapter, we use Peterson's stages of conflict as a loose organizational framework for organizing the burgeoning empirical work on conflict: expression versus avoidance of conflict, affective reactions to conflict, attributions of disputes and disputants, and some musings on conflict management as a social skill.

Peterson's Stage Model

Peterson (1983) suggests that, in general, arguments follow a fairly standard progression, an orderly patterned exchange, with predictable outcomes (see Figure 13.1). Peterson suggests that there are three distinct stages to an argument, with different paths leading to one of three possible outcomes: stalemate, escalation, or resolution.

The first, or beginning, stage of a conflict includes the predisposing conditions, initiating event(s), and then a decision on the part of the couple to engage in the confrontation or to avoid it. *Predisposing conditions* include the sources of conflict we have discussed earlier. Potentially problematic issues do not simply present themselves prior to an argument (e.g., gender differences are a constant); thus, although these sources of conflict can be present without leading to a conflict, there is usually some event (i.e., the straw that breaks the camel's back) that precipitates the confrontation.

Initiating events refer to the specific event that triggers the conflict, such as a buildup of annoying behaviors, undue criticism, illegitimate demands, and rebuffs. Once the argument has been set into motion, couples have a choice between *avoidance* or *engagement*. If avoidance is chosen, the sequence stops here. If, on the other hand, the couple chooses engagement, they move on to the second, or middle, stage of conflict.

In the middle stage of conflict, couples address the conflict issue(s) through engagement in one or more of the following actions: escalation, negotiation, and conciliation. Little skirmishes may escalate into complete warfare for many

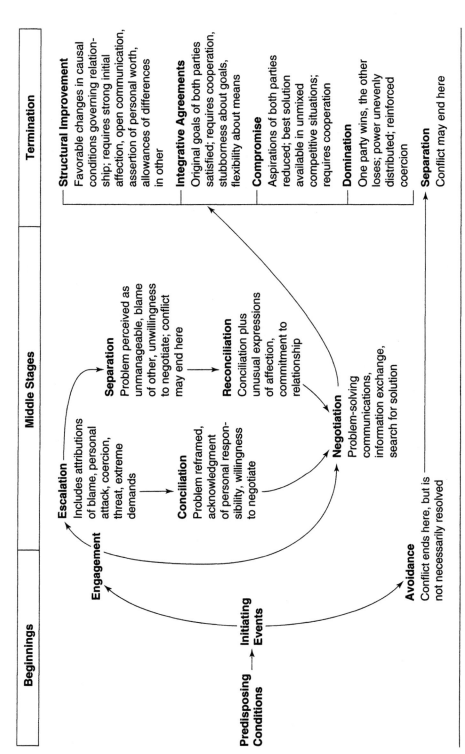

FIGURE 13.1 *Peterson's Model of Conflict*

Source: Adapted from Peterson, 1983. Used by permission.

239

reasons. As we will discuss later, the types of attributions partners make play a role in either escalating or diffusing the situation. Further, our physiological reactions to threats and problems may also lead to escalation.

Two possible outcomes occur after a conflict escalates. In one scenario, the couple moves from an intense angry fight to conciliation, in which partners acknowledge responsibility for their actions and, if resolution is to be truly successful, forgive each other for whatever problems, real or imagined, have occurred. Interestingly, recent research has revealed a link between forgiving and empathy, such that forgiveness is most likely to occur when the injured party feels empathy for the offender (McCullough, Worthington, & Rachal, 1997). The forgiveness-empathy model proposes that an apology, if met with empathy, will lead to forgiveness, which in turn leads to constructive acts, such as conciliation. However, not only does forgiveness increase conciliatory acts but it also *reduces* destructive avoidance behaviors. Such is the power of forgiveness!

In another possible reaction to escalation, couples may actually separate (avoidance), in which the conflict ends on a sour note (e.g., Bill and Kristen go to bed without kissing and making up). On the other hand, this separation might be a prelude to a reconciliation and then negotiation (e.g., after tossing and turning in bed for hours, Bill and Kristen turn the lights on and try to work things out). Thus, this type of "time out" may be helpful to some couples in that it allows them time to cool off and perhaps time to think through more creative solutions to their problems. Yet, there is also the risk that the separation will be accompanied by aggressive hurtful gestures that can further damage the relationship. Peterson observes that withdrawal, in and of itself, offers no solution to problems. If no negotiation has occurred, couples reunite only to find that as the memory of battle fades, the same problems crop up to haunt them.

And finally, after several minutes, hours, days, or months of engagement, couples reach the third and final stage of the conflict process. If couples have not either avoided the problem or already separated, Peterson proposes that the five possible outcomes of conflict are separation, domination, compromise, integrative agreements, and structural improvements. We have already discussed separation. *Domination* is a resolution in which one party holds all the power: One wins, the other loses. This outcome is most probable when both parties are committed to the relationship and separation is not possible. And although we are taught in school as well as in corporate settings that to compromise is to be an effective problem solver, Peterson suggests that compromise leads to less than ideal solutions in close relationships. That is, compromise may work well in unmixed competitive situations, but the very idea of having both parties reduce their goals to find a mutually agreed upon common denominator suggests that neither will be fully satisfied with the outcome.

According to Peterson's schema, only integrative agreements and structural improvements lead to truly satisfying outcomes. They are, not surprisingly, also more difficult to achieve; but then again, they are the only ones that yield win-win results for both parties. *Integrative agreements* are those that incorporate the desires of both parties and include an outcome that is mutually satisfying (as opposed to a compromise in which one or both partners gives up something in the end). For example, imagine a couple in which both are very career oriented. Suppose, further, that the wife got a promotion to a job in another city. A compromise might include a move to that city, resulting in a less satisfactory job for her husband or a long-distance marriage. An integrative agreement might include a move to a home midway between the two jobs.

Structural improvements are the result of a restructuring of the relationship. In these cases, the conflict leads the couple to make changes to the way they view their relationship. In the preceding example, a structural improvement might mean a reassessment of the importance of the couple's careers to the definition of their relationship. A structural improvement might include one or both of the partners giving up their careers to perhaps start a family or working in more low-key jobs.

Interestingly, integrative agreements are more likely to be the result of intermediate levels of conflict intensity, whereas structural improvements are usually the consequence of severe conflicts. Indeed, although we may think of integrative agreements as a complex assimilation of goals and aspirations to a couple's existing schema of their relationship, structural improvement includes basic changes to existing schema to incorporate divergent goals and expectations (i.e., accommodation). Thus, the very worst of our conflicts can lead to growth and an evolution of the relationship in a transformational process.

Expression versus Avoidance

Peterson's (1983) model includes, in its beginning stage, the issues of engagement and avoidance. The use of expression and avoidance has been widely investigated as two general reactions to conflict (Deutsch, 1969). An underlying assumption of this research area is that conflict, unless dispelled, will lead to utter destruction, an explosion. Similar to a hydraulic model, the analogy is that the steam in the engine (the conflict) must be released at regular intervals in order to prevent a dangerous buildup or backlog of negativity (emotion). If release of these negative forces is not accomplished, an explosion or breakdown will occur. Thus, expression is viewed as positive and constructive; whereas avoidance as dysfunctional.

Though the notion that it is good to express negative emotions and to release conflict may seem contrary to what our mothers taught us as children, it actually reflects a commonly held belief. Perhaps some of the clearest evidence of this can be found in the many Hollywood movies (e.g., *Sea of Love* and *The Postman Always Rings Twice*) in which the leading man and the leading woman experience a series of frustrating events that eventually lead to an inevitable knock-down, drag-out brawl. Just as unavoidably, our leading couple suddenly make up through an intense session of equally furious lovemaking. A humorous illustration of this principle is provided by George Costanza, of *Seinfeld* fame. In one episode, George purposefully instigates confrontations with his girlfriend because of his understanding of and belief in makeup sex. However, sometimes avoidance may be the better choice in a conflict; we will return to this issue later in the chapter.

Not only does expression release steam but it may also serve to increase intimacy. That is, expression leads to openness and sharing, which in turn are important to the development of intimacy. Furthermore, transformational perspectives (i.e., conflict is positive) also view conflict as a social skill that can be learned and an event that can be managed successfully (cf. Rubin, Pruitt, & Kim, 1994; Sillars & Weisberg, 1987). Most Americans and westerners in general are comfortable with these assumptions. Many of us tend to agree that keeping our feelings to ourselves, guarding secrets, or hiding our emotions is generally counterproductive to the development of intimacy and closeness. This, however, may not always be true!

Communications researchers (e.g., Baxter, 1990; Rawlins, 1983a, 1983b) suggest that our need for intimacy, expressiveness, and openness is balanced by the complementary drive for privacy, protectiveness, and closedness. That is, on the one hand, we feel a need to openly share and reveal ourselves to another, yet at the same time, we may also have the urge to conceal personal feelings and our own vulnerability. Surely, discussions of intimate and personal topics, those usually involved in interpersonal conflicts, foster clashes between these opposing urges. One implication of this perspective of conflicts is that expression is not automatic or easy, nor is it always desired or ideal. We will return to this issue and other criticisms in our discussion of conflict resolution as a learnable skill.

For now, though, it seems that a simple dichotomy of expression/engagement versus avoidance/escape may be an oversimplification. In a further refinement of this issue, Rusbult and colleagues suggest an additional dimension to consider in our investigation of reactions to conflict (Drigotas, Whitney, & Rusbult, 1995; Rusbult & Zembrodt, 1983; Rusbult, Zembrodt, & Gunn, 1982). That is, in addition to their correlate of the expression-avoidance dimension (what they identify as activity/passivity), they suggest that a second dimension, that of constructiveness/destructiveness, be considered when attempting to understand reactions to conflict. These two basic dimensions were derived from four distinct responses to conflict: exit, voice, loyalty, and neglect (see Figure 13.2).

In addition to identifying these four reactions, Rusbult, Zembrodt, and Gunn (1982) also predict *when* each will be used. They generally find that satisfied

	Constructive	Destructive
Passive	Loyalty	Neglect
Active	Voice	Exit

FIGURE 13.2 *Reactions to Conflict*

Source: Rusbult, Zembrodt, and Gunn (1982). Reprinted by permission.

couples will be more likely to use constructive strategies, whereas dissatisfied couples will be more likely to enact destructive ones. Somewhat consistent with these findings, Ptacek and Dodge (1995) find that couples who use similar types of constructive coping strategies experience greater relationship satisfaction. Thus, it may not be one's conflict resolving skills that are as important as the types of conflicts that arise and one's satisfaction with the relationship.

Affect Reciprocity and Attributions as Predictors of Dissolution

Whether our reactions to conflict are loud or soft, hot or cold, part of our affective response has to do with how we reciprocate what we perceive as negativity from our partner. If your partner yells at you, do you yell back, ignore the exchange, leave the room (house, state, country), or approach the problem calmly and rationally? Which approach is the best? Should we meet fire with fire, or do we calm the beast with Mozart and reason?

Much of the research on how we react emotionally, physiologically, and psychologically to perceived threats from our partners is incorporated in Peterson's middle stages of conflict. What happens during direct negotiations or when conflicts escalate? How do we react to separation? Is conciliation and reconciliation possible? Gottman and colleagues have researched the reasons behind our physiological and affective responses to what happens at these stages of marital conflict.

Not surprisingly, relationship strife causes us to feel bad. However, Levenson and Gottman (1983) have found, once again, that our reactions to conflict depends on how satisfied we are with our relationship. In particular, distressed couples were found to experience more physiological arousal, experience more negative affect, and reciprocate negative affect. Further, Levenson and Gottman (1985) found marital satisfaction to be linked to affect reciprocity, such that satisfaction decreased the *most* when husbands reciprocated their wives' negative affect but wives did *not* reciprocate their husbands' negativity.

Indeed, negative affect reciprocity is one of the main warning signs that indicate if a relationship is headed for the rocks. Levenson and Gottman (1983, 1985) found predictable patterns of affective reactions that differentiated dissatisfied from satisfied couples. According to their research, not only do dissatisfied couples demonstrate higher levels of physiological arousal but they also have more negative affect as well as a greater degree of reciprocity of this negative affect.

In a longitudinal study involving 73 married couples, Gottman and Levenson (1992) identified several physiological, psychological, and behavioral predictors of relationship dissolution. They found that dissatisfied couples evaluated their problems as being more negative and severe, had poorer health, experienced more negative and fewer positive emotional exchanges, had greater defensiveness, and demonstrated more stubbornness and withdrawal from the relationship.

These findings jibe with research that links attributions we make to behaviors we enact (Bradbury & Fincham, 1992). For example, spouses who make negative attributions for problems in their marriage react more destructively to conflict than do spouses making positive, more benevolent attributions. Additionally, the relationship between attributions and behaviors are more strongly correlated in unhappy than in happy marriages. Reciprocity of negative interactions were more easily and reliably predicted in the cases of distressed wives than in nondistressed wives. It seems that negative, malevolent attributions foster reciprocity of negativity.

In summary, the question of whether expression is preferable to avoidance is fraught with *ifs* and *it depends*. In addition to the importance of the types of attributions we make, we might also ask what types of sentiments and affect are expressed. Angry, bitter, hostile, and hurtful expressions can surely be worse than silence and avoidance. Thus, it may be that there are certain skills that we can learn to help us express things the "right" way.

The Social Skill of Conflict Resolution

A fair number of researchers and a large part of commonsense advice portray reactions to conflict in terms such as *managing* conflict, making *strategic choices*, or lacking *communication skills*. One assumption reflected in these terms is that we can *learn* how to manage conflicts through the acquisition of the proper skills and techniques. Thus, constructive conflict would be the result of good communication and conflict resolving skills, whereas destructive outcomes would be the result of poor conflict management abilities. Counseling would include mastery of the methods necessary to communicate and handle discord successfully. Several approaches are consistent with this thinking.

Deutsch (1969) found that the type of conflict strategy used in a dispute determines whether the conflict is constructive or destructive. Couples involved in *constructive conflict* processes concentrate on the issue at hand and use mutual problem-solving approaches, such as persuasion, openness to each other's views, mutual enhancement, and minimization of both threat and deception. These arguments tend to be orderly and predictable. (As discussed earlier, Rusbult and colleagues found similar patterns of conflict outcomes in their studies.)

Couples involved in *destructive conflicts*, on the other hand, use escalating conflict processes such as threat, coercion, and deception. Further, participants in destructive interactions were found to reciprocate these negative conflict strategies, such that disputes often expand beyond the original initiating event or issue. The most obvious inference from these findings is that by using problem-focused, rational, open methods of conflict engagement, we should be able to have better relationships. However, what is not entirely clear is whether the use of these different conflict strategies leads to satisfaction or dissatisfaction with the relationship, or if the types of problems encountered in good versus destructive relationships lead to different types of conflicts and conflict processes.

Indeed, as mentioned earlier, even the use of expression may not be a universally desirable method of dealing with conflict. Inherent in this notion is the underlying assumption that "if we hold it in, we'll explode." This hydraulic model of emotion was tested in aggression research: Expressing aggression (releasing steam) would decrease aggression through a process of catharsis. Unfortunately, quite the contrary was found. Instead of decreasing aggression, clobbering a punching bag while thinking of one's ex would often lead to increased levels of arousal and aggression! Expression of negative affect may also have similar effects.

Cross-cultural research has also supported the notion that expression should not be advanced as the default panacea to conflict. For example, differences in communication styles have been found between Israeli and U.S. couples. Israeli couples are more emotional, more verbally aggressive, and less calm; U.S. couples, on the other hand, are more likely to use rational approaches to problem solving (Winkler & Doherty, 1983). These cultural differences in conflict styles translate directly into what types of coping strategies should be effective for each group. In fact, improving communication skills was more positively related to increases in relationship satisfaction in the U.S. couples but not in the Israeli couples.

Likewise, Sillars and Weisberg (1987) proposed that other cultural or group values are as important as the ideology of intimacy and expression: Values such as harmony maintenance (versus confrontation), the need for privacy and mystery, and the notion that we should "leave well enough alone" also need to be considered in our investigations of conflict in intimate relationships. Certainly, many conflicts eventually "go away," even when we do not take active steps to solve them. In other cases, we may not use expression and rational problem solving to deal with conflict, but may instead employ subtler methods, such as joking or gentle hints (Sillars & Weisberg, 1987).

Although each of these reactions to conflict can be found in any town, city, or country, there are certainly cultural differences along similar dimensions. That is, cultures also differ in the degree to which its members are expressive or reticent. Definite differences exist in the norms that govern the purpose and acceptability of conflict in society as well as how one should go about the conflict process. Thus, in New York, we are free to express ourselves with assertiveness and verve, whereas in southern states, civility is valued above the self-expression of anger and discord.

Finally, Rusbult and colleagues' work on accommodation supports this argument against a hands-down endorsement of expression as a conflict strategy. They suggest that avoidance, or at least the inhibition of impulsive and destructive behaviors, often leads to better conflict management (Rusbult et al., 1991; Yovetich & Rusbult, 1994). Of course, accommodation is more than simply the reining in of negative reactions. It also includes engagement in constructive conflict management strategies—even in the face of hostility and destructive acts from one's partner.

Thus, the expression-avoidance dichotomy may be an overly simplistic one. Interestingly, this division may be perpetuated by the types of research methodologies used in our data collection (Sillars & Weisberg, 1987). Studies using self-reports tend to support the positive correlation between expression and relationship satisfaction. Couples believe that good communication leads to great relationships and, conversely, that poor communication is to blame for weaknesses and failings in relationships. On the other hand, studies using observational techniques reveal that satisfied couples do not always use expression to work through problems (Pike & Sillars, 1985; Rausch et al., 1974). Instead, they often use avoidance and a variety of responses, such as jokes, changing the topic, and even denial of conflict, to name a few.

Outcomes of Conflict

Although conflict may lead to the strengthening of relationships, breakup and dissolution are equally likely to occur. Other consequences of conflict are property damage, physical and emotional abuse, domestic violence, stalking, and even murder. Further, marital conflict has been found to leave deep imprints on the most innocent of bystanders.

Researchers, for example, find that children need not experience parental divorce or separation to manifest the ill effects of conflict. Indeed, divorce is only a gross index of conflict in a relationship. That is, most divorces usually occur because of marital strife and combat; however, some marriages may end amicably with little outward evidence of discord. In support of the notion that even conflict in the absence of divorce can have damaging effects, researchers have found that the specific type of conflict resolution strategy used by parents has direct effects on children's ability to regulate emotions (Gottman & Katz, 1989) as well as whether children internalize or externalize their behaviors (Katz & Gottman, 1993). Children who bear witness to disruptive conflicts between their parents are less able to successfully regulate their emotions. For example, their experience of positive emotions tends to be in excess of the event, and they are unable to "rein in" their emotions. We probably think it charming and not a deficiency when, upon receiving a gift, this type of child is inordinately happy and remains so for a longer period of time than usual. However, rather than a sign of deep gratitude, this behavior pattern is an indication that the child is unable to pull out of the emotional experience (or any emotional experience, good or bad). Thus, it is not surprising that conflict is serious business.

Although the sources of conflict have been discussed at length, it is important to reiterate that conflict does not necessarily lead to or cause dissolution. In other words, conflicts arise from and involve an almost infinite variety of issues, but they may not always be directly implicated or causally responsible for relationship dissolution. Further, as previously suggested, perhaps bad relationships foment particularly bad conflicts, whereas good relationships engender a completely different class of conflict.

Toward a Balanced Theory
of Marriage and Conflict

Gottman's (1993) balance theory of marriage integrates the various conflict styles with what type of person uses each style and what outcomes we can expect from them. Based on a longitudinal study using both observational and self-report data, Gottman identified five different types of couples based on their communication patterns and their conflict engagement styles.

The three types of stable couples (those whose relationships remained intact) were labeled *validators*, *volatiles*, and *avoiders*. *Validators* reacted to problems with a "let's talk it out" approach and were generally positive and constructive. As the label implies, validators were supportive listeners and considerate speakers. Emotional expression, not surprisingly, was moderate. These couples were calm and comfortable in their discussions.

Volatiles, while also stable, had communication patterns that might lead you to think otherwise. Like Ralph and Alice Kramden in the classic television show, *The Honeymooners*, volatiles expressed a high degree of both positive and negative affect. They actually embraced disagreements and conflict engagement; however, in addition to vocalizing negative affect, there was an abundance of humor and affection, as well.

Avoiders used the passage of time as a conflict strategy. Seldom did these couples delve into their problems; rather, each person might state his or her position and then let the conversation come to an end. Moreover, avoiders seemed to feel that no matter what the problem or differences they experienced, what they had in common was greater than what they did not. This attitude allowed them to let issues and problems simply unfold on their own.

The two types of unstable couples, hostile and hostile/detached, were extremely combative in their interactions. *Hostile couples* engaged in a great deal of direct conflict, were highly defensive, and concerned themselves with mind reading tinged with a judgmental or blaming overtone. *Hostile/detached couples* had similar communication patterns but were generally more emotionally detached and uninvolved.

One of the most compelling aspects of the balance theory of marriage is that it goes beyond labeling coping styles as either good or bad, effective or ineffective. That is to say, avoiding a conflict is not necessarily a sign of social weakness, just as enjoying an argument doesn't mean a couple wants to end their marriage. According to Gottman, what is most predictive of relationship stability is the ratio of positive to negative affective experiences. Thus, in the three types of stable couples, Gottman found a five to one ratio of positive to negative affect. Thus, expressing negativity and experiencing intense conflict are not problematic or harmful, so long as the expression of positivity outweighs it by a factor of five! This model is satisfying for many reasons. Intuitively, it seems to encompass our personal experiences of different types of couples and relationships that we have experienced firsthand, as well as those we know indirectly through observation and hearsay. Many are the celluloid couples (e.g., *The Honeymooners*) that fight tooth-and-nail yet seem to have that perfect romantic love chemistry between them.

Summary

Issues.   We have addressed several different issues in the examination of conflict. First, as is true of many social constructs, defining what we mean by conflict is not only difficult but essential. Second, contrary to popular belief, not all outcomes of conflict are negative. In fact, some conflicts are actually like the silver lining of the proverbial dark cloud: beneficial and positive.

Attempting to uncover the sources of conflict reveals a plethora of potential causes, origins, and antecedents. Perhaps the most critical element to determining the source of conflict lies not so much in a particular act or episode, but rather in the type of attribution that is made. Is blame assigned to the partner or placed somewhere else? Thus, the impact of a grave transgression may be lessened by positive attributions ("You didn't do that on purpose; it's not your fault"), and a trivial act may be the straw that breaks the relationship's back ("You always make that awful clicking, sucking sound with your teeth just to annoy me").

Finally, the matter of whether it is better to express our unhappiness or to avoid confrontation was dealt with at length. Suffice it to say that, after our exhaustive investigation, this issue cannot be broken down to a simple either-or situation. Expression is good, depending on who you are and what you have to say. For example, expression of negative affect (negative affect reciprocity) is highly correlated with dissatisfaction and even a deterioration of the relationship. Likewise, avoidance might be better for addressing certain topics and may be a better fit for the communication styles of some couples.

Theories.   Several different theoretical approaches have given the study of conflict a solid grounding in good scientific research. The entailment model of relationships (Fincham & Bradbury, 1987, 1988), for example, integrates what we know about the causes of conflicts with an attributional approach. Thus, this model suggests that we need to consider causal attributions and their consequent judgments of responsibility in our determinations of conflict origination and cause.

Peterson's (1983) stage model provides us with an effective means of laying out and understanding the conflict process. From beginning to middle to termination, Peterson illustrates the dynamics of conflict and its potential outcomes. In a similar vein, Rusbult provides a model that helps us understand our reactions to conflicts. Different behavioral dimensions predict whether we will try to improve our relationship, stay and be unhappy, or leave.

Finally, Gottman provides a compelling and integrative model of marriage and conflict. In his balance model, he proposes that it is not conflict *per se* that disrupts our relationships, but the ratio of the good to the bad. That is, a couple who fights frequently and with great intensity but who also experiences five times as many intensely wonderful, intimate, passionate moments might actually be better off than the couple who fights only once a month but shares no other moments of happiness or joy. Thus, this model answers many of the issues of the expression/avoidance dimension and negative affect reciprocity by putting conflicts in the larger framework of the relationship as a whole.

Research.   Empirical research supporting the theories and issues in this chapter is varied and interesting. Surra and Longstreth (1990) found that, in dating couples, conflict stemmed from differing priorities between men and women. Specifically, men tended to prefer physical activities such as sex, whereas women preferred communal activities that would bring greater intimacy and closeness.

Gottman and Levenson (1992) discovered that, more than gender differences in activity preference or communication, other characteristics of couples lead to conflict and dissolution. Generally, they found that dissatisfied couples had more pessimistic views of their problems and relationships, and consequently reacted more negatively, both physiologically as well as behaviorally, to conflicts.

14

Dissolution and Its Aftermath

Rocker Rod Stewart once said of model Rachel Stewart, his wife of eight years, "I can't find any fault with her at all." Apparently she felt otherwise; last week the couple, who have two kids, announced a separation. Stewart, 54, has a history of woman-hopping, but Hunter, 30, reportedly broke it off because Rod got old and boring, watching TV and hanging out with his middle-aged mates.

—Newsweek, January 18, 1999

Long-suffering Jerry Hall has finally decided her Stone has gone rolling once too often. . . . Hall's attorney filed papers last week seeking a divorce . . . from Mick Jagger after eight years of marriage—and 21 years together. The long-standing problem: the 55-year-old rocker's insatiable womanizing.

—Newsweek, January 25, 1999

Dissolution of Intimate Relationships: The End of Romance

The natural cycle of relationships mandates not only the inevitability of conflict but also the eventual demise of each and every liaison—whether through mutual agreement, combat, external circumstances, or death. Although we generally welcome the blossoming of love and have even developed the unshakeable belief and expectation that we will all find that "happily ever after" relationship, we seem endlessly disappointed, dismayed, and perhaps even surprised by the dissolution of those same romantic relationships. Must all relationships end? Let us look more closely at some theories on the breakdown of relationships.

Causes of Dissolution

Breakups do not occur out of the blue. However, even though the destructive type of conflict may be one of the conditions that precipitates relationship dissolution (see Chapter 12), there are many other factors that determine the longevity and viability of a relationship. Duck (1982), for example, identified three conditions that lead to dissolution: preexisting doom, mechanical failure/process loss, and sudden death.

In *preexisting doom*, the partners are so ill matched that breakup is inevitable. We can think of certain celebrity couples—such as Dennis Rodman and Carmen Electra, Michael Jackson and Lisa Marie Presley, and Sylvester Stallone and Brigitte Nelson—as cases of doomed couples, where odds makers in Las Vegas were probably laying odds on the longevity of these relationships. Some breakups seem to engender shock in those around the troubled couple; however, in these instances, onlookers are usually more surprised that the couple has formed a liaison in the first place and are actually not at all surprised by the demise of the relationship. In other words, the seeds of dissolution or longevity are planted when Romeo first proposes to Juliet: The odds lie in the unique characteristics of the romantic duo and the chemistry that results from the combination of their dispositions, expectations, and interactions.

As seems to be the case for Rod Stewart and Rachel Hunter, dissolution of a relationship may be caused not by mismatched personalities, but by boredom or a sense that the relationship has grown stale and is lacking in excitement. The *mechanical failure/process loss* condition describes couples who just do not seem able to work things out. Like couples in soap operas, these relationships are sabotaged by miscommunication, suspicion, and power struggles. These types of breakups are caused by poor social skills, an inability to experience intimacy, and perhaps difficulties arising from problems adjusting to changes in the relationship (e.g., moving, employment changes, changes in family composition, etc.).

Communication is often cited as one of the most important components of successful relationships (see Chapter 5). The exact mechanism through which the quality of communication can either facilitate or destroy a relationship can be explained in part by the *uncertainty reduction theory (URT)* (Berger, 1987). In a nutshell, URT assumes that people are constantly striving to reduce the uncertainty in their day-to-day lives; this would, of course, include the reduction of uncertainty in their social relationships. Perhaps the aversiveness of uncertainty lies in the fact that, historically and phylogenetically, certainty has led to more favorable outcomes (i.e., predictability, control, greater success, and ultimately survival). What implications does URT hold for the dissolution of relationships?

Parks and Adelman (1983) extended these concepts to close interpersonal relationships. They surveyed 172 college-aged dating pairs and then followed up three months later to determine whether communication and certainty were correlated with relationship dissolution. Consistent with URT predictions, they found that partners who communicated often, not only with their partners but also with family and friends of their partners, had greater certainty about their relationships. Further, based on uncertainty measures, the researchers were then able to predict relationship dissolution with an almost 90 percent accuracy rate. Thus, effective communication is one way of preventing relationship dissolution because of mechanical or process failure.

However, even though certainty is clearly more desirable than uncertainty, and communication can obviously enhance certainty, there is, unfortunately, no one-to-one relationship between communication and certainty. That is, when determining the effectiveness of communication at reducing uncertainty, we must consider not only volume or quantity of communication but also clarity, quality, and motives. For example, we have all observed instances in which a person, perhaps with poor social skills, speaks at great length without communicating anything of significance (or anything that makes sense). On the other hand, it is also fairly obvious that *decreased* levels of communication generally serve to increase uncertainty.

Sudden death is Duck's (1982) graphic description of the third condition leading to relationship termination. Here, one partner betrays the other by breaking the cardinal rules of the relationship, such as engaging in behaviors that culminate in the betrayal of trust, committing adultery, or abusing the partner. As Jerry Hall no doubt discovered, deception and rule breaking destroy trust and rend a relationship beyond repair. Thus, Duck sees the source of dissolution either within the individuals, in the type of interactions (and ultimately in the relationship that develops), and in the types of rule-breaking behaviors in which couples engage.

Barrier Models of Dissolution.   Duck (1982) pinpoints relationship dynamics as a source of dissolution; Thibaut and Kelley's (1959) social exchange model also takes an interpersonal approach to explain the reasons for and types of breakups. It provides a preliminary framework for understanding attraction, satisfaction, as well as dissolution. Further, the social exchange model and other barrier models examine the importance of factors external as well as internal to the couples' relationships.

Recall from our discussion of social exchange theory in Chapter 6 that Thibaut and Kelley (1959) are able to predict the continuation or dissolution of a relationship. Briefly, the comparison level for alternatives enables us to predict how dependent a person is on his or her current relationship. If there are no attractive alternatives, a person will remain in the relationship no matter how unsatisfactory it is. On the other hand, if highly attractive alternatives exist, a person will leave even a good relationship.

The social exchange model presents us with the raw outlines of a "barrier" explanation of dissolution. For example, no matter how unhappy we are with our current relationship, we will not leave until a suitable alternative situation is present. In other words, the absence of an attractive alternative provides a barrier to our exiting our current, loveless relationship.

Its roots deeply embedded in the social exchange model, Levinger's (1976) barrier model pushes beyond it and specifies the specific factors of attraction, alternative attractions, and barriers that define the dynamics of marriage. Thus, not only does Levinger recognize the forces of attraction that impel us to love one another but he also charts the material, psychological, and emotional elements that prevent us from exiting a relationship (see Table 14.1).

Quite simply, Levinger (1976) has portrayed attractions, alternative attractions, and barriers as forces of varying strength that act on individuals in a marriage. Marital cohesion or dissolution depends on the relative strength of each one. For example, attraction to one's partner may be low, and alternatives may look more appealing (e.g., other more attractive partners, independence from an unsatisfying relationship), but the barriers to leaving the relationship may be too costly. Any or all of the following material and psychological costs can prevent dissolution and act as barriers to exiting an unhappy marriage: a domineering father ("We don't believe in divorce in this family!"), the high monetary cost of

TABLE 14.1   *Factors Differentiating High- and Low-Cohesive Marriages*

Attractions	Barriers	Alternate Attractions
Material Rewards Family income Home ownership	**Material Costs** Financial expenses	**Material Rewards** Wife's independent social and economic status
Symbolic Rewards Educational status Occupational status Social similarity	**Symbolic Costs** Obligation toward marital bond Religious constraints Pressures from primary groups Pressures from the community	**Symbolic Rewards** Independence and self-actualization
Affectional Rewards Companionship and esteem Sexual enjoyment	**Affectional Costs** Feelings toward dependent children	**Affectional Rewards** Preferred alternate sex partner Disjunctive kin affiliations

starting out on your own, or family obligations ("We will stay together for the sake of the children").

Barriers, then, hold us secure in great relationships and prevent us from leaving unhappy ones. However, if the forces of attraction are lowered, if alternative attractions are even stronger, and/or if barriers are weakened, dissolution (separation or divorce) occurs. Anthropological evidence provides an illustration of this point. Societies in which men and women are self-sufficient and both economically independent have higher divorce rates than societies in which men and women have greater economic interdependence (Levinger, 1976).

According to the barrier model, when both men and women are on equal economic footing, alternative attractions are increased, especially in terms of material rewards where women have the potential to gain economically and socially by leaving the relationship (Levinger, 1976). Further, if divorce is accepted as a fairly standard practice, one of the symbolic barriers against dissolution is eliminated. Thus, in societies in which both of these conditions exist, divorce rates are high (roughly 40 to 50 percent).

By contrast, in agricultural societies, where husbands and wives are highly dependent on one another for survival, there are fewer alternative attractions for either person. A couple's wealth is not portable; instead, their labor and the returns of their labor are literally planted in their land. Thus, when people leave relationships, they leave behind their economic lifelines. Furthermore, in agricultural societies, divorce is viewed as an unacceptable practice. So, in this case, we have lower alternative attractions and greater barriers. Divorce rates are generally lower in agricultural societies.

For example, think of Mel Gibson as the stalwart farmer, clinging to his flooded fields and desperately holding his family together while his stolid wife, Cissy Spacek, is courted by a wealthy interloper in *The River*. Of course they neither give up their land nor their marriage. Their investment in the family homestead is almost overwhelming. Indeed, a beneficial implication of these models is that barriers hold otherwise good relationships together through the dry spells and bad moments of a relationship.

Lund (1985) examined the finer points of the dynamics of barrier models. In an investigation that mirrored the "magnetic" debate in attraction (i.e., are we drawn to desired others or are we repelled by undesirable others?), she questioned whether we are kept in relationships by forces that "pull" us and adhere us to one another (i.e., attraction, passion, love) or whether, as the barrier model would suggest, we are prevented from leaving a relationship by various internal and external forces such as commitment, investments, and social approval. Lund's research has thus far supported the barrier model as the best predictor of whether relationships will be maintained. Thus, as the folk wisdom goes and contrary to Captain and Tennille, love alone is not enough to keep us together.

Other Models of Dissolution.   Duck (1982) proposed an alternate model of relationship dissolution based on his assumption that dissolution represents the continual evolution of a relationship rather than the reversal or cessation of its development. Duck presented a stage model of dissolution that includes four phases through which unhappy couples pass in a progressive fashion: intrapsychic phase, dyadic phase, social phase, and grave dressing phase. This model is notable for its inclusion of all levels of personal and social interaction. For example, the *intrapsychic phase* represents the personal, internal ruminations of the disaffected partner. It is a self-focused, introspective phase of assessment and evaluation in which the person tallies the good and bad points of the relationship and his or her partner. This phase continues until the musings culminate in the feeling that there is sufficient justification for ending the relationship (Duck, 1982).

The *dyadic phase* represents the interpersonal phase of dissolution. The previously private ruminations are now made public, the cards are on the table, confrontation is achieved, and the whole conflict process begins. The couple may seesaw back and forth between fighting and futilely attempting to repair the relationship. This wavering, along with the bickering and hostile attacks, continues until the next threshold is surmounted: The unhappy initiator of the conflict feels cornered into demonstrating his or her resolve and proving his or her unhappiness through the enactment of separation (Duck, 1982).

The next stage, the *social phase*, is group oriented. Here, partners reach beyond their immediate relationship to manage their social impressions. Separating partners seek out family and friends to attempt to control and shape social reality—to mold the story of "how and why we're splitting up." Interestingly, as demonstrated by Levinger (1976) and Lund (1985), family and community might provide barriers to exiting a relationship, but they might also facilitate the breakup! According to Duck (1982), once the couple makes the move toward divorce or separation, members of their social network may hasten and ease this process (through gossip) by providing coinciding explanations, justifications, and support for the breakup.

The *grave dressing phase* refers to what happens after "all's been said and done." Partners busy themselves with the private and public process of creating the story of the relationship and its end (Weber & Harvey, 1994). It includes the process of justifying the relationship and its termination as well as bridges the chasm between the failed relationship to potential future couplings. This "story" includes assurances that, although their relationship failed, the partners continue to be good relationship material. This type of "account making" (Weber & Harvey, 1994) serves several functions. It helps the individuals understand what happened in the relationship and achieve closure about the breakup. Further, in addition to facilitating recovery from the dissolution, account making helps the partners maintain current relationships and move forward to new ones. Thus, this model of dissolution includes the personal, dyadic, and social steps involved in the process of tearing a relationship asunder.

Evolutionary Approaches to Dissolution.   Another cause for dissolution may lie not in the kinds of conflicts we have, the type of relationship, or the kind of social network, but rather, it may lie in an interaction between our evolutionarily determined makeup and our behavior. Anthropologists have long studied the gamut of human behavior across countless cultures. Not only have they studied the ins and outs of marriage but they have also compiled an interesting array of evidence to support an evolutionary explanation of divorce. One such theory suggests that divorce is not an aberrant event, but one that fits an evolutionary perspective on human reproduction.

One of the motives at the heart of evolutionary explanations is the perpetuation and therefore the strengthening of an organism's gene pool—in other words, the continuation and proliferation of our progeny. According to this perspective, divorce is as natural as marriage (i.e., it is a naturally selected behavior). Citing brain chemical changes, sex researchers suggest that we experience the intense passion of love for only a couple of years, but those few years should provide enough time for procreation to occur. However, since the advent of bipedal ambulation and the consequent narrowing of the pelvic region, humans, unlike quadruped animals, evolved to give birth to highly immature offspring. That is, the more immature and thus smaller the baby, the greater the likelihood of successful birth. And because of the highly immature state of the human infant, parents (and mothers in particular) need to invest a great deal of time and energy into raising and supporting their young. Thus, the relational bond between men and women must be long enough to ensure conception, birth, and the nurturing of their offspring until independence.

Scientists suggest that the length of the human breeding cycle is roughly four years. This hypothesis is supported by a couple of different findings. For instance, these estimates are based on studies of the !Kung and Australian Aborigines who nurse their young for three to four years. Since lactation (coupled with the spartan diet of these tribes) serves as a natural although imperfect method of birth control, subsequent births tend to be suppressed during this period of nursing. Other evidence supporting this hypothesis can be found in the U.S. Census Bureau. Statistics reveal that the largest number of couples separate or divorce after three or four years of marriage, unless a child is born (Fisher, 1987).

In other words, if the union is not "fruitful," dissatisfaction with the relationship increases as the natural passion-inducing brain chemicals wear off and yield to their replacement—attachment hormones. In fact, evolutionary explanations would suggest that the seven-year itch would more accurately be construed as a *four*-year itch (Fisher, 1987). Thus, it is not conflict that leads to dissolution; rather, it is the absence of the proper relationship structures and their resultant brain chemicals that lead to the weakening of passion and the increasing interest in alternative relationships.

Just as the ebb and flow of brain chemicals are naturally occurring events, proponents of this view consider divorce a normal adaptive response to the environment. Indeed, divorce is considered to be just as evolutionarily adaptive as monogamy. However, whereas the adaptiveness of monogamy may be obvious (i.e., children raised within the bounds of a solid union have an increased probability of survival and therefore success in producing and raising their own young), there are also evolutionary advantages to divorce.

Childless unions bode ill for one's gene pool, and therefore those who move on to more bountiful waters are more likely to pass on their genetic material to future generations. Furthermore, once the four-year breeding cycle is over, separation and childrearing with another partner would serve to add genetic diversity (and therefore strength) to one's gene pool. Thus, according to the evolutionary perspective, the major source of conflict and dissolution would be the presence or absence of offspring. Additionally, the idea of marriage as a lifelong union is, from this model, more *abnormal* than that of divorce.

In sum, although the evolutionary perspective presents us with compelling explanations for social behavior, we hasten to add that this type of explanation is a distal one. The previously discussed psychological models can be viewed not only as more proximal explanations for the same behaviors but also more parsimonious. Further, we know by now that, just as a single theory does not always capture the phenomena, there is also no one factor or cause that will unequivocally lead to separation. Rather, it is more likely that a complex interplay of variables are at work in determining whether the relationship is a match made in heaven or hell.

Gender Differences in Dissolution

Is there a gender difference between who ends a relationship? Are women rejected more frequently, or are they more frequently the rejectors? Although most of us have probably been on both sides of the eject button (either pressing it or finding ourselves flying through the great wide open), research does offer support for our perception that there are gender differences in who is more likely to initiate breakups. Hill, Rubin, and Peplau (1976) examined the dating trajectory of college students for a two-year period. They found that breakups were highly correlated with external, structural factors, such as the school calendar. Further, women were also more likely to initiate the breakup, regardless of their boyfriends' dispositions toward this turn of events.

In a study of long-distance relationships among college-aged students, women were not only more likely to initiate breakups but they were also better able to adjust to the dissolutions (Helgeson, 1994). This pattern of dissolution (i.e., women more frequently being the initiator of relationship dissolution) has also been found to be true for the termination of marital relationships, as well (Helgeson, 1994).

The Aftermath of Relationship Dissolution

> *"I was delivered by God when he left." Actress Linda Hamilton, on her pending divorce from* Titanic *director James Cameron, whom she called a "miserable, unhappy man"*
>
> —*Newsweek,* February 8, 1999

We commonly assume that many of us experience sadness in the aftermath of the dissolution of a relationship, but undoubtedly some of us experience a great deal of relief when a bad relationship ends. However, this relief may be short-lived as we find ourselves reassessing and readjusting our lives in ways that we may not have anticipated or predicted. That is, the initial experience of dissolution later gives ways to more complex and complicated feelings and outcomes. Thus, as we shall see, a host of outcomes (mostly negative) are associated with dissolution—whether it be in the breakup of a dating relationship, through divorce, or with the death of a spouse.

Although some of our most painful breakups may have occurred before we turned age 18, there is definitely a distinction to be made between the dissolution of premarital as opposed to wedded relationships. Youth and naiveté may make the wound left by the departure of a loved one seem mortal, but the breakup of a marriage involves so much more: the possible severing of extended relationships, violation of social norms, economic hardship, and changes in status and identity are among the issues. Understandably, the majority of research on aftermath examines divorce; however, let us start with an examination of some of the common elements of relationship breakups—whether it be the dissolution of a dating relationship, an engagement, or a marriage.

Emotional Distress

Several factors contribute to the severity of the trauma and pain of separation: the loss of a close and valued other, lowered self-esteem, dependency, length of the relationship, external sources of stress, and availability of social support, to name a few. In order to sort through the many possible factors that contribute to postrelationship misery, Simpson (1987) studied the history of college-aged dating couples over a three-month period. In addition to discovering variables that contribute to relationship stability (i.e., exclusivity, nature of sexual relationship, orientation of the partners toward sex, self-monitoring, and satisfaction with partner), he also identified several factors that mediated the emotional experience of dissolution. While also good indicators of the stability of relationships, three factors—closeness, duration of the relationship, and the possibility of obtaining a suitable alternative partner—were especially potent predictors of the level of emotional distress experienced following a breakup. In other words, individuals who felt very close to their partners, who had been dating their partners for longer periods of time, or who believed that they could not find a better partner experienced the most distress upon the termination of their relationships.

Some of the emotional turmoil experienced by couples in failed relationships may include distress, sadness, depression, guilt, anger, and loneliness. As we've already discovered in Chapter 10 (Fidelity and Jealousy), one of the emotional fallouts of the dissolution of a romantic relationship may be jealousy. However, several other emotional outcomes become apparent besides jealousy. For example, Baumeister, Reis, and Delespaul (1995) suggested that guilt feelings are linked very closely to intimate relationships and especially to interpersonal conflict, rejection, and loneliness. Two other emotional factors that have received much attention in the research literature are loneliness and the trauma of unrequited love.

Loneliness

One of the obvious outcomes of separation is being single again—alone. Of course, being alone is not always tied to being lonely, but the loss of a constant companion usually triggers feelings of loneliness. Further, our need for attachment, affiliation, and belonging underscore the essence of our humanity. Thus, loneliness, the flip side of attraction and belonging, is generally an aversive, unpleasant state. Indeed, case studies of religious hermits, prisoners of war, and castaways reveal the devastating effects of social isolation and loneliness. The Unabomber, Theodore Kaczynski, although suffering from mental illness as well, may not have been so dangerous had he not had more fulfilling human contact. No doubt, being isolated in his cabin in the mountains of Montana exacerbated his delusional thinking and paranoia.

Who Are the Lonely Hearts?   Clearly, humans are social animals. It is almost a given, therefore, that most of us have experienced loneliness at one time or another in our lives. Yet, despite the commonness of loneliness, we all know people who seem to be consistently more lonely and others who are hardly lonely at all. Who are the lonely, and what causes loneliness?

Contrary to stereotypes, our elders are not lonelier than their children and grandchildren. Through the use of different loneliness measurement scales (see

Figure 14.1), researchers have found that, generally speaking, the younger, the lonelier (Ostrov & Offer, 1980). Adolescents and young adults score higher on loneliness indices than do older adults and the elderly (Peplau et al., 1982; Rubenstein & Shaver, 1982). In fact, loneliness is a very common experience in college students (Shaver, Furman, & Buhrmester, 1985). And although marriage is not a shield against loneliness, the dissolution of marital relationships leads to much higher levels of loneliness (Perlman & Peplau, 1981).

Researchers have found that in addition to age and marital status, personality variables are also correlated with the experience of loneliness. Shyness and social anxiety (Leary, 1983), distrust (Vaux, 1988), hostility (Check, Perlman, & Malamuth, 1985), depression (Lobdell & Perlman, 1986), and poor social and communication skills (Solano & Koester, 1989; Jones, Hobbs, & Hackenbury, 1982) are among the personality factors that have been linked with loneliness. Imagine yourself engaged in a conversation with someone who fails to make eye contact with you, is slow to respond to your queries and then replies in only short monosyllabic answers, makes few statements, fails to continue conversing on topics

FIGURE 14.1 *The Revised UCLA Loneliness Scale*

Directions: Indicate how often you feel the way described in each of the following statements. Use the numbers to respond, where 1 = never, 2 = rarely, 3 = sometimes, and 4 = often.

1. I feel in tune with the people around me.*
2. I lack companionship.
3. There is no one I can turn to.
4. I do not feel alone.*
5. I feel part of a group of friends.*
6. I have a lot in common with the people around me.*
7. I am no longer close to anyone.
8. My interests and ideas are not shared by those around me.
9. I am an outgoing person.*
10. There are people I feel close to.*
11. I feel left out.
12. My social relationships are superficial.
13. No one really knows me well.
14. I feel isolated from others.
15. I can find companionship when I want it.*
16. There are people who really understand me.*
17. I am unhappy being so withdrawn.
18. People are around me but not with me.
19. There are people I can talk to.*
20. There are people I can turn to.*

Note: The total score is the sum of all the items. Higher scores indicate greater loneliness.

*Item should be reversed (i.e., 1 = 4, 2 = 3, 3 = 2, 4 = 1) before scoring.

Source: Russell, Peplau, and Cutrona (1980). Reprinted by permission.

you have introduced, does not ask you about yourself, and is highly self-focused. What would you do? Most of us would search desperately for the first opportunity to flee this situation, leaving our poor conversational partner alone. Indeed, Jones and colleagues (1982) found that unresponsiveness and insensitivity tend to sow loneliness.

Feelings and Sources of Loneliness.   Given the universality of loneliness, it would be a mistake to believe that it stems from age and personality variables alone. There must be more to loneliness than bad breath and poor social skills. Although all types of loneliness derive from the deprivation or perceived deprivation of close contact with others, there are nuances to our feelings of isolation. For example, Mikulincer and Segal (1990) suggested that there are four distinct types of feelings of loneliness: social estrangement, which arises from a lack of ties to one's surroundings; emotional isolation, which is the result of being rejected by others; depressive loneliness, which involves longing for a loved one; and esteem loneliness, which is connected to alienation, shame, and fear. Dissolution of a romantic relationship can thus lead to feelings of depressive loneliness as well as esteem loneliness. However, for couples who have been dating for longer periods of time, and for whom a high degree of social interconnections have been established (i.e., sharing of friends, family integration, etc.), feelings of social estrangement and emotional isolation may also occur. Thus, we can see from this typology how the duration of a relationship may increase the severity of postrelationship distress and loneliness.

Researchers have explored not only the types of loneliness that we experience but also the different causes of loneliness. In an extensive survey that included over 600 participants from all walks of life and ranging from 17 to 79 years of age, Rokach and Brock (1995) concluded that there are five causal factors that contribute to loneliness: personal inadequacies, developmental deficits, unfulfilling intimate relationships, relocation/significant separation, and social marginality. At least two factors, personal inadequacies and developmental deficits, probably make it difficult for individuals to establish friendships and other close or intimate relationships in the first place. Two other factors, unfulfilling intimate relationships and relocation/significant separation, are more directly linked to relationship dissolution.

Shaver and Buhrmester's (1983) conceptualization of loneliness overlaps nicely with the other work on loneliness discussed here. They have suggested that there are two types of loneliness: one that results from emotional isolation (lack or loss of psychological intimacy) and one that results from social isolation (loss or lack of integrated, group involvement). *Psychological intimacy* is met through close interpersonal relationships, such as through romantic love, one's family, and friendship groups. *Integrated involvement*, on the other hand, includes participation in groups, such as committees, long-term work groups, athletic teams, and communes. According to Shaver and Buhrmester's work, membership in an ideal community can meet the needs for both psychological intimacy and group involvement (see Figure 14.2). Romantic couplings, however, though great at alleviating emotional isolation, are very poor at providing integrated involvement. Thus, this conceptualization of loneliness suggests that even though we may be very happy having found the romance of a lifetime, we might still experience loneliness if we lack group involvement. By the same token, loneliness caused by the breakup of a beautiful romance will not be alleviated through involvement in church groups, the Rotary, or soccer clubs.

Breaking up with a loved one, then, results in emotional isolation. Further, this separation can lead to a breakdown in integrated involvement in cases of a divorce or termination of other long-term relationships. Here, one of the partners may relocate, change jobs, or move out of integrated friendship groups. Thus, not only will some couples experience a deep sense of emotional isolation but they may also find themselves without access to previously enjoyed group activities.

Once again, this model is useful in that it can predict how we will feel after the loss of a loved one and how effective some of our coping strategies might be. Specifically, it suggests that turning to friendship groups, special-interest clubs, hobbies, or workplace involvement cannot fully compensate for the loss of a close and cherished partner. Although these activities may provide us with companionship and social support, the level of psychological intimacy provided by the company of others cannot match that which was lost. Thus, substituting friends' or

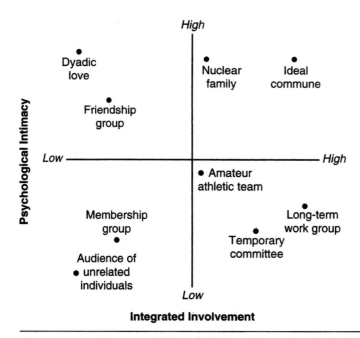

FIGURE 14.2 *Groups and Their Relationship to Psychological Intimacy and Social Integration*

Source: Shaver and Buhrmeister (1983). Reprinted by permission.

family members' consoling words and sympathy for the presence of a loved one can help, but it cannot fill the emotional void and isolation created by the former partner's departure. Together, these elements make it clear that the dissolution of long-term relationships, and especially marital dissolution, can be extremely distressing, particularly in terms of the intensity of loneliness that can be experienced (Mastekaasa, 1997).

Unrequited Love

We have discussed at length the emotional distress of dissolution, jealousy, and loneliness. However, the emotional trauma and turmoil of dissolution may not be symmetrically distributed across the rejected and the rejector. So, how does our role in the breakup influence our postdissolution experience and interpretation of the relationship? Baumeister and colleagues' research on unrequited love provides an excellent framework for investigating the emotional experience of the rejector and the would-be lover (Baumeister & Wotman, 1992; Baumeister, Wotman, & Stillwell, 1993; Bratslavsky, Baumeister, & Sommer, 1998).

Through careful analyses and dissection of autobiographical accounts, Baumeister and colleagues identified two distinct behavioral and emotional reactions to unrequited love (Bratslavsky et al., 1998). At first, most of us would empathize with the spurned lover, for we have all experienced the anguish of rejection. However, Baumeister and colleagues' work reveals a much more complex and interesting picture. The emotional and behavioral aftermath of relationship dissolution depends very much on whose shoes you are in: those of the rejector or those of the rejected.

Essentially, unrequited affection can be the result of three different types of relationships (Bratslavsky et al., 1993). First, *lopsided relationships* can result when a person, inferior in attractiveness and desirability, chooses a love interest who is much more popular, successful, attractive, and desirable than himself or herself (e.g., John Hinckley's obsessive infatuation for Jodi Foster). A second source of unbalanced love relationships results when a *platonic friendship* turns into something more for one (but not both) of its participants (e.g., Niles's love for Daphne on *Frasier*). And finally, *uneven feelings of love* often appear in the early stages of romantic relationships when partners are still trying to figure each other out and sort through their feelings for one another. At first, both may be very interested in the prospect of sharing an intimate relationship; however, after a few months or a couple of dates, it becomes clear that feelings of love are not in fact shared and cannot be reciprocated. It is at this point, when the uninterested dating partners try to extricate themselves from the dyad, that the process of unrequited love swings into action.

One of the paradoxical conclusions drawn from Baumeister's research is that, despite the rejection, the would-be lover's (i.e., the rejected) situation is much more appealing than that of the rejector. Although would-be lovers experience the pain of rejection, they also have many positive emotional experiences, such as hope, anticipation, and the elation of infatuation. The emotional experiences of rejecters, on the other hand, are much more restricted and largely negative, such as guilt, confusion, and uncertainty.

Not surprisingly, the nature of the situation (i.e., one person pursuing with abandon, the other trying simultaneously to avoid the issue, reduce hurt feelings, and separate) shapes the focus of its participants. Would-be lovers tend to be self-focused, largely attentive to their feelings of love and their experience of rejection. Rejectors, on the other hand, tend to be other-focused, quite concerned about how their actions affect their would-be lovers. Let us examine how these differences play out in terms of the emotional experiences of the couple as well as the behavioral options available to them.

One of the central experiences of would-be lovers is damage to their self-esteem. Consistent with their self-focus, would-be lovers internalize their rejection and feel unattractive, inferior, silly, stupid, foolish, and embarrassed (Baumeister & Wotman, 1992). On the other hand, they have no sense of guilt over any discomfort they may have inflicted on their rejectors. They are focused on their own feelings of love and hope, while completely ignoring the distress of their rejector.

The central experience of rejectors, on the other hand, is guilt. This guilt results from two sources: empathy for the would-be lover and anxiety over having to engage in the actual act of rejecting another person's overtures of love. Rejectors report experiencing a great deal of guilt over having to inflict pain—even though it is done unintentionally. The experience of guilt is entirely consistent with the fact that rejectors are other-focused (Baumeister & Wotman, 1992).

The behavioral outcomes of unrequited love are also consistent with the self-versus-other orientation of the rejected and the rejector. Would-be lovers attempt to repair their damaged self-esteem in a variety of ways. For example, they may attempt to bolster their self-esteem by derogating their rivals (in the case of love triangles) or by finding an attractive and loving alternative lover. Interestingly, although friends of the jilted may have harsh words for rejectors, would-be lovers rarely derogate their rejectors. Rejectors, on the other hand, suffer from a sense of scriptlessness (i.e., not having well-defined norms that guide one through the dissolution of relationships). They attempt to escape their feelings of guilt by creating justifications for their actions. That is, rejectors must work very hard to justify their rejection: derogating the would-be lover, painting themselves as victims, suggesting that they are doing "what's best" for the other, and so forth (Bratslavsky et al., 1998; Baumeister & Wotman, 1992).

One factor underlying much of these differences is the fact that, as a society, we place a great emphasis on love and being in love. This, coupled with our need for belongingness (Baumeister & Leary, 1995), makes relationship termination and the refusal of someone's affections extremely difficult and very near contrary to our natural inclinations. Indeed, societal exaltation of love provides ample justification for the would-be lover's actions while providing none for the rejector's. Thus, not only is rejection difficult and almost antinormative but, by this definition, it also leads to scriptlessness. Rejectors are often confused and uncertain as to how to rebuff their hopeful lovers and must search doggedly for justifications for their lack of love and desire for separation.

In sum, people experience a great deal of turmoil and emotional distress in the aftermath of a failed relationship. Loneliness and jealousy are among the emotions they experience. However, as we have just seen, how a person weathers the aftermath of relationship dissolution depends not only on the longevity of the relationship but also on the nature of the relationship (happy, conflicted) and whether the person is the rejector or the rejected. In the next section, we will see how the degree of commitment can also affect our experience of relationship dissolution.

In the Wake of Divorce

> *Police who responded to Marilyn Lemak's 911 call not only found the bodies of her three smothered children but also discovered macabre hints of the motive she would soon describe in a Naperville [Illinois] hospital room. . . . Crumpled on a bathroom floor was a wedding dress. . . . Also inside the home, where her path from room to room was traced in the blood from her suicide attempt, police found a wedding photograph with an X-acto knife stuck through it, the blade piercing the image of her estranged husband, David Lemak, in the chest. . . . Although attorneys had said the divorce was proceeding amicably, law-enforcement sources said that Marilyn Lemak indicated the dissolution of her marriage was one of the primary factors that precipitated the slayings.*
>
> —*Chicago Tribune*, March 10, 1999

Despite the social stigma and emotional trauma associated with separation and divorce, we are dissolving our marriages almost as fast as we are entering them. In fact, recent statistics show a steady increase in divorce rates since the mid-1800s, when roughly 5 percent of marriages ended in divorce, to almost 50 percent in 1985 (Cherlin, 1992). Interestingly, more detailed research reveals that one in three marriages end within four years, while a full one in every two marriages end in divorce within seven years (Bumpass, Sweet, & Castro Martin, 1990). (These statistics, by the way, are consistent with evolutionary explanations of relationship duration.)

Although lessening, there continues to be some degree of stigma tied to divorce. As discussed earlier, the termination of relationships is not a well-scripted procedure in U.S. society. We possess elaborate schemas that guide our perceptions and experiences of falling in love, but we seem to possess less well-developed mental representations of why, when, and how to end it all. How do we know if our unhappiness is temporary? How do we repair and improve our relationships? When do we call it quits? How do we go about ending a relationship? Each question, although very clear, is a difficult and personal one. As we have seen in our discussion of the different theories of dissolution, this ambiguity compels us to turn to others in our social networks to help us construct an explanation and story for these events, to make personal and interpersonal sense of the whole dissolution process. In more traditional societies, of course, these issues are firmly embedded in culture and tradition.

Generally, the economic consequences of divorce are more devastating for women and children than for men. Although designed to give legal equality to women, the advent of no-fault divorce (as opposed to contested divorce) has had the paradoxical effect of worsening the economic welfare of women and children. The economic well-being of divorced women has been estimated to drop by a rate of between 30 to 73 percent, whereas men's economic status improves by an average of 15 to 42 percent (Hoffman & Duncan, 1988; Weitzman, 1985). Loss of income, along with loss of home, relocation, perhaps reentering the job market, and changes in social groups can be devastating not only for women but also for their children.

Losing one's position in society, perhaps experiencing poverty, home loss, custody battles, and stigma, can have ruinous effects on mental, emotional, and physical health. As we see in the tragic story of Marilyn Lemak, divorce can lead to horrifying outcomes, not only psychologically and emotionally but also in terms of mortality. In the next section, we will examine some of the effects of divorce.

Divorce and Health

Given the severity of distress that precedes most divorces as well as research identifying marital dissolution as one of the most potent life stressors, it shouldn't be surprising that divorce also takes a toll on the health and mortality of its participants. That is, in addition to the loneliness and emotional distress that accompany the termination of any relationship, divorce encompasses much more: the termination of a long-term relationship, the involvement of children in addition to family and friends, and societal disapproval. These factors, plus others, may easily exacerbate the loneliness, distress, damage to esteem, and stress brought on by a relationship's end.

Although divorce has been correlated with higher mortality risks, it is difficult to pinpoint the exact nature of this relationship. It is difficult to say with absolute certainty whether divorce itself causes a higher risk of premature mortality. In addition to the hypothesis that the stress and trauma of divorce itself are life-span reducing, an alternative explanation might be that unhealthy individuals or those with propensities for high-risk behaviors (e.g., alcoholism, risk taking) are self-selected for divorce. That is, divorce may not threaten one's health so much as the possibility that certain risk-prone individuals are more likely to get divorced in the first place. A third alternative might be that divorce eliminates an important, life-enhancing, health-promoting component from the divorced person's arsenal of life-support mechanisms: marriage itself. Let us explore each possibility.

First, the idea that divorce may increase premature mortality risks (even years after the divorce) has been documented by many different researchers. Divorce presents its participants with a unique situation, qualitatively different from the breakup of a dating relationship. Holmes and Rahe's (1967) Social Readjustment Rating Scale identifies divorce as the second most stressful life event, second only to the death of a spouse. Further, marital separation is ranked the third most stressing life event. All three are tied not only to the loss of a partner but also to the dissolution of a marital relationship. More recent research supports this portrayal of marital dissolution as a major life stressor (Mastekaasa, 1997).

In a large sample of divorcing or separating Norwegian couples, Mastekaasa (1997) found a dramatic increase in stress and a marked decline in feelings of subjective well-being throughout the preseparation period. Further, one of the key reasons why marital dissolution can be so distressing is because of the intense loneliness experienced by divorced individuals. Undoubtedly, the very stress of separation and divorce can have an adverse impact on one's health.

Thus, while this explanation may make intuitive sense, remember that the supporting evidence is correlational. It may be equally likely that high-risk behavior mediates the relationship between divorce and health, such that individuals who engage in high-risk behaviors (e.g., smoking, drinking, etc.) are more likely to get divorced (because of their risk taking) and are also more likely to experience greater threats to their health (also because of their risk taking). That is, rather than suggesting that divorce leads to poor health, it may be that risk-taking individuals who are also less healthy are more likely to get divorced.

Proponents of the protection hypothesis suggest that the institution of marriage offers protective factors that promote longevity (Anson, 1989; Hemström, 1996). According to Anson, the health benefits of marriage are threefold: Marriage provides social integration through social ties that satisfy intimacy needs; it provides clearer social roles, which in turn lead to reductions in risk taking and other unhealthy behaviors; and, finally, marriage bestows higher social status on its participants. Thus, divorce for some might have the combined effect of the stress due to the separation in addition to the elimination of the protective benefits of marriage. Even in cases where the divorce may be amicable and civil, the couple will nonetheless experience the loss of the mortality protection offered by marriage. Thus, divorcing couples experience not only an increase in stress due to the separation but they also find that the stress-reducing, social support and health-enhancing components found within marriage are now eliminated. Thus, there can be little doubt that marital dissolution leads to psychological and emotional distress.

And as difficult as childrearing may be, and although their presence reduces subjective measures of happiness and well-being (Myers & Diener, 1995), the presence of small children in marriage has been found to increase mortality protection (Hemström, 1996). One reason for this finding may be due to the fact that children also tend to forestall marital dissolution (Castro Martin & Bumpass, 1989). Further, couples with three or more biological children were found to be the least likely to divorce (Spanier & Glick, 1981).

Structural and Sociological Factors Related to Divorce

Sociological analyses reveal several individual-level factors related to the reasons for divorce. Census data reveal that age at time of marriage is one of the strongest predictors of divorce. As compared to marriages in older couples (i.e., those older than age 20), teenagers tying the knot are two to three times more likely to untie it soon thereafter (Norton & Moorman, 1987). This is generally accounted for by the lack of maturity of the teenaged couple and the fact that many of these youths may mature into adults who would have made very different mate selections. Duck's (1982) notion of preexisting doom (discussed earlier) might best describe this reason for divorce among teens. Additionally, the following factors are also somewhat related to divorce in the very young.

Generally, researchers find that these factors, both in combination and independently, lead to higher-than-average divorce rates: having a working-class background, being of lower socioeconomic status, having low-status jobs, and having attained lower levels of education (Norton & Miller, 1992; Castro Martin & Bumpass, 1989). Not only might these variables contribute to the high divorce rate among teenagers but they are also intertwined. For example, a lack of (or a poor) education is often associated with having low-status jobs and therefore lower income. Likewise, low income as well as working-class values can precipitate low participation in educational opportunities. Nonetheless, it is clear that any of these aforementioned variables, singly or in combination, can contribute to or exacerbate stress on a marriage and therefore lead to higher-than-average divorce rates.

Children of Divorce

Not only is the trauma of relationship dissolution felt by its primary protagonists, but it ripples through those around them: children, extended family members, friends, and even neighbors. Perhaps the most vulnerable are the children. For example, although marital partners can look forward to new lives, new beginnings, children have nothing to look forward to; all they see is the dissolution of their family. Thus, over the past several decades, many researchers have examined the effects of divorce on children.

Although the presence of children reduces divorce and increases the protective benefits of marriage, couples with children nonetheless do separate and end their relationships. Although children no longer suffer the social stigma of being children of divorce, its devastation is nonetheless felt in many ways: emotionally, psychologically, and even physically. Indeed, we have already discussed research that showed how exposure to conflict, even in the absence of divorce, leads to emotional and behavioral adjustment problems in children. Thus, it is not surprising that conventional wisdom counsels that ongoing parental conflict and unhappiness are more damaging to the affected children's well-being than would be a divorce; but is this really true? Obviously, in extremely conflict-ridden relationships, such as those in which physical and emotional abuse are present, this belief could not be more true. However, more recent research evidence suggests that the formula and solution are, not surprisingly, much more complex.

Some of the unintended effects of divorce are manifested in the relationships of the children of divorce. Many studies find that children of divorce are themselves much more likely to get divorced as adults (White, 1990). Other researchers have found even more serious effects of divorce on children. In regions and cultures where divorce stigma is still high (e.g., traditional cultures), the effects on children are proportionately worse. Studies in traditional and highly religious cultures (e.g., Iran) find that children of divorce exhibit higher rates of emotional problems and delinquency (Aghajanian & Moghadas, 1998). And even more dramatic, researchers in a recent Canadian study found that along with economic factors, divorce and other family disruptions were the best predictors of youth suicide (Leenaars & Lester, 1995).

Perhaps some of the most compelling revelations of the ill effects of divorce on children come from a recent set of longitudinal studies. Surprisingly, one of the more serious effects of divorce is that children of divorce are more likely than their peers to experience a higher mortality risk: They die younger (Stattin & Romelsjoe, 1995; Tucker et al., 1997). What could be at the root of this startling finding? In a longitudinal study, Tucker and colleagues found that the adult children of divorce had great difficulty maintaining long-term relationships. Both male and female children of divorce were more likely to get divorced themselves. And divorce, as we have already seen, puts one at risk for premature mortality (Friedman et al., 1995; Schwartz et al., 1995).

Additionally, sons of divorce were found to attain lower levels of education—also a correlate of divorce. Female children of divorce, on the other hand, were more likely to engage in high-risk behaviors, such as smoking. Tucker and colleagues (1997) have suggested that the antecedents of these problems may be that children of divorce not only engage in high-risk behaviors but they also generally have poorer social skills, which leads to a greater likelihood that they will experience more failures in their intimate relationships. Without the protective benefits of marriage, these children flounder as adults.

Thus, current research entreats us to examine more closely our motives for divorce, especially when children are involved. Indeed, lawyers and family friends of Marilyn and David Lemak believed their separation to be amicable and proceeding smoothly. The horrible outcomes of their divorce point to the depth of trauma that can be experienced by husbands, wives, their children, and even the community. Thus, our commonsense ideas of the benefits of divorce and our optimistic hopes that our children will benefit from exiting a conflict-ridden family are naive at best, and, at worst, potentially deleterious to our health and the health of our children.

In sum, although these data suggest that children of divorce are simply going to have a difficult time, we can learn several important things from them. First, we might consider developing better interventions for children of divorce. Knowing what can happen is the first step in committing to the proper care and assistance. Another implication of these data are that we, as parents, need to more carefully weigh our responsibilities to ourselves, our spouses, and our children when making separation decisions. And finally, although divorce clearly has negative ramifications for all involved, we cannot and usually do not let it cloud the larger fact that relationships are more essential to us than their dissolution is harmful. Relationships, and intimate relationships in particular, are beautiful, often fulfilling, sometimes exciting, frequently painful (both good and bad pain), but always a part of who we are and who we hope to be.

Widowhood: The Loss of a Committed Partner

The inevitable cycle of life and death also makes the ending of relationships equally inescapable. Thus, whether a relationship ends through breakup, separation, divorce, or death, all relationships end. And although we have considered the aftermath of relationship dissolution, the loss of a partner through death presents a unique constellation of circumstances that merit special attention.

One of the major differences of relationship dissolution through death is the permanence of the loss. Widows and widowers experience loneliness, threats to health, greater mortality risk, and disruption and change in personal relationships and finances (Lopata, 1996), but there are also individual differences in the severity of the distress and the length of grieving (Stroebe & Stroebe, 1987). Much of the current research on bereavement is focused on identifying these differences in coping and recovery (Folkman, 1997).

One of the central components of widowhood is grief. Most readers are likely well acquainted with Kübler-Ross's (1969) model of grieving, which suggests that we pass through five stages, progressing from denial to acceptance. Although it provides a useful heuristic for some, this model also sets up expectations for the stages and for the amount of time the grief process should take. Well-intentioned family and friends embrace these expectations and watch the bereaved closely for signs that his or her grief is progressing in the "proper" fashion and in the allotted time frame (Lopata, 1996). These expectations, and the demand that they create, can disrupt the personal process of grieving and the successful recovery from the loss. Indeed, grief is a much more complex and multidimensional process than a stage model might suggest.

Shuchter (1986) proposed a cognitive-emotional model in which there are five different dimensions to the grieving process: emotional, cognitive/behavioral, performance, relationship with dead spouse, and interpersonal relationship with surviving friends and family. The first dimension, *emotional experience of the bereaved*, runs the gamut from relief to shock to loneliness to intense pain and anger. The survivor's emotional experience includes a veritable jumble of different emotions. Indeed, the bereaved is overwhelmed not only by the actual events surrounding the partner's death but also by his or her own emotional response to the death and its aftermath. Not only does the bereaved react to the actual loss but the individual also grieves for what might have been (regret), experiences guilt over past events and for having survived the loved one, and feels anxiety and fear about the future (Shuchter, 1986). As we will see, how we deal with these emotions has important implications for grieving, recovery, and, ultimately, health.

A second dimension of grief includes the *cognitive/behavioral component of coping with the emotional pain* (Shuchter, 1986). Survivors engage in a cognitive appraisal of their emotional experience and attempt to rein in and control their raw emotions. This dimension is marked by feelings of numbness and disbelief as well as attempts to suppress strong emotions and use other coping strategies. The widow or widower may alternate between avoidance of any reminders of the loved one to wanting to express and share his or her memories of the deceased. Other coping strategies include keeping busy, using passive distractors, and engaging in pleasurable activities. But which coping strategy works best?

The work of Nolen-Hoeksema and colleagues (e.g., Nolen-Hoeksema, Parker, & Larson, 1994; Nolen-Hoeksema, McBride, & Larson, 1997) investigated how ruminating on one's distress, grief, and unhappiness can interfere with recovery. Their research revealed that use of a ruminative coping style in which the bereaved focuses passively on his or her own distress ("Will I ever feel better?" "Why am I such a mess?") interfered with recovery and precipitated depression in a six-month follow-up (Nolen-Hoeksema et al., 1994).

Nolen-Hoeksema and colleagues (1997) extended their investigation of bereavement and rumination to homosexual couples in committed relationships. In a longitudinal study of gay men whose partners' had succumbed to AIDS, Nolen-Hoeksema found only partial support for her earlier findings with regard to the damaging effects of rumination. Her results, nonetheless, suggest that it is maladaptive to think either too much or too little about our emotions and emotional progress (Nolen-Hoeksema et al., 1997). In any case, this analysis, as well as that of Weiss and Richards (1997), is significant in that the research validates the extension of bereavement in heterosexual couples to couples in committed homosexual relationships.

In a related vein, Pennebaker, Mayne, and Francis (1997) used text analysis to study the writings of several different samples, including narrative data collected from the gay men just described. Pennebaker and colleagues have long been investigating the mental health benefits of writing about personal, emotional experiences, such as the deepest thoughts about a topic or the most traumatic event in one's life (Pennebaker & Beall, 1986; Pennebaker & Francis, 1996). Generally, Pennebaker and colleagues found positive effects of disclosure and expression. Further, in the sample of bereaved gay men, Pennebaker, Mayne, and Francis (1997) found results consistent with the work on rumination. They found that narratives that included the fewest past-tense verbs were associated with the poorest recovery and higher levels of distress. In other words, the hesitation to revisit the past, the tendency to suppress memories or pain, and the concentration on negative internal states have negative implications for coping and recovery. The use of cognitive processing words indicating insight and causation lead to better coping. Specifically, the expression of high rates of positive emotion word usage and a low rate of negative emotion word usage revealed the best coping.

The third dimension of Shuchter's (1986) model revolves around the actual *performance and functioning of the bereaved*. Generally, emotional turmoil, distraction, and mental disorganization lead to poor cognitive functioning and hence poor execution of day-to-day activities. Work performance suffers, as does the completion of other even more mundane activities. Mourners experience a loss of motivation and even worsening health.

The fourth and fifth dimensions deal with the interpersonal relationships of the bereaved (Shuchter, 1986). One dimension revolves around the bereaved's *continued relationship with the dead spouse.* This relationship can continue through dreams, daily conversation, and hallucinations. Other forms of "contact" can take place through symbolic representation. A link to the deceased is maintained through contact with the personal possessions of the departed (e.g., clothing and other personal objects). Finally, memories, the continuation of family rituals, or the establishment of new rituals that continue to include the deceased also serve to maintain a relationship with the dead spouse.

The final dimension is comprised of the *interpersonal relationships the bereaved has with living family and friends* (Shuchter, 1986). The trauma of death and loss can either improve existing relationships or cause them to deteriorate. Family members may lose patience with the disoriented and perhaps dependent widow or widower. Disputes over wills and subtle changes in family structure may worsen what may already have been poor relationships. In sum, Shuchter's (1986) analysis of grief suggests that the effects of widowhood and grief are far-reaching and multifaceted. Not only are there emotional and cognitive consequences, but the bereaved also experiences behavioral and performance disruptions, deterioration in health, and disruptions in all interpersonal relationships.

The immediate psychological consequences of losing a committed partner can be severe. However, as Linda Hamilton's response to her pending divorce illustrates (earlier in this chapter), under some circumstances, the end of an intimate relationship can set the stage for the initiation of new ones. Being the social animals we are, it is likely that for many, grief will eventually give way to the excitement of a new intimate relationship.

Summary

Issues.   We started this chapter with a look at why relationships end: who will break up and who will not, why some relationships are successful and others are not, and how a relationship falls apart. We also discussed gender differences in relationship termination and found that women were more likely to initiate breakups and fared much better afterward.

The remainder of this chapter examined the aftermath of relationship dissolution. We learned that there are several different types of lonely feelings, each with different causes. Not surprisingly, breaking up with a loved one contributes to more than one type of lonely feeling as well as feelings of distress (sadness, depression, anger, guilt, jealousy, and regret). Our look at the consequences of unrequited love illustrate how complex our reactions to relationship termination can be, depending on whether you are the rejector or the rejected.

Level of commitment is also related to severity of emotional trauma experienced upon separation from a loved one; thus, we addressed the outcomes of divorce. In addition to looking at some of the demographics of divorce, we saw how divorce has deleterious effects on women's economic and social status and is usually detrimental to the health of both husbands and wives. In fact, divorced people as well as their children were found to experience higher rates of premature mortality. Finally, we considered the case of widowhood. The permanence of loss, the confusion and pain of bereavement, and the unique component of grief make the issue of widowhood distinct from other types of separation.

Theories.   Our examination of why relationships dissolve led us to consider Duck's process loss/mechanical failure hypothesis, the idea that poor communication can be a predictor of relationship termination. Berger's (1987) Uncertainty Reduction Theory suggests that good communication in relationships should enhance the relationship through the reduction of uncertainty. Conversely, poor communication may be a predictor of relationship dissolution.

Other models of dissolution revolve around psychological, societal, and interpersonal structures that either keep us in a relationship (i.e., block our exit) or facilitate our departure from relationships. One such barrier model of dissolution was developed by Levinger (1976). Incorporating and integrating elements of the barrier models and other dissolution theories, Duck (1982) presented a stage model of dissolution that illustrates how dissolution includes intrapersonal, interpersonal, and group-oriented dimensions. We considered one final set of theoretical explanations for relationship dissolution: evolutionary explanations.

In our discussion of the emotional repercussions of relationship termination, we examined the painful effects of loneliness. Shaver and Buhrmester (1989) provided a model that enables us to understand better how different types of relationships fulfill our need for psychological intimacy and integrated involvement. Although romantic relationships are good at fulfilling our emotional and intimacy needs, they do not provide integrated, social involvement. The issue of unrequited love is compelling, and Baumeister and colleagues found many interesting and paradoxical facts about this painful situation.

In our study of divorce, we suggested three different hypotheses regarding the link between divorce and health (premature mortality). We investigated the relationship among personality, situational stress, the health-enhancing benefits of marriage, and their role in promoting or reducing the incidence of premature mortality among the divorced population. It is most probable that some combination of these factors explain the relationship of divorce to health and mortality.

Finally, widowhood brings with it the special problem of grief. A cognitive/emotional model presents grief as a multidimensional concept. Coping strategies such as suppression, rumination, avoidance of the past, and concentration on negative emotions were the least effective strategies.

Research.   In our examination of the causes of dissolution, we discussed Parks and Adelman's (1983) application of the Uncertainty Reduction Theory to romantic relationships. In their study of college-aged couples, they found that higher quality and a broader scope of communication networks served to reduce uncertainty in relationships and could also predict relationship dissolution based on the quality of communication among the dating pairs. Hill, Rubin, and Peplau

(1976) also examined breakups in romantic relationships among college students and found that external, structural factors contributed to breakups and that female coeds were more likely to initiate breakups.

A great deal of social psychological research has been devoted to the study of loneliness. Rokach and Brock (1995) surveyed over 600 people from all walks of life and concluded that there are at least five factors that contribute to loneliness: personal inadequacies, developmental deficits, unfulfilling intimate relationships, separation due to relocation, and being on the social fringe. However, in addition to loneliness, Simpson (1987) found in his longitudinal study of college students that other factors such as closeness, duration of the relationship, and the availability of alternative partners also predict emotional distress upon relationship termination.

In examining the effects of divorce, we saw how Norwegian couples experienced increased stress and decreases in feelings of well-being *before* the breakup. Further, children as well as adults are hurt by divorce. In a longitudinal study of Terman's Minnesota sample of gifted children, begun in the 1930s, Tucker and colleagues (1997) found that children of divorce were more likely to engage in high-risk behavior, tended to become divorced themselves, and, most surprisingly, experienced a higher mortality risk than their peers.

References

Abbey, A., & Melby, C. (1986). The effects of nonverbal cues on gender differences in perceptions of sexual intent. *Sex Roles, 15,* 283–298.

Adams, G. R., & Huston, T. L. (1975). Social perception of middle-aged persons varying in physical attractiveness. *Developmental Psychology, 11,* 657–658.

Adams, H. E., Wright, L. W., & Lohr, B. A. (1996). Is homophobia associated with homosexual arousal? *Journal of Abnormal Psychology, 105,* 440–445.

Adams, J. S. (1965). Inequity in social exchange. In L. Berkowitz (Ed.), *Advances in experimental social psychology* (Vol. 2, pp. 266–300). New York: Academic Press.

Aghajanian, A., & Moghadas, A. A. (1998). Correlates and consequences of divorce in an Iranian city. *Journal of Divorce and Remarriage, 28,* 53–71.

Agnew, C. R., Van Lange, P. A., Rusbult, C. E., & Langston, C. A. (1998). Cognitive interdependence: Commitment and the mental representation of close relationships. *Journal of Personality and Social Psychology, 74,* 939–954.

Ainsworth, M. D. S. (1967). *Infancy in Uganda: Infant care and the growth of love.* Baltimore: Johns Hopkins Press.

Ainsworth, M. D. S. (1982). Attachment: Retrospect and prospect. In C. M. Parkes & J. Stevenson-Hinde (Eds.), *The place of attachment in human behavior.* New York: Basic Books.

Ainsworth, M. D. S., Bell, S. M., & Stayton, D. J. (1971). Individual differences in strange-situation behavior of one-year olds. In H. R. Schaffer (Ed.), *The origins of human and social relations.* New York: Academic Press.

Ainsworth, M. D. S., Blehar, M. C., Waters, E., & Wall, S. (1978). *Patterns of attachment: A psychological study of the strange situation.* Hillsdale, NJ: Erlbaum.

Alicke, M. D., Smith, R. H., & Klotz, M. L. (1986). Judgments of physical attractiveness: The role of faces and bodies. *Personality and Social Psychology Bulletin, 12,* 381–389.

Allen, J. B., Kenrick, D. T., Linder, D. E., & McCall, M. A. (1989). Arousal and attraction: A response-facilitation alternative to misattribution and negative-reinforcement models. *Journal of Personality and Social Psychology, 57,* 261–270.

Allen, L. S., & Gorski, R. A. (1992). Sexual orientation and the size of the anterior commisure in the human brain. *Proceedings of the National Academy of Sciences, 89,* 7199–7202.

Altman, I., & Taylor, D. A. (1973). *Social penetration: The development of interpersonal relationships.* New York: Holt, Rinehart and Winston.

Anson, O. (1989). Marital status and women's health revisited: The importance of a proximate adult. *Journal of Marriage and the Family, 51,* 185–194.

Antill, J. K., & Cotton, S. (1987). Self-disclosure between husbands and wives: Its relationship to sex roles and marital happiness. *Australian Journal of Psychology, 39,* 11–24.

Archer, R. L., Hormuth, S. E., & Berg, J. H. (1982). Avoidance of self-disclosure: An experiment under conditions of self-awareness. *Personality and Social Psychology Bulletin, 8,* 122–128.

Aries, E. (1996). *Men and women in interaction: Reconsidering the differences.* New York: Oxford University Press.

Aron, A., & Aron, E. N. (1986). *Love and the expansion of self: Understanding attraction and satisfaction.* New York: Hemisphere.

Aron, A., & Aron, E. N. (1997). Self-expansion motivation and including other in the self. In S. Duck (Ed.), *Handbook of personal relationships: Theory, research and interventions* (2nd ed., pp. 251–270). Chichester, England: John Wiley & Sons.

Aron, A., Aron, E. N., Tudor, M., & Nelson, G. (1991). Close relationships as including other in the self. *Journal of Personality and Social Psychology, 60,* 241–253.

Aron, A., & Henkemeyer, L. (1995). Marital satisfaction and passionate love. *Journal of Social and Personal Relationships, 12,* 139–146.

Aronson, E. (1992). *The social animal* (6th ed.). New York: Freeman.

Aronson, E., & Cope, V. (1968). My enemy's enemy is my friend. *Journal of Personality and Social Psychology, 8,* 8–12.

Aronson, E., & Linder, D. (1965). Gain and loss of esteem as determinants of interpersonal attraction. *Journal of Experimental Social Psychology, 1,* 156–171.

Aronson, E., & Mills, J. (1959). The effect of severity of initiation on liking for a group. *Journal of Abnormal and Social Psychology, 59,* 177–181.

Arriaga, X. B., & Rusbult, C. E. (1998). Standing in my partner's shoes: Partner perspective taking and reactions to accommodative dilemmas. *Personality and Social Psychology Bulletin, 24,* 927–948.

Ashton, W. A., & Fuehrer, A. (1993). Effects of gender and gender role identification of participant and type of social support resource on support seeking. *Sex Roles, 28,* 461–476.

Atkinson, J., & Huston, T. L. (1984). Sex role orientation and division of labor in early marriage. *Journal of Personality and Social Psychology, 46,* 330–345.

Bailey, J. M., Kim, P. Y., Hills, A., & Linsenmeyer, J. A. W. (1997). Butch, femme, or straight acting? Partner preferences of gay men and lesbians. *Journal of Personality and Social Psychology, 73,* 960–973.

Bailey, J. M., & Pillard, R. C. (1991). A genetic study of male sexual orientation. *Archives of General Psychiatry, 48,* 1089–1096.

Bailey, J. M., Pillard, R. C., Neale, M. C., & Ageyi, Y. (1993). Heritable factors influence sexual orientation in women. *Archives of General Psychiatry, 50,* 217–223.

Ballswick, J. (1988). *The inexpressive male.* Lexington, MA: Lexington Books/D. C. Heath.

Bandura, A. (1965). Influence of models' reinforcement contingencies on the acquisition of imitative responses. *Journal of Personality and Social Psychology, 1,* 589–595.

Bargh, J. A., & Raymond, P. (1995). The naive misuse of power: Nonconscious sources of sexual harassment. *Journal of Social Issues, 51,* 85–96.

Bargh, J. A., Raymond, P., Pryor, J. B., & Strack, F. (1995). Attractiveness of the underling: An automatic power → sex association and its consequences for sexual harassment and aggression. *Journal of Personality and Social Psychology, 68,* 768–781.

Barry, W. A. (1970). Marriage research and conflict: An integrative review. *Psychological Bulletin, 73,* 41–54.

Baumeister, R. F., & Bratslavsky, E. (1999). Passion, intimacy, and time: Passionate love as a function of change in intimacy. *Personality and Social Psychology Review, 3,* 49–67.

Baumeister, R. F., & Leary, M. R. (1995). The need to belong: Desire for interpersonal attachments as a fundamental human motivation. *Psychological Bulletin, 117,* 497–529.

Baumeister, R. F., Reis, H. T., & Delespaul, P. A. E. G. (1995). Subjective and experiential correlates of guilt in daily life. *Personality and Social Psychology Bulletin, 21,* 1256–1268.

Baumeister, R. F., Stillwell, A. M., & Heatherton, T. F. (1994). Guilt: An interpersonal approach. *Psychological Bulletin, 115,* 243–267.

Baumeister, R. F., & Tice, D. M. (1990). Anxiety and social exclusion. *Journal of Social and Clinical Psychology, 9,* 165–195.

Baumeister, R. F., & Wotman, S. R. (1992). *Breaking hearts: The two sides of unrequited love.* New York: Guilford.

Baumeister, R. F., Wotman, S. R., & Stillwell, A. M. (1993). Unrequited love: On heartbreak, anger, guilt, scriptlessness, and humiliation. *Journal of Personality and Social Psychology, 64,* 377–394.

Baxter, L. A. (1984). An investigation of compliance-gaining as politeness. *Human Communication Research, 10,* 427–456.

Baxter, L. A. (1990). Dialectical contradictions in relationship development. *Journal of Social and Personal Relationships, 7,* 69–88.

Baxter, L. A., & Bullis, C. (1986). Turning points in developing romantic relationships. *Human Communication Research, 12,* 469–493.

Beach, S. R. H., & Tesser, A. (1978). Love in marriage: A cognitive account. In R. J. Sternberg & M. L. Barnes (Eds.), *The psychology of love* (pp. 330–355). New Haven, CT: Yale University Press.

Beach, S. R. H., Tesser, A., Fincham, F. D., Jones, D. J., Johnson, D., & Whitaker, D. J. (1998). Pleasure and pain in doing well, together: An investigation of performance-related affect in close relationships. *Journal of Personality and Social Psychology, 74,* 923–938.

Bell, A. P., Weinberg, S. M., & Hammersmith, S. K. (1981). *Sexual preference: Its development in men and women.* Bloomington: Indiana University Press.

Belsky, J., Rovine, M., & Fish, M. (1989). The developing family system. In M. Gunnar (Ed.), *Systems and development: Minnesota symposium on child psychology* (Vol. 22). Hillsdale, NJ: Erlbaum.

Bem, D. J. (1996). Exotic becomes erotic: A developmental theory of sexual orientation. *Psychological Review, 103,* 320–335.

Bem, S. L. (1974). The measurement of psychological androgyny. *Journal of Consulting and Clinical Psychology, 42,* 155–162.

Benson, P. L., Karabenick, S. A., & Lerner, R. M. (1976). Pretty pleases: The effects of physical attractiveness, race, and sex on receiving help. *Journal of Experimental Social Psychology, 12,* 409–415.

Bentler, P. M., & Huba, G. J. (1979). Simple minitheories of love. *Journal of Personality and Social Psychology, 37,* 124–130.

Berg, J. H. (1984). Development of friendship between roommates. *Journal of Personality and Social Psychology, 46,* 346–356.

Berg, J. H., & Archer, R. L. (1980). Disclosure or concern: A second look at liking for the norm breaker. *Journal of Personality, 48,* 245–257.

Berg, J. H., & Archer, R. L. (1982). Responses to self-disclosure and interaction goals. *Journal of Experimental Social Psychology, 18,* 501–512.

Berg, J. H., & Clark, M. S. (1986). Differences in social exchange between intimate and other relationships: Gradually evolving or quickly apparent? In V. J. Derlega & B. A. Winstead (Eds.), *Friendship and social interaction* (pp. 101–128). New York: Springer-Verlag.

Berg, J. H., & McQuinn, R. D. (1986). Attraction and exchange in continuing and noncontinuing dating relationships. *Journal of Personality and Social Psychology, 50,* 942–952.

Berg, J. H., & Peplau, L. A. (1982). Loneliness: The relationship of self-disclosure and androgyny. *Personality and Social Psychology, 8,* 624–630.

Berger, C. R. (1980). Self-consciousness and the adequacy of theory and research into relationship development. *Western Journal of Speech Communication, 44,* 93–96.

Berger, C. R. (1987). Communicating under uncertainty. In M. E. Roloff & G. R. Miller (Eds.), *Interpersonal processes: New directions in communication research* (Vol. 14, pp. 39–62). Newbury Park: Sage.

Berry, D. S., & McArthur, L. Z. (1985). Some components and consequences of a babyface. *Journal of Personality and Social Psychology, 48,* 312–323.

Berscheid, E. (1983). Emotion. In H. H. Kelley, E. Berscheid, A. Christensen, J. H. Harvey, T. L. Huston, G. Levinger, E. McClintock, L. A. Peplau, & D. R. Peterson (Eds.), *Close relationships* (pp. 110–168). New York: Freeman.

Berscheid, E., Dion, K., Walster, E., & Walster, G. W. (1971). Physical attractiveness and dating choice: A test of the matching hypothesis. *Journal of Experimental Social Psychology, 7,* 173–189.

Berscheid, E., Graziano, W., Monson, T., & Dermer, M. (1976). Outcome dependency: Attention, attribution, and attraction. *Journal of Personality and Social Psychology, 34,* 978–989.

Biden, J. R. (1993). Violence against women: The congressional response. *American Psychologist, 48,* 1059–1061.

Bierhoff, H. (1991). Twenty years of research on love: Theory, results, and prospects for the future. *German Journal of Psychology, 15,* 95–117.

Black, H., & Angelis, V. B. (1974). Interpersonal attraction: An empirical investigation of platonic and romantic love. *Psychological Reports, 34,* 1243–1246.

Blanchard, R., & Bogaert, A. F. (1996). Homosexuality in men and number of older brothers. *American Journal of Psychiatry, 153,* 27–31.

Blanchard, R., & Sheridan, P. M. (1992). Sibship size, sibling ratio, birth order, and parental age in homosexual and nonhomosexual men. *Journal of Nervous and Mental Diseases, 180,* 40–47.

Blumstein, P., & Schwartz, P. (1983). *American couples.* New York: Morrow.

Bossard, J. H. S. (1932). Residential propinquity as a factor in mate selection. *American Journal of Sociology, 38,* 219–224.

Bowerman, C. E., & Day, B. R. (1956). A test of the theory of complementary needs as applied to couples during courtship. *American Sociological Review, 21,* 602–605.

Bowlby, J. (1969). *Attachment and loss: Vol. 1. Attachment.* New York: Basic Books.

Bowlby, J. (1973). *Attachment and loss: Vol. 2. Separation.* New York: Basic Books.

Bowlby, J. (1980). *Attachment and loss: Vol. 3. Loss, sadness, and depression.* New York: Basic Books.

Bowlby, J. (1982). Attachment and loss: Retrospect and prospect. *American Journal of Orthopsychiatry, 52,* 664–678.

Bradbury, T. N., & Fincham, F. D. (1989). Behavior and satisfaction in marriage: Prospective mediating processes. *Review of Personality and Social Psychology, 10,* 119–143.

Bradbury, T. N., & Fincham, F. D. (1990). Attributions in marriage: Review and critique. *Psychological Bulletin, 107,* 3–33.

Bradbury, T. N., & Fincham, F. D. (1992). Attributions and behavior in marital interaction. *Journal of Personality and Social Psychology, 63,* 613–628.

Bratslavsky, E., Baumeister, R. F., & Sommer, K. L. (1998). To love or be loved in vain: The trials and tribulations of unrequited love. In B. H. Spitzberg & W. R. Cupach (Eds.), *The dark side of close relationships* (pp. 307–326). Mahwah, NJ: Erlbaum.

Breckler, S. J. (1984). Empirical validation of affect, behavior, and cognition as distinct components of attitude. *Journal of Personality and Social Psychology, 47,* 1191–1205.

Brehm, S. S. (1992). *Intimate relationships* (2nd ed.). New York: McGraw-Hill.

Brewer, M. B. (1979). In-group bias in the minimal intergroup situation: A cognitive-motivational analysis. *Psychological Bulletin, 86,* 307–324.

Brickman, P. (1974). Rule structures and conflict relationships. In P. Brickman (Ed.), *Social conflict.* Lexington, MA: D. C. Heath.

Bringle, R. G. (1991). Psychosocial aspects of jealousy: A transactional model. In P. Salovey (Ed.), *The psychology of jealousy and envy* (pp. 103–131). New York: Guilford.

Bringle, R. G., & Buunk, B. (1986). Examining the causes and consequences of jealousy: Some recent findings and issues. In R. Gilmour & S. Duck (Eds.), *The emerging field of personal relationships* (pp. 225–240). Hillsdale, NJ: Erlbaum.

Bringle, R. G., Renner, P., Terry, R., & Davis, S. (1983). An analysis of situational and person components of jealousy. *Journal of Research in Personality, 17,* 354–368.

Bringle, R. G., Roach, S., Andier, C., & Evenbeck, S. (1979). Measuring the intensity of jealous reactions. *Catalog of Selected Documents in Psychology* (Vol. 9, MS. 1832, pp. 23–24). Washington, DC: American Psychological Association.

Brockner, J., & Swap, W. C. (1976). Effects of repeated exposure and attitude similarity on self-disclosure and interpersonal attraction. *Journal of Personality and Social Psychology, 33,* 531–540.

Brown, M., & Auerback, A. (1981). Communication patterns in initiation of marital sex. *Medical Aspects of Human Sexuality, 15,* 105–107.

Brown, P., & Levinson, S. (1978). Universals in language usage: Politeness phenomena. In E. N. Goody (Ed.), *Questions and politeness: Strategies in social interaction* (pp. 256–310). Cambridge: Cambridge University Press.

Browne, A. (1993). Violence against women by male partners: Prevalence, outcomes, and policy implications. *American Psychologist, 48,* 1077–1087.

Browne, A., & Williams, K. R. (1989). Exploring the effect of resource availability and the likelihood of female-perpetrated homicides. *Law and Society Review, 23,* 75–94.

Brundage, L. E., Derlega, V. J., & Cash, T. F. (1977). The effects of physical attractiveness and need for approval on self-disclosure. *Personality and Social Psychology Bulletin, 3,* 63–66.

Bumpass, L. L., Sweet, J., & Castro Martin, T. (1990). Changing patterns of remarriage. *Journal of Marriage and the Family, 52,* 747–756.

Burleson, B. R. (1997). A different voice on different cultures: Illusion and reality in the study of sex differences in personal relationships. *Personal Relationships, 4,* 229–241.

Burleson, B. R., Kunkel, A. W., Samter, W., & Werking, K. J. (1996). Men's and women's evaluations of communication skills in personal relationships: When sex differences make a difference—and when they don't. *Journal of Social and Personal Relationships, 13,* 201–224.

Burt, M. R. (1980). Cultural myths and supports for rape. *Journal of Personality and Social Psychology, 38,* 217–230.

Bushman, B. J., & Cooper, H. M. (1990). Effects of alcohol on human aggression: An integrative research review. *Psychological Bulletin, 107,* 341–354.

Buss, D. M. (1989). Sex differences in human mate preferences: Evolutionary hypothesis tested in 37 cultures. *Behavioral and Brain Sciences, 12,* 1–14.

Buss, D. M., Larsen, R. J., Westen, D., & Semmelroth, J. (1992). Sex differences in jealousy: Evolution, physiology, and psychology. *Psychological Science, 3,* 251–255.

Buunk, B. P. (1982). Anticipated sexual jealousy: Its relationship to self-esteem, dependency, and reciprocity. *Personality and Social Psychology Bulletin, 8,* 310–316.

Buunk, B. P. (1991). Jealousy in close relationships: An exchange-theoretical perspective. In P. Salovey (Ed.), *The psychology of jealousy and envy*. New York: Guilford.

Buunk, B. P., Angleitner, A., Oubaid, V., & Buss, D. M. (1996). Sex differences in jealousy in evolutionary and cultural perspective: Tests from the Netherlands, Germany, and the United States. *Psychological Science, 7*, 359–363.

Byers, E. S., & Heinlein, L. (1989). Predicting initiations and refusals of sexual activities in married and cohabiting heterosexual couples. *Journal of Sexual Research, 26*, 210–231.

Byrne, D. (1961). The influence of propinquity and opportunities for interaction on classroom relationships. *Human Relations, 14*, 63–70.

Byrne, D. (1971). *The attraction paradigm*. New York: Academic Press.

Byrne, D., Clore, G. L., & Smeaton, G. (1986). The attraction hypothesis: Do similar attitudes affect anything? *Journal of Personality and Social Psychology, 51*, 1167–1170.

Byrne, D., & Nelson, D. (1965). Attraction as a linear function of proportion of positive reinforcements. *Journal of Personality and Social Psychology, 1*, 659–663.

Byrne, D., & Rhamey, R. (1965). Magnitude of positive and negative reinforcements as a determinant of attraction. *Journal of Personality and Social Psychology, 2*, 884–889.

Caldwell, M. A., & Peplau, L. A. (1982). Sex differences in same-sex friendship. *Sex Roles, 8*, 721–732.

Call, V., Sprecher, S., & Schwartz, P. (1992). *The frequency of sexual intercourse in American couples: Results from a national sample*. Paper presented at the National Council on Family Relations, Orlando, Florida.

Carnegie, D. (1936). *How to win friends and influence people*. New York: Simon and Schuster.

Carpenter, E. M., & Kirkpatrick, L. A. (1996). Attachment style and presence of a romantic partner as moderators of psychophysiological responses to a stressful laboratory situation. *Personal Relationships, 3*, 351–367.

Carstensen, L. L., Gottman, J. M., & Levensen, R. W. (1995). Emotional behavior in long-term marriage. *Psychology and Aging, 10*, 140–149.

Cash, T. L., & Derlega, V. J. (1978). The matching hypothesis: Physical attractiveness among same sexed friends. *Personality and Social Psychology Bulletin, 4*, 240–243.

Castro Martin, T., & Bumpass, L. L. (1989). Recent trends in marital disruption. *Demography, 26*, 37–51.

Caudill, B. D., Wilson, G. T., & Abrams, D. B. (1987). Alcohol and self-disclosure: Analyses of interpersonal behavior in male and female social drinkers. *Journal of Studies on Alcohol, 48*, 401–409.

Chaikin, A. L., & Derlega, V. J. (1974). Liking for the norm breaker in self-disclosure. *Journal of Personality, 42*, 117–129.

Check, J. V. P., Perlman, D., & Malamuth, N. M. (1985). Loneliness and aggressive behavior. *Journal of Social and Personal Relationships, 2*, 243–252.

Cherlin, A. J. (1992). *Marriage, divorce, remarriage*. Cambridge, MA: Harvard University Press.

Christopher, F. S., & Cates, R. M. (1984). Factors involved in premarital sexual decision-making. *Journal of Sex Research, 20*, 363–376.

Christopher, F. S., & Cates, R. M. (1985). Premarital sexual pathways and relationship development. *Journal of Social and Personal Relationships, 2*, 271–288.

Cialdini, R. B., Borden, R. J., Thorne, A., Walker, M. R., Freeman, S., & Sloan, L. R. (1976). Basking in the reflected glory: Three (football) field studies. *Journal of Personality and Social Psychology, 34*, 366–375.

Clark, M. S. (1984). Record keeping in two types of relationships. *Journal of Personality and Social Psychology, 47*, 549–577.

Clark, M. S., & Chrisman, K. (1994). Resource allocation in intimate relationships. In A. Weber & J. H. Harvey (Eds.), *Perspectives on close relationships*. Boston: Allyn and Bacon.

Clark, M. S., & Mills, J. (1979). Interpersonal attraction in exchange and communal relationships. *Journal of Personality and Social Psychology, 37,* 12–24.

Clark, M. S., Mills, J., & Corcoran, D. M. (1989). Keeping track of needs and inputs of friends and strangers. *Personality and Social Psychology Bulletin, 15,* 533–542.

Clark, M. S., Mills, J., & Powell, M. C. (1986). Keeping track of needs in communal and exchange relationships. *Journal of Personality and Social Psychology, 51,* 333–338.

Clark, M. S., & Reis, H. T. (1988). Interpersonal processes in close relationships. *Annual Review of Psychology, 39,* 609–672.

Clark, R. A. (1993). Men's and women's self-confidence in persuasive, comforting, and justificatory communicative tasks. *Sex Roles, 28,* 553–567.

Clark, R. A. (1994). Children's and adolescents' gender preferences for conversational partners for specific communicative objectives. *Journal of Social and Personal Relationships, 11,* 313–319.

Clark, R. D. (1990). The impact of AIDS on gender differences in willingness to engage in casual sex. *Journal of Applied Social Psychology, 20,* 771–782.

Clark, R. D., & Hatfield, E. (1989). Gender differences in receptivity to sexual offers. *Journal of Psychology and Human Sexuality, 2,* 39–55.

Clifford, M. M., & Walster, E. (1973). Research note: The effects of physical attractiveness on teacher expectations. *Sociology of Education, 46,* 248–258.

Clore, G. L., & Byrne, D. (1974). A reinforcement-affect model of attraction. In T. L. Huston (Ed.), *Foundations of interpersonal attraction* (pp. 143–170). New York: Academic Press.

Cole, S. W., Kemeny, M. E., Taylor, S. E., & Visscher, M. E. (1996). Elevated physical health risk among gay men who conceal their homosexual identity. *Health Psychology, 15,* 243–251.

Collins, N. L., & Read, S. J. (1990). Adult attachment, working models, and relationship quality in dating couples. *Journal of Personality and Social Psychology, 58,* 644–663.

Coser, L. A. (1956). *The function of social conflict.* London: Free Press.

Coser, L. A. (1967). *Continuities in the study of social conflict.* New York: Free Press.

Costa, P. T., Zonderman, A. B., McCrae, R. R., Cornoni-Huntley, J., Locke, P., & Barbano, S. (1987). Longitudinal analyses of psychological well-being in a national sample: Stability of mean levels. *Journal of Gerontology, 42,* 50–55.

Cowan, P. A., & Cowan, C. P. (1988). Changes in marriage during the transition to parenthood: Must we blame the baby? In G. Y. Michaels & W. A. Goldberg (Eds.), *The transition to parenthood: Current theory and research.* Cambridge: Cambridge University Press.

Critchlow, B. (1983). Blaming the booze: The attribution of responsibility for drunken behavior. *Personality and Social Psychology Bulletin, 9,* 451–473.

Critchlow, B. (1985). The blame in the bottle: Attributions about drunken behavior. *Personality and Social Psychology Bulletin, 11,* 258–274.

Cunningham, J. D., & Antill, J. K. (1981). Love in developing romantic relationships. In S. Duck & R. Gilmour (Eds.), *Personal relationships. 2: Developing personal relationships* (pp. 27–51). New York: Academic Press.

Cunningham, M. R. (1986). Measuring the physical in physical attractiveness: Quasi-experiments on the sociobiology of female facial beauty. *Journal of Personality and Social Psychology, 50,* 925–635.

Cunningham, M. R. (1988). Does happiness mean friendliness? Induced mood and heterosexual self-disclosure. *Personality and Social Psychology Bulletin, 14,* 283–297.

Cunningham, M. R., Barbee, A. P., & Pike, C. L. (1990). What do women want? Facialmetric assessment of multiple motives in the perception of male physical attractiveness. *Journal of Personality and Social Psychology, 59,* 61–72.

Cunningham, M. R., Roberts, A. R., Barbee, A. P., Druen, P. B., & Wu, C. F. (1995). "Their ideas of beauty are, on the whole, the same as ours": Consistency and variability in the cross-cultural perception of female physical attractiveness. *Journal of Personality and Social Psychology, 68,* 261–279.

Cupach, W. R., & Metts, S. (1991). Sexuality and communication in close relationships. In K. McKinney & S. Sprecher (Eds.), *Sexuality in close relationships* (pp. 93–110). Hillsdale, NJ: Erlbaum.

Daly, M., Wilson, M., & Weghorst, S. J. (1982). Male sexual jealousy. *Ethology and Sociobiology, 3,* 11–27.

Darwin, C. (1871). *The descent of man, and selection in relation to sex.* London: John Murray.

Davidson, B., Balswick, J., & Halverson, C. F. (1983). Affective self-disclosure and marital adjustment: A test of equity theory. *Journal of Marriage and the Family, 45,* 93–102.

Davis, K. E., Kirkpatrick, L. A., Levy, M. B., & O'Hearn, R. E. (1994). Stalking the elusive love style: Attachment styles, love styles, and relationship development. In R. Erber & R. Gilmour (Eds.), *Theoretical frameworks for personal relationships.* Hillsdale, NJ: Erlbaum.

Davis, K. E., & Latty-Mann, H. (1987). Lovestyles and relationship quality: A contribution to validation. *Journal of Social and Personal Relationships, 4,* 409–428.

Davis, M. H., & Franzoi, S. L. (1986). Adolescent loneliness, self-disclosure, and private self-consciousness: A longitudinal investigation. *Journal of Personality and Social Psychology, 51,* 595–608.

DeCecco, J. P., & Elia, J. P. (1993). *If you seduce a straight person, can you make them gay? Issues in biological essentialism versus social constructionism in gay and lesbian identities.* New York: Harrington Park Press.

DeLamater, J. D., & MacCorquodale, P. (1979). *Premarital sexuality: Attitudes, relationships, behaviors.* Madison: University of Wisconsin Press.

DeLongis, A., Folkman, S., & Lazarus, R. S. (1988). The impact of daily stress on health and mood: Psychological and social resources as mediators. *Journal of Personality and Social Psychology, 54,* 486–495.

DePaulo, B. M. (1992). Nonverbal behavior and self-presentation. *Psychological Bulletin, 111,* 203–243.

DePaulo, B. M., Lanier, K., & Davis, T. (1983). Detecting the deceit of the motivated liar. *Journal of Personality and Social Psychology, 52,* 303–315.

DePaulo, B. M., Stone, J. I., & Lassiter, G. D. (1985). Telling ingratiating lies: Effects of target sex and target attractiveness on verbal and nonverbal deceptive success. *Journal of Personality and Social Psychology, 48,* 1191–1203.

Derlega, V. J., Barbee, A. P., & Winstead, B. A. (1994). Friendship, gender, and social support: Laboratory studies of supportive interactions. In B. R. Burleson, T. L. Albrecht, & I. G. Sarason (Eds.), *The communication of social support: Message, interactions, relationships, and community* (pp. 136–151). Newbury Park, CA: Sage.

Derlega, V. J., & Chaikin, A. L. (1976). Norms affecting self-disclosure in men and women. *Journal of Consulting and Clinical Psychology, 44,* 376–380.

Derlega, V. J., Harris, M. S., & Chaikin, A. L. (1973). Self-disclosure reciprocity, liking and the deviant. *Journal of Experimental Social Psychology, 9,* 277–284.

Derlega, V. J., Metts, S., Petronio, S., & Margulis, S. T. (1993). *Self-disclosure.* Newbury Park, CA: Sage.

Dermer, M., & Thiel, D. L. (1975). When beauty may fail. *Journal of Personality and Social Psychology, 31,* 1168–1176.

DeSteno, D. A., & Salovey, P. (1994). Jealousy in close relationships: Multiple perspectives on the Green-ey'd Monster. In A. L. Weber & J. H. Harvey (Eds.), *Perspectives on close relationships.* Boston: Allyn and Bacon.

DeSteno, D. A., & Salovey, P. (1996). Evolutionary origins of sex differences in jealousy? Questioning the "fitness" of the model. *Psychological Science, 7,* 367–372.

Deutsch, M. (1969). Conflicts: Productive and destructive. *Journal of Social Issues, 25,* 7–41.

de Weerth, C., & Kalma, A. P. (1993). Female aggression as a response to sexual jealousy: A sex role reversal? *Aggressive Behavior, 19,* 265–279.

Dickson-Markman, F. (1984). How important is self-disclosure in marriage? *Communication Research Reports, 1,* 7–14.

Dindia, K. (1987). The effects of sex of subject and sex of partner on interruptions. *Human Communication Research, 13,* 345–371.

Dingler-Duhon, M., & Brown, B. B. (1987). Self-disclosure as an influence strategy: Effects of Machiavellianism, androgyny, and sex. *Sex Roles, 16,* 109–123.

Dion, K. K. (1972). Physical attractiveness and evaluation of children's transgressions. *Journal of Personality and Social Psychology, 24,* 207–213.

Dion, K. K. (1974). Children's physical attractiveness and sex as determinants of adult punitiveness. *Developmental Psychology, 10,* 772–778.

Dion, K. K. (1977). The incentive value of physical attractiveness for young children. *Personality and Social Psychology Bulletin, 3,* 67–70.

Dion, K. K. (1986). Stereotyping based on physical attractiveness: Issues and conceptual perspectives. In C. P. Herman, M. P. Zanna, & E. T. Higgins (Eds.), *The Ontario Symposium: Vol. 3. Physical appearance, stigma, and social behavior* (pp. 7–21). Hillsdale, NJ: Erlbaum.

Dion, K. K., Berscheid, E., & Walster, E. (1972). What is beautiful is good. *Journal of Personality and Social Psychology, 24,* 285–290.

Dion, K. K., & Dion, K. L. (1975). Self-esteem and romantic love. *Journal of Personality, 43,* 39–57.

Dizard, J. E., & Gadlin, H. (1990). *The minimal family.* Amherst: University of Massachusetts Press.

Doherty, K., Weingold, M. F., & Schlenker, B. R. (in press). Self-serving interpretations of motives. *Personality and Social Psychology Bulletin.*

Downy, J. L., & Damhave, K. W. (1991). The effects of place, type of comment, and effort expended on the perception of flirtation. *Journal of Social Behavior and Personality, 6,* 35–43.

Drigotas, S. M., Whitney, G. A., & Rusbult, C. E. (1995). On the peculiarities of loyalty: A diary study of responses to dissatisfaction in everyday life. *Personality and Social Psychology Bulletin, 21,* 596–609.

Driscoll, R., Davis, K. W., & Lipetz, M. E. (1972). Parental interference and romantic love. *Journal of Personality and Social Psychology, 24,* 1–10.

Dryer, D. C., & Horowitz, L. M. (1997). When do opposites attract? Interpersonal complementarity versus similarity. *Journal of Personality and Social Psychology, 72,* 592–603.

Duck, S. (1982). A topography of relationship disengagement and dissolution. In S. Duck (Ed.), *Personal relationships 4: Dissolving personal relationships.* New York: Academic Press.

Duck, S. (1988). *Relating to others.* Pacific Grove, CA: Brooks/Cole.

Duck, S. (1991). Diaries and logs. In B. M. Montgomery & S. Duck (Eds.), *Studying interpersonal interaction* (pp. 141–161). New York: Guilford.

Duck, S., & Montgomery, B. M. (1991). The interdependence among interaction substance, theory, and methods. In B. M. Montgomery & S. Duck (Eds.), *Studying interpersonal interaction* (pp. 3–15). New York: Guilford.

Duck, S., & Sants, H. (1983). On the origin of the specious: Are personal relationships really interpersonal states? *Journal of Social and Clinical Psychology, 1,* 27–41.

Duffy, S. M., & Rusbult, C. E. (1986). Satisfaction and commitment in homosexual and heterosexual relationships. *Journal of Homosexuality, 12,* 1–23.

Duncan, S. (1974). On the structure of speaker-auditor interaction during speaking turns. *Language in Society, 2,* 161–180.

Dunn, J., Slomkowski, C., Donelan, N., & Herrera, C. (1995). Conflict, understanding, and relationships: Developments and differences in the preschool years. Special Issue: Conflict resolution in early social development. *Early Education and Development, 6,* 303–316.

Dutton, D. G., & Aron, A. P. (1974). Some evidence for heightened sexual attraction under conditions of high anxiety. *Journal of Personality and Social Psychology, 30,* 510–517.

Dutton, M. A. (1992). Assessment and treatment of PTSD among battered women. In D. Foy (Ed.), *Treating PTSD: Procedure for combat veterans, battered women, adult and child sexual assault.* New York: Guilford.

Eagly, A. H., Ashmore, R. D., Makhijani, M. G., & Longo, L. C. (1991). What is beautiful is good, but . . . : A meta-analytic review of research on the physical attractiveness stereotype. *Psychological Bulletin, 110,* 109–128.

Eagly, A. H., & Wood, W. (1999). The origins of sex differences in human behavior: Evolved dispositions versus social roles. *American Psychologist, 54,* 408–423.

Eberle, P. A. (1982). Alcohol abusers and non-users: A discriminant analysis of differences between two subgroups of batterers. *Journal of Health and Social Behavior, 23,* 260–271.

Efran, M. G. (1974). The effect of physical appearance on the judgment of guilt, interpersonal attraction, and severity of recommended punishment in a simulated jury task. *Journal of Research in Personality, 8,* 45–54.

Eibl-Eibesfeldt, I. (1974). *Love and hate.* New York: Schocken.

Eisenman, R. (1993). Professor Anita Hill versus Judge Clarence Thomas: The view of students at a southern university. *Bulletin of the Psychonomic Society, 31,* 179–180.

Eiser, J. R. (1986). *Social psychology: Attitudes, cognition, and social behavior.* New York: Cambridge University Press.

Elicker, J., Englund, M., & Sroufe, L. A. (1992). Predicting peer competence and peer relationships in childhood from early parent-child relationships. In R. Parke & G. Ladd (Eds.), *Family-peer relationships: Modes of linkage.* Hillsdale, NJ: Erlbaum.

Ellis, L., & Ames, M. A. (1987). Neurohormonal functioning and sexual orientation: A theory of homosexuality and heterosexuality. *Psychological Bulletin, 101,* 233–258.

Ellis, S., Rogoff, B., & Cramer, C. C. (1981). Age segregation in children's social interactions. *Developmental Psychology, 17,* 399–407.

Ellsberg, M., Caldera, T., Herrera, A., Winkvist, A., & Kullgren, G. (1999). Domestic violence and emotional distress among Nicaraguan women: Results from a population-based study. *American Psychologist, 54,* 30–36.

Erber, R. (1991). Affective and semantic priming: Effects of mood on category accessibility and inference. *Journal of Experimental Social Psychology, 27,* 480–498.

Erber, R., & Fiske, S. T. (1984). Outcome dependency and attention to inconsistent information. *Journal of Personality and Social Psychology, 47,* 709–726.

Erber, R., & Tesser, A. (1994). Self-evaluation maintenance: A social psychological approach to interpersonal relationships. In R. Erber & R. Gilmour (Eds.), *Theoretical frameworks for personal relationships* (pp. 211–234). Hillsdale, NJ: Erlbaum.

Esses, V., & Webster, C. D. (1988). Physical attractiveness, dangerousness, and the Canadian Criminal Code. *Journal of Applied Social Psychology, 18,* 1017–1031.

Fagan, R. W., Barnett, O. W., & Patton, J. B. (1988). Reasons for alcohol use in maritally violent men. *American Journal of Drug and Alcohol Abuse, 14,* 371–392.

Farina, A., Fischer, E. H., Sherman, S., Smith, W. T., Groh, T., & Mermin, P. (1977). Physical attractiveness and mental illness. *Journal of Abnormal Psychology, 86,* 510–517.

Fausto-Sterling, A. (1985). *Myths of gender: Biological theories about women and men.* New York: Basic Books.

Feeney, B. C., & Kirkpatrick, L. A. (1996). Effects of adult attachment and presence of romantic partners on physiological responses to stress. *Journal of Personality and Social Psychology, 70,* 255–270.

Feeney, J. A. (1995). Adult attachment and emotional control. *Personal Relationships, 2,* 143–159.

Feeney, J. A., & Noller, P. (1990). Attachment style as a predictor of adult romantic relationships. *Journal of Personality and Social Psychology, 58,* 281–291.

Fehr, B. (1988). Prototype analysis of the concepts of love and commitment. *Journal of Personality and Social Psychology, 55,* 557–579.

Feingold, A. (1988). Matching for attractiveness in romantic partners and same-sex friends: A meta-analysis and theoretical critique. *Psychological Bulletin, 104,* 226–235.

Feingold, A. (1990). Gender differences in effects of physical attractiveness on romantic attraction: A comparison across five research paradigms. *Journal of Personality and Social Psychology, 59,* 981–993.

Feingold, A. (1991). Sex differences in the effects of similarity and physical attractiveness on opposite-sex attraction. *Basic and Applied Social Psychology, 12,* 357–367.

Feingold, A. (1992). Good looking people are not what we think. *Psychological Bulletin, 111,* 304–341.

Felmlee, D. H. (1995). Fatal attractions: Affection and disaffection in intimate relationships. *Journal of Social and Personal Relationships, 12,* 295–311.

Felmlee, D. H. (1998a). "Be careful what you wish for . . .": A quantitative and qualitative investigation of "fatal attractions." *Personal Relationships, 5,* 235–253.

Felmlee, D. H. (1998b). Fatal attraction. In B. H. Spitzberg & W. R. Cupach (Eds.), *The dark side of close relationships* (pp. 3–31). Mahwah, NJ: Erlbaum.

Felmlee, D. H., Sprecher, S., & Bassin, E. (1990). The dissolution of intimate relationships: A hazard model. *Social Psychology Quarterly, 53,* 13–30.

Festinger, L. (1956). *A theory of cognitive dissonance.* Stanford, CA: Stanford University Press.

Festinger, L., Schachter, S., & Back, K. W. (1950). *Social pressures in informal groups: A study of human factors in housing.* New York: Harper & Brothers.

Fincham, F. D., & Bradbury, T. N. (1987). Cognitive processes and conflict in close relationships: An attribution-efficacy model. *Journal of Personality and Social Psychology, 53,* 1106–1118.

Fincham, F. D., & Bradbury, T. N. (1988). The impact of attributions in marriage: An experimental analysis. *Journal of Social and Clinical Psychology, 7,* 147–162.

Fincham, F. D., & Jaspers, J. M. (1980). Attribution of responsibility: From man the scientist to man as lawyer. In L. Berkowitz (Ed.), *Advances in experimental social psychology* (Vol. 13, pp. 81–138). New York: Academic Press.

Fisher, H. E. (1987). The four-year itch. *Natural History*, 22–33.

Fisher, H. E. (1989). Evolution of human serial pair-bonding. *American Journal of Physical Anthropology, 78*, 331–354.

Fishman, P. M. (1980). Conversational insecurity. In H. Giles, W. P. Robinson, & P. M. Smith (Eds.), *Language: Social psychological perspectives* (pp. 127–132). Oxford: Pergamon.

Fiske, S. T., & Taylor, S. E. (1991). *Social cognition* (2nd ed.). New York: McGraw-Hill.

Fitzgerald, L. F. (1993). Sexual harassment: Violence against women in the workplace. *American Psychologist, 48*, 1070–1076.

Fitzgerald, L. F., Swan, S., & Fisher, K. (1995). Why didn't she just report him? The psychological and legal implications of women's responses to sexual harassment. *Journal of Social Issues, 51*, 117–138.

Folkman, S. (1997). Use of bereavement narratives to predict well-being in gay men whose partner died of AIDS—Four theoretical perspectives. *Journal of Personality and Social Psychology, 72*, 851–854.

Foner, P. S. (1947). *History of the labor movement in the United States.* New York: International Publishers.

Footlick, J. K. (1990, Winter/Spring). What happened to the family? *Newsweek Special Edition*, pp. 14–20.

Ford, C. S., & Beach, F. A. (1951). *Patterns of sexual behavior.* New York: Harper and Row.

Forgas, J. P., & Bower, G. H. (1987). Mood effects on person perception judgments. *Journal of Personality and Social Psychology, 53*, 53–60.

Franzoi, S. L., & Herzog, M. E. (1987). Judging physical attractiveness: What body aspects do we use? *Personality and Social Psychology Bulletin, 13*, 19–33.

Frazier, P. A., Byer, A. L., Fisher, A. R., Wright, D. M., & DeBord, K. A. (1996). Adult attachment style and partner choice: Correlational and experimental findings. *Personal Relationships, 3*, 117–136.

Freud, S. (1922). Certain neurotic mechanisms in jealousy, paranoia, and homosexuality. In *Collected papers* (Vol. 2). London: Hogarth Press

Friedman, H. S., Tucker, J. S., Schwartz, J. E., Tomlinson-Keasey, C., et al. (1995). Psychosocial and behavioral predictors of longevity: The aging and death of the "Termites." *American Psychologist, 50*, 69–78.

Fuller, T. L., & Fincham, F. D. (1995). Attachment style in married couples: Relation to current marital functioning, stability over time, and method of assessment. *Personal Relationships, 2*, 17–34.

Gartrell, N. (1982). The lesbian as a "single" woman. *American Journal of Psychotherapy, 35*, 502–509.

Geiselman, R. E., Haight, N. A., & Kimata, L. G. (1984). Context effects in the perceived physical attractiveness of faces. *Journal of Experimental Social Psychology, 20*, 409–424.

Gelles, R. J. (1979). Violence in the family: A review of research in the seventies. *Journal of Marriage and the Family, 42*, 873–885.

Gelles, R. J. (1988). Violence and pregnancy: Are pregnant women at greater risk of abuse? *Journal of Marriage and the Family, 42*, 873–885.

Gerdes, E. G., Dammann, E. J., & Heilig, K. E. (1988). Perceptions of rape victims and assailants: Effects of physical attractiveness, acquaintance, and subject gender. *Sex Roles, 19*, 141–153.

Gilbert, D. T., Pelham, B. W., & Krull, D. S. (1988). On cognitive busyness: When person perceivers meet persons perceived. *Journal of Personality and Social Psychology, 54,* 733–740.

Gilligan, C. (1982). *In a different voice.* Cambridge, MA: Harvard University Press.

Givens, D. B. (1978). The nonverbal basis of attraction: Flirtation, courtship, and seduction. *Psychiatry, 41,* 346–359.

Gladue, B. A., & Delaney, H. J. (1990). Gender differences in perception of attractiveness of men and women in bars. *Personality and Social Psychology Bulletin, 16,* 378–391.

Glass, S. P., & Wright, T. L. (1985). Sex differences in type of extramarital involvement and marital dissatisfaction. *Sex Roles, 12,* 1101–1120.

Goethals, G. R. (1986). Social comparison theory: Psychology from the lost and found. *Personality and Social Psychology Bulletin, 12,* 261–278.

Goffman, E. (1959). *The presentation of self in everyday life.* Garden City, NY: Doubleday, Anchor.

Gold, J. A., Ryckman, R. M., & Mosly, N. R. (1984). Romantic mood induction and attraction to a dissimilar other: Is love blind? *Personality and Social Psychology Bulletin, 10,* 358–368.

Goldsmith, D. J., McDermott, V., & Hawkins, M. (1996). *Gender differences in perceived supportiveness of conversations about problems: A preliminary report of results.* Paper presented at the annual meeting of the International Communication Association, Chicago.

Gondolf, E. W., & Foster, R. A. (1991). Pre-program attrition in batterer programs. *Journal of Family Violence, 6,* 337–349.

Goodwin, J. S., Hunt, W. C., Key, C. R., & Samet, J. M. (1987). The effect of marital status on stage, treatment and survival of cancer patients. *Journal of the American Medical Association, 258,* 3125–3130.

Gormly, A. V. (1979). Behavioral effects of receiving agreement or disagreement from a peer. *Personality and Social Psychology Bulletin, 5,* 405–408.

Gottman, J. M. (1993). The roles of conflict engagement, escalation, and avoidance in marital interaction: A longitudinal view of five types of couples. *Journal of Consulting and Clinical Psychology, 61,* 6–15.

Gottman, J. M., & Katz, L. F. (1989). Effects of marital discord on young children's peer interaction and health. *Developmental Psychology, 25,* 373–381.

Gottman, J. M., & Krokoff, L. J. (1989). Marital interaction and satisfaction: A longitudinal view. *Journal of Consulting and Clinical Psychology, 57,* 47–52.

Gottman, J. M., & Levenson, R. W. (1992). Marital processes predictive of later dissolution: Behavior, physiology, and health. *Journal of Personality and Social Psychology, 63,* 221–233.

Gouaux, C. (1971). Induced affective states and interpersonal attraction. *Journal of Personality and Social Psychology, 20,* 37–43.

Grauerholz, E., & Serpe, R. T. (1985). Initiation and response: The dynamics of sexual interaction. *Sex Roles, 12,* 1041–1059.

Gray, J. (1992). *Men are from Mars, women are from Venus.* New York: HarperCollins.

Greeley, A. M. (1991). *Faithful attraction: Discovering intimacy, love, and fidelity in American marriage.* New York: Doherty.

Greenblatt, C. S. (1983). The salience of sexuality in the early years of marriage. *Journal of Marriage and the Family, 45,* 289–299.

Griffit, W. B. (1969). Personality similarity and self concept as determinants of interpersonal attraction. *Journal of Social Psychology, 78,* 137–146.

Griffit, W. B., & Veitch, R. (1971). Hot and crowded: Influence of population density and temperature on interpersonal affective behavior. *Journal of Personality and Social Psychology, 17*, 92–98.

Grossmann, K., Grossmann, K. E., Spaengler, S., Suess, G., & Unzner, L. (1985). Maternal sensitivity and newborn orientation responses as related to quality of attachment in Northern Germany. *Monographs of the Society for Research in Child Development, 50*, (1-2 Serial No. 209).

Gruber, J. E., & Smith, M. D. (1995). Women's responses to sexual harassment: A multivariate analysis. *Basic and Applied Social Psychology, 17*, 543–562.

Grush, J. E. (1976). Attitude formation and mere exposure phenomena: A nonartificial explanation of empirical findings. *Journal of Personality and Social Psychology, 33*, 281–290.

Guldner, G. T., & Swenson, C. H. (1995). Time spent together and relationship quality: Long-distance relationships as a test case. *Journal of Social and Personal Relationships, 12*, 313–320.

Gutek, B. A., & Morasch, B. (1982). Sex ratios, sex role spillover, and sexual harassment of women at work. *Journal of Social Issues, 38*, 55–74.

Gutek, B. A., & O'Connor, M. (1995). The empirical basis for the reasonable woman standard. *Journal of Social Issues, 51*, 151–166.

Gutierres, S. E., Kenrick, D. T., & Partch, J. J. (1999). Beauty, dominance, and the mating game: Contrast effects in self-assessment reflect gender differences in mate selection. *Personality and Social Psychology Bulletin, 25*, 1126–1134.

Hackel, L. S., & Ruble, D. N. (1992). Changes in the marital relationship after the first baby is born: Predicting the impact of expectancy disconfirmation. *Journal of Personality and Social Psychology, 62*, 944–957.

Harris, C. R., & Christenfeld, N. (1996). Gender, jealousy, and reason. *Psychological Science, 7*, 364–366.

Harvey, J. H. (1987). Attributions in close relationships: Research and theoretical developments. *Journal of Social and Clinical Psychology, 5*, 420–434.

Hatfield, E. (1988). Passionate and companionate love. In R. J. Sternberg & M. L. Barnes (Eds.), *The psychology of love* (pp. 191–217). New Haven, CT: Yale University Press.

Hatfield, E., Brenton, C., & Cornelius, J. (1989). Passionate love and anxiety in young adolescents. *Motivation and Emotion, 13*, 271–289.

Hatfield, E., & Rapson, R. L. (1987). Passionate love: New directions in research. In W. H. Jones & D. Perlman (Eds.), *Advances in personal relationships* (Vol. 1, pp. 109–139). Greenwich, CT: JAI Press.

Hatfield, E., Schmitz, E., Cornelius, J., & Rapson, R. L. (1988). Passionate love: How early does it begin? *Journal of Psychology and Human Sexuality, 1*, 35–52.

Hatfield, E., & Sprecher, S. (1986). Measuring passionate love in intimate relationships. *Journal of Adolescence, 9*, 383–410.

Hatfield, E., & Sprecher, S. (1986). *Mirror, mirror . . . The importance of looks in everyday life.* Albany, NY: SUNY Press.

Hatfield, E., Utne, M. K., & Traupmann, J. (1979). Equity theory and intimate relationships. In R. L. Burgess & T. L. Huston (Eds.), *Social exchange in developing relationships* (pp. 99–133). New York: Academic Press.

Hazan, C., & Shaver, P. (1987). Romantic love conceptualized as an attachment process. *Journal of Personality and Social Psychology, 52*, 511–524.

Heider, F. (1958). *The psychology of interpersonal relations.* New York: Wiley.

Helgeson, V. S. (1994). Long-distance romantic relationships: Sex differences in adjustment and breakup. *Personality and Social Psychology Bulletin, 20*, 254–265.

Helgeson, V. S., Shaver, P., & Dyer, M. (1987). Prototypes of intimacy and distance in same-sex and opposite-sex relationships. *Journal of Social and Personal Relationships, 4,* 195–233.

Hemström, Ö. (1996). Is marriage dissolution linked to differences in mortality risks for men and women? *Journal of Marriage and the Family, 58,* 366–378.

Hendrick, C., & Hendrick, S. S. (1986). A theory and method of love. *Journal of Personality and Social Psychology, 50,* 392–402.

Hendrick, S. S. (1981). Self-disclosure and marital satisfaction. *Journal of Personality and Social Psychology, 40,* 1150–1159.

Hendrick, S. S., & Hendrick, C. (1993). Lovers as friends. *Journal of Social and Personal Relationships, 10,* 459–466.

Hendrick, S. S., Hendrick, C., & Adler, N. L. (1988). Romantic relationships: Love, satisfaction, and staying together. *Journal of Personality and Social Psychology, 54,* 980–988.

Herek, G. M., & Capitanio, J. P. (1996). "Some of my best friends": Intergroup contact, concealable stigma, and heterosexuals' attitudes toward gay men and lesbians. *Personality and Social Psychology Bulletin, 22,* 412–424.

Herman, J. L. (1992). *Trauma and recovery.* New York: Basic Books.

Herr, P. M., Sherman, S. J., & Fazio, R. H. (1983). On the consequences of priming: Assimilation and contrast effects. *Journal of Experimental Social Psychology, 19,* 323–340.

Hieger, L. J., & Troll, L. E. (1973). A three-generation study of attitudes concerning the importance of romantic love in mate selection. *Gerontologist, 13,* 86.

Hill, C. T., Rubin, Z., & Peplau, L. A. (1976). Breakups before marriage: The end of 103 affairs. *Journal of Social Issues, 32,* 147–168.

Hines, M., Allen, L. S., & Gorski, R. A. (1992). Sex differences in subregions of the amygdala and the bed nucleus of the stria terminalis of the rat. *Brain Research, 579,* 321–326.

Hoffman, S. D., & Duncan, G. J. (1988). What are the economic consequences of divorce? *Demography, 25,* 641–645.

Hollingshead, A. B. (1998). Retrieval processes in transactive memory systems. *Journal of Personality and Social Psychology, 74,* 659–671.

Holmes, J. (1984). Women's language: A functional approach. *General Linguistics, 24,* 149–178.

Holmes, J. G., & Rempel, J. T. (1989). Trust in close relationships. In C. Hendrick (Ed.), *Close relationships: Review of personality and social psychology* (Vol. 10, pp. 187–220). Newbury Park, CA: Sage.

Holmes, T., & Rahe, R. (1967). The social readjustment rating scale. *Journal of Psychosomatic Research, 11,* 213–218.

Holt, P. A., & Stone, G. L. (1997). Needs, coping strategies, and coping outcomes associated with long-distance relationships. *Journal of College Student Development, 29,* 136–141.

Homans, G. C. (1951). *The human group.* New Brunswick, NJ: Transaction.

Homans, G. C. (1961). *Social behavior.* New York: Harcourt, Brace & World.

Horne, S. (1999). Domestic violence in Russia. *American Psychologist, 54,* 55–61.

Horvath, T. (1981). Physical attractiveness: The influence of selected torso parameters. *Archives of Sexual Behavior, 10,* 21–24.

Hotaling, G. T., & Sugarman, D. B. (1990). A risk marker analysis of assaulted wives. *Journal of Family Violence, 5,* 1–13.

Hoyenga, K. B., & Hoyenga, K. T. (1981). *The question of sex differences: Psychological, cultural, and biological issues.* Boston: Little, Brown.

Hupka, R. B. (1984). Jealousy: Compound emotion or label for a particular situation? *Motivation and Emotion, 8,* 141–155.

Hupka, R. B. (1991). The motive for the arousal of romantic jealousy: Its cultural origin. In P. Salovey (Ed.), *The psychology of jealousy and envy* (pp. 252–270). New York: Guilford.

Huston, T. L., McHale, S. M., & Crouter, A. C. (1986). When the honeymoon's over: Changes in the marriage relationship over the first year. In R. Gilmour & S. Duck (Eds.), *The emerging field of personal relationships* (pp. 109–132). Hillsdale, NJ: Erlbaum.

Ickes, W. (1982). A basic paradigm for the study of personality, roles, and social behavior. In W. Ickes & E. S. Knowles (Eds.), *Personality, roles, and social behavior.* New York: Springer-Verlag.

Ickes, W. (1983). A basic paradigm for the study of unstructured dyadi interaction. In H. Reis (Ed.), *New directions for methodology of social and behavioral science* (pp. 5–21). San Francisco: Jossey-Bass.

Ickes, W., Bissonnette, V., Garcia, S., & Stinson, L. L. (1990). Implementing and using the dyadic interaction paradigm. In C. Hendrick & M. S. Clark (Eds.), *Research methods in personality and social psychology* (Vol. 11, pp. 16–44). Newbury Park, CA: Sage.

Isabella, R. A. (1993). Origins of attachment: Maternal interaction behavior across the first year. *Child Development, 64,* 605–621.

Ito, T. A., Miller, N., & Pollock, V. E. (1996). Alcohol and aggression: A meta-analysis on the moderating effects of inhibitory cues, triggering events, and self-focused attention. *Psychological Bulletin, 120,* 60–82.

Izard, C. E. (1991). *The psychology of emotions.* New York: Plenum.

Jacobs, L. E., Berscheid, E., & Walster, E. (1971). Self-esteem and attraction. *Journal of Personality and Social Psychology, 17,* 84–91.

James, D. (1981). The honeymoon effect on marital coitus. *Journal of Sex Research, 17,* 114–123.

James, D., & Clarke, S. (1993). Women, men, and interruptions: A critical review. In D. Tannen (Ed.), *Gender and conversational interaction* (pp. 231–280). New York: Oxford University Press.

James, D., & Drakich, J. (1993). Understanding gender differences in amount of talk: A critical review. In D. Tannen (Ed.), *Gender and conversational interaction* (pp. 281–312). New York: Oxford University Press.

Jellison, J. M., & Oliver, D. F. (1983). Attitude similarity and attraction: An impression management approach. *Personality and Social Psychology Bulletin, 9,* 111–115.

Johnson, D. L., & Rusbult, C. E. (1989). Resisting temptation: Devaluation of alternative partners as a means of maintaining commitment in close relationships. *Journal of Personality and Social Psychology, 57,* 967–980.

Johnson, M. P. (1995). Patriarchal terrorism and common couple violence: Two forms of violence against women. *Journal of Marriage and the Family, 57,* 283–294.

Jones, E. E., & Nisbett, R. E. (1972). The actor and the observer: Divergent perceptions of the causes of behavior. In E. E. Jones, D. E. Kanouse, H. H. Kelley, R. E. Nisbett, S. Valins, & B. Weiner (Eds.), *Attribution: Perceiving the causes of behavior* (pp. 79–94). Morristown, NJ: General Learning Press.

Jones, E. E., & Pittman, T. S. (1982). Toward a general theory of strategic self-presentation. In J. Suls (Ed.), *Psychological perspectives on the self.* Hillsdale, NJ: Erlbaum.

Jones, E. E., & Wortman, C. (1973). *Ingratiation: An attributional approach.* Morristown, NJ: General Learning Press.

Jones, J. T., & Cunningham, J. D. (1996). Attachment styles and other predictors of relationship satisfaction in dating couples. *Personal Relationships, 3,* 387–399.

Jones, W. H., Hanson, R. O., & Phillips, A. L. (1978). Physical attractiveness and judgments of psychopathology. *Journal of Social Psychology, 55,* 79–84.

Jones, W. H., Hobbs, S. A., & Hackenbury, D. (1982). Loneliness and social skills deficits. *Journal of Personality and Social Psychology, 42,* 682–689.

Josephs, R. A., Markus, H. R., & Tafarodi, R. W. (1992). Gender and self-esteem. *Journal of Personality and Social Psychology, 63,* 391–402.

Judd, C. M., Smith, E. R., & Kidder, L. H. (1991). *Research methods in social relations.* Fort Worth, TX: Harcourt Brace Jovanovich.

Kalick, S. M. (1988). Physical attractiveness as a status cue. *Journal of Experimental Social Psychology, 24,* 469–489.

Kandel, D. B. (1978). Similarity in real-life adolescent friendship pairs. *Journal of Personality and Social Psychology, 36,* 306–312.

Katz, L. F., & Gottman, J. M. (1993). Patterns of marital conflict predict children's internalizing and externalizing behaviors. *Developmental Psychology, 29,* 940–950.

Keelan, J. P., Dion, K. L., & Dion, K. K. (1994). Attachment style and heterosexual relationships among young adults: A short-term panel study. *Journal of Social and Personal Relationships, 11,* 201–214.

Kennedy, C. W., & Camden, C. T. (1983). A new look at interruptions. *Western Journal of Speech Communication, 47,* 45–58.

Kenny, D. A. (1988). Interpersonal perception: A multivariate round robin analysis. *Journal of Social and Personal Relationships, 5,* 247–261.

Kenny, D. A. (1994). Using the social relations model to understand relationships. In R. Erber & R. Gilmour (Eds.), *Theoretical frameworks for personal relationships.* Hillsdale, NJ: Erlbaum.

Kenny, D. A., & Kashy, D. A. (1991). Analyzing interdependence in dyads. In B. M. Montgomery & S. Duck (Eds.), *Studying interpersonal interaction* (pp. 275–285). New York: Guilford.

Kenny, D. A., & Malloy, T. E. (1988). Partner effects in social interaction. *Journal of Nonverbal Behavior, 12,* 34–57.

Kenrick, D. T., & Cialdini, R. B. (1977). Romantic attraction: Misattribution versus reinforcement explanations. *Journal of Personality and Social Psychology, 35,* 381–391.

Kenrick, D. T., & Gutierres, S. E. (1980). Contrast effects and judgments of physical attractiveness: When beauty becomes a social problem. *Journal of Personality and Social Psychology, 38,* 131–140.

Kenrick, D. T., & Johnson, G. A. (1979). Interpersonal attraction in aversive environments: A problem for the classical conditioning paradigm? *Journal of Personality and Social Psychology, 37,* 572–579.

Kenrick, D. T., Neuberg, S. L., Zierk, K., & Krones, J. (1994). Evolution and social cognition: Contrast effects as a function of sex, dominance, and physical attractiveness. *Personality and Social Psychology Bulletin, 20,* 210–217.

Kerckhoff, A. C., & Davis, K. E. (1962). Value consensus and need complementarity in mate selection. *American Sociological Review, 27,* 295–303.

Kerns, K. A. (1994). A developmental model of the relations between mother-child attachment and friendship. In R. Erber & R. Gilmour (Eds.), *Theoretical framewords for personal relationships* (pp. 129–156). Hillsdale, NJ: Erlbaum.

Kiecolt-Glaser, J. K., Garner, W., Speicher, C., Penn, G. M., Holliday, J., & Glaser, R. (1984). Psychosocial modifiers of immunocompetence in medical students. *Psychosomatic Medicine, 46,* 7–14.

Kinsey, A. C., Pomeroy, W. B., & Martin, C. E. (1948). *Sexual behavior in the human male.* Philadelphia: Saunders.

Kinsey, A. C., Pomeroy, W. B., Martin, C. E., & Gebhard, P. H. (1953). *Sexual behavior in the human female.* Philadelphia: Saunders.

Kirkpatrick, L. A., & Davis, K. E. (1994). Attachment style, gender, and relationship stability: A longitudinal analysis. *Journal of Personality and Social Psychology, 66,* 502–512.

Kite, M. E. (1994). When perceptions meet reality: Individual differences in reactions to lesbians and gay men. In B. Greene & G. M. Herek (Eds.), *Lesbian and gay psychology: Theory, research, and clinical applications. Psychological perspectives on lesbian and gay issues* (Vol. 1, pp. 25–53). Thousand Oaks, CA: Sage.

Kleck, R. E., & Rubenstein, C. (1975). Physical attractiveness, perceived attitude similarity, and interpersonal attraction in an opposite-sex encounter. *Journal of Personality and Social Psychology, 31,* 107–114.

Kleinke, C. L. (1986). Gaze and eye contact: A research view. *Psychological Bulletin, 100,* 78–100.

Kleinke, C. L., Meeker, F. B., & Staneski, R. A. (1986). Preference for opening lines: Comparing ratings by men and women. *Sex Roles, 15,* 585–600.

Komaromy, M., Bindman, A. B., Haber, R. J., & Sand, M. E. (1993). Sexual harassment in medical training. *New England Journal of Medicine, 328,* 322–326.

Koss, M. P. (1993). Rape: Scope, impact, intervention and public policy response. *American Psychologist, 48,* 1062–1069.

Koss, M. P., Gidycz, C. A., & Wisniewski, N. (1987). The scope of rape: Incidence and prevalence of sexual aggression and victimization in a national sample of higher education students. *Journal of Consulting and Clinical Psychology, 55,* 162–170.

Kozu, J. (1999). Domestic violence in Japan. *American Psychologist, 54,* 50–54.

Krebs, D., & Adinolfi, A. A. (1975). Physical attractiveness, social relations, and personality style. *Journal of Personality and Social Psychology, 31,* 245–253.

Kruglanski, A. W., & Mayseless, O. (1990). Classic and current social comparison research: Expanding the perspective. *Psychological Bulletin, 108,* 195–208.

Kubie, L. S. (1956). Psychoanalysis and marriage: Practical and theoretical issues. In V. W. Eisenstein (Ed.), *Neurotic interaction in marriage* (pp. 10–43). New York: Basic Books.

Kübler-Ross, E. (1969). *On death and dying.* New York: Macmillan.

Kulik, J. A., & Mahler, H. I. M. (1989). Stress and affiliation in a hospital setting: Preoperative roommate preferences. *Personality and Social Psychology Bulletin, 15,* 183–193.

Kunkel, A. W. (1995). *Assessing the adequacy of explanations for gender differences in emotional support: An experimental test of the different cultures and skill deficit accounts.* Paper presented at the annual meeting of the Speech Communication Association, San Antonio, TX.

Kunkel, A. W., & Burleson, B. R. (1998). Social support and the emotional lives of men and women: An assessment of the different cultures perspective. In D. L. Canary & K. Dindia (Eds.), *Sex, gender, and communication: Similarities and differences.* Mahwah, NJ: Erlbaum.

Kunkel, A. W., & Burleson, B. R. (1999). Assessing explanations for sex differences in emotional support: A test of the different cultures and skill specialization accounts. *Human Communication Research, 25,* 307–340.

LaFrance, M., & Hecht, M. A. (1995). Why smiles generate leniency. *Personality and Social Psychology Bulletin, 21,* 207–214.

Lakoff, R. (1973). Language and women's place. *Language in Society, 2,* 45–79.

Lakoff, R. (1975). *Language and woman's place*. New York: Harper and Row.

Lakoff, R. (1977). Women's language. *Language and Style, 10,* 222–247.

Landy, D., & Sigall, H. (1974). Beauty is talent: Task evaluation as a function of the performer's physical attractiveness. *Journal of Personality and Social Psychology, 29,* 299–304.

Lane, J. D., & Wegner, D. M. (1994). Secret relationships: The back alley to love. In R. Erber & R. Gilmour (Eds.), *Theoretical frameworks for personal relationships*. Hillsdale, NJ: Erlbaum.

Lavrakas, P. (1975). Female preferences for male physiques. *Journal of Research in Personality, 9,* 324–334.

Leary, M. R. (1983). *Understanding social anxiety: Social, personality, and clinical perspectives.* Beverly Hills, CA: Sage.

Leary, M. R. (1995). *Self-presentation: Impression management and interpersonal behavior.* Madison, WI: Brown & Benchmark.

Lecky, P. (1945). *Self-consistency: A theory of personality.* Hamden, CT: Shoe String Press.

Lee, J. A. (1973). *The colors of love: An exploration of the ways of loving.* Don Mills, Ontario, Canada: New Press.

Lee, J. A. (1988). Love-styles. In R. J. Sternberg & M. L. Barnes (Eds.), *The psychology of love* (pp. 38–67). New Haven, CT: Yale University Press.

Leenaars, A. A., & Lester, D. (1995). The changing suicide pattern in Canadian adolescents and youth, compared to their American counterparts. *Adolescence, 30,* 539–547.

Leonard, D. W. (1975). Partial reinforcement effects in classical aversive conditioning in rabbits and human beings. *Journal of Comparative and Physiological Psychology, 88,* 596–608.

Lerner, M. J. (1970). The desire for justice and reactions to victims. In J. McCauley & L. Berkowitz (Eds.), *Altruism and helping behavior.* New York: Academic Press.

Lerner, R. M., & Lerner, J. V. (1977). Effects of age, sex, and physical attractiveness on child-peer relations, academic performance, and elementary school adjustment. *Developmental Psychology, 1,* 585–590.

LeVay, S. (1991). A difference in hypothalamic structure between heterosexual and homosexual men. *Science, 253,* 1034–1037.

Levenson, R. W., Carstensen, L. L., & Gottman, J. M. (1993). Long-term marriage: Age, gender, and satisfaction. *Psychology and Aging, 8,* 301–313.

Levenson, R. W., Carstensen, L. L., & Gottman, J. M. (1994). Influence of age and gender on affect, physiology, and their interrelations: A study of long-term marriages. *Journal of Personality and Social Psychology, 67,* 56–68.

Levenson, R. W., & Gottman, J. M. (1983). Marital interaction: Physiological linkage and affective exchange. *Journal of Personality and Social Psychology, 45,* 587–597.

Levenson, R. W., & Gottman, J. M. (1985). Physiological and affective predictors of change in relationship satisfaction. *Journal of Personality and Social Psychology, 49,* 85–94.

Leventhal, G. S., & Michaels, J. W. (1971). Locus of cause and equity motivation as determinants of reward allocation. *Journal of Personality and Social Psychology, 17,* 229–235.

Levinger, G. (1966). Systematic distortion in spouses' reports of preferred and actual sexual behavior. *Sociometry, 29,* 291–299.

Levinger, G. (1976). A social psychological perspective on marital dissolution. *Journal of Social Issues, 32,* 21–47.

Levinger, G. (1994). Figure versus ground: Micro- and macroperspectives on the social psychology of personal relationships. In R. Erber & R. Gilmour (Eds.), *Theoretical frameworks for personal relationships* (pp. 1–28). Hillsdale, NJ: Erlbaum.

Levinger, G., & Huesman, L. R. (1980). An "incremental exchange" perspective on the pair relationship: Interpersonal reward and level of involvement. In K. K. Gergen, M. S. Greenberg, & R. H. Willis (Eds.), *Social exchange: Advances in theory and research* (pp. 165–188). New York: Plenum.

Levinger, G., Senn, D. J., & Jorgensen, B. W. (1970). Progress toward permanence in courtship: A test of the Kerckhoff-Davis hypothesis. *Sociometry, 33,* 427–443.

Levinger, G., & Snoek, J. D. (1972). *Attraction in relationships: A new look at interpersonal attraction.* Morristown, NJ: General Learning Press.

Levy, M. B., & Davis, K. E. (1988). Love styles and attachment styles compared: Their relation to each other and to various relationship characteristics. *Journal of Social and Personal Relationships, 5,* 439–471.

Lewak, R. W., Wakefield, J. A., & Briggs, P. F. (1985). Intelligence and personality in mate choice and marital satisfaction. *Personality and Individual Differences, 6,* 471–477.

Lloyd, S., Cate, R., & Henton, J. (1982). Equity and rewards as predictors of satisfaction in casual and intimate relationships. *Journal of Psychology, 110,* 43–48.

Lobdell, J., & Perlman, D. (1986). The intergenerational transmission of loneliness: A study of college females and their parents. *Journal of Marriage and the Family, 48,* 589–595.

Lopata, H. Z. (1996). *Current widowhood: Myths and realities.* Thousand Oaks, CA: Sage.

Lott, A. J., & Lott, B. E. (1974). The role of reward in the formation of positive interpersonal attitudes. In T. Huston (Ed.), *Foundations of interpersonal attraction* (pp. 171–189). New York: Academic Press.

Ludwig, D., Franco, J. N., & Malloy, T. E. (1986). Effects of reciprocity and self-monitoring on self-disclosure with a new acquaintance. *Journal of Social and Personality Psychology, 50,* 1077–1082.

Lund, M. (1985). The development of investment and commitment scales for predicting continuity of personal relationships. *Journal of Social and Personal Relations, 2,* 3–23.

Lundberg, G. A., & Beazley, V. (1948). "Consciousness of kind" in a college population. *Sociometry, 11,* 59–74.

Lundberg, G. A., Hertzler, V. B., & Dickson, L. (1949). Attraction patterns in a university. *Sociometry, 12,* 158–169.

Lussier, Y., Sabourin, S., & Wright, J. (1993). On causality, responsibility, and blame in marriage: Validity of the entailment model. *Journal of Family Psychology, 7,* 322–332.

Lynch, J. J. (1977). *The broken heart: The medical consequences of loneliness.* New York: Basic Books.

Lyons-Ruth, K., Repacholi, B., McLeod, S., & Silva, E. (1991). Disorganized attachment behavior in infancy: Short-term stability, maternal and infant correlates, and risk-related subtypes. *Development and Psychopathology, 3,* 377–396.

Maccoby, E. E. (1996). Peer conflict and intrafamily conflict: Are there conceptual bridges? *Merrill-Palmer Quarterly, 42,* 165–176.

Main, M., & Weston, D. (1981). The quality of the toddler's relationship to mother and father: Related to conflict behavior and the readiness to establish new relationships. *Child Development, 52,* 932–940.

Major, B., Carrington, P. I., & Carnevale, P. J. D. (1984). Physical attractiveness and self-esteem: Attributions for praise from an other-sex evaluator. *Personality and Social Psychology Bulletin, 10,* 43–50.

Makepeace, J. M. (1987). Social factor and victim-offender differences in courtship violence. *Family Relations: Journal of Applied Family and Child Studies, 36,* 87–91.

Malamuth, N. M., & Brown, L. M. (1994). Sexually aggressive men's perceptions of women's communications: Testing three explanations. *Journal of Personality and Social Psychology, 67,* 699–712.

Maltz, D. N., & Borker, R. A. (1982). A cultural approach to male-female miscommunication. In J. J. Gumperz (Ed.), *Language and social identity* (pp. 196–216). Cambridge: Cambridge University Press.

Mandler, G. (1975). *Mind and emotion.* New York: Wiley.

Margolin, L., & White, L. (1987). The continuing role of physical attractiveness in marriage. *Journal of Marriage and the Family, 49,* 21–28.

Marks, G., & Miller, N. (1987). Ten years of research on the false-consensus effect: An empirical and theoretical review. *Psychological Bulletin, 102,* 72–90.

Marshall, L. L. (1992a). Development of the severity of violence against women scales. *Journal of Family Violence, 7,* 103–121.

Marshall, L. L. (1992b). Development of the severity of violence against men scales. *Journal of Family Violence, 7,* 189–203.

Marshall, L. L., & Rose, P. (1987). Gender, stress and violence in the adult relationships of a sample of college students. *Journal of Social and Personal Relationships, 4,* 299–316.

Marshall, L. L., & Vitanza, S. A. (1994). Physical abuse in close relationships: Myths and realities. In A. L. Weber & J. H. Harvey (Eds.), *Perspectives on close relationships* (pp. 263–284). Boston: Allyn and Bacon.

Martin, L. L. (1986). Set/reset: Use and disuse of concepts in impression formation. *Journal of Personality and Social Psychology, 51,* 493–504.

Mason, A., & Blankenship, V. (1987). Power and affiliation motivation, stress and abuse in intimate relationships. *Journal of Personality and Social Psychology, 52,* 203–210.

Mastekaasa, A. (1997). Marital dissolution as a stressor: Some evidence on psychological, physical, and behavioral changes in the pre-separation period. *Journal of Divorce and Remarriage, 26,* 155–183.

Masters, W. H., & Johnson, V. E. (1966). *Human sexual response.* Boston: Little, Brown.

Masters, W. H., & Johnson, V. E. (1970). *Human sexual inadequacy.* Boston: Little, Brown.

Masters, W. H., & Johnson, V. E. (1979). *Homosexuality in perspective.* Boston: Little, Brown.

Mathes, E. W., Adams, H. E., & Davies, R. M. (1985). Jealousy: Loss of relationship rewards, loss of self-esteem, depression, anxiety, and anger. *Journal of Personality and Social Psychology, 48,* 1552–1561.

May, J. L., & Hamilton, P. A. (1980). Effects of musically evoked affect on women's interpersonal attraction toward and perceptual judgments of physical attractiveness of men. *Motivation and Emotion, 4,* 217–228.

McAdams, D. P. (1982). Intimacy motivation. In A. J. Stewart (Ed.), *Motivation and society* (pp. 133–171). San Francisco: Jossey-Bass.

McAdams, D. P. (1988). Personal needs and personal relationships. In S. Duck (Ed.), *Handbook of personal relationships: Theory, research, and intervention* (pp. 7–22). New York: Wiley.

McAdams, D. P., & Bryant, F. B. (1987). Intimacy motivation and subjective well-being in a nationwide sample. *Journal of Personality, 55,* 395–414.

McAdams, D. P., & Vaillant, G. E. (1982). Intimacy motivation and psychosocial adjustment: A longitudinal study. *Journal of Personality Assessment, 46,* 586–593.

McCarthy, B., & Duck, S. W. (1976). Friendship duration and responses to attitudinal agreement-disagreement. *British Journal of Social and Clinical Psychology, 15,* 377–386.

McClelland, D. (1985). How motives, skills, and values determine what people do. *American Psychologist, 40,* 812–825.

McCormick, N. B. (1979). Come-ons and put-offs: Unmarried students' strategies for having and avoiding sexual intercourse. *Psychology of Women Quarterly, 4,* 194–211.

McCormick, N. B., & Jones, A. J. (1989). Gender differences in nonverbal flirtation. *Journal of Sex Education and Therapy, 15,* 271–282.

McCullough, M. E., Worthington, E. L., & Rachal, K. C. (1997). Interpersonal forgiving in close relationships. *Journal of Personality and Social Psychology, 73,* 321–336.

McDaniel, S. H., Stiles, W. B., & McGaughey, K. J. (1981). Correlations of male college students' verbal response mode use in psychotherapy with measures of psychological disturbance and psychotherapy outcome. *Journal of Consulting and Clinical Psychology, 49,* 571–582.

McWirther, D. P., Sanders, S. A., & Reinisch, J. M. (Eds.). (1990). *Homosexuality/heterosexuality: The Kinsey scale and current research.* New York: Oxford University Press.

Mead, M. (1963). *Sex and temperament in three primitive societies.* New York: Morrow.

Meleshko, K. G. A., & Alden, L. (1993). Anxiety and self-disclosure: Toward a motivational model. *Journal of Personality and Social Psychology, 64,* 1000–1009.

Meritor Savings Bank v. *Vinson,* 477 U.S. 57 (1986).

Michael, R. T., Gagnon, J. H., Laumann, E. O., & Kolata, G. (1994). *Sex in America: A definitive survey.* Boston: Little, Brown.

Mickelson, K. D., Helgeson, V. S., & Weiner, E. (1995). Gender effects on social support provision and receipt. *Personal Relationships, 2,* 211–224.

Middlemist, R. D., Knowles, E. S., & Matter, C. F. (1977). Personal space invasions in the lavatory: Suggestive evidence for arousal. *Journal of Personality and Social Psychology, 33,* 541–546.

Mikulincer, M. (1998). Attachment working models and the sense of trust: An exploration of interaction goals and affect regulation. *Journal of Personality and Social Psychology, 74,* 1209–1224.

Mikulincer, M., & Segal, J. (1990). A multidimensional analysis of the experience of loneliness. *Journal of Social and Personal Relationships, 7,* 209–230.

Miller, D. T., & Ross, M. (1975). Self-serving biases in the attribution of causality: Fact or fiction? *Psychological Bulletin, 82,* 213–225.

Miller, R. S., & Schlenker, B. R. (1985). Egotism in group members: Public and private attributions of responsibility for group performance. *Social Psychology Quarterly, 48,* 85–89.

Mills, J., & Clark, M. S. (1994). Communal and exchange relationships: Controversies and research. In R. Erber & R. Gilmour (Eds.), *Theoretical frameworks for personal relationships.* Hillsdale, NJ: Erlbaum.

Mishler, E. G., & Waxler, N. E. (1968). *Interaction in families: An experimental study of family processes and schizophrenia.* New York: Wiley.

Mittelman, B. (1956). Analysis of reciprocal neurotic patterns in family relationships. In V. W. Eisenstein (Ed.), *Neurotic interaction in marriage* (pp. 81–100). New York: Basic Books.

Miyake, K., Chen, S., & Campos, J. J. (1985). Infant temperament, mother's mode of interaction, and attachment in Japan: An interim report. *Monographs of the Society for Research in Child Development, 50* (1-2 Serial No. 209).

Monsour, M. (1992). Meanings of intimacy in cross and same-sex friendships. *Journal of Social and Personal Relationships, 9,* 277–295.

Mook, D. B. (1987). *Motivation: The organization of action.* New York: Norton.

Mook, D. G. (1980). In defense of external invalidity. *American Psychologist, 38,* 379–388.

Moreland, R. L., & Zajonc, R. B. (1982). Exposure effects in person perception: Familiarity, similarity, and attraction. *Journal of Experimental Social Psychology, 18,* 395–415.

Morrow, P. C., McElroy, J. C., Stamper, B. G., & Wilson, M. A. (1990). The effects of physical attractiveness and other demographic characteristics on promotion decisions. *Journal of Management, 16,* 723–736.

Morton, T. L. (1978). Intimacy and reciprocity of exchange: A comparison of spouses and strangers. *Journal of Personality and Social Psychology, 36,* 72–81.

Mueser, K. T., Grau, B. W., Sussman, S., & Rosen, A. J. (1984). You're only as pretty as you feel: Facial expression as a determinant of physical attractiveness. *Journal of Personality and Social Psychology, 46,* 469–478.

Mullen, P. E. (1991). Jealousy: The pathology of passion. *British Journal of Psychiatry, 158,* 593–601.

Mullen, P. E., & Martin, J. L. (1994). Jealousy: A community study. *British Journal of Psychiatry, 164,* 35–43.

Murphy, C. M., & O'Farrell, T. J. (1994). Factors associated with marital aggression in male alcoholics. *Journal of Family Psychology, 8,* 321–335.

Murphy, C. M., & O'Farrell, T. J. (1996). Marital violence among alcoholics. *Current Directions in Psychological Science, 5,* 183–186.

Murray, H. A. (1938). *Explorations in personality.* New York: Oxford University Press.

Murray, S. L., Holmes, J. G., & Griffin, D. W. (1996a). The benefits of positive illusions: Idealization and the construction of satisfaction in close relationships. *Journal of Personality and Social Psychology, 70,* 79–98.

Murray, S. L., Holmes, J. G., & Griffin, D. W. (1996b). The self-fulfilling nature of positive illusions in romantic relationships: Love is not blind, but prescient. *Journal of Personality and Social Psychology, 71,* 1155–1180.

Murstein, B. I. (1961). A complementary need hypothesis in newlyweds and middle-aged married couples. *Journal of Abnormal and Social Psychology, 63,* 194–197.

Murstein, B. I. (1972). Physical attractiveness and marital choice. *Journal of Personality and Social Psychology, 22,* 8–12.

Murstein, B. I., & Brust, R. G. (1985). Humor and interpersonal attraction. *Journal of Personality Assessment, 49,* 637–640.

Murstein, B. I., & Christy, P. (1976). Physical attractiveness and marital adjustment in middle-aged couples. *Journal of Personality and Social Psychology, 34,* 537–542.

Myers, D. G., & Diener, E. (1995). Who is happy? *Psychological Science, 6,* 10–19.

Nadler, A. (1980). Good looks do not help: Effects of helper's physical attractiveness and expectation for future interaction on help-seeking behavior. *Personality and Social Psychology Bulletin, 6,* 378–383.

Nadler, A., & Dotan, I. (1992). Commitment and rival attractiveness: Their effects on male and female reactions to jealousy-arousing situations. *Sex Roles, 26,* 293–310.

Nahemow, L., & Lawton, M. P. (1975). Similarity and propinquity in friendship formation. *Journal of Personality and Social Psychology, 32,* 204–213.

Newcomb, T. M. (1961). *The acquaintance process.* New York: Holt, Rinehart and Winston.

Nihon Bengoshi Rengokai, Ryoseino Byodoni Kansuru Iinkai [Committee on Gender Equality, Japan Bar Association]. (1996). *Fufukan boryoku 110 ban houkokusho [Report of marital violence hotline].* Tokyo: Author.

Nisbett, R. E., & Wilson, T. D. (1977). Telling more than we can know: Verbal reports on mental processes. *Psychological Review, 84,* 231–259.

Nolen-Hoeksema, S., McBride, A., & Larson, J. (1997). Rumination and psychological distress among bereaved partners. *Journal of Personality and Social Psychology, 72,* 855–862.

Nolen-Hoeksema, S., Parker, L. E., & Larson, J. (1994). Ruminative coping with depressed mood following loss. *Journal of Personality and Social Psychology, 67,* 92–104.

Noller, P. (1993). Gender and emotional communication in marriage: Different cultures or differential social power? *Journal of Language and Social Psychology, 12,* 132–152.

Norton, A. J. (1987, July/August). Families and children in the year 2000. *Children Today,* 6–9.

Norton, A. J., & Miller, L. (1992, October). *Marriage, divorce, and remarriage in the 1990s.* Washington, DC: U.S. Bureau of the Census, Current Population Reports, P23–180.

Norton, A. J., & Moorman, J. E. (1987). Current trends in marriage and divorce among American women. *Journal of Marriage and the Family, 49,* 3–14.

O'Connor, E. M., & Simms, C. M. (1990). Self-revelation as manipulation: The effects of sex and machiavellianism on self-disclosure. *Social Behavior and Personality, 18,* 95–99.

O'Connor, S. C., & Rosenblood, L. K. (1996). Affiliation motivation in everyday experience. *Journal of Personality and Social Psychology, 70,* 513–522.

O'Grady, K. E. (1982). Sex, physical attractiveness, and perceived risk for mental illness. *Journal of Personality and Social Psychology, 43,* 1064–1071.

Olday, D., & Wesley, B. (1988). Dating violence: A comparison of high school and college subsamples. *Free Inquiry in Creative Sociology, 16,* 183–191.

Osofsky, J. D. (1982). *The concept of attachment and psychoanalysis.* Paper presented at the American Psychological Association meeting, Washington, DC.

Ostrov, E., & Offer, D. (1980). Loneliness and the adolescent. In J. Hartog, J. R. Audy, & T. A. Cohen (Eds.), *The anatomy of loneliness* (pp. 170–185). New York: International Universities Press.

Pagelow, M. D. (1984). *Family violence.* New York: Praeger.

Pam, A., & Pearson, J. (1994). The geometry of the eternal triangle. *Family Process, 33,* 175–190.

Park, K. A., & Waters, E. (1989). Security of attachment and preschool friendships. *Child Development, 60,* 1076–1081.

Parks, M. R., & Adelman, M. B. (1983). Communication networks and the development of romantic relationships: An expansion of uncertainty reduction theory. *Human Communication Research, 10,* 55–79.

Parks, M. R., & Floyd, K. (1996). Meanings for closeness and intimacy in friendship. *Journal of Social and Personal Relationships, 13,* 85–107.

Parrott, W. G. (1991). The emotional experiences of envy and jealousy. In P. Salovey (Ed.), *The psychology of jealousy and envy* (pp. 3–30). New York: Guilford.

Parrott, W. G., & Smith, R. H. (1993). Distinguishing the experiences of envy and jealousy. *Journal of Personality and Social Psychology, 64,* 906–920.

Patterson, M. L. (1987). Presentational and affect-management functions of nonverbal involvement. *Journal of Nonverbal Behavior, 11,* 110–122.

Pavlov, I. P. (1927). *Conditioned reflexes.* London: Oxford University Press.

Pence, E., & Paymar, M. (1993). *Education groups for men who batter: The Duluth model.* New York: Springer.

Pennebaker, J. W. (1989). Confession, inhibition, and disease. In L. Berkowitz (Ed.), *Advances in experimental social psychology* (Vol. 22, pp. 211–244). San Diego, CA: Academic Press.

Pennebaker, J. W. (1990). *Opening up: The healing power of confiding in others.* New York: Morrow.

Pennebaker, J. W. (1995). *Emotion, disclosure, and health.* Washington, DC: APA Books.

Pennebaker, J. W., & Beall, S. K. (1986). Confronting a traumatic event: Toward an understanding of inhibition and disease. *Journal of Abnormal Psychology, 95,* 274–281.

Pennebaker, J. W., Dyer, M. A., Caulkins, R. S., Litowitz, D. L., Ackerman, P. L., Anderson, D. B., & McGraw, K. M. (1979). Don't the girls get prettier at closing time: A country and western application to psychology. *Personality and Social Psychology Bulletin, 5,* 122–125.

Pennebaker, J. W., & Francis, M. E. (1996). Cognitive, emotional, and language processes in disclosure. *Cognition and Emotion, 10,* 601–626.

Pennebaker, J. W., Mayne, T. J., & Francis, M. E. (1997). Linguistic predictors of adaptive bereavement. *Journal of Personality and Social Psychology, 72,* 863–871.

Peplau, L. A., Bikson, T. K., Rook, K. S., & Goodchilds, J. D. (1982). Being old and living alone. In L. A. Peplau & D. Perlman (Eds.), *Loneliness: A sourcebook of current theory, research, and therapy* (pp. 327–347). New York: Wiley.

Peplau, L. A., Garnets, L. D., Spalding, L. R., Conley, T. D., & Veniegas, R. C. (1998). A critique of Bem's "Exotic Becomes Erotic" theory of sexual orientation. *Psychological Review, 105,* 387–394.

Peplau, L. A., & Hill, C. T. (1990, July). *Sex-role attitudes and dating relationships: A 15-year follow-up of the Boston couples.* Paper presented at the conference of the International Society for the Sudy of Personal Relationships, Oxford University, UK.

Peplau, L. A., Rubin, Z., & Hill, C. T. (1977). Sexual intimacy in dating relationships. *Journal of Social Issues, 33,* 86–109.

Peretti, P. O., & Pudowski, B. C. (1997). Influence of jealousy on male and female college daters. *Social Behavior and Personality, 25,* 155–160.

Perlman, D., & Peplau, L. A. (1981). Toward a social psychology of loneliness. In S. Duck & R. Gilmour (Eds.), *Personal relationships. 3: Personal relationships in disorder* (pp. 31–56). New York: Academic Press.

Perper, T., & Weis, D. L. (1987). Proceptive and rejective strategies of U.S. and Canadian college women. *Journal of Sex Research, 23,* 455–480.

Peterson, D. R. (1983). Conflict. In H. H. Kelley, E. Berscheid, A. Christensen, J. H. Harvey, T. L. Huston, G. Levinger, E. McClintock, L. A. Peplau, & D. R. Peterson (Eds.), *Close relationships* (pp. 360–396). New York: Freeman.

Pfeiffer, S. M., & Wong, P. T. (1989). Multidimensional jealousy. *Journal of Social and Personal Relationships, 6,* 181–196.

Pike, G. R., & Sillars, A. L. (1985). Reciprocity of marital communication. *Journal of Social and Personal Relationships, 2,* 303–324.

Pipes, R. B., & LeBov-Keeler, K. (1997). Psychological abuse among college women in exclusive heterosexual dating relationships. *Sex Roles, 36,* 585–603.

Pirog-Good, M. A., & Stets, J. E. (1989). The help-seeking behavior of physically and sexually abused college students. In M. A. Pirog-Good & J. E. Stets (Eds.), *Violence in dating relationships: Emerging social issues* (pp. 108–125). New York: Praeger.

Plutchik, R. (1980). *Emotion: A psychoevolutionary analysis.* New York: Harper and Row.

Plutchik, R. (1983). Emotions in early development: A psychoevolutionary approach. In R. Plutchik & H. Kellerman (Eds.), *Emotion: Theory, research, and experience* (Vol. 2). New York: Academic Press.

Price, R. A., & Vandenberg, S. G. (1979). Matching for physical attractiveness in married couples. *Personality and Social Psychology Bulletin, 5,* 398–400.

Pryor, J. B. (1995). The psychosocial impact of sexual harassment on women in the U.S. military. *Basic and Applied Social Psychology, 17,* 605–611.

Pryor, J. B., Giedd, J. L., & Williams, K. B. (1995). Research on sexual harassment: Lingering issues and future directions. *Journal of Social Issues, 51,* 69–84.

Pryor, J. B., & Stoller, L. M. (1994). Sexual cognition processes in men high in the likelihood to sexually harass. *Personality and Social Psychology Bulletin, 20,* 163–169.

Ptacek, J. T., & Dodge, K. L. (1995). Coping strategies and relationship satisfaction in couples. *Personality and Social Psychology Bulletin, 21,* 76–84.

Raines, R. S., Hechtman, S. B., & Rosenthal, R. (1990). Nonverbal behavior and gender as determinants of physical attractiveness. *Journal of Nonverbal Behavior, 14,* 253–267.

Rands, M., Levinger, G., & Mellinger, G. (1981). Patterns of conflict resolution and marital satisfaction. *Journal of Family Issues, 2,* 297–321.

Rapoport, A. (1960). *Fights, games and debates.* Ann Arbor: University of Michigan Press.

Rausch, H. L., Barry, W. A., Hertel, R. K., & Swain, M. A. (1974). *Communication, conflict, and marriage.* San Francisco: Jossey-Bass.

Rawlins, W. K. (1983a). Openness as problematic in ongoing friendships: Two controversial dilemmas. *Communication Monographs, 50,* 1–13.

Rawlins, W. K. (1983b). Negotiating close friendship: The dialectic of conjunctive freedoms. *Human Communication Research, 9,* 255–266.

Reis, H. T. (1990). The role of intimacy in interpersonal relations. *Journal of Social and Clinical Psychology, 9,* 15–30.

Reis, H. T. (1994). Domains of experience: Investigating relationship processes from three perspectives. In R. Erber & R. Gilmour (Eds.), *Theoretical frameworks for personal relationships.* Hillsdale, NJ: Erlbaum.

Reis, H. T., Nezlek, J., & Wheeler, L. (1980). Physical attractiveness in social interaction. *Journal of Personality and Social Psychology, 38,* 604–617.

Reis, H. T., Senchak, M., & Solomon, B. (1985). Sex differences in the intimacy of social interaction: Further examination of potential explanations. *Journal of Personality and Social Psychology, 48,* 1204–1217.

Reis, H. T., Wheeler, L., Spiegel, N., Kernis, M. H., Nezlek, J., & Perri, M. (1982). Physical attractiveness in social interaction: II. Why does appearance affect social experience? *Journal of Personality and Social Psychology, 43,* 979–996.

Reis, H. T., Wilson, I., Monestere, C., Bernstein, S., Clark, A., Seidl, E., Franco, M., Gioioso, E., Freeman, L., & Radoane, K. (1990). What is smiling is beautiful and good. *European Journal of Social Psychology, 20,* 259–267.

Rholes, W. S., Simpson, J. A., & Blakeley, B. S. (1995). Adult attachment styles and mothers' relationships with their young children. *Personal Relationships, 2,* 35–54.

Risman, B. J., Hill, C. T., Rubin, Z., & Peplau, L. A. (1981). Living together in college: Implications for courtship. *Journal of Marriage and the Family, 43,* 77–83.

Robinson v. Jacksonville Shipyards, Inc. (1991). 59 L W1 2470 (DC M Fla).

Robinson, I. E., & Jedlicka, D. (1982). Change in sexual attitudes and behavior of college students from 1965 to 1980: A research note. *Journal of Marriage and the Family, 44,* 237–240.

Rogers, C. R. (1961). *On becoming a person.* Boston: Houghton Mifflin.

Rokach, A., & Brock, H. (1995). The effects of gender, marital status, and the chronicity and immediacy of loneliness. *Journal of Social Behavior and Personality, 10,* 833–848.

Rosell, E., Miller, K., & Barber, K. (1995). Firefighting women and sexual harassment. *Public Personnel Management, 24,* 339–350.

Rosenbaum, M. E. (1986). The repulsion hypothesis: On the nondevelopment of relationships. *Journal of Personality and Social Psychology, 51,* 1156–1166.

Rosenblatt, A., & Greenberg, J. (1988). Depression and interpersonal attraction: The role of perceived similarity. *Journal of Personality and Social Psychology, 55,* 112–119.

Rosenfeld, L. B. (1979). Self-disclosure avoidance: Why I am afraid to tell you who I am. *Communciation Monographs, 46,* 63–74.

Ross, L., Greene, D., & House, P. (1977). The "false consensus effect": An egocentric bias in social perception and attribution processes. *Journal of Experimental Social Psychology, 13,* 279–301.

Ross, M. B., & Salvia, J. (1975). Attractiveness as a biasing factor in teaching judgments. *American Journal of Mental Deficiency, 80,* 96–98.

Rotton, J., Barry, T., Frey, J., & Soler, E. (1978). Air pollution and interpersonal attraction. *Journal of Applied Social Psychology, 8,* 57–71.

Rubenstein, C. M., & Shaver, P. (1982). Loneliness in two northeastern cities. In J. Hartog, J. R. Audy, & Y. A. Cohen (Eds.), *The anatomy of loneliness* (pp. 319–337). New York: International Universities Press.

Rubin, J. Z., Pruitt, D. G., & Kim, S. H. (1994). *Social conflict: Escalation, stalemate, and settlement.* New York: McGraw-Hill.

Rubin, Z. (1970). Measurement of romantic love. *Journal of Personality and Social Psychology, 16,* 265–273.

Rubin, Z. (1973). *Liking and loving.* New York: Holt, Rinehart and Winston.

Rubin, Z., Hill, C. T., Peplau, L. A., & Dunkel-Schetter, C. (1980). Self-disclosure in dating couples: Sex roles and the ethic of openness. *Journal of Marriage and the Family, 42,* 305–317.

Rubin, Z., & Shenker, S. (1978). Friendship, proximity, and self-disclosure. *Journal of Personality, 46,* 1–22.

Ruble, D. N., Fleming, A. S., Hackel, L., & Stangor, C. (1988). Changes in the marital relationship during the transition to first-time motherhood: Effects of violated expectations concerning division of household labor. *Journal of Personality and Social Psychology, 55,* 78–87.

Rudman, L. A., Borgida, E., & Robertson, B. A. (1995). Suffering in silence: Procedural justice versus gender socialization issues in university sexual harassment grievance procedures. *Basic and Applied Social Psychology, 17,* 519–541.

Rusbult, C. E. (1983). A longitudinal test of the investment model: The development (and deterioration) of satisfaction and commitment in heterosexual involvement. *Journal of Personality and Social Psychology, 45,* 101–117.

Rusbult, C. E., Johnson, D. J., & Morrow, G. D. (1986). Impact of couple patterns of problem solving on distress and nondistress in dating relationships. *Journal of Personality and Social Psychology, 50,* 744–753.

Rusbult, C. E., Onizuka, R. K., & Lipkus, I. (1993). What do we really want? Mental models of ideal romantic involvement explored through multidimensional scaling. *Journal of Experimental Social Psychology, 29,* 493–527.

Rusbult, C. E., Verette, J., Whitney, G. A., Slovik, L. F., & Lipkus, I. (1991). Accommodation processes in close relationships: Theory and preliminary empirical evidence. *Journal of Personality and Social Psychology, 60,* 53–78.

Rusbult, C. E., & Zembrodt, I. M. (1983). Responses to dissatisfaction in romantic involvements: A multidimensional scaling analysis. *Journal of Experimental Social Psychology, 19,* 274–293.

Rusbult, C. E., Zembrodt, I. M., & Gunn, L. K. (1982). Exit, voice, loyalty, and neglect: Responses to dissatisfaction in romantic involvements. *Journal of Personality and Social Psychology, 43,* 1230–1242.

Rusbult, C. E., Zembrodt, I. M., & Iwaniszek, J. (1986). The impact of gender and sex-role orientation on responses to dissatisfaction in close relationships. *Sex Roles, 15,* 1–20.

Russell, D., Peplau, L., & Cutrona, C. E. (1980). The revised UCLA Loneliness Scale: Concurrent and discriminant validity evidence. *Journal of Personality and Social Psychology, 39,* 472–480.

Russell, D.E. (1982). *Rape in marriage.* New York: Macmillan.

Sabatelli, R. M., & Cecil-Pigo, E. F. (1985). Relational interdependence and commitment in marriage. *Journal of Marriage and the Family, 47,* 931–937.

Sabini, J., & Silver, M. (1982). *Moralities of everyday life.* New York: Oxford University Press.

Sagrestano, L. (1992). Power strategies in interpersonal relationships. *Psychology of Women Quarterly, 16,* 481–495.

Salovey, P., & Rodin, J. (1985). The heart of jealousy. *Psychology Today,* 22–25, 28–29.

Salovey, P., & Rodin, J. (1986). Differentiation of social-comparison jealousy and romantic jealousy. *Journal of Personality and Social Psychology, 50,* 1100–1112.

Salovey, P., & Rodin, J. (1988). Coping with envy and jealousy. *Journal of Social and Clinical Psychology, 7,* 15–33.

Salovey, P., & Rodin, J. (1991). Provoking jealousy and envy: Domain relevance and self-esteem threat. *Journal of Social and Clinical Psychology, 10,* 395–413.

Scanzoni, J. (1979). A historical perspective on husband-wife bargaining power and marital dissolution. In G. Levinger & O. C. Moles (Eds.), *Divorce and separation: Context, causes, and consequences.* New York: Basic Books.

Scanzoni, J. (1979). Social processes and power in families. In W. R. Burr, R. Hill, F. I. Nye, & I. L. Reiss (Eds.), *Contemporary theories about the family: Research-based theories* (Vol. 1, pp. 295–316). New York: Free Press.

Scanzoni, J., Polonko, K., Teachman, J., & Thompson, L. (1989). *The sexual bond: Rethinking families and close relationships.* Newbury Park, CA: Sage.

Schachter, S. (1959). *The psychology of affiliation: Experimental studies of the sources of gregariousness.* Stanford, CA: Stanford University Press.

Schachter, S., & Singer, J. (1962). Cognitive, social, and physiological determinants of the emotional state. *Psychological Review, 69,* 379–399.

Scheier, M. F., & Carver, C. S. (1985). The self-consciousness scale: A revised version for use with general populations. *Journal of Applied Social Psychology, 15,* 687–699.

Schlenker, B. R., & Leary, M. R. (1982). Audiences' reactions to self-enhancing, self-denigrating, and accurate self-presentations. *Journal of Experimental Social Psychology, 18,* 89–104.

Schuman, H., & Presser, S. (1981). *Questions and answers in attitude surveys.* New York: Academic Press.

Schutz, R. E. (1958). Patterns of personal problems of adolescent girls. *Journal of Educational Psychology, 49,* 1–5.

Schwartz, J. E., Friedman, H. S., Tucker, J. S., Tomlinson-Keasey, C., Wingard, D. L., & Criqui, M. H. (1995). Sociodemographic and psychosocial factors in childhood as predictors of adult mortality. *American Journal of Public Health, 85,* 1237–1245.

Schwartz, N., & Clore, G. L. (1983). Mood, misattribution, and judgments of well-being: Informative and directive functions of affective states. *Journal of Personality and Social Psychology, 45,* 513–523.

Searles, P., & Berger, R. J. (1987). The current status of rape reform legislation: An examination of state statutes. *Women's Rights Law Reporter,* pp. 25–43.

Secord, P. F., & Backman, C. W. (1964). *Social psychology.* New York: McGraw-Hill.

Segal, M. W. (1974). Alphabet and attraction: An unobtrusive measure of the effect of propinquity in a field setting. *Journal of Personality and Social Psychology, 30,* 654–657.

Seligman, C., Brickman, J., & Koulack, D. (1977). Rape and physical attractiveness: Assigning responsibility to victims. *Journal of Personality, 45,* 554–563.

Sergios, P. A., & Cody, J. (1986). Importance of physical attractiveness and social assertiveness skills in male homosexual dating behavior and partner selection. *Journal of Homosexuality, 12,* 71–84.

Seta, J. J., & Seta, C. E. (1982). Personal equity: An intrapersonal comparator system analysis of reward value. *Journal of Personality and Social Psychology, 43,* 222–235.

Seta, J. J., Seta, C. E., & Martin, L. L. (1987). Payment and value: The generation of an evaluation standard and its effect on value. *Journal of Experimental Social Psychology, 23,* 285–301.

Shaffer, D. R., & Ogden, J. K. (1986). On sex differences in self-disclosure during the acquaintance process: The role of anticipated future interaction. *Journal of Personality and Social Psychology, 51,* 92–101.

Shaffer, D. R., Ogden, J. K., & Wu, C. (1987). Effects of self-monitoring and prospect of future interaction on self-disclosure reciprocity during the acquaintance process. *Journal of Personality, 55,* 75–96.

Shaffer, D. R., Smith, J. E., & Tomarelli, M. (1982). Self-monitoring as a determinant of self-disclosure reciprocity during the acquaintance process. *Journal of Personality and Social Psychology, 43,* 163–175.

Shaffer, D. R., & Tomarelli, M. M. (1989). When public and private self-foci clash: Self-consciousness and self-disclosure reciprocity during the acquaintance process. *Journal of Personality and Social Psychology, 56,* 765–776.

Sharpsteen, D. J. (1991). The organization of jealousy knowledge: Romantic jealousy as a blended emotion. In P. Salovey (Ed.), *The psychology of jealousy and envy* (pp. 31–51). New York: Guilford.

Sharpsteen, D. J. (1995). The effects of relationship and self-esteem threats on the likelihood of romantic jealousy. *Journal of Social and Personal Relationships, 12,* 89–101.

Sharpsteen, D. J., & Kirkpatrick, L. A. (1997). Romantic jealousy and adult romantic attachment. *Journal of Personality and Social Psychology, 72,* 627–640.

Shaver, P., & Buhrmester, D. (1983). Loneliness, sex-role orientation, and group life: A social needs perspective. In P. B. Paulus (Ed.), *Basic group processes* (pp. 259–314). New York: Springer-Verlag.

Shaver, P., Furman, W., & Buhrmester, D. (1985). Transition to college: Network changes, social skills, and loneliness. In S. Duck & D. Perlman (Eds.), *Understanding personal relationships: An interdisciplinary approach* (pp. 193–219). London: Sage.

Shaver, P. R., Schwartz, J., Kirson, D., & O'Connor, C. (1987). Emotion knowledge: Further exploration of a prototype approach. *Journal of Personality and Social Psychology, 52,* 1061–1086.

Sheffey, S., & Tindale, R. S. (1992). Perceptions of sexual harassment in the workplace. *Journal of Applied Social Psychology, 22,* 1502–1520.

Sherif, M., Harvey, O. J., White, B. J., Hood, W. R., & Sherif, C. W. (1961). *The Robber's Cave experiment: Intergroup conflict and cooperation.* Middletown, CT: Wesleyan University Press.

Sherman, L. W. (1980). Causes of police behavior: The current state of quantitative research. *Journal of Research in Crime and Delinquency, 17,* 69–100.

Sherman, L. W., & Berk, R. A. (1984). The specific deterrent effects of arrest for domestic assault. *American Sociological Review, 49,* 261–271.

Sherman, L. W., Smith, D. A., Schmidt, J. D., & Rogan, D. P. (1992). Crime, punishment, and stake in conformity: Legal and informal control of domestic violence. *American Sociological Review, 57,* 680–690.

Sherwin, R., & Corbett, S. (1985). Campus sexual norms and dating relationships: A trend analysis. *The Journal of Sex Research, 21,* 258–274.

Shettel-Neuber, J., Bryson, J. B., & Young, L. E. (1978). Physical attractiveness of the "other person" and jealousy. *Personality and Social Psychology Bulletin, 4,* 612–615.

Shively, M., & DeCecco, J. (1977). Components of sexual identity. *Journal of Homosexuality, 3,* 41–48.

Shuchter, S. R. (1986). *Dimensions of grief: Adjusting to the death of a spouse.* San Francisco: Jossey-Bass.

Sigall, H., & Landy, D. (1973). Radiating beauty: The effects of having a physically attractive partner on person perception. *Journal of Personality and Social Psychology, 28,* 218–224.

Sigall, H., & Michela, J. (1976). I'll bet you say that to all the girls: Physical attractiveness and reactions to praise. *Journal of Personality, 44,* 611–626.

Sillars, A. L. (1991). Behavioral observation. In B. M. Montgomery & S. Duck (Eds.), *Studying interpersonal interaction* (pp. 197–218). New York: Guilford.

Sillars, A. L., & Weisberg, J. (1987). Conflict as a social skill. In M. E. Roloff & G. R. Miller (Eds.), *Interpersonal processes: New directions in communication research* (Vol. 14, pp. 140–171). Newbury Park, CA: Sage.

Simmel, G. (1955). *Conflict.* New York: Free Press.

Simon, H. A. (1967). Motivational and emotional controls of cognition. *Psychological Review, 74,* 29–39.

Simpson, J. A. (1987). The dissolution of romantic relationships: Factors involved in relationship stability and emotional distress. *Journal of Personality and Social Psychology, 53,* 683–692.

Simpson, J. A. (1990). The influence of attachment styles on romantic relationships. *Journal of Personality and Social Psychology, 59,* 971–980.

Simpson, J. A., & Gangestad, S. W. (1992). Sociosexuality and romantic partner choice. *Journal of Personality, 60,* 31–51.

Simpson, J. A., Gangestead, S. W., & Lerma M. (1990). Perception of physical attractiveness: Mechanisms involved in the maintenance of romantic relationships. *Journal of Personality and Social Psychology, 59,* 1192–1201.

Simpson, J. A., Rholes, W. S., & Nelligan, J. S. (1992). Support-seeking and support-giving within couple members in an anxiety-provoking situation: The role of attachment styles. *Journal of Personality and Social Psychology, 62,* 434–446.

Singh, D. (1993). Adaptive significance of female physical attractiveness: Role of waist-to-hip ratio. *Journal of Personality and Social Psychology, 65,* 293–307.

Singh, D. (1995). Female judgment of male attractiveness and desirability for relationships: Role of waist-to-hip ratio and financial status. *Journal of Personality and Social Psychology, 69,* 1089–1101.

Singh, R., & Tan, L. S. (1992). Attitudes and attraction: A test of the similarity-attraction and dissimilarity-repulsion hypothesis. *British Journal of Social Psychology, 31,* 227–238.

Snell, W. E., Miller, R. S., & Belk, S. S. (1988). Development of the emotional self-disclosure scale. *Sex Roles, 18,* 59–73.

Snyder, M. (1987). *Public appearances/private realities: The psychology of self-monitoring.* New York: Freeman.

Snyder, M., & Gangestead, S. (1986). On the nature of self-monitoring: Matters of assessment, matters of validity. *Journal of Personality and Social Psychology, 51,* 125–139.

Solano, C. H., Batton, P. G., & Parish, E. A. (1982). Loneliness and patterns of self-disclosure. *Journal of Personality and Social Psychology, 43,* 524–531.

Solano, C. H., & Koester, N. H. (1989). Loneliness and communication problems: Subjective anxiety or objective skills? *Personality and Social Psychology Bulletin, 15,* 126–133.

Solomon, M. R., & Schopler, J. (1978). The relationship of physical attractiveness and punitiveness: Is the linearity assumption out of line? *Personality and Social Psychology Bulletin, 4,* 483–486.

Solomon, R. L., & Corbitt, J. D. (1974). An opponent-process theory of motivation: I. Temporal dynamics of affect. *Psychological Review, 81,* 119–145.

Spanier, G. B., & Glick, P. C. (1981). Marital instability in the United States: Some correlates and recent changes. *Family Relations, 30,* 329–339.

Spence, J., & Helmreich, R. (1978). *Masculinity and femininity: Their psychological dimensions, correlates, and antecedents.* Austin: University of Texas Press.

Spielberger, C. D. (1966). The effects of anxiety on complex learning and academic achievement. In C. D. Spielberger (Ed.), *Anxiety and behavior.* New York: Academic Press.

Spinoza, B. (1981). *The ethics.* Malibu, CA: Simon.

Spinoza, B. (1989). *Ethics.* London: J. M. Dent.

Sprecher, S. (1986). The relation between inequity and emotions in close relationships. *Social Psychology Quarterly, 49,* 309–321.

Sprecher, S. (1988). Investment model, equity, and social support determinants of relationship commitment. *Social Psychology Quarterly, 51,* 318–328.

Sprecher, S. (1989a). The importance to males and females of physical attractiveness, earning potential, and expressiveness in initial attraction. *Sex Roles, 21,* 581–607.

Sprecher, S. (1989b). Expected impact of sex-related events on dating relationships. *Journal of Psychology and Human Sexuality, 2,* 77–92.

Sprecher, S. (1999). "I love you more today than yesterday": Romantic partners' perceptions of changes in love and related affect over time. *Journal of Personality and Social Psychology, 76,* 46–53.

Stattin, H., & Romelsjoe, A. (1995). Adult mortality in the light of criminality, substance abuse, and behavioural and family-risk factors in adolescence. *Criminal Behavior and Mental Health, 5,* 279–311.

Stearns, P. (1989). *Jealousy: The evolution of an emotion in American history.* New York: New York University Press.

Stephan, W., Berscheid, E., & Walster, E. (1971). Sexual arousal and heterosexual perception. *Journal of Personality and Social Psychology, 20,* 93–101.

Sternberg, R. J. (1986). A triangular theory of love. *Psychological Review, 93,* 119–135.

Sternberg, R. J. (1988). Triangulating love. In R. J. Sternberg & M. L. Barnes (Eds.), *The psychology of love* (pp. 119–138). New Haven, CT: Yale University Press.

Stiff, J. B., Miller, G. R., Sleight, C., Mongeau, P., Gardelick, R., & Rogan, R. (1989). Explanations for visual cue primacy in judgments of honesty and deceit. *Journal of Personality and Social Psychology, 56,* 555–564.

Storms, M. D. (1973). Videotape and the attribution process: Reversing actors' and observers' points of view. *Journal of Personality and Social Psychology, 27,* 165–175.

Strachan, C. E., & Dutton, D. G. (1992). The role of power and gender in anger responses to sexual jealousy. *Journal of Applied Social Psychology, 22,* 1721–1740.

Straus, M. A., & Gelles, R. J. (1986). Societal change and change in family violence from 1975 to 1985 as revealed in two national surveys. *Journal of Marriage and the Family, 48,* 465–479.

Straus, M. A., & Gelles, R. J. (1990). *Physical violence in American families: Risk factors and adaptions to violence in 8,145 families.* New Brunswick, NJ: Transaction.

Straus, M. A., Gelles, R. J., & Steinmetz, S. K. (1980). *Behind closed doors: Violence in the American family*. Garden City, NY: Doubleday.

Stroebe, W., & Stroebe, M. S. (1987). *Bereavement and health: The psychological and physical consequences of partner loss*. New York: Cambridge University Press.

Strube, M. J. (1988). The decision to leave an abusive relationship: Empirical evidence and theoretical issues. *Psychological Bulletin, 104*, 236–250.

Sunnafrank, M. (1984). Attitude similarity and interpersonal attraction in communication processes: In pursuit of an ephemeral influence. *Communication Monographs, 50*, 273–284.

Surra, C. A., & Longstreth, M. (1990). Similarity of outcomes, interdependence, and conflict in dating relationships. *Journal of Personality and Social Psychology, 59*, 501–516.

Swaab, D. F., & Hoffman, M. A. (1990). An enlarged suprachiasmatic nucleus in homosexual men. *Brain Research, 537*, 141–148.

Swann, W. B., Jr. (1983). Self-verification: Bringing social reality into harmony with the self. In J. Suls & A. G. Greenwald (Eds.), *Social psychology perspectives* (Vol. 2, pp. 33–66). Hillsdale, NJ: Erlbaum.

Swann, W. B., Jr., Hixon, J. G., & De La Ronde, C. (1992). Embracing the bitter "truth": Negative self-concepts and marital commitment. *Psychological Science, 3*, 118–121.

Swann, W. B., Jr., Hixon, J. G., Stein-Seroussi, A., & Gilbert, D. T. (1990). The fleeting gleam of praise: Cognitive processes underlying behavioral reactions to self-relevant feedback. *Journal of Personality and Social Psychology, 59*, 17–26.

Swann, W. B., Jr., Stein-Seroussi, A., & Giesler, R. B. (1992). Why people self-verify. *Journal of Personality and Social Psychology, 62*, 392–401.

Symons, D. (1979). *The evolution of human sexuality*. New York: Oxford University Press.

Tajfel, H. (1970). Experiments in intergroup discrimination. *Scientific American, 223*, 96–102.

Tan, D. T. Y., & Singh, R. (1995). Attitudes and attraction: A developmental study of the similarity-attraction and dissimilarity-repulsion hypothesis. *Personality and Social Psychology Bulletin, 21*, 975–986.

Tangney, J. P. (1992). Situational determinants of shame and guilt in young adulthood. *Personality and Social Psychology Bulletin, 18*, 199–206.

Tannen, D. (1990). *You just don't understand: Women and men in conversation*. New York: Morrow.

Tannen, D. (1994a). *Talking from 9 to 5—Women and men in the workplace: Language, sex, and power*. New York: Avon Books.

Tannen, D. (1994b). *Gender and discourse*. New York: Oxford University Press.

Tashakorri, A., & Insko, C. A. (1981). Interpersonal attraction and person perception: Two tests of three balance models. *Journal of Experimental Social Psychology, 17*, 266–285.

Taylor, D. A., & Belgrave, F. Z. (1986). The effects of perceived intimacy and valence on self-disclosure reciprocity. *Personality and Social Psychology Bulletin, 12*, 247–255.

Taylor, S. E., & Brown, S. E. (1988). Illusion and well-being: A social psychological perspective on mental health. *Psychological Bulletin, 103*, 193–210.

Taylor, S. E., & Fiske, S. T. (1975). Point of view and perceptions of causality. *Journal of Personality and Social Psychology, 32*, 439–445.

Taylor, S. E., Fiske, S. T., Close, M., Anderson, C., & Ruderman, A. (1977). *Solo status as a psychological variable: The power of being distinctive*. Unpublished manuscript, Harvard University.

Tesser, A. (1978). Self-generated attitude change. In L. Berkowitz (Ed.), *Advances in experimental social psychology* (Vol. 11, pp. 289–338). New York: Academic Press.

Tesser, A. (1988). Toward a self-evaluation maintenance model of social behavior. In L. Berkowitz (Ed.), *Advances in experimental social psychology* (Vol. 21, pp. 181–227). New York: Academic Press.

Tesser, A., Campbell, J., & Smith, M. (1984). Friendship choice and performance: Self-evaluation maintenance in children. *Journal of Personality and Social Psychology, 46,* 561–574.

Tesser, A., & Paulhus, D. L. (1976). Toward a causal model of love. *Journal of Personality and Social Psychology, 34,* 1095–1105.

Tesser, A., & Shaffer, D. (1990). Attitudes and attitude change. *Annual Review of Psychology, 44,* 672–682.

Tharp, R. G. (1963). Psychological patterning in marriage. *Psychological Bulletin, 60,* 97–117.

Thibaut, J. W., & Kelley, H. H. (1959). *The social psychology of groups.* New York: Wiley.

Thornhill, R., & Thornhill, N. W. (1992). The evolutionary psychology of men's coercive sexuality. *Behavioral and Brain Sciences, 15,* 363–421.

Tidwell, M. O., Reis, H. T., & Shaver, P. R. (1996). Attachment, attractiveness, and social interaction: A diary study. *Journal of Personality and Social Psychology, 71,* 729–745.

Tolstedt, B. E., & Stokes, J. P. (1984). Self-disclosure, intimacy, and the depenetration process. *Journal of Personality and Social Psychology, 46,* 84–90.

Tomkins, S. S. (1991). *Affect, imagery, consciousness, Vol. 3: The negative affects: Anger and fear.* New York: Springer

Tourangeau, R., & Rasinski, K. A. (1988). Cognitive processes underlying context effects in attitude measurement. *Psychological Bulletin, 103,* 299–314.

Tov-Ruach, L. (1980). Jealousy, attention, and loss. In A. O. Rorty (Ed.), *Explaining emotions* (pp. 465–488). Berkeley: University of California Press.

Triandis, H. C. (1994). The self and social behavior in differing cultural contexts. In N. R. Goldberger & J. B. Veroff (Eds.), *The culture and psychology reader* (pp. 326–365). New York: New York University Press.

Trivers, R. L. (1972). Parental investment and sexual selection. In B. Campbell (Ed.), *Sexual selection and the descent of man* (pp. 136–179). Chicago: Aldine.

Trobst, K. K., Collins, R. L., & Embree, J. M. (1994). The role of emotion in social support provision: Gender, empathy and expressions of distress. *Journal of Social and Personal Relationships, 11,* 45–62.

Tucker, J. S., Friedman, H. S., Schwartz, J. E., Criqui, M. H., Tomlinson-Keasey, C., Wingard, D. L., & Martin, L. R. (1997). Parental divorce: Effects on individual behavior and longevity. *Journal of Personality and Social Psychology, 73,* 381–391.

Tucker, J. S., Friedman, H. S., Wingard, D. L., & Schwartz, J. E. (1996). Marital history at midlife as a predictor of longevity: Alternative explanations to the protective effect of marriage. *Health Psychology, 15,* 94–101.

Tucker, P., & Aron, A. (1993). Passionate love and marital satisfaction at key transition points in the family life cycle. *Journal of Social and Clinical Psychology, 12,* 135–147.

Turner, J. L., Foa, E. B., & Foa, U. G. (1971). Interpersonal reinforcers: Classification, interrelationship, and some differential properties. *Journal of Personality and Social Psychology, 19,* 168–180.

Tyler, T. R., & Sears, D. O. (1977). Coming to like obnoxious people when we must live with them. *Journal of Personality and Social Psychology, 35,* 200–211.

U.S. Merit System Protection Board. (1981). *Sexual harassment of federal workers: Is it a problem?* Washington, DC: U.S. Government Printing Office.

Vangelisti, A. L., & Daly, J. A. (1997). Gender differences in standards for romantic relationships. *Personal Relationships, 4,* 203–219.

Van Horn, K. R., Arnone A., Nesbitt, K., Desilets, L., Sears, T., Giffin, M., & Brudy, R. (1998). Physical distance and interpersonal characterisitcs in college students' romantic relationships. *Personal Relationships, 4,* 25–34.

Vaughan, D. (1986). *Uncoupling.* New York: Oxford University Press.

Vaughn, B. E., Lefever, G. B., Seifer, R., & Barglow, P. (1989). Attachment behavior, attachment security, and temperament during infancy. *Child Development, 60,* 728–737.

Vaux, A. (1985). Variations in social support associated with gender, ethnicity, and age. *Journal of Social Issues, 41,* 89–110.

Vaux, A. (1988). Social and personal factors in loneliness. *Journal of Social and Clinical Psychology, 6,* 462–471.

Veitch, R., & Griffit, W. (1976). Good news-bad news: Affective and interpersonal effects. *Journal of Applied Social Psychology, 6,* 69–75.

Victor, J. S. (1980). *Human sexuality: A social psychological approach.* Englewood Cliffs, NJ: Prentice-Hall.

Walker, L. E. A. (1979). *The battered woman.* New York: Harper and Row.

Walker, L. E. A. (1984). *The battered woman syndrome.* New York: Springer.

Walster, E., Aronson, V., Abrahams, D., & Rottman, L. (1966). Importance of physical attractiveness in dating behavior. *Journal of Personality and Social Psychology, 4,* 508–516.

Walster, E., Berscheid, E., & Walster, G. W. (1973). New directions in equity. *Journal of Personality and Social Psychology, 25,* 151–176.

Walster, E., Walster, G. W., & Berscheid, E. (1978). *Equity: Theory and research.* Boston: Allyn and Bacon.

Walster, E., Walster, G. W., Pilliavin, J., & Schmitt, L. (1973). "Playing hard-to-get": Understanding an elusive phenomenon. *Journal of Personality and Social Psychology, 26,* 113–121.

Walster, E., Walster, G. W., & Traupman, J. (1978). Equity and premarital sex. *Journal of Personality, 36,* 82–92.

Watson, J. B. (1924). *Behaviorism.* New York: Norton.

Watts, B. L. (1982). Individual differences in circadian activity rhythms and their effects on roommate relationships. *Journal of Personality, 50,* 374–384.

Weber, A. L., & Harvey, J. H. (1994). Accounts in coping with relationship loss. In A. Weber and J. H. Harvey (Eds.), *Perspectives on close relationships* (pp. 285–306). Boston: Allyn and Bacon.

Weber, M. (1976). *Wirtschaft und Gesellschaft.* Tuebingen, Germany: Mohr.

Wedell, D. H., Parducci, A., & Geiselman, R. E. (1987). A formal analysis of ratings of physical attractiveness: Successive contrast and simultaneous assimilation. *Journal of Experimental Social Psychology, 23,* 230–249.

Wegner, D. M. (1986). Transactive memory: A contemporary analysis of the group mind. In B. Mullen & G. R. Goethals (Eds.), *Theories of group behavior* (pp. 185–208). New York: Springer-Verlag.

Wegner, D. M. (1994). Ironic processes of mental control. *Psychological Review, 101,* 34–52.

Wegner, D. M., & Erber, R. (1992). The hyperaccessibility of suppressed thoughts. *Journal of Personality and Social Psychology, 63,* 903–912.

Wegner, D. M., Erber, R., & Raymond, P. (1991). Transactive memory in close relationships. *Journal of Personality and Social Psychology, 61,* 923–929.

Wegner, D. M., Guiliano, T., & Hertel, P. (1985). Cognitive interdependence in close relationships. In W. J. Ickes (Ed.), *Compatible and incompatible relationships* (pp. 252–276). New York: Springer-Verlag.

Wegner, D. M., Lane, J. D., & Dimitri, S. (1994). The allure of secret relationships. *Journal of Personality and Social Psychology, 66,* 287–300.

Wegner, D. M., Schneider, D. J., Carter, S., III, & White, L. (1987). Paradoxical effects of thought suppression. *Journal of Personality and Social Psychology, 58,* 409–418.

Weiss, R. S. (1969). The fund of sociability. *Transaction, 7,* 36–43.

Weiss, R. S. (1979). The emotional impact of marital separation. In G. Levinger & O. C. Moles (Eds.), *Divorce and separation: Context, causes, and consequences* (pp. 201–210). New York: Basic Books.

Weiss, R. S. (1982). Attachment in adult life. In C. M. Parkes & J. Stevenson-Hinde (Eds.), *The place of attachment in human behavior* (pp. 171–184). New York: Basic Books.

Weiss, R. S., & Richards, T. A. (1997). A scale for predicting quality of recovery following the death of a partner. *Journal of Personality and Social Psychology, 72,* 885–891.

Weitzman, L. J. (1985). *The divorce revolution: The unexpected social and economic consequences for women and children in America.* New York: Free Press.

Werner, C. M., Brown, B. B., Altman, I., & Staples, B. (1992). Close relationships in their physical and social contexts: A transactional perspective. *Journal of Social and Personal Relationships, 9,* 411–431.

West, C., & Zimmerman, D. H. (1983). Small insults: A study of interruptions in conversations between unacquainted persons. In B. Thorne, C. Kramarae, & N. Henley (Eds.), *Language, gender, and society* (pp. 102–117). Rowley, MA: Newbury House.

West, D. J. (1977). *Homosexuality re-examined.* Minneapolis: University of Minnesota Press.

West, S. T., & Brown, T. J. (1975). Physical attractiveness, the severity of the emergency, and helping: A field experiment and interpersonal simulations. *Journal of Experimental Social Psychology, 11,* 531–538.

Wheeler, L., & Kim, Y. (1997). What is beautiful is culturally good. The physical attractiveness stereotype has different content in different cultures. *Personality and Social Psychology Bulletin, 23,* 795–800.

Wheeler, L., & Nezlek, J. (1977). Sex differences in social participation. *Journal of Personality and Social Psychology, 35,* 742–754.

Wheeler, L., & Reis, H. T. (1991). Self-recording of events in everyday life. *Journal of Personality, 59,* 339–354.

Wheeler, L., Reis, H., & Nezlek, J. (1983). Loneliness, social interactions, and sex roles. *Journal of Personality and Social Psychology, 45,* 943–953.

Wheeless, L. R., & Grotz, J. (1977). The measurement of trust and its relationship to self-disclosure. *Human Communication Research, 3,* 250–257.

White, G. L. (1980). Physical attractiveness and courtship progress. *Journal of Personality and Social Psychology, 39,* 660–668.

White, G. L. (1981). A model of romantic jealousy. *Motivation and Emotion, 5,* 295–310.

White, G. L. (1991). Self, relationship, friends, and family: Some applications of systems theory to romantic jealousy. In P. Salovey (Ed.), *The psychology of jealousy and envy* (pp. 231–251). New York: Guilford.

White, G. L., & Kight, T. D. (1984). Misattribution of arousal and attraction: Effects of salience of explanations of arousal. *Journal of Experimental Social Psychology, 20,* 55–64.

White, L. K. (1990). Determinants of divorce: A review of research in the eighties. *Journal of Marriage and the Family, 52,* 904–912.

White, S. G., & Hatcher, C. (1984). Couple complementarity and similarity: A review of the literature. *American Journal of Family Therapy, 12,* 15–25.

Wills, T. A. (1991). Similarity and self-esteem in downward comparison. In J. Suls & T. A. Wills (Eds.), *Social comparison: Contemporary theory and research* (pp. 51–78). Hillsdale, NJ: Erlbaum.

Wilson, E. O. (1975). *Sociobiology.* Cambridge, MA: Belknap Press.

Winch, R. F. (1958). *Mate selection: A theory of complementarity of needs.* New York: Harper & Brothers.

Winkler, I., & Doherty, W. J. (1983). Communication styles and marital satisfaction in Israeli and American couples. *Family Process, 22,* 221–228.

Winstead, B. A., Derlega, V. J., & Wong, P. T. (1984). Effects of sex-role orientation on behavioral self-disclosure. *Journal of Research in Personality, 18,* 541–553.

Winter, D. G. (1988). The power motive in women—and men. *Journal of Personality and Social Psychology, 54,* 510–519.

Wood, J. T. (1994). *Who cares? Women, care, and culture.* Carbondale: Southern Illinois University Press.

Wood, J. T. (1997). *Gendered lives: Communication, gender, and culture* (2nd ed.). Belmont, CA: Wadsworth.

Wood, J. V., & Taylor, K. L. (1991). Serving self-relevant goals through social comparison. In J. Suls & T. A. Wills (Eds.), *Social comparison: Contemporary theory and research* (pp. 51–78). Hillsdale, NJ: Erlbaum.

Yovetich, N. A., & Rusbult, C. E. (1994). Accomodative behavior in close relationships: Exploring transformation of motivation. *Journal of Experimental Social Psychology, 30,* 138–164.

Zajonc, R. B. (1968). Attitudinal effects of mere exposure. *Journal of Personality and Social Psychology Monograph Supplement, 9,* Part 2, 1–27.

Zebrowitz, L. A., Montepare, J. M., & Lee, H. K. (1993). They don't all look alike: Individuated impressions of other racial groups. *Journal of Personality and Social Psychology, 65,* 85–101.

Zillmann, D., & Bryant, J. (1988). Pornography's impact on sexual satisfaction. *Journal of Applied Social Psychology, 18,* 438–453.

Zimmerman, D. H., & West, C. (1975). Sex roles, interruptions and silences in conversation. In B. Thorne & N. Henley (Eds.), *Language and sex: Difference and dominance* (pp. 105–129). Rowley, MA: Newbury House.

Zuckerman, M., Spiegel, N. H., DePaulo, B. M., & Rosenthal, R. (1982). Nonverbal strategies for decoding deception. *Journal of Nonverbal Behavior, 6,* 171–187.

Author Index

Subject Index